SINGER/RANDOM HOUSE LITERATURE SERIES

SINGER / RANDOM HOUSE LITERATURE SERIES

PATTERNS OF LITERATURE - VOLUME ONE

The
Short Story

SINGER/RANDOM HOUSE LITERATURE SERIES

PATTERNS OF LITERATURE - VOLUME ONE

The
Short Story

Julian L. Maline, James Berkley, *General Editors*

Paul A. Thetreau
Thomas J. Shanahan
Dwight L. Burton
John S. Simmons

Dictionary of Questions for Understanding Literature
by Vernon Ruland

Random House, Inc.
New York

SINGER / RANDOM HOUSE LITERATURE SERIES

Contents

Unit Two - Medieval Prose Narratives

Unit Three - Nineteenth-Century Short Stories

Unit Four - Twentieth-Century Short Stories

Introduction

While storytelling is as old as man himself, the short story, as an art form, is of relatively recent vintage. For a long time, the short story appeared only as either an illustration of a moral lesson (as in fables and the parables from the New Testament) or as one incident in a long adventurous account of the deeds and exploits of some heroic figure (as in *The Iliad, The Song of Roland,* or the Arthurian legend). During these early times, other forms of literature, drama, poetry, and prose nonfiction, were being widely used and the major literary productions of Western Man appeared in these forms until about the nineteenth century.

It might be said, therefore, that the art form known as the short story grew in importance along with the development of what is commonly known as the Modern Era. This, the twentieth century, is clearly an age of prose fiction. A large number of the most significant works of the last one hundred years have been written in the prose narrative form. The short story, a kind of offshoot of the novel, probably had its beginnings when readers noticed with interest "stories within stories," appealing incidents contained within the longer work. With the growth of an educated, story-loving, reading public, however, opportunity increased for the writing of these single incidents. Today literally thousands of short stories are being written and published in a great variety of books and magazines all over the world.

Thus the short story of the mid-twentieth century is an extremely popular form of literature. Brevity accounts for part of this popularity. Readers who lose patience with the sustained attention required by the novel can gain satisfaction through the short story which they can read at one "sitting." Nor are they bothered by the interruptions of acts, scenes, and stage directions found in dramatic literature or by the unique organization of statements found in poetry. There is usually some action in a story and almost always a build-up of suspense toward some climactic moment. Also, the story is most often based on some contemporary situation with which the reader has at least some familiarity.

In spite of the popularity, freedom from mechanical distractions, and the interest of the short story, readers must distinguish among *purposes* for reading short stories or any other literary form. Those who sit on a bus or in a restaurant and pick up a short story are probably reading purely for enjoyment or to pass the time. They are seldom involved in the study of the work as representative of an art form called the short story. As a student of literature, your purposes for reading the selections in this book are quite different. Of course you may well enjoy the works; the enjoyment of literature is one of the most important hoped-for results of a high school English program. But of equal importance is that through the *study* of the short story, you become more aware of the nature of human expression in literature — language — which is one of the most significant aspects of any culture. Also, as you learn about the structure of the short story through the reading, analyzing, and comparing of several stories, it is hoped that you will become a more discriminating reader of short stories; in other words, that you will be better able to distinguish the excellent from the ordinary.

In order to accomplish these ends, you must take a somewhat different approach to the reading of the work than would the man on the bus or in the restaurant. You must concentrate first on what a particular writer is saying both in and through his story. You must decide whether the story has been written purely for entertainment or whether the incidents described are being employed in the service of a theme of general significance. Then you must consider carefully the manner in which the writer develops his incidents and ideas. Since the writer of a short story, unlike the novelist, limits his scope, in time and space, he must choose his details with great care and purposefulness. As a student of this form, it will be necessary for you to look carefully at both the narrative parts in the story and the ways in which these parts relate to the whole.

There are many suggestions to be made for the effective study of the short story. Possibly the most important one is that each story be read slowly and carefully. A swift, preliminary reading for the overall "feel" of the work is generally useful, but in order to deal with the meaning and structure of the stories in this volume, you must avoid rapid, cursory reading. Nothing can be skimmed or skipped. Since most writers lean heavily on a comparatively few details, the reader's responsibility to assess the relative importance of each of these details becomes proportionately greater. Some important events, incidents, and situations are frequently presented with a minimum of description or exposition. In such passages, the reader must analyze the details that are there in order to determine what actually happened and to what extent this happening affects the story as a whole. For example, in the story "In Greenwich There Are Many Gravelled Walks" by the modern American writer Hortense Calisher, the main character goes to a beatnik-type party in an apartment in Greenwich Village where he encounters among the guests a very despondent young man. During the party the despondent young man commits suicide. The following passage shows Miss Calisher's means of relating the turn of events:

> In the triangular silence, Mario stepped past Peter and slid the window up softly. He leaned out to listen, peering sidewise at the window to the right. As he was pulling himself back in, he looked down. His hands stiffened on the ledge. Very slowly he pulled himself all the way in and stood up. Behind him a tin ventilator clattered inward and fell to the floor. In the shadowy lamplight his too classic face was like marble which moved numbly. He swayed a little, as if with vertigo.
>
> "I'd better get out of here!"
>
> They heard his heavy breath as he dashed from the room. The slam of the outer door blended with Robert's battering, louder now, on the door down the hall.
>
> "What's down there?" She was beside Peter, otherwise he could not have heard her. They took hands, like strangers

met on a narrow footbridge or on one of those steep places where people cling together more for anchorage against their own impulse than for balance. Carefully they leaned out over the sill. Yes—it was down there, the shirt, zebra-striped, just decipherable on the merged shadow of the courtyard below.°

It is obvious that the writer has employed a rather unusual means of describing the actual events. Without deliberate reading, one could miss the entire event and its impact.

Careful reading of a story is essential throughout, but it is frequently of vital importance in the opening passages of selections. A characteristic of many short story writers is *compression*. Because of their limited space, they say much in a few words. These compressed passages, often evident in the early stages of a story, are carefully placed because so many stories pick up a character's life, not at its beginning, but somewhere during its course. When much has obviously happened to the character before we meet him at the outset of the story, how can we know what his condition and outlook on things are when we meet him? Much of this information is provided in the opening of the story and usually in a fairly compact statement. Read the opening paragraph of Edgar Allan Poe's famous story, "The Cask of Amontillado":

The thousand injuries of Fortunato I had borne as I best could, but when he ventured upon insult, I vowed revenge. You, who so well know the nature of my soul, will not suppose, however, that I gave utterance to a threat. *At length* I would be avenged; this was a point definitely settled—but the very definitiveness with which it was resolved precluded the idea of risk. I must not only punish, but punish with impunity. A wrong is unredressed when retribution overtakes its redresser. It is equally unredressed when the avenger fails to make himself felt as such to him who has done the wrong.

In this short statement, the reader learns that (1) the narrator is a major figure in the story, (2) he has apparently been wronged by another man and is plotting revenge, (3) this plot will be slowly and carefully developed, (4) the narrator's revenge is to be the "perfect crime," (5) it is important that the avenger make himself clearly known to the man who has wronged him.

More important, the reader, by inference, gains some insight into the character of the narrator. The idea of revenge has obviously possessed him. Even from these few statements he may be interpreted as a potentially violent man, a man who seems to be taking real delight in the harm he is planning to do to another human being. In the obvious dedication of the narrator to his goal, a distinct *mood* is suggested. Without this information and this insight, the reader does not gain full appreciation for the kind of act perpetrated by the narrator and the manner of its unfolding. Without this opening paragraph clearly in mind, the story has less meaning.

Another problem in reading the short story lies in the manner in which sequences of events are presented. While many stories begin at the beginning and follow conventionally to an end point, many do not. Time sequences are juggled with abandon in the short story. Since the writer is presenting only a relatively small segment of life he may "play around with his clock," as the British writer E. M. Forster would say. The writer does this in order to place in sharpest focus those details which he wishes to emphasize. The result is often a series of abrupt transitions in scenes, unexpected flashbacks, and puzzling underdeveloped situations. In his story "The Body of an American," John Dos Passos has presented an image of the personality of the Unknown Soldier of World War I. Because the soldier is literally unknown, Dos Passos can do a good deal of supposing. He does not start at the beginning, but introduces the story with a description of the ceremonies being conducted for this anonymous, dead soldier in Arlington National Cemetery. From there he unexpectedly moves back in time to the random choosing in France of the box containing the soldier's remains. From there he moves back again to a description of what might have been the circumstances of the soldier's birth. For the rest of the story (about four pages), Dos Passos describes the possible life of the soldier up to the point of his death. But, in order to keep the reader's attention on the significance of the man, he frequently leaves this chronological recapitulation to describe briefly part of the ceremonies at the tomb. Then he ends where he began, and dwells momentarily on the true meaning of the event.

Whether or not Dos Passos is successful in communicating his theme in this story is not important in this discussion. The fact is that he does use an unconventional means of telling the story and that this approach may create a problem for some readers. The reader must unscramble the narrative if he is to understand what actually happens, let alone what the happening implies.

The use to which dialogue is put can also be a source of confusion in many stories, particularly those written during this century. The writer of fiction can know more about his characters than we can ever know about those around us. When he says of his character, "he thought," or "she felt," he is exploring the inner nature of people in a way that we can never do. Thus there are often two kinds of statements made by characters in fiction: those which they make outwardly and those which they make to themselves. Some short story writers signal these statements with *he said, he thought, he felt.* The identification and nature of dialogue is clarified in many works by the use of quotation marks. There are some stories, however, in which no such aids are provided, and the reader must be alert to separate characters' statements from the rest of the narrative, one character's statements from those of another, and the overt comments of a character from what he is thinking to himself. Once again careful reflection and rereading are the best means of making these distinctions.

Just as stories tend to begin in the middle of things, they may often end that way. Once again it must be remembered that the short story covers only a small part, frequently one major incident, in the lives of the people portrayed. When the story itself ends, the people involved presumably go on to other experiences. Furthermore, it is often not stated or even suggested in short story endings that a major conclusion has been reached or a great change has been accomplished in the situation under consideration. The reader is most often left to speculate as to what substantial effect, if any, the experiences described within the story will have on the character who has undergone them. There is much *anti-climax* to be found in the concluding phases of the short story since it is only a part of life which is being described.

For the reasons given above, many short story endings may be abrupt or left "hanging in the air." For the student seeking certainty in the fiction he reads, many of the works in the latter part of this volume may be disappointing. The main reason for this kind of ending is a simple one: the writer is trying to provide his readers with a faithful account of life, and since life is usually extended and almost always complex, no one single incident may necessarily produce a lasting or complete effect on a given person. Therefore, unless the reader is willing (1) to relate thoroughly the ending of the story to the details of the entire work and (2) base any predictions for the future beyond the story limits on a careful sifting of all the evidence found in it, he may well be frustrated by certain stories in the nineteenth- and twentieth-century sections of the volume. A story (not included in this book) which provides such an ending is Ernest Hemingway's famous "The Killers." In this story Nick Adams, a young man living with his friend George in a small town, meets two hired big-city killers in his favorite café. The killers, temporarily taking over the café, announce that they have been hired to "take care" of an ex-prizefighter who has sought seclusion in the town. As soon as he can, Nick leaves the café, rushes to Ole Andersen, at the ex-fighter's boarding house, and informs him of the plot. Ole seems resigned to his fate and tells Nick that there's not much that can be done. Nick returns to the café where he tells George of his mission. The dialogue that follows illustrates how understatement can provide an intensity and force that overstatement cannot.

"Yes," said Nick. "He's in his room and he won't go out."
The cook opened the door from the kitchen when he heard Nick's voice.
"I don't even listen to it," he said and shut the door.
"Did you tell him about it?" George asked.
"Sure. I told him but he knows what it's all about."
"What's he going to do?"
"Nothing."
"They'll kill him."
"I guess they will."
"He must have got mixed up in something in Chicago."
"I guess so," said Nick.
"It's a hell of a thing."
"It's an awful thing," Nick said.
They did not say anything. George reached down for a towel and wiped the counter.
"I wonder what he did?" Nick said.
"Double-crossed somebody. That's what they kill them for."
"I'm going to get out of this town," Nick said.
"Yes," said George. "That's a good thing to do."
"I can't stand to think about him waiting in the room and knowing he's going to get it. It's too damned awful."
"Well," said George, "you better not think about it."*

There isn't much satisfaction in this ending, but in the writing of Hemingway and many other writers of short stories, life is not necessarily satisfying, and things don't always come out all right (or, for that matter, even come *out*) in the end. As a matter of fact, the reader should be wary of the happy, all's-well-that-ends-well finale of the short stories he reads. These conclusions may well be forced or contrived; they may be unsupported by the text of the work. In this respect, the ending may furnish a means of judging whether the story represents or distorts life as it actually is. In any event, the reader must be aware of the omnipresent need in short fiction to scrutinize the events of the *entire* work in order to grasp the "why" of the conclusion.

Thus readers of the short story must be aware of several structural characteristics which may cause difficulty in

*Excerpt from "The Killers" (Copyright 1927 Ernest Hemingway; renewal copyright © 1955) is reprinted with the permission of Charles Scribner's Sons from *Men Without Women* by Ernest Hemingway.

understanding. It is a good idea to reread, to discuss, to summarize in writing your ideas about the works for better understanding. In the case of each work, the "Dictionary of Questions" contains several suggestions for particular kinds of investigation. These questions are designed for intensive inquiry into thematic, structural, and historical aspects of the selection. They also provide a guide for personal or subjective evaluation. Although those Dictionary questions referred to after each selection represent what the editors believe to be the major points to consider in a given selection, other Dictionary questions may be equally as useful and should be used. Problem Questions, highlighting basic issues in the unit, will be found at the end of each of the four units of the volume. Finally, consult the two fiction models, the Prose Narrative Model on page 33, and the Short Story Model on page 156, for ideas as to how the significant aspects of the selections you read can be analyzed, specifically in terms of the "Dictionary of Questions." If you observe the suggestions on reading the short story as described previously, and you make an honest attempt to apply the questions asked to the works in question, you should learn a great deal about the nature of short fiction.

ANCIENT PROSE NARRATIVES

Fiction, in its beginnings, was almost entirely oral in nature. There can be little doubt that from earliest times, man has been a storytelling creature, and the relating of narratives in prose and other forms had probably been going on a long time before someone sat down to put in writing stories which he had heard from one or more sources. Thus, in its most rudimentary form, the short story goes back in time about as far as man himself.

In the first unit of this book, representative selections from those forms which record the earliest written prose narratives have been included. They are not at all alike in nature; thus the modern short story can be said to have a long and diverse tradition.

The poet Horace states in *Ars Poetica* that the purpose of literature is to please, persuade, and instruct. As you read the first short selections in this unit, you will note that some early forms of prose narrative were read largely for instructional purposes. Fables, for instance, have been consistently used for the illustration of some moral precept. You will note in this unit that one group of Aesop's *Fables* is labeled "Without Morals," a precaution taken by the modern translator so that the reader will not search in vain for a specifically defined message. Greek *myths* (or fables) generally are attempts to explain the mystery of natural phenomena as well as the consequences of human behavior. In the Biblical selections we find further use of the narrative form for didactic purposes. The New Testament, for instance, is filled with *parables,* the recounting of a tale containing an obvious moral followed by the direct statement of that moral. Notice at this point that a most important

11

and fruitful source of literature is and has always been the Holy Bible. Besides being a source of religious inspiration, information, and authority, the Bible is also a great landmark in the literary tradition.

Most fables and parables are quite short. Some few, however, of those found in this unit are excerpts from longer works. The battle between Hector and Achillês, for instance, is really only one incident from the long epic work, *The Iliad.* This kind of narrative structure, the anecdote or short story found within a longer work, is characteristic also of much short prose fiction. Since many ancient works were long and *episodic* (the joining together of several episodes which have been experienced by one or more major characters), early narratives have the same basic *form* as the modern story and provide us with many incidents which themselves form separate, interesting stories. These stories from the longer ancient works are largely for the pleasure of the reader.

Thus the stories in this unit emanate from several sources and were used for several purposes. There are fables, parables, narratives from the Bible, and excerpts from the two great epics of Homer. Although they are quite different in nature, they do present some of the important characteristics of the short story form which is so familiar to readers of our time. Some of these characteristics are the following:

1. The focusing by the writer on one character and usually on one important action.

2. The rapid but clearly defined build-up of suspense within the story toward a climactic moment.

3. Careful description of some significant outer action; that is, there is almost always some physical event which is crucial to the story.

4. The use by the writer of the element of *compression.* Much is identified or intimated in relatively few words. The reader is therefore often left to draw his own *inferences.*

As you read the selections which follow, notice the presence of the features described above. They are in virtually every selection in this volume.

Fables

AESOP

THE MAN, THE BOY, AND THE DONKEY

A Man and his son were once going with their Donkey to market. As they were walking along by its side a country-man passed them and said: "You fools, what is a Donkey for but to ride upon?"

So the Man put the Boy on the Donkey and they went on their way. But soon they passed a group of men, one of whom said: "See that lazy youngster, he lets his father walk while he rides."

So the Man ordered his Boy to get off, and got on himself. But they hadn't gone far when they passed two women, one of whom said to the other: "Shame on that lazy lout to let his poor little son trudge along."

Well, the Man didn't know what to do, but at last he took his Boy up before him on the Donkey. By this time they had come to the town, and the passers-by began to jeer and point at them. The Man stopped and asked what they were scoffing at. The men said: "Aren't you ashamed of yourself for overloading that poor Donkey of yours—you and your hulking son?"

The Man and Boy got off, and tried to think what to do. They thought and they thought, till at last they cut down a pole, tied the Donkey's feet to it, and raised the pole and the Donkey to their shoulders. They went along amid the laughter of all who met them till they came to Market Bridge, when the Donkey, getting one of his feet loose, kicked out and caused the Boy to drop his end of the pole. In the struggle, the Donkey fell over the bridge, and, his forefeet being tied together, he was drowned.

"That will teach you," said an old man who had followed them:

"PLEASE ALL, AND YOU WILL PLEASE NONE."

BELLING THE CAT

Long ago, the mice had a general council to consider what measures they could take to outwit their common enemy, the Cat. Some said this, and some said that; but at last a young mouse got up and said he had a proposal to make, which he thought would meet the case. "You will all agree," said he, "that our chief danger consists in the sly and treacherous manner in which the enemy approaches us. Now, if we could receive some signal of her approach, we could easily escape from her. I venture, therefore, to propose that a small bell be procured, and attached by a ribbon around the neck of the Cat. By this means we should always know when she was about, and could easily retire while she was in the neighborhood."

This proposal met with general applause, until an old mouse got up and said: "This is all very well, but who is to bell the Cat?" The mice looked at one another and nobody spoke. Then the old mouse said:

"IT IS EASY TO PROPOSE IMPOSSIBLE REMEDIES."

THE WOLF IN SHEEP'S CLOTHING

A Wolf found great difficulty in getting at the sheep owing to the vigilance of the shepherd and his dogs. But one day it found the skin of a sheep that had been flayed° and thrown aside, so it put it on over its own pelt° and strolled down among the sheep. The Lamb that belonged to the sheep, whose skin the Wolf was wearing, began to follow the Wolf in the Sheep's clothing; so, leading the Lamb a little apart, he soon made a meal off her, and for some time he succeeded in deceiving the sheep, and enjoying hearty meals.

"APPEARANCES ARE DECEPTIVE."

THE DOG IN THE MANGER

A Dog looking out for its afternoon nap jumped into the Manger of an Ox and lay there cosily upon the straw. But

soon the Ox, returning from its afternoon work, came up
to the Manger and wanted to eat some of the straw. The
Dog in a rage, being awakened from its slumber, stood up
and barked at the Ox, and whenever it came near attempted
to bite it. At last the Ox had to give up the hope of getting
at the straw, and went away muttering:

"AH, PEOPLE OFTEN GRUDGE OTHERS WHAT THEY CANNOT
ENJOY THEMSELVES."

THE LION AND THE STATUE

A Man and a Lion were discussing the relative strength of
men and lions in general. The Man contended that he and
his fellows were stronger than lions by reason of their
greater intelligence. "Come now with me," he cried, "and
I will soon prove that I am right." So he took him into the
public gardens and showed him a statue of Hercules overcoming the Lion and tearing his mouth in two.

"That is all very well," said the Lion, "but proves
nothing, for it was a man who made the statue."

"WE CAN EASILY REPRESENT THINGS
AS WE WISH THEM TO BE."

Aesop's Fables
Without Morals

Translated by Lloyd W. Daly

THE FOX AND THE GRAPES

A hungry fox saw some grapes hanging from a vine in a
tree and, although he was eager to reach them, was unable
to do so. As he went away, he said to himself, "They're
sour grapes."

From "Aesop Without Morals" translated by Lloyd W. Daly and reprinted with the
permission of A. S. Barnes & Company, Inc., and Thomas Yoseloff.

THE BLIND MAN

A blind man used to be able to tell by the feel of any animal
that was put into his hands what kind it was. Once when a
baby lynx° was given him, he stroked it and felt it all over
and said, "I don't know whether you're a wolf or a fox or
the whelp° of some such animal, but this I do know well,
that it is not a good idea for such an animal as you to be
with a flock of sheep."

THE OLD WOMAN AND THE DOCTOR

An elderly woman who was having eye trouble called in a
doctor. Every time he came to see her, he would apply
some ointment, and while her eyes were still closed, he
would carry off some of her household utensils. When he
had carried off all she had and successfully completed his
treatment, he asked her for the fee they had agreed on. She
would not pay it, and he took her before the magistrates.
She said that she had promised to pay the fee if he restored
her sight, but that now, as a result of the treatment, she was
in a worse condition than before. "As it was," she said, "I
could see all the utensils in my house, but now I can't see
them at all."

THE DEER AT THE WATER HOLE

A deer was very thirsty and came to a spring. As she drank,
she saw her reflection in the water and was delighted to see
the size and beauty of her horns, but she was much distressed at how slight and insecure her legs were. While
she was still pondering this, a lion appeared and put her to
flight. As she started to run, she easily left him behind. As
long as the land was clear she stayed a safe distance ahead,
but when she came to wooded country, as luck would have
it, her horns became entangled in the branches, and since
she couldn't run, she was caught. As she was about to be
killed, she said to herself, "Poor fool, I was being saved by
the limbs I thought would fail me, and now I am ruined by
those in which I had so much confidence."

For each fable do especially Questions 11, 32, 44, 50, and 150.
Consult the Prose Narrative Model on page 33.

AESOP   *6th Century B.C.*

To give a detailed biographical sketch of Aesop's life is impossible, for, like Homer, Aesop has only a legendary past. In fact,
many scholars say Aesop never lived, and many of the fables at
first attributed to Aesop were later traced to Egyptian and Indian
origins. However, tradition says Aesop was a slave of Iadmon of
Samos who taught moral values through simple stories in which
the main characters are animals with human qualities and human
weaknesses. Phaedrus, a Macedonian slave whom Augustus freed,
translated the fables of Aesop into Latin verse. In the thirteenth
century a Byzantine monk compiled a collection of the fables in
prose form. And Jean de La Fontaine (1668-1694) gave us the
most polished version in his *Fables.*

The Man and the Adder

PILPAY

A Man mounted upon a Camel once rode into a thicket, and
went to rest himself in that part of it from whence a caravan°
was just departed, and where the people having left a fire,
some sparks of it, being driven by the wind, had set a bush,
wherein lay an Adder, all in flame. The fire environed the
Adder in such a manner that he knew not how to escape,
and was just giving himself over to destruction, when he
perceived the Man already mentioned, and with a thousand
mournful conjurations° begged of him to save his life. The
Man, on this, being naturally compassionate, said to himself, "It is true these creatures are enemies to mankind;
however, good actions are of great value, even of the very
greatest when done to our enemies; and whoever sows the
seed of good works, shall reap the fruit of blessings." After
he had made this reflection, he took a sack, and tying it to
the end of his lance, reached it over the flame to the Adder,
who flung himself into it; and when he was safe in, the

"The Man and the Adder" by Pilpay, reprinted with the permission of Philosophical
Library, Publishers.

traveler pulled back the bag, and gave the Adder leave°
to come forth, telling him he might go about his business;
but hoped he would have the gratitude to make him a promise never to do any more harm to men, since a man had done
him so great a piece of service.

To this the ungrateful creature answered, "You much
mistake both yourself and me; think not that I intend to be
gone so calmly; no, my design is first to leave thee a parting
blessing, and throw my venom° upon thee and thy Camel."

"Monster of ingratitude!" replied the Traveler, "desist
a moment at least, and tell me whether it be lawful to re-
compense° good with evil."

"No," replied the Adder, "it certainly is not; but in acting
in that manner I shall do no more than what yourselves do
every day; that is to say, retaliate° good deeds with wicked
actions, and requite° benefits with ingratitude."

"You cannot prove this slanderous and wicked asper-
sion," replied the Traveler: "nay, I will venture to say that
if you can show me any one other creature in the world that
is of your opinion, I will consent to whatever punishment
you think fit to inflict on me for the faults of my fellow-
creatures."

"I agree to this willingly," answered the Adder; and at
the same time spying a Cow, "Let us propound our question," said he, "to this creature before us, and we shall
see what answer she will make." The Man consented; and
so both of them accosting the Cow, the Adder put the question to her, how a good turn was to be requited. "By its
contrary," replied the Cow, "if you mean according to the
customs of men; and this I know by sad experience. I
belong," said she, "to a man to whom I have long been
several ways extremely beneficial; I have been used to
bring him a calf every year, and to supply his house with
milk, butter, and cheese; but now I am grown old, and no
longer in a condition to serve him as formerly I did, he has
put me in this pasture to fat me, with a design to sell me to
a butcher, who is to cut my throat, and he and his friends
are to eat my flesh: and is not this requiting good with evil?"

On this, the Adder, taking upon him to speak, said to the

Man, "What say you now? are not your own customs a sufficient warrant for me to treat you as I intend to do?"

The Traveler, not a little confounded at this ill-timed story, was cunning enough, however, to answer, "This is a particular case only, and give me leave to say, one witness is not sufficient to convince me; therefore pray let me have another."

"With all my heart," replied the Adder; "let us address ourselves to this Tree that stands here before us." The Tree, having heard the subject of their dispute, gave his opinion in the following words: "Among men, benefits are never requited but with ungrateful actions. I protect travelers from the heat of the sun, and yield them fruit to eat, and a delightful liquor° to drink; nevertheless, forgetting the delight and benefit of my shade, they barbarously cut down my branches to make sticks, and handles for hatchets, and saw my body to make planks and rafters. Is not this requiting good with evil?"

The Adder, on this, looking upon the Traveler, asked if he was satisfied. But he was in such a confusion that he knew not what to answer. However, in hopes to free himself from the danger that threatened him, he said to the Adder, "I desire only one favor more; let us be judged by the next beast we meet; give me but that satisfaction, it is all I crave: you know life is sweet; suffer me therefore to beg for the means of continuing it." While they were thus parlaying° together, a Fox passing by was stopped by the Adder, who conjured° him to put an end to their controversy.

The Fox, upon this, desiring to know the subject of their dispute, said the Traveler, "I have done this Adder a signal piece of service, and he would fain persuade me that, for my reward, he ought to do me a mischief." "If he means to act by you as you men do by others, he speaks nothing but what is true," replied the Fox; "but, that I may be better able to judge between you, let me understand what service it is that you have done him."

The Traveler was very glad of this opportunity of speaking for himself, and recounted the whole affair to him: he told him after what manner he had rescued him out of the flames with that little sack, which he showed him.

"How!" said the Fox, laughing outright, "would you pretend to make me believe that so large an Adder as this could get into such a little sack? It is impossible!" Both the Man and the Adder, on this, assured him of the truth of that part of the story; but the Fox positively refused to believe it. At length said he, "Words will never convince me of this monstrous improbability; but if the Adder will go into it again, to convince me of the truth of what you say, I shall then be able to judge the rest of this affair."

"That I will do most willingly," replied the Adder; and at the same time, put himself into the sack.

Then said the Fox to the Traveler, "Now you are the master of your enemy's life: and, I believe, you need not be long in resolving what treatment such a monster of ingratitude deserves of you." With that the Traveler tied up the mouth of the sack, and, with a great stone, never left off beating it till he had pounded the Adder to death; and, by that means, put an end to his fears and the dispute at once.

Do especially Questions 11, 14, 21, 47, 73, 88, 90, and 150. Consult the Prose Narrative Model on page 33.

PILPAY

Pilpay, the author of "The Man and the Adder," wrote in Sanskrit. This legendary fabulist is known through an ancient Sanskrit collection called *The Panchatantra*, but the dates of his birth and death are unknown. About 550 A.D. his work was translated into Pahlevi, later into Arabic. Still other versions exist in Mongol, Malay, and Afghan.

The Iliad: The Battle of Achillês and Hector

HOMER Translated by W. H. D. Rouse

The old King Priam was the first to see Achillês speeding
over the plain. His armour shone on his breast, like the
star of harvest whose rays are most bright among many
stars, in the murky night: they call it Orion's Dog.[1] Most
brilliant is that star, but he is a sign of trouble, and brings
many fevers for unhappy mankind.

The old man groaned, and lifting up his hands beat them
upon his head as he groaned, and cried aloud to his son
entreating him; but his son was standing before the gates
immovable, and determined to meet Achillês face to face.

"O Hector!" the old man cried in piteous tones as he
stretched out his hands, "Hector my beloved son! Do not
face that man alone, without a friend, or fate will soon find
you out! Do not be so hard-hearted! Peleion[2] will destroy
you, for he is stronger than you are. O that the gods loved
him as I do! Soon would vultures° and dogs feast on him
lying on the ground! Then this cruel pain would pass from
my heart. He has bereaved me of many sons, and good
sons, killing and selling to far-off islands.

"Now again there are two sons that I cannot see amongst
those who are crowded here in the city — Lycaon and Poly-
doros; their mother was the princess Laothoê. If they are
alive in the enemy camp, they shall be ransomed; there is
gold and bronze enough here, for she had plenty from her
old father Altês. If they are dead already and in the house
of Hadês,[3] there is grief for their mother and me their
father; but for the rest of the people the grief will not last
so long if only you do not die with them by the hands of
Achillês.

[1] The brightest star, Rigel, in the equatorial constellation Orion.
[2] The son of Peleus, that is, Achillês.
[3] The Greek underworld, the home of the dead.

Selections from *The Iliad* and *The Odyssey*, Homer, translated by W.H.D. Rouse.
Published by Nelson, London, and the New American Library of World Literature,
New York. Reprinted by permission of Thomas Nelson & Sons, Ltd., Publishers.

"Do come within these walls, my son! Save the men and women of our city; life is sweet—do not let Achillês rob you of life and win glory for himself! Pity me also—an old man, but not too old to know, not too old to be unhappy! A miserable portion indeed Father Cronidês[4] will give me then—to perish in my old age, after I have lived to see many troubles, seen my sons destroyed and my daughters dragged into slavery, my house ransacked, little children dashed on the ground in fury, my sons' wives dragged away by Achaian hands! And my self last of all—someone shall strike me down or pierce my body, and leave me dead at my door for carrion° dogs to devour; my own table-dogs, my watchdogs, which I have fed with my own hands, will go mad and lap my blood, and lie sated° by the door where they used to watch. For a young man all is decent when he is killed in battle; he may be mangled with wounds, all is honourable in his death whatever may come. But a hoary head, and a white beard, and nakedness violated by dogs, when an old man is killed, there is the most pitiable sight that mortal eyes can see."

As the old man spoke he tore the white hairs from his head; but Hector would not listen. His mother stood there also, weeping; she loosened the folds of her dress, and with the other hand bared her breast, and through her tears cried out the secrets of her heart:

"O Hector my own child, by *this* I beseech you, have pity on me, if ever I gave you the soothing breast! Remember this, my love, and come behind these walls—let these walls keep off that terrible man! Do not stand out in front against him, do not be so hard! For if he kill you, never shall I lay you on your bier,° never shall I mourn over you, my pretty bud, son of my own body! Nor your precious wife—we shall both be far away, and Danaän[5] dogs will devour you in the Danaän camp!"

But their tears and their prayers availed nothing with

[4]Cronos, the supreme ruler of the earth and its inhabitants before Zeus deposed him. He was still called upon, occasionally, as the supreme ruler in the time of Homer.
[5]Pertaining to Argos. Since the men of Argos were allies of the Achaeans, *Danaän* equals Achaean here.

Hector's proud spirit. He stood fast, and awaited the coming of his tremendous foe. Like a serpent of the mountains over his hole, fed full of poisons and imbued° with bitter hate, who lies in wait coiled about the hole and fiercely glaring, so Hector imbued with unquenchable° passion would not retreat, but stood, leaning his shield against a bastion° of the wall. Then deeply moved he spoke to his own heart:

"What shall I do? If I retreat behind these walls, Polydamas[6] will be the first to heap reproaches on me, for he advised me to lead the army back to the city on that dread night when Achillês rose up. I would not listen—it would have been better if I had! And now that I have ruined them all by my rashness, I am ashamed to face the men and women of Troy, or some base fellows may say—Hector thought too much of his own strength, and ruined us all! They will say that: and my better part is to face him for life and death. Either I shall kill him and return in triumph, or I shall die with honour before the gate.

"Shall I lay down my shield and helmet and lean my spear against the wall, and go to meet him alone, and promise to yield Helen with all her wealth, all that Alexandros brought with her to Troy?—yield the woman who was the cause of the great war, let the princes of Argos take her away, offer to pay besides half the treasure of our city, make the elders of the city take oath to hide nothing but to divide honestly all we possess? But what good would that be? Suppose I should approach him, and then he would not have pity and would not spare me? Suppose I should strip off my armour, and then he should just kill me naked like a woman? This is no place for fairy tales, or lovers' pretty prattle,° the way of a man with a maid, when man and maid prattle so prettily together! Better get to work at once; we'll see which of us the Olympian[7] makes the winner!"

So he mused and stood his ground, while Achillês drew near, like Enyalios the warrior god, shaking over his right

[6]A valiant leader of the Trojans.
[7]Zeus.

shoulder that terrible Pelian ashplant:[8] the armour upon
him shone like flaming fire or beams of the rising sun.
Hector trembled to see him. He could stand no longer but
took to flight, and Peleidês[9] was upon him with a leap:
Hector fled swiftly under the walls of Troy and Peleidês
flew after him furiously, as a falcon swoops without effort
after a timid dove, for he is the swiftest of flying things,
and he darts upon her with shrieking cries close behind,
greedy for a kill. They passed the look-out and the wind-
beaten fig tree, keeping ever away from the wall along the
cartroad, until they reached the two fountains which are the
sources of eddying Scamandros.[10] One is a spring of hot
water, with steam rising above it as if it were boiling over
a fire; one even in summer is cold as hail or snow or frozen
ice. Near these are the tanks of stone, where the Trojan
women and girls used to wash their linen in peace-time,
before the Achaians came.

So far they came in their race, fleeing and pursuing, a
strong man fleeing and a far stronger in pursuit: they ran
hard, for Hector's life was the prize of this race, not such
prizes as men run for, a beast or an oxhide shield. Thrice°
round the city of Priam they ran, like champion racehorses
running round the turningpost for a tripod° or a woman or
some great stake, when a man is dead and the games are
given in his honour. All the gods were watching, and the
Father of gods and men exclaimed:

"Confound it, I love that man whom I see hunted round
those walls! I am deeply grieved for Hector, who has
sacrificed many an ox on the heights of Ida[11] or the citadel
of Troy! and now there is prince Achillês, chasing him
round the city of Priam. What do you think, gods? Just
consider, shall we save him from death, or shall we let
Achillês beat him now? He is a brave man."

Athena Brighteyes replied:

[8]Achilles' spear (ashplant) was made of the tall, straight ash growing on
Mt. Pelion, a mountain in eastern Thessaly.
[9]Son of Peleus, again a reference to Achillês.
[10]A river flowing from Troy into the Dardanelles. Today it is called the
Menderes River.
[11]Mt. Ida, not far from ancient Troy.

"O Father Flashingbolt, O Thundercloud, you must never say that! A mortal man, long doomed by fate, and you will save him from death? Do as you please, but the rest of us cannot approve."

Zeus Cloudgatherer answered:

"Never mind, Tritogeneia, my love. I did not really mean it and I want to be kind to you. Wait no longer but do what you wish."

Athena was ready enough, and shot away down the slopes of Olympos.[12]

Achillês was now following at full speed and gave Hector no chance. He watched him like a hound which has put up a hart° from his lair, and gives chase through the dingles° and the dells;° let the hart hide and crouch in the brake,° the hound tracks him out till he finds. If Hector going by the road made a dash at the city gates for refuge, hoping his friends might help him with a volley from the walls above, Achillês would take a short cut and get before him, running under the walls and turning him back towards the open ground. It was like some race in a dream, where one chases another, and he cannot catch or the other escape; so Achillês could never catch Hector, or Hector escape Achillês. How indeed could Hector have escaped his fleet pursuer so far, if Apollo[13] had not then for the last time been near, to give him strength and speed? And Achillês had signalled to his own men that no one should let fly a shot at Hector, and take his own credit away if he came in second.

But when the fourth time they drew near the two fountains, see now, the Father laid out his golden scales and placed in them two fates of death, one for Achillês and one for Hector. He grasped the balance and lifted it: Hector's doom sank down, sank down to Hadês, and Apollo left him.

At that moment Athena was by the side of Achillês, and she said in plain words:

[12]The home of the gods, on Mt. Olympus in northern Greece.
[13]In Greek mythology, the god of music, poetry, prophecy, and medicine. He had a special liking for Hector and had protected him many a time from harm.

"Now you and I will win, my splendid Achillês! Now I hope we shall bring great glory to our camp before the Achaian nation, by destroying Hector, for all his insatiable° courage. Now there is no chance that he can escape, not if Apollo Shootafar should fume and fret and roll over and over on the ground before Zeus Almighty! Rest and take breath, and I will go and persuade the man to stand up to you."

Achillês was glad of a rest, and stood still leaning on his barbed ashplant.

Athena now took the form and voice of Deïphobos:[14] she went over to Hector and said to him simply:

"Achillês is giving you a hard time, old fellow, chasing you like this round the city. Let us stand and defend ourselves."

Hector answered:

"O Deïphobos, I always liked you best of all the sons of my father and mother! But now I shall think more of you than ever, for daring to come outside for my sake when you saw me here. All the rest keep inside!"

Athena said:

"My dear old fellow, father and mother and all our friends begged and besought me to stay, they are so terribly afraid of him; but I had not the heart to desert you. Now then let us have at him! No sparing of spears—let us see whether he will kill us both and carry off our bloodstained spoils, or if your spear shall bring him down!"

So the deceiver led him towards Achillês; and when they were near him Hector spoke:

"I will fly from you no more, Peleidês. Three times I raced round the city of Priam and would not await your attack; but now my heart bids me stand and face you, for death or for life. But first come near and let us give our troth,° the gods shall be the best witnesses and sentinels of our agreement. If Zeus gives me endurance, and if I take your life, I will do no vile outrage to your body; I will

[14]One of Hector's many brothers.

take your armour, Achillês, and your body I will give back to your people. You do the same."

Achillês answered with a frowning face:

"Hector, I cannot forget. Talk not to me of bargains. Lions and men make no truce, wolves and lambs have no friendship—they hate each other for ever. So there can be no love between you and me; and there shall be no truce for us, until one of the two shall fall and glut° Arês[15] with his blood. Call up all your manhood; now you surely need to be a spearman and a bold man of war. There is no chance of escape now; this moment Pallas[16] Athena shall bring you low by my spear. Now in one lump sum you shall pay for all my companions, whom you have slain and I have mourned."

With the words he poised and cast his long spear. But Hector saw it coming and crouched down, so that it flew over and stuck in the earth. Pallas Athena pulled it out and gave it back to Achillês, but Hector saw nothing. Then Hector said:

"A miss! I am not dead yet as you thought, most magnificent Achillês! So there was something Zeus did not tell you about me, as it seems. You are only a rattletongue° with a trick of words, trying to frighten me and make me lose heart. I am not going to run and let you pierce my back —I will charge you straight, and then you may strike me in the breast if it be God's will, but first see if you avoid *my* spear! I pray that you may take it all into your body! The war would be lighter for Troy if you were dead, for you are our greatest danger."

He poised his spear and cast it, and hit the shield fair in the middle; but the spear rebounded and fell away. Hector was troubled that the cast had failed; he had no second spear, and he stood discomfited.° Then he shouted to Deïphobos and called for another, but no Deïphobos was there. Now Hector knew the truth, and cried out:

"All is lost! It is true then, the gods have summoned me

[15]In Greek mythology, the god of war.
[16]A poetic epithet often attached to Athena's name.

to death. Deïphobos was by my side I thought—but he is in the city and I have been deceived by Athena. Now then, death is near me, there can be no delay, there is no escape. All this while such must have been the pleasure of Zeus and his son Shootafar, who have kindly protected me so far: but now fate is upon me. Yet I pray that I may die not without a blow, not inglorious. First may I do some notable thing that shall be remembered in generations to come!"

With these words he drew the sword that hung by his side, sharp and strong, gathered himself and sprang, like an eagle flying high and swooping down from the clouds upon a lamb or cowering hare.° Achillês moved to meet him full of fury, covering his chest with the resplendent° shield while the thick golden plumes nodded upon his flashing helmet. His right hand held poised the great spear, which gleamed like the finest of all the stars of heaven, the star of evening brilliant in the dark night;[17] he scanned Hector with ruthless heart, to see where the white flesh gave the best opening for a blow. Hector was well covered with that splendid armour which he had stript from Patroclos,[18] but an opening showed where the collar-bones join the neck to the shoulder, the gullet, where a blow brings quickest death. There Achillês aimed, and the point went through the soft neck; but it did not cut the windpipe, and Hector could still answer his foe. He fell in the dust, and Achillês cried in triumph:

"There, Hector! You thought no doubt while you were stripping Patroclos that you would be safe; you cared nothing for me far away. Fool! There was an avenger,° a stronger man than Patroclos, waiting far away! I was there behind in the camp, and I have brought you low! Now you shall be mauled by vultures and dogs, and he shall be buried by a mourning nation!"

Hector half-fainting answered:

"I beseech you by your soul and by your knees, by your father and your mother, do not leave me for dogs to mangle

[17]The planet Venus; sometimes called Hesperus.
[18]The brave companion of Achillês who was killed by Hector earlier in *The Iliad.*

among your ships—accept a ransom, my father and my
mother will provide gold and treasure enough, and let them
carry home my body, that my people may give me the fire,
which is the rightful due of the dead."

Achillês said with an angry frowning face:

"Knee me no knees, you cur, and father me no fathers!
No man living shall keep the dogs from your head—not if
they bring ransom ten times and twenty times innumerable,
and weigh it out, and promise more, not if Priamos Dar-
danidês[19] pay your weight in gold—not for that ransom
shall your mother lay you out on the bier and mourn for
the son of her womb, but carrion dogs and carrion birds
shall devour you up! For what you have done to me I wish
from the bottom of my heart that I could cut you to pieces
and eat you raw myself!"

Hector answered him dying:

"Ah, I know you well, and I forbode° what will be. I was
not likely to persuade you, for your heart is made of iron.
But reflect! or I may bring God's wrath upon you, on that
day when Paris and Phoibos[20] Apollo shall slay you by the
Scaian Gate, although you are strong."

As he spoke, the shadow of death encompassed° him; and
his soul left the body and went down to Hadês, bewailing
his fate, bidding a last farewell to manhood and lusty
strength. Hector was dead, but even so Achillês again
spoke:

"Lie there dead! My fate I will accept, whenever it is
the will of Zeus and All Gods to fulfill it."

He drew the spear out of the body and laid it aside. Then
he stript off the armour, and the other Achaians came
crowding round. How they gazed in wonder at Hector's
noble form and looks! Yet no one came near without a
stab; they beat him and stabbed him, saying to each other:

"Ha ha! Hector feels very much softer now than when he
burnt our ships with his blazing brands!"

Achillês, when he finished stripping the spoils, turned to

[19]Priam, son of Dardanos.
[20]A poetic epithet often attached to Apollo's name. Phoibus means
brilliant.

the crowd, and made them a speech in his downright manner.

"My friends," he said, "princes and captains of the nation, since as you see the gods have granted me to kill this man who has done us more damage than all the rest put together, let us go round the city ready for battle, and find out what they mean to do: whether they will leave their fortress now this man is dead, or whether they will still confront us although they have no Hector.—But stay, what am I thinking about! Patroclos lies beside our ship unmourned, unburied! Patroclos I can never forget so long as I live and move! And even if in the house of Hadês men forget their dead, yet I will remember my dear comrade even there. Come on, my lads, let us march back to our ships singing our hymn of victory, and bring this man with us. We have won a great triumph; we have killed Hector, to whom the Trojans prayed as if he were a god!"

And then he thought of a shameful outrage. He cut behind the sinews° of both Hector's feet from ankle to heel and strapt them together with leather thongs, and fastened them to his chariot leaving the head to drag. Then he laid the armour in the car, and got in himself and whipt up the horses. Away they flew: the dust rose as the body was dragged along, the dark hair spread abroad, there in the dirt trailed the head that was once so charming, which now Zeus gave to his enemies to maltreat in his own native land. And as the head was bedabbled thus in the mire, his mother tore her hair and threw away the covering veil, and wailed aloud seeing her son; his father lamented sore, the people wailed, and lamentation filled the city. Such lamentation there might have been, if all frowning Ilios were smouldering in ashes.

The people had much ado to keep the old King in his frenzy from rushing out of the Dardanian[21] Gate. He rolled in the dung-heap and appealed to all, naming each by his name:

"Have done, my friends! I know you love me, but let me

[21]Trojan.

go out alone and visit the Achaian camp—let me pray to
this terrible violent man! He may have shame before his
fellows, and pity an old man—yes, I think he has an old
father like me, Peleus, who begat him and bred him to be
the ruin of Troy! And for me more than all he has brought
trouble—so many of my sons he has killed in their prime!
I mourn for them, but not for them all so much as one, who
will bring me down with sorrow to the grave, my Hector.
Would that he had died in my arms! Then we could have
mourned and wept till we could weep no more, the unhappy mother who bore him, and I his father."

As he spoke, he wept, and the people lamented with
him. Then Hecabê led the women's lamentation, herself
weeping the while:

"My child, I am desolate: how shall I live in sorrow when
you are dead? Night and day you were my boast in the city,
and a blessing to all, both men and women, who used to
welcome you as one divine. Truly you were a great glory
to them also while you lived, but now death and fate has
come upon you!"

But Hector's wife had not yet heard anything of her
husband; no messenger had told her the truth, that he
remained outside the gate. She was busy with her loom
in a far corner of the house, embroidering pretty flowers on
a wide purple web. She called to the servants to put a
cauldron° to boil on the fire, that Hector might have a warm
bath when he came in from the battle. Poor creature, she
knew not that he was far away from all baths, brought low
by the hands of Achillês and the will of Brighteyes Athena.

But when she heard lamentation and wailing from the
wall, her limbs quivered and the shuttle° fell to the ground
out of her hand, and she called to her maids:

"Here, come with me two of you and let me see what has
happened. That was the voice of my honoured good-
mother![22] My heart is in my mouth—my knees are turned
to stone! Some trouble is at hand for the sons of Priam!
Far from my ear be that word! But I am terribly afraid

[22]Mother-in-law; Hecabê.

prince Achillês has cut off my rash Hector by himself and driven him away to the plain! Ah, he will put an end to the fatal pride that always possessed him, for Hector would never stay in the crowd—he would always run out in front and yield in courage to no man!"

She tore out like a mad woman with beating heart, and the maids followed. When she came to the crowd of men on the battlements, she stood peering about—then she saw him dragged along in front of the city; the horses were dragging him at full speed towards the Achaian camp, careless what they did. Then the darkness of night came over her eyes, and she fell backwards fainting and gasping; the coverings fell from her head—diadem,° coif,° braided circlet, and the veil which golden Aphroditê[23] had given her, on the day when Hector paid his rich bride-gifts and led her away from Eëtion's house. Crowding round her were Hector's sisters and goodsisters holding her up, distracted unto death.

When she came to herself and revived, she cried out amid her sobs:

"O Hector, I am unhappy! So we were both born to one fate, you in Troy in the palace of Priam, I in Thebê under woody Placos, in the house of Eëtion who brought me up as a tiny tot—doomed father, doomed child! Would I had never been born! Now you have gone to the house of Hadês deep down under the earth; but I am left in bitter grief a widow in our home. And our son is still only a baby—O doomed father, doomed mother! Never will you be a blessing to him, Hector, or he to you: for you are dead. Even if he escapes from this miserable war, yet his portion shall be always labour and sorrow, for strangers will rob him of his lands.

"The day of orphanhood makes a child wholly friendless. He must always hang his head, his cheeks are slobbered with tears, he goes begging to his father's friends, and plucks one by the cloak, another by the shirt; if one has pity he puts a cup to his mouth for a sip, wets the lips but

[23]The goddess of love; Venus.

not the palate.° The boy who has both father and mother slaps him and drives him away from the table with unkind words — 'Just get out! Your father does not dine with us.' Then the boy runs crying to his widowed mother — yes, Astyanax, who once sat on his own father's knee and ate only marrow° and richest fat of sheep! And when he felt sleepy and did not want to play any more, he slept on a bedstead, with nurse's arms round him, with a soft bed under him, full and satisfied.

"But now he will have plenty to suffer since his father is gone — my Astyanax as they all call him in this city, because you alone saved their gates and walls. And now you are in the enemy camp, far from your father and mother, and when the dogs have had enough, crawling worms will eat your body — naked, although there is nice soft linen in your house made by your own women. But I will make a bonfire of the whole store; it is of no use to you, for your body will not lie out in that, but it will do you honour in the eyes of the people of Troy."

She wept while she spoke, and the women lamented with her.

PROSE NARRATIVE MODEL

The Battle of Achillês and Hector approached from the Seven Views of the *Dictionary of Questions*

FIRST VIEW

1. What is my first impression of the work as a total unit? Upon first reading about the battle between Hector and Achillês, I was interested only in the outcome. I had no trouble trying to visualize the fight because many details and descriptions are given. The characters seem very real, but the constant interference of the gods and the strange names bothered me somewhat, but not enough to dampen my interest in the story.

SECOND VIEW

2. Under which type in the following scheme would I classify the work from a first reading? Why? From my first reading, I can determine that the battle between Hector and Achillês is an excerpt from *The Iliad,* a long narrative epic. The battle incident, written in prose, is a *short story* within the longer narrative.

TYPES OF LITERATURE

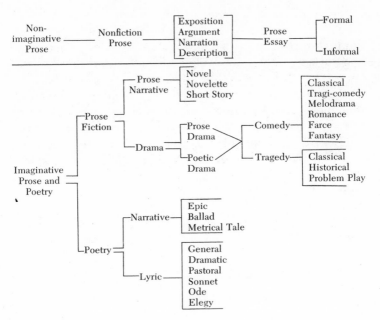

THIRD VIEW

15. What does the author want me to generalize about the central character? The author wants me to consider whether Hector, who apparently decides to confront Achillês for reasons of personal pride and honor, is actually a victim of predetermined fate and whimsical gods or the victim of his own personality. Hector, a doomed mortal, is alone when he fights the godlike Achillês who is armed with the favor and protection of Athena.

17. Next, what of major importance happened to him? The happening of major significance is not so much Hector's death, or his valiant, but futile defense, as it is the dishonorable desecration of his body. Hector has become the object of Achillês' insatiable revenge; consequently, Hector's dying plea for ransom, which would insure his proper burial, is savagely denied. The significance of this flagrant disregard for the rights of the dead is amplified by the agonizing lamentations of Hector's family.

FOURTH VIEW

42. Can I construct a graph giving the exposition, rising action, climax, falling action, and catastrophe? What are the various inciting forces to account for the hero's rising action,... the turning point in the climax, etc.? As I conceive my chart, I am aware that Priam's plea introduces the ideas that will set the stage for future action. His plea foreshadows Hector's death at the hands of a stronger adversary, and reveals the fact that neither Hector nor himself will receive proper burial. Hector's resolution leads to his meeting Achillês, while divine interference leads to the climactic battle. Achillês' refusal and victory result in the utter helplessness of Troy and Hector's family, since they are now without a champion or protector.

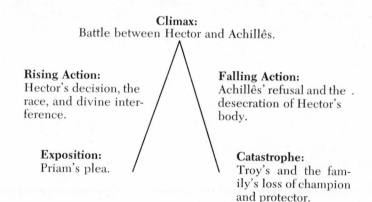

Climax:
Battle between Hector and Achillês.

Rising Action:
Hector's decision, the race, and divine interference.

Falling Action:
Achillês' refusal and the desecration of Hector's body.

Exposition:
Priam's plea.

Catastrophe:
Troy's and the family's loss of champion and protector.

FIFTH VIEW

75. Is the work primarily one of incident and surprise, character problems, or mood and local color; or are plot, character, and setting of equal importance? I think that character problems are of primary importance in this work. Hector is faced with the dilemma of choosing between public and personal dishonor or probable death and honor. His decision to fight Achillês precipitates his most important problem — preventing the desecration of his remains. But neither of Hector's problems are solved. He is helpless against the combined forces of fate, Athena, and the anger of Achillês. Not only does he lose his life, but his body is publicly dishonored; he is denied a proper funeral, and his city and family are left without a protector.

89. What conflicts constitute the main action of the story? One emotion or state of mind against another, or one man against another, or man against his physical environment and society — or a combination of these conflicts? I first find Hector in conflict with himself. It is not easy for Hector to disregard the emotional pleas of his parents or to disregard his own knowledge that Achillês is a "tremendous foe." Internal strife is also reflected in his keen awareness of peer criticism and its implication with regard to the most honorable course of action. As the defender of Troy, Hector has caused the Achaians heavy casualties; consequently, he has incurred the wrath of an entire nation. In killing Patroclos, he has incited the hatred of Achillês. Not only is Hector in conflict with a nation and a man, but also with himself. He knows his former "rashness" in battle and his refusal to take Polydamas' advice has led to ruin, and yet he must fight with courage.

92. *Foreshadowing and suspense* — What is their function in the work? Instances foreshadowing Hector's death are numerous. Priam's agonizing plea reveals Achillês' superior strength. Athena's remark to Zeus that Hector's doom has long since been decreed by fate is reinforced by the golden scales of Zeus, Apollo's abandonment of Hector, and Athena's deception. Even though Hector's death is foreshadowed, the suspense of anticipating subsequent action is maintained.

107. What is the character's philosophy of life — his convictions and beliefs about man, the world, and human destiny? Does the author seem favorably inclined, critical, or noncommittal towards this philosophy? It seems to me that Hector sums up the typically Greek attitude toward man, the world, and human destiny. He is distrustful of men, but longs for their praise. Honor and courage are the ideals most sought after. Even though Hector is more or less certain that Achillês will kill him, he cannot allow himself to shirk battle. Although he considers begging for mercy and surrendering, and does run from Achillês when he meets him, his manhood is always uppermost in his mind. He is unmoved by the pleas of women and old men for, to the Greek, they can know nothing of manhood.

Hector understands destiny in a truly Greek way. Although fate decrees the manner and end of life, Hector knows that his own "rashness," his stubbornness in not leading his army back to camp on the night Achillês was angered by Trojan excesses, his slaughter of Patroclos and wearing his armor has sealed his doom. Hector fears, but probably understands, Achillês' insatiable wrath because he himself has been ruthless. Even his wife (when she fears her husband is dead) mentions her "rash Hector," his "fatal pride," and how he would never stay in a crowd.

In spite of the interference of the gods, fate, to the Greeks, seems to be the result of the combination of circumstances and a human's own behavior.

109. Who are the important subordinate characters? What are their chief traits? Are they distinct personalities, or are they mere surface types? Achillês at first seems to function as a foil to Hector's hopes of an honorable death. His savage desire for revenge seems unnatural and suggests a distinct personality who perverts the concept of duty to a friend and violates human decency. Priam emerges as a distinct personality whose concern for the safety of his son, and whose own helplessness as an old man, seem convincing. Hector's wife, a surface type, reinforces the idea of helplessness and the horrible effects of war on the innocent.

SIXTH VIEW

133. How does my knowledge of elements outside the work contribute to further understanding of the work itself? It is significant for me to learn that Achillês was the son of a goddess, Thetis, who made him, with the exception of his heel, physically invincible. Even his magnificent armor had been forged by Hephaestus, a god. It is little wonder then that any mortal, even one as brave as Hector, would be awed by this half-god who enjoyed divine protection. Upon reading the complete work, I would reëvaluate Achillês' role and I note the phrase "the wrath of Achillês" which begins *The Iliad*. Achillês' wrath, extreme vengeance, when provoked, is the guiding force of the whole book. Certainly his excesses are well known to the Trojans and are as deciding a factor in Hector's doom as Athena and fate. Even though the gods play important and decisive roles in the events that occur during this ten-year war, I am aware that the true invincibility and vulnerability of Achillês are his wrath and pride; that "fate" is really the probable outcome of certain kinds of events imposed on certain kinds of human personalities. The gods emerge as superhumans, themselves powerless before fate. Although they actively take sides, the outcome of the war is clearly known by them. An uneasy truce for the funeral of Hector, which concludes *The Iliad,* is brought about through the violent interference of gods friendly to the Trojan cause.

SEVENTH VIEW

148. How does a final reading of the work (considering it as a total unit after all of the analytical study has been completed) compare with my first unanalyzed impressions in the First View? The more I think about this story the more I see in it. At first I was

interested only in the battle—then the people in the story. Later
I found much more to think about: what the Greeks were really
like, how much of what they felt and did is what people today feel
and do. I am surprised that even though I felt greatest sympathy
for Hector, I can also sympathize with Achillês. I can understand,
in part, why so much space is devoted to descriptions of weapons
and why the Greeks admired and were excited by well-constructed
weapons—they thought of them not only as powerful instruments,
but as beautiful objects of art.

The story made me think about war, then and now; about what
the women, children, and older men feel about it; what courage
and honor means. I know that *The Iliad* is called a classic, and I
begin to understand what that word means and what is meant by
"universality": even though these things, if they happened at all,
happened a long time ago, they are no less thought provoking or
enjoyable for readers today. Even though Homer's work is not
"realistic" in one sense, it is very real in another.

The Odyssey: Odysseus Visits the Lotus-Eaters and the Cyclops

HOMER Translated by W. H. D. Rouse

Then Odysseus began his tale:

"What a pleasure it is, my lord," he said, "to hear a
singer like this, with a divine voice! I declare it is just the
perfection of gracious life: good cheer and good temper
everywhere, rows of guests enjoying themselves heartily
and listening to the music, plenty to eat on the table, wine
ready in the great bowl, and the butler ready to fill your cup
whenever you want it. I think that is the best thing men can
have. —But you have a mind to hear my sad story and make
me more unhappy than I was before. What shall I begin
with, what shall I end with? The lords of heaven have
given me sorrow in abundance.

"First of all I will tell you my name, and then you may
count me one of your friends if I live to reach my home,

although that is far away. I am Odysseus Laërtiadês,[1] a name well known in the world as one who is ready for any event. My home is Ithaca, that bright conspicuous isle, with Mount Neriton rising clear out of the quivering forests. Round it lie many islands clustering close, Dulichion and Samê and woody Zacynthos. My island lies low, last of all in the sea to westward, the others away toward the dawn and the rising sun. It is rough, but a nurse of good lads; I tell you there is no sweeter sight any man can see than his own country. Listen now: a radiant goddess Calypso[2] tried to keep me by her in her cave and wanted me for a husband; Circê[3] also would have had me stay in her mansion, and a clever creature she was, and she also wanted me for a husband, but she never could win my heart. How true it is that nothing is sweeter than home and kindred, although you may have a rich house in a foreign land far away from your kindred! Ah well, but you are waiting to hear of my journey home and all the sorrows which Zeus laid upon me after I left Troy.

"From Ilion the wind carried me to Ismaros of the Ciconians. There I destroyed the city and killed the men. We spared the women and plenty of cattle and goods, which we divided to give each man a fair share. I told the men we must show a light heel and be off, but the poor fools would not listen. Plenty of wine was drunk, plenty of sheep were killed on that beach, and herds of cattle! Meanwhile some of the enemy got away and shouted to other Ciconians, neighbors of theirs inland, more men and better men, who knew how to fight from the chariot against a foe, and on foot if need be.

"A multitude of these men swarmed down early in the morning, as many as leaves and flowers in the season of the year. Surely Zeus sent us a hard fate that day, to bring trouble on a lot of poor devils! They drew up near the ships, and then came volleys° on both sides. All through the

[1]Son of Laërtes.
[2]A sea nymph who did not permit Odysseus to leave her island for seven years.
[3]An enchantress who turned men into swine.

morning while the day grew stronger we stood our ground and held them off, although they outnumbered us; but when the sun began to change course, about ox-loosing time,[4] the Ciconians got the upper hand and bent our line. Six men-at-arms from each vessel were killed; and the rest of us were saved alive.

"From that place we sailed onward much discouraged, but glad to have escaped death, although we had lost good companions. Yet we did not let the galleys° go off, until we had called thrice on the name of each of our hapless comrades who died in that place. But Zeus Cloudgatherer sent a norwester upon our fleet with a furious tempest, bringing clouds over land and sea; and night rushed down from the sky. The ships were blown plunging along, the sails were split into shreds and tatters by the violence of the wind. We let down the sails in fear of death and rowed the bare hulls to shore. There we lay two days and two nights on end, eating out our hearts with hardship and anxiety. But when the third day showed welcome streaks of light, we stept° the masts and hoisted new sails, and sat still, while the wind drove us on and the steersman held the way. Then I might have come safe to my native land, but the sea and the current and the northwest wind caught me as I was doubling Cape Malea, and drifted me outside Cythera.[5]

"Nine days after that I was beaten about on the sea by foul winds, and on the tenth day we made land in the country of the Lotus-eaters, who get their food from flowers.[6] We went ashore and took in water, and the men made their meal on the spot close to the ships. When we had eaten and drunk, I sent some of them to find out who the natives were: two picked men with a speaker. Before long they came across some of the Lotus-eaters. However, they did no harm to the men, only gave them some of their lotus to eat. As soon as they tasted that honey-sweet fruit,

[4]About noon, when the day's plowing is done.
[5]One of the Ionian islands south of Greece called Cerigo today.
[6]Not the lotus grass, but some kind of berry like a small date or poppy-pod. This fruit produced a dreamy languor and forgetfulness.

they thought no more of coming back to us with news, but chose rather to stay there with the lotus-eating natives, and chew their lotus, and good-by to home. I brought them back to the ships by main force, grumbling and complaining, and when I had them there, tied them up and stowed them under the benches. Then I ordered the rest to hurry up and get aboard, for I did not want them to have a taste of lotus and say good-by to home. They were soon on board and sitting on their benches and rowing away over the sea.

"From that place we sailed on in low spirits. We came next to the Cyclopians,[7] the Goggle-eyes, a violent and lawless tribe. They trust to providence, and neither plant nor plow, but everything grows without sowing or plowing; wheat and barley and vines which bear grapes in huge bunches, and the rain from heaven makes them grow of themselves. These Cyclopians have no parliament° for debates and no laws, but they live on high mountains in hollow caves; each one lays down the law for wife and children, and no one cares for his neighbors.

"Now a low flat island lies across their harbor, not very near the land and not very far, covered with trees. In this are an infinite number of wild goats, for no man walks there to scare them away, and no hunters frequent° the place to follow their toilsome trade in the forests and the hills. So it has neither flocks nor tillage;° but unsown and unplowed, untrodden of men, it feeds the bleating goats. For the Goggle-eyes have no ships with their crimson cheeks,[8] and no shipwrights among them to build boats for them to row in and visit the cities of the world, like men who traverse the seas on their lawful occasions. Such craftsmen might have civilized the island: for it is not a bad island. It could produce all the kindly fruits of the earth; there are meadows along the shore, soft land with plenty of water; there might be no end of grapes. There is smooth land for the plow; the soil is very rich, and they might always stack a good harvest in the season of the year. There is a harbor with easy riding;

[7] A race of giants supposedly living in Sicily, who had only one eye in the middle of the forehead.
[8] Sails.

no cable is wanted,° no anchor-stones or stern-hawsers.°
You just beach your ship and stay till the sailors have a
fancy to go and the wind blows fair. Moreover, at the head
of the harbor there is glorious water, a spring running out
of a cave, with poplars growing all round.

"Some providence guided us in through the dark night,
with not a thing to be seen; for a thick mist was about our
ships, and the moon showed no light through the clouds.
At that time we did not catch a glimpse of the island:
indeed we saw no long breakers rolling towards the land,
before our ships ran up on the beach. When they were safe
there, we lowered the sails and got out on the shore and
slept heavily until the dawn.

"As soon as dawn gleamed through the mist, we roamed
about and admired the island. Then those kindly daughters
of Zeus, the Nymphs, sent down goats from the hills to
give us all a good meal. We lost no time, got our bows and
long spears out of the ships, divided into three bands, and
let fly at the quarry.° Very soon God gave us as much as we
wanted. I had twelve ships with me, and nine goats were
given to each by lot, but ten were picked out for me alone.
So all day long we sat there feasting, with plenty of meat
and delicious wine. For the good red wine was not all used
up yet, but some was left; when we took the Ciconian city,
each crew had supplied themselves with plenty in large
two-handled jars. We gazed at the country of the Goggle-
eyes, which was quite close; we could see the smoke and
hear the bleating of sheep and goats. When the sun set
and darkness came, we lay down on the beach to sleep.

"But with the first rosy streaks of the dawn, I called a
meeting and made a speech to the men. 'My good fellows,'
I said, 'the rest of you stay here, while I take my ship and
crew and see who these people are; whether they are wild
savages who know no law, or hospitable men who know
right from wrong.'

"So I went aboard and told my crew to cast loose; they
were soon in their places and rowing along. The land was
not far off, and when we reached it we saw a cave there on a
headland° close by the sea, high and shaded with laurels,°

in which numbers of animals were housed by night, both sheep and goats. Outside was an enclosure with high walls round it, made of great stones dug into the earth and the trunks of tall pines and spreading oaks. These were the night-quarters of a monstrous man, who was then tending his flocks a long way off by himself; he would not mix with the others, but kept apart in his own lawless company. Indeed he was a wonderful monster, not like a mortal man who eats bread, but rather like a mountain peak with trees on the top standing up alone in the highlands.

"Then I told the rest of my men to wait for me and look after the ship, but I picked out twelve of the best men I had, and we set out. I took with me a goatskin of ruby wine, delicious wine, which I had from Maron Euanthidês, priest of Apollo who was the protecting god of Ismaros. We had saved him and his wife and child out of reverence, because he lived in the sacred grove of Phoibos Apollo. I had glorious gifts from him: he gave me seven talents'° weight of worked gold, he gave me a mixing-bowl of solid silver, but besides that, he gave me great jars of wine, a whole dozen of them, delicious wine, not a drop of water in it, a divine drink! Not a soul knew about this wine, none of the servants or women, except himself and his own wife and one cellarer. When they drank of this wine, he used to pour one cup of it into twenty measures of water, and a sweet scent was diffused abroad from the mixer, something heavenly; no one wanted to be an abstainer then! I had filled a skin with this wine, and brought it with me, also a bag of provisions; for from the first I had a foreboding that I should meet a man of mighty strength, but savage, knowing neither justice nor law.

"We walked briskly to the cave, but found him not at home; he was tending his fat flocks on the pasture. So we entered the cave and took a good look all round. There were baskets loaded with cheeses, there were pens stuffed full of lambs and kids.° Each lot was kept in a separate place; firstlings° in one, middlings° in another, yeanlings° in another. Every pot and pan was swimming with whey,° all the pails and basins into which he did the milking. The men begged me first to let them help themselves to the cheeses and be off; next they wanted to make haste and drive the kids and lambs out of the pens and get under sail. But I would not listen — indeed it would have been much better if I had! but I wanted to see himself and claim the stranger's gift. As it turned out, he was destined to be anything but a vision of joy to my comrades.

"So we lit a fire and made our thank offering, and helped ourselves to as many cheeses as we wanted to eat; then we sat inside till he should come back with his flocks. At last in he came, carrying a tremendous load of dry wood to give light for supper. This he threw down inside the cave with a crash that terrified us and sent us scurrying° into the corners. Then he drove his fat flocks into the cave, that is to say, all he milked, leaving the rams and billy goats outside the cave but within the high walls of the enclosure. Then he picked up a huge great stone and placed it in the doorway: not two and twenty good carts with four wheels apiece could have lifted it off the ground, such was the size of the precipitous° rock which he planted in front of the entrance. Then he sat down and milked the goats and ewes,° bleating loudly, all in order, and put her young under each. Next he curdled half of the white milk and packed it into wicker° baskets, leaving the other half to stand in bowls, that he might have some to drink for supper or whenever he wanted. At last after all this busy work, he lighted the fire and saw us.

"'Who are you?' he called out. 'Where do you come from over the watery ways? Are you traders, or a lot of pirates ready to kill and be killed, bringing trouble to foreigners?'

"While he spoke, our hearts were wholly broken within us to see the horrible monster and to hear that beastly voice. But I managed to answer him:

"'We are Achaians from Troy, driven out of our course over the broad sea by all the winds of heaven. We meant to sail straight home, but we have lost our way altogether: such was the will of Zeus, I suppose. We have the honor to be the people of King Agamemnon Atreidês,[9] whose fame is greatest of all men under the sky, for the strong city he sacked and the many nations he conquered. But we have found you and come to your knees to pray if you will give us the stranger's due or anything you may think proper to give to a stranger. Respect the gods, most noble sir; see, we are your suppliants!° Strangers and suppliants have their guardian strong. God walks with them to see they get no wrong.'

"He answered me with cruel words: 'You are a fool, stranger, or you come from a long way off, if you expect me to fear gods. We Cyclopians care nothing for them, we are stronger than they are. I should not worry about Zeus if I wanted to lay hands on you or your companions. But tell me, where did you moor your ship—far off or close by? I should be glad to know that.'

"He was just trying it on, but I knew something of the world and saw through it; so I answered back, 'My ship was wrecked by Poseidon Earthshaker,[10] who cast us on the rocks near the boundary of your country; the wind drove us on a lee° shore. But I was saved with these others.'

"The cruel monster made no answer, but just jumped up and reached out towards my men, grabbed two like a pair of puppies and dashed them on the ground: their brains ran out and soaked into the earth. Then he cut them up limb by limb and made them ready for supper. He devoured them like a mountain lion, bowels and flesh and marrow-bones, and left nothing. We groaned aloud, lifting our hands to Zeus, when we saw this brutal business; but there was nothing to be done.

"When Goggle-eye had filled his great belly with his meal of human flesh, washed down with a draught of milk neat,° he lay and stretched himself among the sheep. But I did not lose heart. I considered whether to go near and draw my sharp sword and drive it into his breast; I could

[9]King Agamemnon was the King of Mycenae and commander-in-chief of the Achaeans during the Trojan War. He was the son of Atreus.
[10]Greek god of the sea and of horses.

feel about till I found the place where the midriff encloses
the liver. But second thoughts kept me back. We should
have perished ourselves in that place, dead and done for;
we could never have moved the great stone which he had
planted in the doorway. So we lay groaning and awaited
the dawn.

"Dawn came. He lit the fire, milked his flocks, all in
order, put the young under each, then he grabbed two more
men and prepared his breakfast. That done, he drove out
the fat flocks, moving away the great stone with ease; but
he put it back again, just as you fit cover to quiver.° With
many a whistle Goggle-eye turned his fat flocks to the hills;
but I was left brooding and full of dark plans, longing to
have my revenge if Athena would grant my prayer.

"Among all my schemes and machinations,° the best plan
I could think of was this. A long spar° was lying beside the
pen, a sapling of green olive wood; Goggle-eye had cut it
down to dry it and use as a staff. It looked to us about as
large as the mast of a twenty-oar ship, some broad hoy° that
sails the deep sea; it was about that length and thickness.
I cut off a fathom° of this and handed it over to my men to
dress down. They made it smooth, then I sharpened the
end and charred it in the hot fire and hid it carefully under
the dung which lay in a great mass all over the floor. Then
I told the others to cast lots who should help me with the
pole and rub it into his eye while he was sound asleep.
The lot fell on those four whom I would have chosen
myself, which made five counting me.

"In the evening, back he came with his flocks. This time
he drove them all into the cave and left none outside in the
yard; whether he suspected something, or God made him
do it, I do not know. Then he lifted the great stone and set
it in place, sat down and milked his ewes and nannies°
bleating loudly, all in order, put her young under each, and
when all this was done, grabbed two more men and made
his meal.

"At this moment I came near to Goggle-eye, holding in
my hand an ivywood cup full of the red wine, and I said:
"'Cyclops, here, have a drink after that jolly meal of

mansmutton! I should like to show you what drink we had on board our ship. I brought it as a drink offering for you, in the hope that you might have pity and help me on my way home. But you are mad beyond all bearing! Hard heart, how can you expect any other men to pay you a visit? For you have done what is not right.'

"He took it and swallowed it down. The good stuff delighted him terribly and he asked for another drink:

"'Oh, please give me more, and tell me your name this very minute! I will give you a stranger's gift which will make you happy! Mother Earth does give us wine in huge bunches, even in this part of the world, and the rain from heaven makes them grow; but this is a rivulet of nectar and ambrosia!'[11]

"Then I gave him a second draught.° Three drinks I gave him; three times the fool drank. At last, when the wine had got into his head, I said to him in the gentlest of tones:

"'Cyclops, do you ask me my name? Well, I will tell you, and you shall give me the stranger's due, as you promised. Noman is my name; Noman is what mother and father call me and all my friends.'

"Then the cruel monster said, 'Noman shall be last eaten of his company, and all the others shall be eaten before him! That shall be your stranger's gift.'

"As he said this, down he slipped and rolled on his back. His thick neck drooped sideways, and all-conquering sleep laid hold on him; wine dribbled out of his gullet with lumps of human flesh, as he belched in his drunken slumbers. Then I drove the pole deep under the ashes to grow hot, and spoke to hearten my men that no one might fail me through fear.

"As soon as the wood was on the point of catching fire and glowed white-hot, green as it was, I drew it quickly out of the fire while my men stood round me: God breathed great courage into us then. The men took hold of the stake and thrust the sharp point into his eye; and I leaned hard on it from above and turned it round and round. As a man

[11]The drink and the food of the gods. Hence, any drink or food of exceptionally good quality.

bores a ship's timber with an auger, while others at the lower part keep turning it with a strap which they hold at each end, and round and round it runs: so we held the fire-sharpened pole and turned it, and the blood bubbled about its hot point. The fumes singed eyelids and eyelashes all about as the eyeball burnt and the roots crackled in the fire. As a smith plunges an ax or an adze in cold water, for that makes the strength of steel, and it hisses loud when he tempers it, so his eye sizzled about the pole of olive wood.

"He gave a horrible bellow till the rocks rang again, and we shrank away in fear. Then he dragged out the post from his eye dabbled and dripping with blood, and threw it from him, wringing his hands in wild agony, and roared aloud to the Cyclopians who lived in caves round about among the windy hills. They heard his cries and came thronging from all directions, and stood about the cave, asking what his trouble was:

"'What on earth is the matter with you, Polyphemos?' they called out. 'Why do you shout like this through the night and wake us all up? Is any man driving away your flocks against your will? Is anyone trying to kill you by craft or main force?'

"Out of the cave came the voice of mighty Polyphemos: 'O my friends, Noman is killing me by craft and not by main force!'

"They answered him in plain words:

"'Well, if no man is using force, and you are alone, there's no help for a bit of sickness when heaven sends it; so you had better say your prayers to Lord Poseidon your father!'

"With these words away they went, and my heart laughed within me, to think how a mere nobody had taken them all in with my machinomanations!

"But the Cyclops, groaning and writhing in agony, fumbled about with his hands until he found the stone and pushed it away from the entrance. There he sat with his hands outspread to catch anyone who tried to go out with the animals. A great fool he must have thought me!

"But I had been casting about what to do for the best, if I

could possibly find some escape from death for my comrades and myself. All kinds of schemes and machinations I wove in my wits, for it was life or death, and perdition° was close by. The plan that seemed to me best was this. The rams were well grown, large and fine, with coats of rich dark wool. In dead silence I tied them together with twisted withies,° which the monster used for his bed. I tied them in threes, with a man under the middle one, while the two others protected him on each side. So three carried each of our fellows; but for myself—there was one great ram, the finest of the whole flock; I threw my arms over his back and curled myself under his shaggy belly, and there I lay turned upwards, with only my hands to hold fast by the wonderful fleece in patience. So we all waited anxiously for the dawn.

"At last the dawn came. The rams and billies surged out to pasture, but the nannies and ewes unmilked went bleating round the pens; for their udders were full to bursting. Their master, still tormented with pain, felt over the backs of all the animals as they passed out; but the poor fool did not notice how my men were tied under their bellies. Last of all the great ram stalked to the door, cumbered with the weight of his wool and of me and my teeming° mind. Polyphemos said as he pawed him over:

"'Hullo, why are you last today, you lazy creature? It is not your way to let them leave you behind! No, no, you go first by a long way to crop the fresh grass, stepping high and large, first to drink at the river, first all eagerness to come home in the evening; but now last! Are you sorry perhaps for your master's eye, which a villain has blinded with his cursed companions, after he had fuddled° me with wine? Noman! who hasn't yet escaped the death in store for him, I tell him that! If you only had sense like me, if you could only speak and tell me where the man is skulking from my vengeance! Wouldn't I beat his head on the ground, wouldn't his brains go splashing all over the place! And then I should have some little consolation for the trouble which this nobody of a Noman has brought upon me!'

"So he let the ram go from him out of the cave. A little way from the cave and its enclosure, I shook myself loose first from under my ram; then I freed my companions, and with all speed we drove the fat animals trotting along, often looking round, until we reached our ship. Glad indeed our friends were to see us, all of us that were left alive; they lamented the others and made such a noise that I had to stop it, frowning at them and shaking my head. I told them to look sharp and throw on board a number of the fleecy beasts, and get away. Soon they were in their places paddling along; but when we were about as far off from the shore as a man can shout, I called out in mockery:

"'I say, Cyclops! He didn't turn out to be such a milksop after all, did he, when you murdered his friends, and gobbled them up in your cave? Your sins were sure to find you out, you cruel brute! You had no scruple to devour your guests in your own house, therefore vengeance has fallen upon you from Zeus and the gods in heaven!'

"This made him more furious than ever. He broke off the peak of a tall rock and threw it; the rock fell in front of the ship; the sea splashed and surged up as it fell; it raised a wave which carried us back to the land, and the rolling swell drove the ship right upon the shore. I picked up a long quant° and pushed her off, and nodded to the men as a hint to row hard and save their lives. You may be sure they put their backs into it! When we were twice as far as before, I wanted to shout again to Goggle-eye, although my comrades all round tried to coax me not to do it—

"'Foolhardy man! Why do you want to provoke the madman? Just now he threw something to seaward of us and drove back the ship to land, and we thought all was up with us. And if he had heard one sound of us speaking or making a sound, he would have thrown a jagged rock and smashed our timbers and our bones to smithereens!° He throws far enough!'

"But I was determined not to listen and shouted again in my fury:

"'I say, Cyclops! if ever anyone asks you who put out your ugly eye, tell him your blinder was Odysseus, the con-

queror of Troy, the son of Laërtês, whose address is in
Ithaca!'

"When he heard this he gave a loud cry, and said, 'Upon
my word, this is the old prophecy come true! There was a
soothsayer here once, a fine tall fellow, Telemos Eury-
medês, a famous soothsayer who lived to old age prophe-
sying amongst our people. He told me what was to happen,
that I should lose my sight at the hands of Odysseus. But I
always expected that some tall handsome fellow would
come this way, clothed in mighty power. Now a nobody,
a weakling, a whippersnapper, has blinded my eye after
fuddling me with wine! Come to me, dear Odysseus,
and let me give you the stranger's gift, let me beseech
the worshipful Earthshaker to grant you a happy voyage!
For I have the honor to be his son, and he declares he is
my father. He will cure me, if he chooses, all by himself,
without the help of blessed gods or mortal man.'

"I answered at once, 'I wish I could kill you and send
you to perdition as surely as no one will ever unblind your
eye, not even the Earthshaker!'

"At this he held out his hand to heaven, and prayed to
Lord Poseidon:

"'Hear me, Poseidon Earthholder Seabluehair! If I am
truly thy son, and thou art indeed my father, grant that
Odysseus the conqueror of Troy—the son of Laërtês—
whose address is in Ithaca, may never reach his home! But
if it is his due portion to see his friends and come again
to his tall house and his native land, may he come there late
and in misery, in another man's ship, may he lose all his
companions, and may he find tribulation° at home!'

"This was his prayer, and Seabluehair heard it. Then
once again he lifted a stone greater than the other and
circled it round his head, gathering all his vast strength
for the blow, and flung it; down it fell behind our ship, just
a little, just missed the end of the steering oar. The sea
splashed and surged up as it fell, and the wave carried her
on and drove her to shore on the island.

"When we came safe to the island, where the other ships
were waiting for us, we found our companions in great

anxiety, hoping against hope. We drew up our ship on the sand, and put the sheep of old Goggle-eye ashore and divided them so as to give everyone a fair share. But by general consent the great ram was given to me. I sacrificed him on the beach to Zeus Cronidês;[12] clouds and darkness are round about him, and he rules over all. I made my burnt-offering, but Zeus regarded it not; for as it turned out, he intended that all my tight° ships and all my trusty companions should be destroyed.

"We spent the rest of the day until sunset in feasting, eating full and drinking deep; and when the sun set and darkness came on, we lay to rest on the seashore. Then at dawn I directed the men in all haste to embark and throw off the moorings. They were soon aboard and rowing away in good fettle over the sea.

"So we fared onwards, thankful to be alive, but sorrowing for our comrades whom we had lost."

[12]Zeus, son of Cronus.

Do especially Questions 11, 41, 58, 59, 60, 75, 82, 83, 84, 95, 96, 102, 112, and 114. Consult the Prose Narrative Model on page 33.

HOMER

Some authorities argue that Homer the poet was not one man, but several. Other authorities, and this is the view most widely accepted by contemporary scholars, say that Homer the poet was a single individual. Since *The Iliad* and *The Odyssey* were composed before the advent of written records, no absolutely definitive information is available regarding the life of Homer. Herodotus, the Greek historian, was one of the first to set down in writing biographical data about Homer. According to Herodotus, as well as other early accounts, Homer was born somewhere in Ionia. He was a poor, blind poet who traveled from city to city recounting the epic tales about the Trojan War. Recent studies tend to place his life and works in the ninth century, although Herodotus says he died in 1102 B.C. While *The Iliad* and *The Odyssey* have no

doubt been somewhat altered because they were for many generations handed down by word of mouth, nevertheless, they still
represent the work and genius of the great Greek epic poet Homer.

The Story of Europa

Retold by Edith Hamilton

Io[1] was not the only girl who gained geographical fame
because Zeus[2] fell in love with her. There was another,
known far more widely — Europa, the daughter of the King
of Sidon.[3] But whereas the wretched Io had to pay dearly
for the distinction,[4] Europa was exceedingly fortunate.
Except for a few moments of terror when she found herself
crossing the deep sea on the back of a bull she did not
suffer at all. The story does not say what Hera was about at
the time, but it is clear that she was off guard and her
husband free to do as he pleased.

Up in heaven one spring morning as he idly watched the
earth, Zeus suddenly saw a charming spectacle. Europa
had waked early, troubled just as Io had been by a dream,
only this time not of a god who loved her but of two Con-
tinents who each in the shape of a woman tried to possess
her, Asia saying that she had given her birth and therefore
owned her, and the other, as yet nameless, declaring that
Zeus would give the maiden to her.

Once awake from this strange vision which had come at
dawn, the time when true dreams oftenest visit mortals,

[1] Ionia, the Ionian Islands, and the Ionian Sea, it is said, derive their names
from this girl's name.
[2] In Greek mythology, the king of the gods and of men; equivalent to
Jupiter in Roman mythology.
[3] The capital of ancient Phoenicia in Asia Minor.
[4] Io was turned into a heifer by the jealous Hera, Zeus's wife, and was
guarded by the hundred-eyed dog Argus. Finally she reached Egypt and
regained her natural form upon the death of Argus.

Europa decided not to try to go to sleep again, but to summon her companions, girls born in the same year as herself
and all of noble birth, to go out with her to the lovely bloom-
ing meadows near the sea. Here was their favorite meeting
place, whether they wanted to dance or bathe their fair
bodies at the river mouth or gather flowers.

This time all had brought baskets, knowing that the
flowers were now at their perfection. Europa's was of gold,
exquisitely chased° with figures which showed, oddly
enough, the story of Io, her journeys in the shape of a cow,
the death of Argus, and Zeus lightly touching her with his
divine hand and changing her back into a woman. It was,
as may be perceived, a marvel worth gazing upon, and had
been made by no less a personage than Hephaestus,[5] the
celestial workman of Olympus.

Lovely as the basket was, there were flowers as lovely to
fill it with, sweet-smelling narcissus° and hyacinths° and
violets and yellow crocus,° and most radiant of all, the
crimson splendor of the wild rose. The girls gathered them
delightedly, wandering here and there over the meadow,
each one a maiden fairest among the fair; yet even so,
Europa shone out among them as the Goddess of Love[6]
outshines the Sister Graces.[7] And it was that very Goddess
of Love who brought about what next happened. As Zeus
in heaven watched the pretty scene, she who alone can
conquer Zeus—along with her son, the mischievous boy
Cupid—shot one of her shafts into his heart, and that very
instant he fell madly in love with Europa. Even though
Hera was away, he thought it well to be cautious, and before
appearing to Europa he changed himself into a bull. Not
such a one as you might see in a stall or grazing in a field,
but one beautiful beyond all bulls that ever were, bright
chestnut in color, with a silver circle on his brow and
horns like the crescent° of the young moon. He seemed so

[5]In Greek mythology, the god of fire and the forge, son of Zeus and Hera.
[6]Aphrodite; Venus.
[7]In Greek mythology, the three sister goddesses who had control over
pleasure, charm, elegance, and beauty in human life and in nature:
Aglaia (Brilliance), Euphrosyne (Joy), and Thalia (Bloom).

gentle as well as so lovely that the girls were not frightened at his coming, but gathered around to caress him and to breathe the heavenly fragrance that came from him, sweeter even than that of the flowery meadow. It was Europa he drew toward, and as she gently touched him, he lowed° so musically no flute could give forth a more melodious sound.

Then he lay down before her feet and seemed to show her his broad back, and she cried to the others to come with her and mount him.

> For surely he will bear us on his back,
> He is so mild and dear and gentle to behold,
> He is not like a bull, but like a good, true man,
> Except he cannot speak.[8]

Smiling she sat down on his back, but the others, quick though they were to follow her, had no chance. The bull leaped up and at full speed rushed to the seashore and then not into, but over, the wide water. As he went, the waves grew smooth before him and a whole procession rose up from the deep and accompanied him—the strange sea-gods, Nereids[9] riding upon dolphins,° and Tritons[10] blowing their horns, and the mighty Master of the Sea himself,[11] Zeus's own brother.

Europa, frightened equally by the wondrous creatures she saw and the moving waters all around, clung with one hand to the bull's great horn and with the other caught up her purple dress to keep it dry, and the winds

> Swelled out the deep folds even as a sail
> Swells on a ship, and ever gently thus
> They wafted° her.

No bull could this be, thought Europa, but most certainly a god; and she spoke pleadingly to him, begging him to pity her and not leave her in some strange place all alone. He spoke to her in answer and showed her she had guessed rightly what he was. She had no cause to fear, he told her.

[8]The verse quotations are from Moschus, a third-century Alexandrian poet.
[9]Sea-nymphs; there were fifty of them.
[10]Attendants of the sea-gods.
[11]Poseidon.

He was Zeus, greatest of gods, and all he was doing was from love of her. He was taking her to Crete,[12] his own island, where his mother[13] had hidden him from Cronus[14] when he was born, and there she would bear him

> Glorious sons whose sceptres° shall hold sway
> Over all men on earth.

Everything happened, of course, as Zeus had said. Crete came into sight; they landed, and the Seasons, the gate-keepers of Olympus, arrayed her for her bridal. Her sons were famous men, not only in this world but in the next— where two of them, Minos and Rhadamanthus, were re-warded for their justice upon the earth by being made the judges of the dead. But her own name remains the best known of all.

[12]Greek island in the eastern Mediterranean.
[13]Rhea, the mother of the gods.
[14]Zeus's father. Cronus had overthrown his father to become ruler of the universe; he, in turn, was overthrown by his son, Zeus.

Do especially Questions 2, 11, 73, 83, 112, and 133. Consult the Prose Narrative Model on page 33.

The Story of Phaethon

Retold by Edith Hamilton

The palace of the Sun was a radiant place. It shone with gold and gleamed with ivory and sparkled with jewels. Everything without and within flashed and glowed and glittered. It was always high noon there. Shadowy twi-light never dimmed the brightness. Darkness and night were unknown. Few among the mortals could have long endured that unchanging brilliancy of light, but few had ever found their way thither.

Nevertheless, one day a youth, mortal on his mother's side, dared to approach. Often he had to pause and clear his dazzled eyes, but the errand which had brought him was so urgent that his purpose held fast and he pressed on, up to the palace, through the burnished° doors, and into the throne-room where, surrounded by a blinding, blazing splendor, the Sun-god sat. There the lad was forced to halt. He could bear no more.

Nothing escapes the eyes of the Sun. He saw the boy instantly and he looked at him very kindly. "What brought you here?" he asked. "I have come," the other answered boldly, "to find out if you are my father or not. My mother said you were, but the boys at school laugh when I tell them I am your son. They will not believe me. I told my mother and she said I had better go and ask you." Smiling, the Sun took off his crown of burning light so that the lad could look at him without distress. "Come here, Phaethon," he said, "you are my son. Clymene[1] told you the truth. I expect you will not doubt my word too? But I will give you a proof. Ask anything you want of me and you shall have it. I call the Styx[2] to be witness to my promise, the river of the oath of the gods."

No doubt Phaethon had often watched the Sun riding through the heavens and had told himself with a feeling, half awe, half excitement, "It is my father up there." And then he would wonder what it would be like to be in that chariot, guiding the steeds along that dizzy course, giving light to the world. Now at his father's words this wild dream had become possible. Instantly he cried, "I choose to take your place, Father. That is the only thing I want. Just for a day, a single day, let me have your car to drive."

The Sun realized his own folly. Why had he taken that fatal oath and bound himself to give in to anything that happened to enter a boy's rash young head? "Dear lad," he said, "this is the only thing I would have refused you. I know I cannot refuse. I have sworn by the Styx. I must yield if you persist. But I do not believe you will. Listen while I tell you what this is you want. You are Clymene's son as well as mine. You are mortal and no mortal could

[1]The wife of Merops, King of the Ethiopians. Through her union with Helios, the sun-god, she gave birth to seven daughters, the Heliades, and one son, Phaethon.
[2]The chief river of the Greek underworld.

drive my chariot. Indeed, no god except myself can do that. The ruler of the gods[3] cannot. Consider the road. It rises up from the sea so steeply that the horses can hardly climb it, fresh though they are in the early morning. In midheaven it is so high that even I do not like to look down. Worst of all is the descent, so precipitous° that the Sea-gods[4] waiting to receive me wonder how I can avoid falling headlong. To guide the horses, too, is a perpetual struggle. Their fiery spirits grow hotter as they climb and they scarcely suffer° my control. What would they do with you?

"Are you fancying that there are all sorts of wonders up there, cities of the gods full of beautiful things? Nothing of the kind. You will have to pass beasts, fierce beasts of prey, and they are all that you will see. The Bull, the Lion, the Scorpion, the great Crab,[5] each will try to harm you. Be persuaded. Look around you. See all the goods the rich world holds. Choose from them your heart's desire and it shall be yours. If what you want is to be proved, my son, my fears for you are proof enough that I am your father."

But none of all this wise talk meant anything to the boy. A glorious prospect opened before him. He saw himself proudly standing in that wondrous car, his hands triumphantly guiding those steeds which Jove himself could not master. He did not give a thought to the dangers his father detailed. He felt not a quiver of fear, not a doubt of his own powers. At last the Sun gave up trying to dissuade him. It was hopeless, as he saw. Besides, there was no time. The moment for starting was at hand. Already the gates of the east glowed purple, and Dawn had opened her courts full of rosy light. The stars were leaving the sky; even the lingering morning star[6] was dim.

There was need for haste, but all was ready. The Seasons, the gatekeepers of Olympus, stood waiting to fling

[3]Zeus; Jupiter; Jove.
[4]Poseidon, the Tritons, the Nereids.
[5]Four of the imaginary creatures forming the zodiac. They were believed to live in an imaginary belt in the heavens extending eight degrees on either side of the apparent path of the sun.
[6]The planet Venus.

the doors wide. The horses had been bridled and yoked to the car. Proudly and joyously Phaethon mounted it and they were off. He had made his choice. Whatever came of it he could not change now. Not that he wanted to in that first exhilarating rush through the air, so swift that the East Wind was outstripped and left far behind. The horses' flying feet went through the low-banked clouds near the ocean as through a thin sea mist and then up and up in the clear air, climbing the height of heaven. For a few ecstatic moments Phaethon felt himself the Lord of the Sky. But suddenly there was a change. The chariot was swinging wildly to and fro; the pace was faster; he had lost control. Not he, but the horses were directing the course. That light weight in the car, those feeble hands clutching the reins, had told them their own driver was not there. They were the masters then. No one else could command them. They left the road and rushed where they chose, up, down, to the right, to the left. They nearly wrecked the chariot against the Scorpion; they brought up short and almost ran into the Crab. By this time the poor charioteer was half fainting with terror, and he let the reins fall.

That was the signal for still more mad and reckless running. The horses soared up to the very top of the sky and then, plunging headlong down, they set the world on fire. The highest mountains were the first to burn, Ida and Helicon, where the Muses dwell, Parnassus, and heaven-piercing Olympus.[7] Down their slopes the flame ran to the low-lying valleys and the dark forest lands, until all things everywhere were ablaze. The springs turned into steam; the rivers shrank. It is said that it was then the Nile fled and hid his head, which still is hidden.[8]

In the car Phaethon, hardly keeping his place there, was wrapped in thick smoke and heat as if from a fiery furnace. He wanted nothing except to have this torment and terror ended. He would have welcomed death. Mother Earth,[9]

[7]All four of these mountains were found in the ancient Greek world. All of them were, in some way, sacred to the gods.
[8]Because the river Nile is four thousand miles long, the ancients were never able to discover its source.
[9]Gaea, the mother and wife of Uranus; the queen of the gods.

too, could bear no more. She uttered a great cry which reached up to the gods. Looking down from Olympus[10] they saw that they must act quickly if the world was to be saved. Jove seized his thunderbolt and hurled it at the rash, repentant driver. It struck him dead, shattered the chariot, and made the maddened horses rush down into the sea.

Phaethon all on fire fell from the car through the air to the earth. The mysterious river Eridanus, which no mortal eyes have ever seen, received him and put out the flames and cooled the body. The Naiads,[11] in pity for him, so bold and so young to die, buried him and carved upon the tomb:

> Here Phaethon lies who drove the Sun-god's car.
> Greatly he failed, but he had greatly dared.[12]

His sisters, the Heliades, the daughters of Helios, the Sun, came to his grave to mourn for him. There they were turned into poplar trees, on the bank of the Eridanus,

> Where sorrowing they weep into the stream forever.
> And each tear as it falls shines in the water
> A glistening drop of amber.°

[10]The home of the gods.
[11]Sea-nymphs, goddesses, living in springs, fountains, rivers, and lakes.
[12]This and the following quotation are from Ovid, a Roman poet (43 B.C.-17 A.D.).

Do especially Questions 15, 17, 18, 41, 74, 89, 90, 91, and 102.
Consult the Prose Narrative Model on page 33.

The Story of Perseus

Retold by Edith Hamilton

King Acrisius of Argos[1] had only one child, a daughter, Danaë. She was beautiful above all the other women of the land, but this was small comfort to the King for not having a

[1]A city in eastern Peloponnesus, Greece.

son. He journeyed to Delphi[2] to ask the god if there was any hope that some day he would be the father of a boy. The priestess told him no, and added what was far worse: that his daughter would have a son who would kill him.

The only sure way to escape that fate was for the King to have Danaë instantly put to death—taking no chances, but seeing to it himself. This Acrisius would not do. His fatherly affection was not strong, as events proved, but his fear of the gods was. They visited with terrible punishment those who shed the blood of kindred.° Acrisius did not dare slay his daughter. Instead, he had a house built all of bronze and sunk underground, but with part of the roof open to the sky so that light and air could come through. Here he shut her up and guarded her.

> So Danaë endured, the beautiful,
> To change the glad daylight for brass-bound walls.
> And in that chamber secret as the grave
> She lived a prisoner. Yet to her came
> Zeus[3] in the golden rain.

As she sat there through the long days and hours with nothing to do, nothing to see except the clouds moving by overhead, a mysterious thing happened, a shower of gold fell from the sky and filled her chamber. How it was revealed to her that it was Zeus who had visited her in this shape we are not told, but she knew that the child she bore was his son.

For a time she kept his birth secret from her father, but it became increasingly difficult to do so in the narrow limits of that bronze house and finally one day the little boy—his name was Perseus—was discovered by his grandfather. "Your child!" Acrisius cried in great anger. "Who is his father?" But when Danaë answered proudly, "Zeus," he would not believe her. One thing only he was sure of, that the boy's life was a terrible danger to his own. He was afraid to kill him for the same reason that had kept him from killing her, fear of Zeus and the Furies[4] who pursue such

[2]A city in ancient Phocis, Greece; it was the site of the celebrated oracle of Apollo.
[3]The chief of the gods.
[4]The three terrible female spirits with snaky hair (Alecto, Tisiphone, and Megaera) who punished the doers of unavenged crimes.

murderers. But if he could not kill them outright, he could put them in the way of tolerably certain death. He had a great chest made, and the two placed in it. Then it was taken out to sea and cast into the water.

In that strange boat Danaë sat with her little son. The daylight faded and she was alone on the sea.

> When in the carven° chest the wind and waves
> Struck fear into her heart she put her arms,
> Not without tears, round Perseus tenderly.
> She said, "O Son, what grief is mine.
> But you sleep softly, little child,
> Sunk deep in rest within your cheerless home,
> Only a box, brass-bound. The night, this darkness visible,
> The scudding° waves so near to your soft curls,
> The shrill voice of the wind, you do not heed,
> Nestled in your red cloak, fair little face."

Through the night in the tossing chest she listened to the waters that seemed always about to wash over them. The dawn came, but with no comfort to her for she could not see it. Neither could she see that around them there were islands rising high above the sea, many islands. All she knew was that presently a wave seemed to lift them and carry them swiftly on and then, retreating, leave them on something solid and motionless. They had made land; they were safe from the sea, but they were still in the chest with no way to get out.

Fate willed it—or perhaps Zeus, who up to now had done little for his love and his child—that they should be discovered by a good man, a fisherman named Dictys. He came upon the great box and broke it open and took the pitiful cargo home to his wife who was as kind as he. They had no children and they cared for Danaë and Perseus as if they were their own. The two lived there many years, Danaë content to let her son follow the fisherman's humble trade, out of harm's way. But in the end more trouble came. Polydectes, the ruler of the little island, was the brother of Dictys, but he was a cruel and ruthless man. He seems to have taken no notice of the mother and son for a long time, but at last Danaë attracted his attention. She was still radiantly beautiful even though Perseus by now was full grown, and Polydectes fell in love with her. He wanted her, but he did not want her son, and he set himself to think out a way of getting rid of him.

There were some fearsome monsters called Gorgons who lived on an island and were known far and wide because of their deadly power. Polydectes evidently talked to Perseus about them; he probably told him that he would rather have the head of one of them than anything else in the world. This seems practically certain from the plan he devised for killing Perseus. He announced that he was about to be married and he called his friends together for a celebration, including Perseus in the invitation. Each guest, as was customary, brought a gift for the bride-to-be, except Perseus alone. He had nothing he could give. He was young and proud and keenly mortified.° He stood up before them all and did exactly what the King had hoped he would do, declared that he would give him a present better than any there. He would go off and kill Medusa and bring back her head as his gift. Nothing could have suited the King better. No one in his senses would have made such a proposal. Medusa was one of the Gorgons,

> And they are three, the Gorgons, each with wings
> And snaky hair, most horrible to mortals,
> Whom no man shall behold and draw again
> The breath of life,

for the reason that whoever looked at them was turned instantly into stone. It seemed that Perseus had been led by his angry pride into making an empty boast. No man unaided could kill Medusa.

But Perseus was saved from his folly. Two great gods were watching over him. He took ship as soon as he left the King's hall, not daring to see his mother first and tell her what he intended, and he sailed to Greece to learn where the three monsters were to be found. He went to Delphi, but all the priestess would say was to bid him seek the land where men eat not Demeter's[5] golden grain, but only acorns. So he went to Dodona,[6] in the land of oak trees,

[5]The goddess of agriculture and fruitfulness.
[6]A town in Epirus where there was a famous oracle of Zeus.

where the talking oaks were which declared Zeus's will and where the Selli lived who made their bread from acorns. They could tell him, however, no more than this, that he was under the protection of the gods. They did not know where the Gorgons lived.

When and how Hermes[7] and Athena[8] came to his help is not told in any story, but he must have known despair before they did so. At last, however, as he wandered on, he met a strange and beautiful person. We know what he looked like from many a poem, a young man with the first down upon his cheek when youth is loveliest, carrying, as no other young man ever did, a wand of gold with wings at one end, wearing a winged hat, too, and winged sandals. At sight of him hope must have entered Perseus' heart, for he would know that this could be none other than Hermes, the guide and the giver of good.

This radiant personage told him that before he attacked Medusa he must first be properly equipped, and that what he needed was in the possession of the nymphs[9] of the North. To find the nymphs' abode, they must go to the Gray Women who alone could tell them the way. These women dwelt in a land where all was dim and shrouded in twilight. No ray of sun looked ever on that country, nor the moon by night. In that gray place the three women lived, all gray themselves and withered as in extreme old age. They were strange creatures, indeed, most of all because they had but one eye for the three, which it was their custom to take turns with, each removing it from her forehead when she had had it for a time and handing it to another.

All this Hermes told Perseus and then he unfolded his plan. He would himself guide Perseus to them. Once there Perseus must keep hidden until he saw one of them take the eye out of her forehead to pass it on. At that moment, when none of the three could see, he must rush forward and seize the eye and refuse to give it back until they told him how to reach the nymphs of the North.

[7]The messenger of the gods and a god himself.
[8]The goddess of wisdom, skills, and warfare.
[9]Goddesses.

He himself, Hermes said, would give him a sword to attack Medusa with—which could not be bent or broken by the Gorgon's scales, no matter how hard they were. This was a wonderful gift, no doubt, and yet of what use was a sword when the creature to be struck by it could turn the swordsman into stone before he was within striking distance? But another great deity was at hand to help. Pallas Athena stood beside Perseus. She took off the shield of polished bronze which covered her breast and held it out to him. "Look into this when you attack the Gorgon," she said. "You will be able to see her in it as in a mirror, and so avoid her deadly power."

Now, indeed, Perseus had good reason to hope. The journey to the twilight land was long, over the stream of Ocean[10] and on to the very border of the black country where the Cimmerians dwell, but Hermes was his guide and he could not go astray. They found the Gray Women at last, looking in the wavering light like gray birds, for they had the shape of swans. But their heads were human and beneath their wings they had arms and hands. Perseus did just as Hermes had said, he held back until he saw one of them take the eye out of her forehead. Then before she could give it to her sister, he snatched it out of her hand. It was a moment or two before the three realized they had lost it. Each thought one of the others had it. But Perseus spoke out and told them he had taken it and that it would be theirs again only when they showed him how to find the nymphs of the North. They gave him full directions at once; they would have done anything to get their eye back. He returned it to them and went on the way they had pointed out to him. He was bound, although he did not know it, to the blessed country of the Hyperboreans,[11] at

[10]The primitive Greeks imagined that the earth was bounded by an immense river. This was the River Ocean, or Oceanus, which, having no source or outlet, gave birth to all the rivers, the entire sea, to all the water which gushed from the earth, to all deep wells. On the shores of the River Ocean lived the virtuous Ethiopians, the fog-bound Cimmerians, the minute Pygmies.
[11]These people inhabit a region of sunshine and everlasting spring, beyond the mountains of the North Wind.

the back of the North Wind, of which it is said: "Neither by ship nor yet by land shall one find the wondrous road to the gathering place of the Hyperboreans." But Perseus had Hermes with him, so that the road lay open to him, and he reached that host of happy people who are always banqueting and holding joyful revelry. They showed him great kindness; they welcomed him to their feast, and the maidens dancing to the sound of flute and lyre paused to get for him the gifts he sought. These were three: winged sandals, a magic wallet which would always become the right size for whatever he carried in it, and, most important of all, a cap which made the wearer invisible. With these and Athena's shield and Hermes' sword Perseus was ready for the Gorgons. Hermes knew where they lived, and leaving the happy land the two fled back across Ocean and over the sea to the Terrible Sisters' island.

By great good fortune they were all asleep when Perseus found them. In the mirror of the bright shield he could see them clearly, creatures with great wings and bodies covered with golden scales and hair a mass of twisting snakes. Athena was beside him now as well as Hermes. They told him which one was Medusa and that was important, for she alone of the three could be killed; the other two were immortal. Perseus on his winged sandals hovered above them, looking, however, only at the shield. Then he aimed a stroke down at Medusa's throat and Athena guided his hand. With a single sweep of his sword he cut through her neck and, his eyes still fixed on the shield with never a glance at her, he swooped low enough to seize the head. He dropped it into the wallet which closed around it. He had nothing to fear from it now. But the two other Gorgons had awakened and, horrified at the sight of their sister slain, tried to pursue the slayer. Perseus was safe; he had on the cap of darkness and they could not find him.

> So over the sea rich-haired Danaë's son,
> Perseus, on his winged sandals sped,
> Flying, swift as thought.
> In a wallet of silver,

A wonder to behold,
He bore the head of the monster,
While Hermes, the son of Maia,
The messenger of Zeus,
Kept ever at his side.

On his way back he came to Ethiopia and alighted there. By this time Hermes had left him. Perseus found, as Hercules[12] was later to find, that a lovely maiden had been given up to be devoured by a horrible sea serpent. Her name was Andromeda and she was the daughter of a silly vain woman,

That starred Ethip queen who strove
To set her beauty's praise above
The sea-nymphs, and their power offended.

She had boasted that she was more beautiful than the daughters of Nereus, the Sea-god. An absolutely certain way in those days to draw down on one a wretched fate was to claim superiority in anything over any deity; nevertheless people were perpetually doing so. In this case the punishment for the arrogance the gods detested fell not on Queen Cassiopeia, Andromeda's mother, but on her daughter. The Ethiopians were being devoured in numbers by the serpent; and, learning from the oracle that they could be freed from the pest only if Andromeda were offered up to it, they forced Cepheus, her father, to consent. When Perseus arrived the maiden was on a rocky ledge by the sea, chained there to wait for the coming of the monster. Perseus saw her and on the instant loved her. He waited beside her until the great snake came for its prey; then he cut its head off just as he had the Gorgon's. The headless body dropped back into the water; Perseus took Andromeda to her parents and asked for her hand, which they gladly gave him.

[12]The Greek mythical hero renowned for feats of strength, particularly for the twelve labors imposed on him by Hera. One of Hercules' exploits was to rescue Hesione, daughter of Laomedon, King of Troy. Hesione was chained to a rock as an expiatory victim against an epidemic. She would have been eaten by a sea-dragon, except for the intervention of Hercules.

With her he sailed back to the island and his mother, but
in the house where he had lived so long he found no one.
The fisherman Dictys' wife was long since dead, and the
two others, Danaë and the man who had been like a father
to Perseus, had had to fly and hide themselves from Polydectes, who was furious at Danaë's refusal to marry him.
They had taken refuge in a temple, Perseus was told. He
learned also that the King was holding a banquet in the
palace and all the men who favored him were gathered
there. Perseus instantly saw his opportunity. He went
straight to the palace and entered the hall. As he stood at
the entrance, Athena's shining buckler on his breast, the
silver wallet at his side, he drew the eyes of every man
there. Then before any could look away he held up the
Gorgon's head; and at the sight one and all, the cruel King
and his servile courtiers, were turned into stone. There
they sat, a row of statues, each, as it were, frozen still in
the attitude he had struck when he first saw Perseus.

When the islanders knew themselves freed from the
tyrant it was easy for Perseus to find Danaë and Dictys. He
made Dictys king of the island, but he and his mother
decided that they would go back with Andromeda to Greece
and try to be reconciled with Acrisius, to see if the many
years that had passed since he had put them in the chest
had not softened him so that he would be glad to receive
his daughter and grandson. When they reached Argos,
however, they found that Acrisius had been driven away
from the city, and where he was no one could say. It happened that soon after their arrival Perseus heard that the
King of Larissa, in the North, was holding a great athletic
contest, and he journeyed there to take part. In the discus-
throwing when his turn came and he hurled the heavy
missile, it swerved and fell among the spectators. Acrisius
was there on a visit to the King, and the discus struck him.
The blow was fatal and he died at once.

So Apollo's oracle was again proved true. If Perseus felt
any grief, at least he knew that his grandfather had done
his best to kill him and his mother. With his death their
troubles came to an end. Perseus and Andromeda lived

happily ever after. Their son, Electryon, was the grandfather of Hercules.

Medusa's head was given to Athena, who bore it always
upon the aegis, Zeus's shield, which she carried for him.

---

*Do especially Questions 2, 16, 17, 73, 83, 84, 88, 95, 99, and 111.
Consult the Prose Narrative Model on page 33.*

Noah and the Flood (From *The King James Bible*)°

CHAPTER 6

And it came to pass, when men began to multiply on the
face of the earth, and daughters were born unto them, that
the sons of God saw the daughters of men that they were
fair; and they took them wives of all which they chose.
And the Lord said, My spirit shall not always strive with
man, for that he also is flesh: yet his days shall be an hundred and twenty years. There were giants in the earth in
those days; and also after that, when the sons of God came
in unto the daughters of men, and they bare children to
them, the same became mighty men which were of old,
men of renown.

And God saw that the wickedness of man was great in the
earth, and that every imagination of the thoughts of his
heart was only evil continually. And it repented the Lord
that he had made man on the earth, and it grieved him at
his heart. And the Lord said, I will destroy man whom I
have created from the face of the earth; both man, and
beast, and the creeping thing, and the fowls of the air; for
it repenteth me that I have made them. But Noah found
grace in the eyes of the Lord.

These are the generations of Noah: Noah was a just man
and perfect in his generations, and Noah walked with God.
And Noah begat three sons, Shem, Ham, and Japheth. The
earth also was corrupt before God, and the earth was filled

°From Genesis, Chapters 6-9.

with violence. And God looked upon the earth, and, behold, it was corrupt; for all flesh had corrupted his way
upon the earth. And God said unto Noah, The end of all
flesh is come before me; for the earth is filled with violence
through them; and, behold, I will destroy them with the
earth.

Make thee an ark of gopher wood; rooms shalt thou make
in the ark, and shalt pitch it within and without with pitch.
And this is the fashion which thou shalt make it of: The
length of the ark shall be three hundred cubits, the breadth
of it fifty cubits, and the height of it thirty cubits. A window
shalt thou make to the ark, and in a cubit shalt thou finish
it above; and the door of the ark shalt thou set in the side
thereof; with lower, second, and third stories shalt thou
make it. And, behold, I, even I, do bring a flood of waters
upon the earth, to destroy all flesh, wherein is the breath of
life, from under heaven; and every thing that is in the earth
shall die. But with thee will I establish my covenant; and
thou shalt come into the ark, thou, and thy sons, and thy
wife, and thy sons' wives with thee. And of every living
thing of all flesh, two of every sort shalt thou bring into the
ark, to keep them alive with thee; they shall be male and
female. Of fowls after their kind, and of cattle after their
kind, of every creeping thing of the earth after his kind, two
of every sort shall come unto thee, to keep them alive. And
take thou unto thee of all food that is eaten, and thou shalt
gather it to thee; and it shall be for food for thee, and for
them. Thus did Noah; according to all that God commanded him, so did he.

CHAPTER 7

And the Lord said unto Noah, Come thou and all thy house
into the ark; for thee have I seen righteous before me in this
generation. Of every clean beast thou shalt take to thee by
sevens, the male and his female: and of beasts that are not
clean by two, the male and his female. Of fowls also of the
air by sevens, the male and the female; to keep seed alive
upon the face of all the earth. For yet seven days, and I will

cause it to rain upon the earth forty days and forty nights; and every living substance that I have made will I destroy from off the face of the earth. And Noah did according unto all that the Lord commanded him. And Noah was six hundred years old when the flood of waters was upon the earth.

And Noah went in, and his sons, and his wife, and his sons' wives with him, into the ark, because of the waters of the flood. Of clean beasts, and of beasts that are not clean, and of fowls, and of every thing that creepeth upon the earth, there went in two and two unto Noah into the ark, the male and the female, as God had commanded Noah. And it came to pass after seven days, that the waters of the flood were upon the earth.

In the six hundredth year of Noah's life, in the second month, the seventeenth day of the month, the same day were all the fountains of the great deep broken up, and the windows of heaven were opened. And the rain was upon the earth forty days and forty nights. In the selfsame day entered Noah, and Shem, and Ham, and Japheth, the sons of Noah, and Noah's wife, and the three wives of his sons with them, into the ark; they, and every beast after his kind, and all the cattle after their kind, and every creeping thing that creepeth upon the earth after his kind, and every fowl after his kind, every bird of every sort. And they went in unto Noah into the ark, two and two of all flesh, wherein is the breath of life. And they that went in, went in male and female of all flesh, as God had commanded him: and the Lord shut him in. And the flood was forty days upon the earth; and the waters increased, and bare up the ark, and it was lift up above the earth. And the waters prevailed, and were increased greatly upon the earth; and the ark went upon the face of the waters. And the waters prevailed exceedingly upon the earth; and all the high hills, that were under the whole heaven, were covered. Fifteen cubits upward did the waters prevail; and the mountains were covered. And all flesh died that moved upon the earth, both of fowl, and of cattle, and of beast, and of every creeping thing that creepeth upon the earth, and every man: all in whose nostrils was the breath of life, of all that was in the

dry land, died. And every living substance was destroyed
which was upon the face of the ground, both man, and
cattle, and the creeping things, and the fowl of the heaven;
and they were destroyed from the earth: and Noah only
remained alive, and they that were with him in the ark. And
the waters prevailed upon the earth an hundred and fifty
days.

CHAPTER 8

And God remembered Noah, and every living thing, and
all the cattle that was with him in the ark: and God made a
wind to pass over the earth, and the waters asswaged;° the
fountains also of the deep and the windows of heaven were
stopped, and the rain from heaven was restrained; and the
waters returned from off the earth continually: and after the
end of the hundred and fifty days the waters were abated.
And the ark rested in the seventh month, on the seventeenth day of the month, upon the mountains of Ararat.
And the waters decreased continually until the tenth
month, on the first day of the month, were the tops of
the mountains seen.
  And it came to pass at the end of forty days, that Noah
opened the window of the ark which he had made: and he
sent forth a raven, which went forth to and fro, until the
waters were dried up from off the earth. Also he sent forth
a dove from him, to see if the waters were abated from off
the face of the ground; but the dove found no rest for the
sole of her foot, and she returned unto him into the ark, for
the waters were on the face of the whole earth: then he put
forth his hand, and took her, and pulled her in unto him into
the ark. And he stayed yet other seven days; and again
he sent forth the dove out of the ark; and the dove came in
to him in the evening; and, lo, in her mouth was an olive
leaf pluckt off: so Noah knew that the waters were abated
from off the earth. And he stayed yet other seven days; and
sent forth the dove; which returned not again unto him any
more.
  And it came to pass in the six hundredth and first year, in

the first month, the first day of the month, the waters were dried up from off the earth: and Noah removed the covering of the ark, and looked, and, behold, the face of the ground was dry. And in the second month, on the seven and twentieth day of the month, was the earth dried.

And God spake unto Noah, saying, Go forth of the ark, thou, and thy wife, and thy sons, and thy sons' wives with thee. Bring forth with thee every living thing that is with thee, of all flesh, both of fowl, and of cattle, and of every creeping thing that creepeth upon the earth; that they may breed abundantly in the earth, and be fruitful, and multiply upon the earth. And Noah went forth, and his sons, and his wife, and his sons' wives with him: every beast, every creeping thing, and every fowl, and whatsoever creepeth upon the earth, after their kinds, went forth out of the ark.

And Noah builded an altar unto the Lord; and took of every clean beast, and of every clean fowl, and offered burnt offerings on the altar. And the Lord smelled a sweet savour; and the Lord said in his heart, I will not again curse the ground any more for man's sake; for the imagination of man's heart is evil from his youth; neither will I again smite any more every thing living, as I have done. While the earth remaineth, seedtime and harvest, and cold and heat, and summer and winter, and day and night shall not cease.

CHAPTER 9

And God blessed Noah and his sons, and said unto them, Be fruitful, and multiply, and replenish the earth. And the fear of you and the dread of you shall be upon every beast of the earth, and upon every fowl of the air, upon all that moveth upon the earth, and upon all the fishes of the sea; into your hand are they delivered. Every moving thing that liveth shall be meat for you; even as the green herb have I given you all things. But flesh with the life thereof, which is the blood thereof, shall ye not eat. And surely your blood of your lives will I require; at the hand of every beast will I require it, and at the hand of man; at the hand of every man's brother will I require the life of man. Whoso sheddeth man's blood, by man shall his blood be shed: for in the image of God made he man. And you, be ye fruitful, and multiply; bring forth abundantly in the earth, and multiply therein.

And God spake unto Noah, and to his sons with him, saying, And I, behold, I establish my covenant with you, and with your seed after you; and with every living creature that is with you, of the fowl, of the cattle, and of every beast of the earth with you; from all that go out of the ark, to every beast of the earth. And I will establish my covenant with you; neither shall all flesh be cut off any more by the waters of a flood; neither shall there any more be a flood to destroy the earth. And God said, This is the token of the covenant which I make between me and you and every living creature that is with you, for perpetual generations: I do set my bow in the cloud, and it shall be for a token of a covenant between me and the earth. And it shall come to pass, when I bring a cloud over the earth, that the bow shall be seen in the cloud: and I will remember my covenant, which is between me and you and every living creature of all flesh; and the waters shall no more become a flood to destroy all flesh. And the bow shall be in the cloud; and I will look upon it, that I may remember the everlasting covenant between God and every living creature of all flesh that is upon the earth. And God said unto Noah, This is the token of the covenant, which I have established between me and all flesh that is upon the earth.

And the sons of Noah, that went forth of the ark, were Shem, and Ham, and Japheth: and Ham is the father of Canaan. These are the three sons of Noah: and of them was the whole earth overspread. And Noah began to be an husbandman, and he planted a vineyard: and he drank of the wine, and was drunken; and he was uncovered within his tent. And Ham, the father of Canaan, saw the nakedness of his father, and told his two brethren without. And Shem and Japheth took a garment, and laid it upon both their shoulders, and went backward, and covered the nakedness of their father; and their faces were backward, and they saw not their father's nakedness. And Noah awoke from his wine, and knew what his younger son had done unto him. And he said, Cursed be Canaan; a servant of servants shall he be unto his brethren. And he said, Blessed be the Lord God of Shem; and Canaan shall be his servant. God shall enlarge Japheth, and he shall dwell in the tents of Shem; and Canaan shall be his servant.

And Noah lived after the flood three hundred and fifty years. And all the days of Noah were nine hundred and fifty years: and he died.

> *Do especially Questions 2, 11, 15, 41, 73, 109, and 133. Consult the Prose Narrative Model on page 33.*

The Book of Ruth (From *The King James Bible*)

CHAPTER 1

Now it came to pass in the days when the judges ruled, that there was a famine in the land. And a certain man of Beth-lehem-judah went to sojourn in the country of Moab, he, and his wife, and his two sons. And the name of the man was Elimelech, and the name of his wife Naomi, and the name of his two sons Mahlon and Chilion, Ephrathites of Beth-lehem-judah. And they came into the country of Moab, and continued there. And Elimelech Naomi's husband died; and she was left, and her two sons. And they took them wives of the women of Moab; the name of the one was Orpah, and the name of the other Ruth: and they dwelled there about ten years. And Mahlon and Chilion died also both of them; and the woman was left of her two sons and her husband.

Then she arose with her daughters in law, that she might return from the country of Moab: for she had heard in the country of Moab how that the Lord had visited his people in giving them bread. Wherefore she went forth out of the place where she was, and her two daughters in law with her; and they went on the way to return unto the land of Judah. And Naomi said unto her two daughters in law, Go,

return each to her mother's house; the Lord deal kindly
with you, as ye have dealt with the dead, and with me. The
Lord grant you that ye may find rest, each of you in the
house of her husband. Then she kissed them; and they
lifted up their voice, and wept. And they said unto her,
Surely we will return with thee unto thy people. And
Naomi said, Turn again, my daughters: why will ye go with
me? are there yet any more sons in my womb, that they may
be your husbands?. Turn again, my daughters, go your way;
for I am too old to have an husband. If I should say, I have
hope, if I should have an husband also to night, and should
also bear sons; would ye tarry for them till they were
grown? would ye stay for them from having husbands? nay,
my daughters; for it grieveth me much for your sakes that
the hand of the Lord is gone out against me. And they
lifted up their voice, and wept again: and Orpah kissed
her mother in law; but Ruth clave unto her. And she said,
Behold, thy sister in law is gone back unto her people, and
unto her gods: return thou after thy sister in law. And Ruth
said, Intreat me not to leave thee, or to return from following after thee: for whither thou goest, I will go; and where
thou lodgest, I will lodge: thy people shall be my people,
and thy God my God: Where thou diest, will I die, and
there will I be buried: the Lord do so to me, and more
also, if ought but death part thee and me. When she saw
that she was stedfastly minded to go with her, then she left
speaking unto her.

So they two went until they came to Beth-lehem. And
it came to pass, when they were come to Beth-lehem, that
all the city was moved about them, and they said, Is this
Naomi? And she said unto them, Call me not Naomi, call
me Mara: for the Almighty hath dealt very bitterly with me.
I went out full, and the Lord hath brought me home again
empty: why then call ye me Naomi, seeing the Lord hath
testified against me, and the Almighty hath afflicted me?
So Naomi returned, and Ruth the Moabitess, her daughter
in law, with her, which returned out of the country of Moab:
and they came to Beth-lehem in the beginning of barley
harvest.

CHAPTER 2

And Naomi had a kinsman of her husband's a mighty man of
wealth, of the family of Elimelech; and his name was Boaz.
And Ruth the Moabitess said unto Naomi, Let me now go to
the field, and glean ears of corn after him in whose sight I
shall find grace. And she said unto her, Go, my daughter.
And she went, and came, and gleaned in the field after the
reapers: and her hap° was to light on a part of the field
belonging unto Boaz, who was of the kindred of Elimelech.

And, behold, Boaz came from Beth-lehem, and said unto
the reapers, The Lord be with you. And they answered
him, The Lord bless thee. Then said Boaz unto his servant
that was set over the reapers, Whose damsel is this? And
the servant that was set over the reapers answered and said,
It is the Moabitish damsel that came back with Naomi out
of the country of Moab: And she said, I pray you, let me
glean and gather after the reapers among the sheaves: so
she came, and hath continued even from the morning until
now, that she tarried a little in the house. Then said Boaz
unto Ruth, Hearest thou not, my daughter? Go not to glean
in another field, neither go from hence, but abide here fast
by my maidens: let thine eyes be on the field that they do
reap, and go thou after them: have I not charged the young
men that they shall not touch thee? and when thou art
athirst, go unto the vessels, and drink of that which the
young men have drawn. Then she fell on her face, and
bowed herself to the ground, and said unto him, Why have
I found grace in thine eyes, that thou shouldest take knowledge of me, seeing I am a stranger? And Boaz answered
and said unto her, It hath fully been shewed me, all that
thou hast done unto thy mother in law since the death of
thine husband: and how thou hast left thy father and thy
mother, and the land of thy nativity, and art come unto a
people which thou knewest not heretofore. The Lord
recompense thy work, and a full reward be given thee of the
Lord God of Israel, under whose wings thou art come to
trust. Then she said, Let me find favour in thy sight, my

lord; for that thou hast comforted me, and for that thou
hast spoken friendly unto thine handmaid, though I be not
like unto one of thine handmaidens. And Boaz said unto
her, At mealtime come thou hither, and eat of the bread,
and dip thy morsel in the vinegar. And she sat beside the
reapers: and he reached her parched corn, and she did eat,
and was sufficed, and left. And when she was risen up to
glean, Boaz commanded his young men, saying, Let her
glean even among the sheaves, and reproach her not: And
let fall also some of the handfuls of purpose for her, and
leave them, that she may glean them, and rebuke her not.
So she gleaned in the field until even, and beat out that she
had gleaned: and it was about an ephah° of barley.

And she took it up, and went into the city: and her mother
in law saw what she had gleaned: and she brought forth,
and gave to her that she had reserved after she was sufficed.
And her mother in law said unto her, Where hast thou
gleaned to day? and where wroughtest thou? blessed be he
that did take knowledge of thee. And she shewed her
mother in law with whom she had wrought, and said, The
man's name with whom I wrought to day is Boaz. And
Naomi said unto her daughter in law, Blessed be he of the
Lord, who hath not left off his kindness to the living and to
the dead. And Naomi said unto her, The man is near of
kin unto us, one of our next kinsmen. And Ruth the Moabitess said, He said unto me also, Thou shalt keep fast by my
young men, until they have ended all my harvest. And
Naomi said unto Ruth her daughter in law, It is good, my
daughter, that thou go out with his maidens, that they meet
thee not in any other field. So she kept fast by the maidens
of Boaz to glean unto the end of barley harvest and of
wheat harvest; and dwelt with her mother in law.

CHAPTER 3

Then Naomi her mother in law said unto her, My daughter,
shall I not seek rest for thee, that it may be well with thee?
And now is not Boaz of our kindred, with whose maidens
thou wast? Behold, he winnoweth barley to night in the

threshingfloor. Wash thyself therefore, and anoint thee, and put thy raiment upon thee, and get thee down to the floor: but make not thyself known unto the man, until he shall have done eating and drinking. And it shall be, when he lieth down, that thou shalt mark the place where he shall lie, and thou shalt go in, and uncover his feet, and lay thee down; and he will tell thee what thou shalt do. And she said unto her, All that thou sayest unto me I will do.

And she went down unto the floor, and did according to all that her mother in law bade her. And when Boaz had eaten and drunk, and his heart was merry, he went to lie down at the end of the heap of corn: and she came softly, and uncovered his feet, and laid her down.

And it came to pass at midnight, that the man was afraid, and turned himself: and, behold, a woman lay at his feet. And he said, Who art thou? And she answered, I am Ruth thine handmaid. . . . And he said, Blessed be thou of the Lord, my daughter: for thou hast shewed more kindness in the latter end than at the beginning, inasmuch as thou followedst not young men, whether poor or rich. And now, my daughter, fear not; I will do for thee all that thou requirest: for all the city of my people doth know that thou art a virtuous woman. And now it is true that I am thy near kinsman: howbeit there is a kinsman nearer than I. Tarry this night, and it shall be in the morning, that if he will perform unto thee the part of a kinsman, well; let him do the kinsman's part: but if he will not do the part of a kinsman to thee, then will I do the part of a kinsman to thee, as the Lord liveth: lie down until the morning.

And she lay at his feet until the morning: and she rose up before one could know another. And he said, Let it not be known that a woman came into the floor. Also he said, Bring the vail that thou hast upon thee, and hold it. And when she held it, he measured six measures of barley, and laid it on her: and she went into the city. And when she came to her mother in law she said, Who art thou, my daughter? And she told her all that the man had done. And she said, These six measures of barley gave he me; for he said to me, Go not empty unto thy mother in law. Then said she, Sit still, my daughter, until thou know how the matter will fall: for the man will not be in rest, until he have finished the thing this day.

CHAPTER 4

Then went Boaz up to the gate, and sat him down there: and, behold, the kinsman of whom Boaz spake came by; unto whom he said, Ho, such a one! turn aside, sit down here. And he turned aside, and sat down. And he took ten men of the elders of the city, and said, Sit ye down here. And they sat down. And he said unto the kinsman, Naomi, that is come again out of the country of Moab, selleth a parcel of land, which was our brother Elimelech's: And I thought to advertise thee, saying, Buy it before the inhabitants, and before the elders of my people. If thou wilt redeem it, redeem it: but if thou wilt not redeem it, then tell me, that I may know: for there is none to redeem it beside thee; and I am after thee. And he said, I will redeem it. Then said Boaz, What day thou buyest the field of the hand of Naomi, thou must buy it also of Ruth the Moabitess, the wife of the dead, to raise up the name of the dead upon his inheritance.

And the kinsman said, I cannot redeem it for myself, lest I mar mine own inheritance: redeem thou my right to thyself; for I cannot redeem it. Now this was the manner in former time in Israel concerning redeeming and concerning changing, for to confirm all things; a man plucked off his shoe, and gave it to his neighbour: and this was a testimony in Israel. Therefore the kinsman said unto Boaz, Buy it for thee. So he drew off his shoe.

And Boaz said unto the elders, and unto all the people, Ye are witnesses this day, that I have bought all that was Elimelech's, and all that was Chilion's and Mahlon's, of the hand of Naomi. Moreover Ruth the Moabitess, the wife of Mahlon, have I purchased to be my wife, to raise up the name of the dead upon his inheritance, that the name of the dead be not cut off from among his brethren, and from the gate of his place: ye are witnesses this day. And all the people that were in the gate, and the elders, said, We are witnesses. The Lord make the woman that is come into thine house like Rachel and like Leah, which two did build the house of Israel: and do thou worthily in Ephratah, and be famous in Beth-lehem: and let thy house be like the house of Pharez, whom Tamar bare unto Judah, of the seed which the Lord shall give thee of this young woman.

So Boaz took Ruth, and she was his wife; and when he went in unto her, the Lord gave her conception, and she bore a son. And the women said unto Naomi, Blessed be the Lord, which hath not left thee this day without a kinsman, that his name may be famous in Israel. And he shall be unto thee a restorer of thy life, and a nourisher of thine old age: for thy daughter in law, which loveth thee, which is better to thee than seven sons, hath born him. And Naomi took the child, and laid it in her bosom, and became nurse unto it. And the women her neighbours gave it a name, saying, There is a son born to Naomi; and they called his name Obed: he is the father of Jesse, the father of David.
· Now these are the generations of Pharez: Pharez begat Hezron, and Hezron begat Ram, and Ram begat Amminadab, and Amminadab begat Nahshon, and Nahshon begat Salmon, and Salmon begat Boaz, and Boaz begat Obed, and Obed begat Jesse, and Jesse begat David.

Do especially Questions 9, 16, 17, 33, 44, 52, 77, 78, 79, 139, and 140. Consult the Prose Narrative Model on page 33.

The Death of Absalom (From The King James Bible)

II SAMUEL: 18

And David numbered the people that were with him, and set captains of thousands and captains of hundreds over them. And David sent forth a third part of the people under the hand of Joab, and a third part under the hand of Abishai the son of Zeruiah, Joab's brother, and a third part under the hand of Ittai the Gittite. And the king said unto the people, I will surely go forth with you myself also. But the people answered, Thou shalt not go forth: for if we flee away, they will not care for us; neither if half of us die, will they care for us: but now thou art worth ten thousand of us: therefore now it is better that thou succour us out of the city. And the king said unto them, What seemeth you best I will do. And the king stood by the gate side, and all the people came out by hundreds and by thousands. And the king commanded Joab and Abishai and Ittai, saying, Deal gently for my sake with the young man, even with Absalom. And all the people heard when the king gave all the captains charge concerning Absalom.

So the people went out into the field against Israel: and the battle was in the wood of Ephraim; where the people of Israel were slain before the servants of David, and there was there a great slaughter that day of twenty thousand men. For the battle was there scattered over the face of all the country: and the wood devoured more people that day than the sword devoured.

And Absalom met the servants of David. And Absalom rode upon a mule, and the mule went under the thick boughs of a great oak, and his head caught hold of the oak, and he was taken up between the heaven and the earth; and the mule that was under him went away. And a certain man saw it, and told Joab, and said, Behold, I saw Absalom hanged in an oak. And Joab said unto the man that told him, And, behold, thou sawest him, and why didst thou not smite him there to the ground? and I would have given thee ten shekels of silver, and a girdle. And the man said unto Joab, Though I should receive a thousand shekels of silver in mine hand, yet would I not put forth mine hand against the king's son: for in our hearing the king charged thee and Abishai and Ittai, saying, Beware that none touch the young man Absalom. Otherwise I should have wrought falsehood against mine own life: for there is no matter hid from the king, and thou thyself wouldest have set thyself against me. Then said Joab, I may not tarry thus with thee. And he took three darts in his hand, and thrust them through the heart of Absalom, while he was yet alive in the midst of the oak. And ten young men that bare Joab's armour compassed about and smote Absalom, and slew him. And Joab blew the trumpet, and the people returned from pursuing after Israel: for Joab held back the people. And they took Absalom, and cast him into a great pit in the wood, and laid a very great heap of stones upon him: and all Israel fled every one to his tent.

Now Absalom in his lifetime had taken and reared up for himself a pillar, which is in the king's dale: for he said, I have no son to keep my name in remembrance: and he called the pillar after his own name: and it is called unto this day, Absalom's place.

Then said Ahimaaz the son of Zadok, Let me now run, and bear the king tidings, how that the Lord hath avenged him of his enemies. And Joab said unto him, Thou shalt not bear tidings this day, but thou shalt bear tidings another day: but this day thou shalt bear no tidings, because the king's son is dead. Then said Joab to Cushi, Go tell the king what thou hast seen. And Cushi bowed himself unto Joab, and ran. Then said Ahimaaz the son of Zadok yet again to Joab, But howsoever, let me, I pray thee, also run after Cushi. And Joab said, Wherefore wilt thou run, my son, seeing that thou hast no tidings ready? But howsoever, said he, let me run. And he said unto him, Run. Then Ahimaaz ran by the way of the plain, and overran Cushi. And David sat between the two gates: and the watchman went up to the roof over the gate unto the wall, and lifted up his eyes, and looked, and behold a man running alone. And the watchman cried, and told the king. And the king said, If he be alone, there is tidings in his mouth. And he came apace, and drew near. And the watchman saw another man running: and the watchman called unto the porter, and said, Behold another man running alone. And the king said, He also bringeth tidings. And the watchman said, Me thinketh the running of the foremost is like the running of Ahimaaz the son of Zadok. And the king said, He is a good man, and cometh with good tidings. And Ahimaaz called, and said unto the king, All is well. And he fell down to the earth upon his face before the king, and said, Blessed be the Lord thy God, which hath delivered up the men that lifted up their hand against my lord the king. And the king said, Is the young man Absalom safe? And Ahimaaz answered, When Joab sent the king's servant, I saw a great tumult, but I knew not what it was. And the king said unto him, Turn aside, and stand here. And he turned aside, and stood still. And, behold, Cushi came; and Cushi said, Tidings, my lord the king: for the Lord hath avenged thee this day of all them that rose up against thee. And the king said unto Cushi, Is the young man Absalom safe? And Cushi answered, The enemies of my lord the king, and all that rise against thee to do thee hurt, be as that young man is.

And the king was much moved, and went up to the chamber over the gate, and wept: and as he went, thus he said, O my son Absalom, my son, my son Absalom! would God I had died for thee, O Absalom, my son, my son!

Do especially Questions 9, 16, 17, 44, 52, 58, 77, 78, 79, 80, 81, 139, and 140. Consult the Prose Narrative Model on page 33.

The Parable of the Labourers

(From *The New English Bible*)

MATTHEW 20*

. . . Peter said, "Here are we who left everything to become your followers. What will there be for us?" Jesus replied, "I tell you this: in the world that is to be, when the Son of Man is seated on his throne in heavenly splendour, you my followers will have thrones of your own, where you will sit as judges of the twelve tribes of Israel. And anyone who

*Jesus, aware of the fate that awaits him, is on his way to Jerusalem with his disciples. As he goes, he stops to heal or to answer questions about civil affairs, domestic affairs, and salvation.

has left brothers or sisters, father, mother, or children, land or houses for the sake of my name will be repaid many times over, and gain eternal life. But many who are first will be last, and the last first.

"The kingdom of Heaven is like this. There was once a landowner who went out early one morning to hire labourers for his vineyard; and after agreeing to pay them the usual day's wage he sent them off to work. Going out three hours later he saw some more men standing idle in the market-place. 'Go and join the others in the vineyard,' he said, 'and I will pay you a fair wage'; so off they went. At noon he went out again, and at three in the afternoon, and made the same arrangement as before. An hour before sunset he went out and found another group standing there; so he said to them, 'Why are you standing about like this all day with nothing to do?' 'Because no one has hired us,' they replied; so he told them, 'Go and join the others in the vineyard.' When evening fell, the owner of the vineyard said to his steward, 'Call the labourers and give them their pay, beginning with those who came last and ending with the first.' Those who had started work an hour before sunset came forward, and were paid the full day's wage. When it was the turn of the men who had come first, they expected something extra, but were paid the same amount as the others. As they took it, they grumbled at their employer: 'These late-comers have done only one hour's work, yet you have put them on a level with us, who have sweated the whole day long in the blazing sun!' The owner turned to one of them and said, 'My friend, I am not being unfair to you. You agreed on the usual wage for the day, did you not? Take your pay and go home. I choose to pay the last man the same as you. Surely I am free to do what I like with my own money. Why be jealous because I am kind?' Thus will the last be first, and the first last."

Jesus was journeying towards Jerusalem, and on the way he took the Twelve[1] aside, and said to them, "We are going to Jerusalem, and the Son of Man will be given up to the

---

[1] The twelve disciples.

chief priests and the doctors of the law; they will condemn him to death and hand him over to the foreign power, to be mocked and flogged and crucified, and on the third day he will be raised to life again."

The mother of Zebedee's[2] sons then came before him, with her sons. She bowed low and begged a favour. "What is it you wish?" asked Jesus. "I want you," she said, "to give orders that in your kingdom my two sons here may sit next to you, one at your right, and the other at your left." Jesus turned to the brothers and said, "You do not understand what you are asking. Can you drink the cup that I am to drink?" "We can," they replied. Then he said to them, "You shall indeed share my cup; but to sit at my right or left is not for me to grant; it is for those to whom it has already been assigned by my Father."

When the other ten heard this, they were indignant° with the two brothers. So Jesus called them to him and said, "You know that in the world, rulers lord it over their subjects, and their great men make them feel the weight of authority; but it shall not be so with you. Among you, whoever wants to be great must be your servant, and whoever would be first must be the willing slave of all — like the Son of Man; he did not come to be served, but to serve, and to surrender his life as a ransom° for many."

As they were leaving Jericho he was followed by a great crowd of people. At the roadside sat two blind men. When they heard it said that Jesus was passing they shouted, "Have pity on us, Son of David." The people rounded° on them and told them to be quiet. But they shouted all the more, "Sir, have pity on us, have pity on us, Son of David." Jesus stopped and called the men. "What do you want me to do for you?" he asked. "Sir," they answered, "we want our sight." Jesus was deeply moved, and touched their eyes. At once their sight came back, and they went on after him.

[2]The father of the disciples James and John.

Do especially Questions 2, 11, 15, 61, and 147. Consult the Prose Narrative Model on page 33.

The Prodigal Son (From *The New English Bible*)

LUKE 15

Another time, the tax-gatherers and other bad characters were all crowding in to listen to him;[1] and the Pharisees and the doctors of the law began grumbling among themselves: "This fellow," they said, "welcomes sinners and eats with them." He answered them with this parable:° "If one of you has a hundred sheep and loses one of them, does he not leave the ninety-nine in the open pasture and go after the missing one until he has found it? How delighted he is then! He lifts it on to his shoulders, and home he goes to call his friends and neighbours together. 'Rejoice with me!' he cries. 'I have found my lost sheep.' In the same way, I tell you, there will be greater joy in heaven over one sinner who repents than over ninety-nine righteous people who do not need to repent.

"Or again, if a woman has ten silver pieces and loses one of them, does she not light the lamp, sweep out the house, and look in every corner till she has found it? And when she has, she calls her friends and neighbours together, and says, 'Rejoice with me! I have found the piece that I lost.' In the same way, I tell you, there is joy among the angels of God over one sinner who repents."

Again he said: "There was once a man who had two sons; and the younger said to his father, 'Father, give me my share of the property.' So he divided his estate° between them. A few days later the younger son turned the whole of his share into cash and left home for a distant country, where he squandered it in reckless living. He had spent it all, when a severe famine fell upon that country and he began to feel the pinch. So he went and attached himself to one of the local landowners, who sent him on to his farm

[1]Jesus.

to mind the pigs. He would have been glad to fill his belly with the pods° that the pigs were eating; and no one gave him anything. Then he came to his senses and said, 'How many of my father's paid servants have more food than they can eat, and here am I, starving to death! I will set off and go to my father, and say to him, "Father, I have sinned against God and against you; I am no longer fit to be called your son; treat me as one of your paid servants.'" So he set out for his father's house. But while he was still a long way off his father saw him, and his heart went out to him. He ran to meet him, flung his arms round him, and kissed him. The son said, 'Father, I have sinned, against God and against you; I am no longer fit to be called your son.' But the father said to his servants, 'Quick! fetch a robe, my best one, and put it on him; put a ring on his finger and shoes on his feet. Bring the fatted calf and kill it, and let us have a feast to celebrate the day. For this son of mine was dead and has come back to life; he was lost and is found.' And the festivities began.

"Now the elder son was out on the farm; and on his way back, as he approached the house, he heard music and dancing. He called one of the servants and asked what it meant. The servant told him, 'Your brother has come home, and your father has killed the fatted calf because he has him back safe and sound.' But he was angry and refused to go in. His father came out and pleaded with him; but he retorted, "You know how I have slaved for you all these years; I never once disobeyed your orders; and you never gave me so much as a kid, for a feast with my friends. But now that this son of yours turns up, after running through your money with his women, you kill the fatted calf for him.' 'My boy,' said the father, 'you are always with me, and everything I have is yours. How could we help celebrating this happy day? Your brother here was dead and has come back to life, was lost and is found.'"

Do especially Questions 12, 15, 19, 20, 44, 45, 88, 90, 91, and 146. Consult the Prose Narrative Model on page 33.

PROBLEM QUESTIONS

1. What is the most obvious aspect of the story form to be found in the Fables?

2. What favors asked of Jesus in *Matthew* 20 prove that parables were the best means he could have chosen in which to speak to the masses?

3. Both the New Testament selections and Aesop present rather obvious morals in their stories. What circumstances prevailed then which made these direct statements necessary?

4. It might seem that the fight between Achillês and Hector is long and drawn out, particularly in the preliminary stages. Also, there are many long speeches. Why were these details included?

5. In classical mythology, Odysseus is most frequently characterized as being shrewd and cunning. Find places in the selection from *The Odyssey* in which this is demonstrated to be true.

6. Think of some of the ways in which the selections you have read in this unit differ from the kinds of short stories you read in both magazines and anthologies you study in school. List them. Do they seem important to you? Why?

7. Compare the effect and circumstances of Absalom's death, in *II Samuel*, to Hector's death in *The Iliad*.

MEDIEVAL PROSE NARRATIVES

During the Medieval and Early Modern Periods of literary history, the oral tradition was still a strong one. Troubadours and minstrels roamed the European continent singing and reciting stories on many topics and from many sources. Most of the famous medieval legends and epics of that period, like their ancient predecessors, were apparently sung or recited long before they were written down. There was, however, during the Medieval Period a great increase in the production of written literary materials, many of which were prose narratives in nature. This was the period of growth of many centers of learning at European city universities and monasteries. It marks the time when great quantities of literature of all kinds came to be recorded and preserved.

You will note that all of the selections in this unit are excerpts from longer works. The Medieval Period was noteworthy for its production of long narratives, largely in the epic, folk tale, and legendary form. Within these long narratives can be found many anecdotes, sagas, and descriptions of incidents which can be classified as stories in their own right. Probably the biggest contributions of this period to the development of the modern short story were that it extended certain aspects of narrative style which had been started in the earlier era, and that it developed certain tendencies which were then carried on by writers of later years.

Prose narratives written in the Medieval Period took as points of departure certain stylistic approaches which were developed in the period of Ancient literature and utilized them thoroughly. First among these is the use of the highly developed anecdote in the context of the longer, episodic work. In the case of all four selections in this unit, the incident around which the narrative is built is but one of several in the longer work. These incidents have in part proved useful to later writers of narrative style because they could be taken from a text as essentially whole stories. The writers could then through intensification, dramatization, and enlargement develop their own story from the anecdote chosen. This is an excellent example of how the story writer could create a whole new selection through the use of his imagination.

The development of topics for good stories was also extended during the Medieval Period. Much material in folklore, legendry, and mythology was added during the Middle Ages. The significance of the hero as a central figure in prose narrative gained further eminence. Since the works were long and the characters were portrayed as heroic, the number of incidents within a given narrative was enlarged. Thus writers of short prose fiction who came after the Medieval Period had a rather large storehouse of topics ready for exploration. The material from all four works in this unit, in addition to the Robin Hood and Arthurian legends (and several others), have furnished many writers ever since with characters and plot structure for short fictional works.

Narratives of the Medieval and Early Modern Periods continued to emphasize the quest, action, suspense, and adventure, which were characteristics of ancient works. Like these earlier narratives, medieval stories provided engrossing plots with many action-packed situations and obvious climaxes so characteristic of later short stories.

Along with those aspects of modern short fiction which were continued in the Medieval Period, an important one originated. In the several episodes in *Don Quixote*, prose fiction is used for a specific social purpose. In this work Cervantes used satire to build a case against the social order in which he lived. Like the Roman satirist Juvenal, he did this by piling up his evidence, using event after event to justify his conviction that the way of life practiced by his contemporaries was inadequate, obsolete, and ridiculous. Each incident, then, was used specifically for the purpose of suggesting the need for social reform. This narrative provided a model for modern writers who sought also to effect social, economic, or political change through their works. *Don Quixote* reveals the nature of contemporary life, not that of the past.

One final note should be made about the nature of literature in this period. The development of certain modern short story techniques was still a long way off. In the following unit you will read three examples of the form as it slowly emerged. *The Nibelungenlied, The Song of Roland,* and *The Legend of the Cid,* like Chaucer's *Canterbury Tales,* were written as poems. The short story form *per se* had not yet been developed. While the form of these three works was originally poetic, they are presented here as what they are in function and essence — prose narratives.

How Siegfried Fought with the Saxons (From *The Nibelungenlied*)

Translated by Helen M. Mustard

[*Completed in 1203 by an unknown poet,* The Nibelungenlied *(the song of the Nibelungs) is an ancient German epic based on the adventures of Siegfried, a brave Netherland warrior. At an early age, Siegfried won much honor and fame by killing a dragon and seizing the Nibelungen treasure. Young Siegfried was invulnerable (except for a small spot on his shoulder), but was eventually murdered because of a woman's vengeance and treachery.*

Although Siegfried enjoyed the amorous sighs of every maiden in Netherland, he fell in love with the renowned beauty of Kriemhild, a Burgundian princess. To win her hand in marriage, Siegfried offered his services to Kriemhild's father, King Gunther of Burgundy.]

Strange news now approached Gunther's land, brought by envoys° who had been sent to the Burgundians from far away by warriors they did not know but who bore° them hate. When they heard the message, they were greatly dismayed.

I will tell you their names. They were Liudeger, a mighty prince from the land of the Saxons, and King Liudegast of Denmark. They took with them on their campaign many an excellent fighter.

The envoys had arrived in Gunther's land, sent there by his enemies, and people asked the strangers what message they brought and bade them to go quickly to court to see the king.

He greeted them kindly and said, "You are welcome. Tell me who sent you here. I have not been informed of this."

Thus the king spoke, but they were much afraid of his anger. "If you will permit us, O King, to give you the message we bring, we will not be silent but will name you the lords who sent us here — Liudegast and Liudeger. They intend to invade your land. You have earned their wrath. In fact, we have been told that both rulers bear you great hate. They plan to march against Worms on the Rhine,[1] and many warriors will aid them — of this we assure you. Within twelve weeks the campaign will take place. If you have good friends who will help you protect your castles and your lands, you had better show this speedily, for many a helmet and shield will be slashed here by our lords. Or if you wish to negotiate° with them, send them word, and the vast hosts of your powerful enemies will not ride so near to you to do you grievous injury from which many a good knight must lose his life."

"Wait for a while," said the king, "until I consider the matter further. Then I will announce my intention to you. If I have loyal friends, I shall not conceal this important news from them but shall make lament of it."

[1]Worms is a city in Germany situated on the Rhine river.

"How Siegfried Fought with the Saxons" from *The Nibelungenlied*, translated by Helen M. Mustard, copyright © 1963, from *Medieval Epics*, Modern Library. Reprinted with permission of Random House, Inc.

Deeply troubled, Gunther kept the message a secret in his heart. He summoned Hagen and others of his men and also sent for Gernot to come to court at once. Then came the most distinguished men, as many as could be found there.

"Our land is to be attacked by powerful armies," said Gunther. "Take this to heart."

Gernot made answer, "We'll prevent that with our swords. Only those destined° for death will fall. Let them die — I can't forget my honor for their sake. Our enemies shall be welcome."

"I don't agree," said Hagen. "Liudegast and Liudeger are very arrogant.° And we cannot summon all our men in such a short time. Why don't you tell Siegfried about it?"

Orders were given to quarter² the messengers in the town. Gunther bade that they be well cared for, no matter how hostile one felt toward them — and this was well done — until he learned from his friends who among them would assist him. Yet with his fears the king was very troubled. Then a good knight,³ who could not know what had happened, saw him grieving and asked the king to tell him about the matter.

"I am greatly surprised," said Siegfried, "at how you have changed the joyful manner that has long been your custom with us until now."

Gunther answered, "I cannot confide to everyone the sorrow I must bear secretly in my heart. Only to steadfast friends should one lament his heart's distress."

At this Siegfried's color turned first pale, then red, and he said to the king, "I have never refused you anything. I will help you ward off all your sorrows. If you are seeking friends, I shall be one of them and am certain of fulfilling this pledge with honor as long as I live."

"May God reward you, Lord Siegfried. Your words please me. And even if your prowess° should never aid me, I am happy to hear that you are so friendly toward me. If I live a while longer, you will be rewarded for this. I will tell you why I am sad. I have heard from messengers of my enemies

²To provide housing for.
³Siegfried.

that they intend to make war on me. Never before did warriors do that to us in this land."

"Don't be concerned about it," said Siegfried. "Put your mind at ease and do as I request—let me win for you honor and profit, and command your men to come to your aid. Even if your mighty enemies had thirty thousand warriors to help them, I would withstand them if I had only a thousand. Rely on me for that."

"I shall always repay you with my service," said King Gunther.

"Then summon a thousand of your men, since I have only twelve of my own with me, and I will protect your land. Siegfried's[4] hand shall always serve you loyally. Hagen shall help us, and also your good warriors Ortwin, Dankwart, and Sindolt. And brave Volker shall ride along. He shall carry the banner. There's no one I'd rather entrust it to. Let the messengers ride home to their master's lands, and send word that they will see us soon so that our castles may be left in peace."

The king gave orders to summon both kinsmen° and vassals.° Liudeger's envoys now came to court. They were overjoyed that they were to return home. King Gunther offered them rich gifts and provided them with safe conduct. At this their spirits rose.

"Tell my enemies," said Gunther, "to give up their journey and remain at home. But if they insist on invading my lands, they will come to grief unless my friends desert me."

Costly gifts were brought out for the messengers. Of these Gunther had an abundance to give, and Liudeger's men dared not refuse them. When they had been dismissed, they went away happy.

Now when the envoys had arrived in Denmark and King Liudegast was told with what message they had come from the Rhine, he was extremely annoyed at the great arrogance of the Burgundians. The envoys reported that they had many valiant men and that among them they had seen a

---

[4]This practice of referring to oneself in the third person is frequently used in *The Nibelungenlied.*

warrior called Siegfried, a hero from Netherland. Liudegast was not pleased to hear this news.

When the men of Denmark learned of it, they hastened to fetch even more of their friends, until at last Lord Liudegast had gathered twenty thousand of his brave warriors for his journey. King Liudeger of Saxony also summoned his men till they had forty thousand or more with whom they meant to ride to Burgundy.

Here at home likewise King Gunther had assembled his kinsmen and his brother's vassals, whom they intended to lead to battle, and also Hagen's men. Because of this, warriors were soon to meet their death. They prepared for the journey, and when they were ready to ride from Worms across the Rhine, bold Volker bore the banner, and Hagen of Troneg was marshal of the troop. With them rode Sindolt and Hunolt, who knew well how to earn Gunther's gold, and Hagen's brother Dankwart and Ortwin, too, served with honor in the campaign.

"Sir King, remain here at home," said Siegfried, "since your warriors are willing to follow me. Stay with the ladies and have full confidence. I assure you, I will protect both your honor and possessions. I'll see to it that those who planned to attack you at Worms on the Rhine will have reason to stay at home. We'll ride into their land so close to them that their overbearing pride will turn to fear."

From the Rhine they rode with their warriors through Hesse toward Saxony, where battle later took place. With fire and pillage° they so ravaged the land that both princes were deeply distressed when they were told of it.

They had now reached the border. The squires came marching along.

"Who shall take command of this following?" asked Siegfried.

"Have Dankwart protect the lads on the way," they said. "He is a valiant fighter. We'll lose all the less through Liudeger's men. Have him and Ortwin guard the rear."[5]

"Then I will ride myself," said Siegfried, "and reconnoiter° until I discover where our enemies are."

[5]When preparing for battle, the squires stayed behind to guard the troops.

He was soon armed, and when he was ready to leave, he placed the troops in Hagen's and Gernot's charge. Then he rode alone into the Saxon land, and many a helmet strap did he sever that day. Soon he saw the mighty host that was encamped upon the plain and far outnumbered his own forces. There were forty thousand or even more. Siegfried, in high spirits, rejoiced at the sight.

There also a warrior, fully armed, had set out toward the enemy to reconnoiter. Lord Siegfried caught sight of him, and he saw Siegfried too. Each began to eye the other hostily.° I will tell you who it was who was scouting there. He bore a bright shield of gold in his hand. It was King Liudegast, guarding his troops. The noble stranger[6] urged his horse toward him. Lord Liudegast had also watched him with enmity.° Both now dug the spurs into their horses' flanks and couched their spears against their shields. At this the mighty king was seized with great fear. After the thrust the horses carried the princes past each other as if blown by the wind. Then in true knightly fashion, using the bridles, the two fierce men wheeled about and took a try with their swords. Lord Siegfried struck so hard that the whole plain resounded, and from the helmet flew flame-red sparks as if from mighty fires. Each had met his match in the other. Lord Liudegast, too, dealt Siegfried many a furious blow. The strength of both fell heavy on the shields.

Meanwhile thirty of Liudegast's men had ridden out on patrol, but before they could come to his aid, Siegfried gained the victory with three severe wounds which he dealt the king through his splendid, gleaming breastplate. Along both edges the sword drew blood from the wounds, and King Liudegast was sad at heart. He begged Siegfried to let him live and offered him his lands and told him his name was Liudegast.[7] His warriors now came up, having seen clearly what happened between the two on their scouting trip. As Siegfried was about to take Liudegast away, he was set upon by the thirty men, but he guarded his royal

[6]Siegfried.
[7]The loser in a battle gives his name as a sign of his surrender.

hostage with mighty blows. Then he did them even worse harm. In self-defense he killed the thirty warriors. He left only one alive, who speedily rode away and brought the news of what had happened there.[8] The truth of his story could be seen by his reddened helmet. The men of Denmark were deeply grieved when they heard that their lord had been taken prisoner. His brother was told of it too, and he began to rage with a boundless wrath at the injury that had been done him.

Siegfried took Liudegast by force to Gunther's men and delivered him into Hagen's charge. When they were told it was the king, they were but moderately grieved. The Burgundians were ordered to tie on their pennants.[9]

"Up now," called Siegfried. "More shall be done here before the day ends, if I am still alive, and it will sadden many a woman in the Saxon land. Listen to me, warriors from the Rhine. I can guide you well to Liudeger's host, and you will see helmets slashed by the hands of good fighters. They'll learn what fear is before we return home."

Gernot and his men hastened to their horses. At once Lord Volker, the stalwart minstrel, seized the banner and rode at the head of the troops. The whole army was splendidly equipped for battle. Yet they had no more than a thousand men, and Siegfried's twelve warriors besides. Clouds of dust rose up from the roads as they galloped across the land. Many a fine shield could be seen glittering from their ranks.

The Saxon troops had also come up, with well-sharpened swords, as I have since been told, that cut fearfully in the warriors' hands. They meant to defend castles and land against the strangers. Marshals of the two rulers led the troops forward.

Now Siegfried came up with his men whom he had brought from Netherland. Many hands were bloodied that day in battle. Sindolt and Hunolt, and Gernot as well, struck many a warrior dead in combat before he actually

---

[8]Siegfried kills the thirty but one is left alive. There is no explanation for this error in number.
[9]This was a signal for the attack.

realized how courageous they were. Noble ladies later wept over this. Volker and Hagen, and Ortwin too, these battle-bold men, dulled with streaming blood the gleam of many a helmet. And Dankwart performed marvelous deeds.

The men of Denmark put their hands to the test, and shields were heard resounding from the hurtling clash and from the sharp swords wielded there. The daring Saxons did damage enough in the fray. As the Burgundians pressed forward to the fight, they hewed° many a gaping wound, and blood flowed across the saddles. Thus the brave knights strove for honor. Their keen-edged weapons ringing loudly in their hands, the men of Netherland pushed through the mighty host to follow their lord. Valiantly they made their way with Siegfried, but not one of the men from the Rhine was able to keep up with him. Bloody streams were seen pouring through the bright helmets from the strength of Siegfried's hand before he came upon Liudeger at the head of his battle comrades. Three times he had fought his way through the host from end to end. Now Hagen appeared and helped him to satisfy his thirst for strife. Many excellent knights were to die at their hands that day.

When the mighty Liudeger caught sight of Siegfried and saw that he held the good sword Balmung[10] high in his hand and was killing so many of the Saxons, he became fiercely angry. There was a great press and loud clang of swords as their followers thrust against each other. The two warriors now tried their mettle on one another. The troops gave way for them, and a savage combat began. The ruler of the Saxons had been told that his brother was a prisoner, and he was deeply grieved. He did not know[11] that Siegelind's[12] son had done it. People had blamed Gernot, but he later learned the truth. Liudeger's blows were so powerful that Siegfried's war horse staggered beneath the saddle. When the horse had recovered, Siegfried turned

[10]Warriors traditionally gave names to their weapons.
[11]Although the manuscripts say "he knew well," Liudeger obviously does not know at this point that Siegfried had captured his brother, nor does he recognize Siegfried until later.
[12]Siegfried's mother.

furiously to the attack. Hagen and Gernot helped him well, and Dankwart and Volker too. Many a man fell at their hands. And Sindolt, Hunolt, and Ortwin struck down many in the struggle. The princes remained unseparated in the battle. Hurled by warriors' hands, spears flew above helmets right through the bright shields, many of which were stained with blood. Many men dismounted from their horses during the violent battle, and Siegfried and Liudeger also rushed at one another. Then off flew the shield plates from the force of Siegfried's blow. He thought to win the victory over the valiant Saxons, many of whom were wounded. Oh, how many shining armor rings the bold Dankwart broke! Now Lord Liudeger recognized a crown painted on the shield in Siegfried's hand and knew who this mighty warrior was.

He began to call out loudly to his friends, "Cease your fighting, all my vassals. I have seen Siegmund's[13] son here. I have recognized the powerful Siegfried. The wicked devil sent him here to Saxony."

He bade the banners be lowered and asked for peace. It was then granted him, but he had to become a hostage to Gunther's land. To this Siegfried had compelled him. By mutual agreement they put an end to the battle and laid aside their riddled helmets and their broad, battered shields, all of them red with blood. The Burgundians took prisoner whomever they wished, for they had the power. Gernot and Hagen gave orders for the wounded to be placed on stretchers. Five hundred knights they took with them as prisoners to the Rhine. The defeated warriors now rode back to Denmark.[14] Nor had the Saxons fought so well that one could give them any praise, and they were downcast. The dead were greatly mourned by their friends.

[13]Siegfried's father.
[14]Except for the prisoners and the wounded, the opposing armies were allowed to return home.

*Do especially Questions 10, 15, 17, 80, 83, 95, 103, and 109.
Consult the Prose Narrative Model on page 33.*

FROM *The Song of Roland*

Translated by Norma Lorre Goodrich

[*Of controversial date and unknown authorship,* The Song
of Roland, *based on the historical framework of Charlemagne's life, portrays the heroic exploits of Roland, the
French national ideal. The best known legend about
Roland tragically begins and ends with the Battle of
Roncesvalles in the Pyrenees. Charlemagne, on his march
homeward after an unsuccessful attempt to conquer the
Basques and the Spanish province of Saragossa, has been
treacherously deceived into letting Roland, along with
twelve peers and twenty thousand knights, form the rear
guard which is subsequently ambushed.*]

Clear is the day in Spain, and radiant the sun! Four hundred thousand Sarrazins, under King Marsilie of Saragossa,
spur their horses northward! Crimson, blue, and white
flash their banners in the sun. A thousand trumpets shrill
as they ride in serried° ranks. Their clarions° call through
the thin mountain air, and alert the rear guard of the Franks,[1]
who are almost at the pass.

"Sir Companion," asked Oliviers of his friend Rollanz,[2]
"can it be that the Sarrazins have followed?"

"If they have," Rollanz answered Oliviers, "then it is the
will of God. We shall make our stand here. Every vassal
knows what he must suffer for his king—distress, and heat
and cold. Let every baron strike great blows for Carlemagne!"

Oliviers climbed a hill to look toward the south. There
he saw such a host of Sarrazins coming that he could not
even count them. Their helmets glittered in the sun and
their shields; their satin banners floated over a sea of rhyth-

---

[1]Early inhabitants of what is now France.
[2]Names are left in Old French to preserve their musical effect.

mic, mounted knights. "Rollanz, sound the horn!" cried
Oliviers. "Carlemagne will hear it and come back!"

"I shall not call for aid! I shall not sound the horn!"
Rollanz answered his friend. "In doing so I would lose my
good name in my beloved France. Durendal[3] will run in
blood today up to its golden hilt! Let the pagans spur
northward to the portals! I swear to you here; they are bent
unto death. May neither God nor the angels suffer shame
because of us! Halt! Let us wheel about and fight them!"

Among the twelve peers[4] was the Archbishop Turpins.
Standing on a hillock, he called the Franks to him. "Dismount and pray, for the battle draws near." Then he blessed
the valiant knights and gave them absolution. "As penance
I command you to strike a blow for God!"

The sunny-faced, the smiling Rollanz reviewed the peers.
He rode his swift war charger and brandished high his
lance. Its pennants were pure white with long, streaming
tassels. "Sir Barons, before evening we shall have won a
wealthy prize. These pagans that spur after us are seeking
martydom."° As Rollanz, sheathed in armor, cantered
Veillantif[5] down the line of the Franks, their battle cry
"Mountjoy" rose from twenty thousand throats. They knew
Guenes[6] had sold them to King Marsilie of Saragossa. Then
Guenes had appointed Rollanz to the rear guard. They
knew they were betrayed.

Opposite the Franks lined up the hosts from Spain,
vassals and allies of Marsilie of Saragossa. "Cowardly
French, ride forth and tilt with us! Today your Carlemagne
will lose his *right hand*. Foolish was your king to leave his
nephew Rollanz at the pass! Do you know you were sold
and betrayed into our ambush by your own Baron Guenes?"

Rollanz struck the first blow that day at Roncevals. With
his sword Durendal he split the taunter's body. "No, son
of a slave, our King Carles knew whom to trust! No shame

[3]Roland's sword, given to him by Charlemagne.
[4]Noblemen. There were twelve French peers and twelve Spanish peers.
[5]Roland's famous war horse.
[6]Guenes was a Frankish peer whose envy of Roland led him to treachery.

shall fall on him, on us, or on our gentle France!" Second to Rollanz, Oliviers marked out his man, dug his golden spurs into his horse's flanks and charged the pagan foe. Third into their ranks lumbered the Archbishop Turpins, marked out a prince of Barbary, and slew him with his boar spear. Then the good Sir Gerin sent a heathen's soul to Satan. Gerin's friend, the Knight Gerier, next pierced a pagan peer. Duke Sansun attacked next, and after him Anseïs. "That was a worthy arm," cheered Rollanz. Then Engelers of Gascony, Oton, and Berengier accounted for three more. Of the twelve Spanish peers, only Margariz and Chernubles still lived a few minutes more.

The twelve peers of France fought like lions on that field. With each blow Rollanz split a Sarrazin's skull, sectioned his body, and severed the horse's spine. He swung about him in scythe strokes. At one moment he passed Oliviers, who was braining enemies with his shivered lance. "Where's Halteclere, your sword?" Oliviers had been too busy to unsheathe it! . . . By hundreds, then by thousands, they strewed the field with pagan dead. Many a gallant French knight also gave up his young life at Roncevals.

Across the Pyrenees all France waited. All France knew that it was a tragic day. From the Mont-Saint-Michel to Saints, and from Besançon to Ouessant, walls crumbled in every house! At noon there grew a darkness in the sky and a great hush broken only by streaks of chainfire and thunder. A hollow wind swept from mountain to seacoast. Huge chunks of hail rattled on the thatch.° People crowded together for comfort. They spoke only in whispers. "Here has come the day of judgment and the end of the world!" They did not know and therefore could not say the truth: it was grief sweeping across fair France for the coming death of Rollanz!

Even as the Frankish peers stood masters of the field, they heard a distant rumbling like the waves of the seacoast. Then hove into sight the main body of the Spanish army, twenty battalions on the double, and seven thousand trumpets sounding the charge. At their head galloped, his dragon pennant streaming in the hot summer sun, Abisme,

the daring leader of the infidels. The Archbishop Turpins
marked him well. "That Sarrazin is a heretic.° Much better
I should kill him, for I have always hated cowards!"
Turpins spurred his yellow-maned Danish charger and
smashed his lance into the amethysts and topazes that
gleamed on Abisme's shield. Turpins ran him through.
Then he wheeled back and encouraged the Franks, "Sir
Barons, go not with somber thoughts! Beyond this last day
we shall live no more on earth. Therefore strike your
blows today for God and for France! I am here to guarantee
you all a seat in Paradise."

Then a count of Saragossa, Climborins by name — he who
had kissed Guenes on the mouth for his treason — unhorsed
and killed Engelers of Gascony. What a loss was that for
the Franks! Oliviers saw it and took revenge. Then the
heathen Valdabrun — he who had taken Jerusalem by treachery, violated the temple of Solomon, and killed the Patriarch
before his fonts — slaughtered the distinguished Duke
Sansun. "God! What a baron was he!" moaned the Franks.
Rollanz struck down Valdabrun, split his skull, his byrnie,°
his jeweled saddle, and his horse's spine. Then charged
from the Spanish ranks an African son of a king, who cut the
vermilion-and-azure shield of Anseïs, killed that noble
baron. "Baron Anseïs, what a pity is your death!" moaned
the Franks. Then from the middle rode out the Archbishop
Turpins. Never tonsured° priest ever did such deeds of
prowess. "You have just killed a baron whom my heart
regrets," said Turpins as he struck the African dead.

Grandonie, the heathen son of Cappadocia's king, crushed
the crimson shield of Gerin, then killed Gerier his companion, and after them Berengier. "See how our numbers
dwindle!" moaned the Franks. Rollanz saw those heathen
blows. Grandonie had never seen Rollanz in his life, and
yet he recognized him. Despite the noise and confusion of
battle, Grandonie knew Rollanz at once. Rollanz was the
open-faced, proud-eyed, the graceful, handsome knight. All
at once Grandonie was afraid. Rollanz did not let him
escape. With one stroke of Durendal he slit the helmet of
Toledo steel as far as the nose, then cut through the teeth

and lips, unthreaded the chain mail,° ripped through the silver pommel, and crushed the horse's spine. Then cried the Franks, "Carles's *right hand* guarantees us!" Drops of bright blood trickled through the green field of Roncevals.

In the Book of Deeds it is well written that the Franks had killed up to this moment four thousand of their foes. They stemmed the first four attacks, but the fifth one cost them dear. All the Franks were dead, except for sixty knights whom God had thus far spared. They saw what there was to do: they must fetch a high price!

"Sir Knight and dear companions," shouted Rollanz to Oliviers, "with all these knights dead, France will remain a desert! I shall now wind the horn!"

"To sound it now would be unworthy of us all! . . . How bloody are your arms, dear Rollanz!"

"I have been dealing bloody blows. . . . Why are you angry with me now?"

"All this carnage°is your fault! You outstretched yourself today. If you had listened when I spoke, King Carles would be here now. You have lost us by your pride, Rollanz. Before evening you and I will say farewell."

As Rollanz and Oliviers stood quarreling, the Archbishop Turpins came between them. "Sir Rollanz! Sir Oliviers! By God, I beg you to stop! The horn can no longer save us. Yet, on the other hand, it would still be better for Rollanz to sound it. Why? Because the Franks will return with our army. They will gather up our bodies and carry them over the mountains. They will not leave us as carrion° for wild dogs and wolves. They will inter us in the crypts of our cathedrals."

"Sir, well spoken" answered Rollanz. He lifted the horn to his lips and blew with all his might, until his temples burst and the salt blood burst through his throat.

High are the peaks and loud the voice of the horn! For thirty leagues around its shrill tongue blared. Far up on the passes of the Pyrenees, Carlemagne heard it and halted. "Our men do battle!" cried King Carles.

"No," answered the traitor Guenes. "You know how playful Rollanz is. He'd blow his horn all day on the track of a hare. Who'd dare to attack our rear guard? Let's ride forward into France."

"Listen," commanded Carles. "That horn was winded long!"

Duke Naimes agreed with Carles. "Rollanz does battle. I am sure of it. And that man, Guenes, beside you, Sir King, has betrayed him! God, Sire, do you hear that desperate horn?"

"Answer Rollanz," cried Carles. "Sound the horns and arm yourselves all!" In haste the Franks dismounted, slipped on their mail shirts, grasped their spears, and mounted their war horses. Under their breaths they prayed Rollanz would live to see their avenging arms. What is the use of words? They were too late. . . .

High are the hills and shadowy and dark, the valleys deep and the torrents swift! Rollanz looked over his shoulder toward the mountain peaks and then at the dead lords of France who lay at his feet. "I saw you lay your sweet lives down for me, and yet I could not save you. May God bear you all to Paradise. May he rest your gallant souls in sainted flowers! Greater barons than you have I never seen." Then Rollanz returned to battle, so terrible and swift that the archbishop gasped to see him drive the heathen like packs of yelping dogs before him.

"That's what a true knight should be," thought Turpins, "either strong and proud like Rollanz, or else I wouldn't give four cents for him. Either let him be like Rollanz, or let him go to a monastery and pray for our sins." Rollanz gave no quarter that day and took no prisoners. Through the thick of battle he spied the King of Saragossa. "May God damn you!" cried Rollanz as he struck off King Marsilie's right hand. Then he cut off his prince's head. At that one hundred thousand pagans, screaming to Mohammed for aid, fled from the field of battle. . . . Call them, as you will! They will not return!

Then Marsilie's uncle, a king who held lands all the way from Carthage to Ethiopia, led his troops against the Franks. His warriors were black and fierce; only their teeth showed white under their helms. When Rollanz saw them coming, he knew that he was lost. They were gallant, those men! Rallying the few remaining Franks, however, Rollanz plunged dauntlessly into their midst. As the African king rode past on his sorrel,° he struck Oliviers a deathblow in the back. Before he fell, however, Oliviers turned and killed that king. "You shall never go brag to some lady how you killed Oliviers," he cried. Then he summoned Rollanz, for he knew he soon would die.

Hurrying to Oliviers' side, Rollanz scanned° his friend's face sadly. Oliviers' cheeks were already pale and blood- less. Great clots of blood dripped from his body to the ground. Rollanz' eyes blurred, and his head swam at the sight. Oliviers did not even recognize Rollanz. Thinking he was an enemy knight, Oliviers swung his sword at him and dented his helmet. When Rollanz spoke, then Oliviers came to his senses, knew the voice, and asked forgiveness. "I have no injury, Oliviers," said Rollanz gently. "I pardon you here and before God." Then each knight bowed to the other. So did Rollanz and Oliviers part in their life- times....

There were only three French barons left alive. One was Gualter of Hum, who had fought all day on the mountains. Now, a sole survivor, he rode down to the plain toward Rollanz. "Where are you, gentle Count? Where are you, Rollanz? I was never afraid when I could fight beside you!" Side by side, Rollanz, Gualter, and the Archbishop Turpins of Rheims faced the Sarrazin host. None of them would abandon the others. Forty thousand mounted Sarrazins face them, and one thousand on foot. No pagan stirs a foot to meet them. Instead, they shower volleys° of spears, lances, arrows, and darts; Gualter falls. The archbishop's horse falls. The archbishop's body is pierced through with four spears!

Yet the gallant archbishop still struggled to his feet. His eyes sought Rollanz. He gasped, "I am not defeated! I do not surrender!" Then the huge Turpins advanced boldly toward the enemy, swinging his sword about his head in a frenzy of anger and will to defy them. The Book says he injured four hundred more, and so says the eyewitness, the Baron Gilie who built the monastery at Laon. Anyone who doesn't know this, understands nothing about History!

Count Rollanz stood alone. He trembled from fatigue, from the heat of battle, and from his bursting temples. He still did not know whether or not Carlemagne had heard his call. He tried once more to sound the horn, but his strength was almost gone. Even so, the emperor heard the feeble notes. "Sirs!" called King Carles. "That was my nephew's last breath! I can tell by the sound that he is near death! Ride on, whoever wishes to see him yet alive! Sound all our horns at once!" Then sixty thousand trumpets blared full-tongued through the hills and echoing vales.

On the plain of Roncevals the pagans stopped to hear that blast. "Carles will soon be upon us! Then there will be havoc.° If Rollanz lives one hour more, we are lost and so is Spain." Then four hundred banded together and advanced toward Turpins and Rollanz.

Count Rollanz of France, nephew of the king, drew himself up cold and haughty. He clenched his teeth and waited. He would never retreat an inch while breath stayed in his lungs. "I am on horseback while you have lost your mount." said Rollanz to the archbishop. "Therefore let Durendal bear the brunt. Know only that I am beside you, whatever happens."

Turpins laughed and answered stanchly,° "He is a felon° who will still not strike them hard! Carles is coming. He will avenge us."

The four hundred Sarrazins stood face to face with Rollanz. Not a man of them dared attack, and yet there was not a moment to lose. Even then they could hear the advance body of the Franks thundering down the mountain. The blaring war cry "Mountjoy" floated to their ears. Instead of rushing the two French barons, the Sarrazins let fly another volley of spears, arrows, lances, and beribboned darts. Then they turned tail and fled for their lives across the field.

Rollanz stood alone on the field of battle. His armor, his helmet, his mail were pierced and shattered. His valiant war horse Veillantif was dead of thirty wounds. Rollanz turned to the archbishop. As gently as he could, he lifted off his armor and stanched° his wounds. Then raising the prelate° in his arms, Rollanz laid him on thick grass. "Take leave of me, gentle sir," pleaded Rollanz. "All our friends and companions, all are dead. I shall go and carry their bodies here before you. I shall lay them in a row here on the sod."

Still the archbishop lived and so did his great heart. "Go and return, Rollanz. This field is ours, thank God—yours and mine!"

Rollanz walked across the battlefield. He searched through the vales and he searched through the hills. First he found Sir Gerin and Sir Gerier, then Sir Berengier, Sir Anseïs, and Sir Sansun. Then he found the body of that great hero Sir Gerard of Rusillun. These he laid at the archbishop's feet so that they could be blessed. Then Rollanz sought and found his dear friend, Sir Oliviers the Wise. As he carried Oliviers in his arms, Rollanz spoke soft words to his friend, and wept. After he had laid Oliviers on the earth, Rollanz could endure no more. His face became drained and white. He sank to the ground.

"How I pity you, Baron," said the Archbishop Turpins. The compassion he felt for Rollanz was the sharpest pain he had felt all that day. Unsteadily the worthy prelate rose to his feet. He wanted to bring water for Rollanz from the little stream that flows at Roncevals, but he had lost too much blood. Before he had traversed° the length of an acre, his heart faltered and stopped beating. The throes of death gripped him. He fell forward on the grass. . . .

Rollanz feels death very close. His brains bubble out through his ears. His every thought is a prayer to God to summon to Him the dead peers of France. He prays to the Angel Gabriel, who is near. Then taking his ivory war horn in one hand, and his sword Durendal in the other, Rollanz walks in the direction of Spain toward a hill where there are four marble steps. There he falls over backward on the green turf.

Do especially Questions 11, 15, 17, 58, 61, 83, 89, 93, and 106.
Consult the Prose Narrative Model on page 33.

How the Cid Won
His Knighthood (From *The Legend of the Cid*)

Translated by Robert Goldston

[El Poema Del Cid, *written in 1140 by an unknown Castil-
lian poet just forty years after The Cid's death, is a tribute
to Rodrigo de Vivar, the champion and protector of Spain
and Christianity who became a legend during his own lifetime. Rodrigo's life of honor and fame began when King
Fernando of Castille sent his heralds to proclaim a Council
of State to be attended by his loyal nobles.*]

One of the lesser of these nobles was don Diego de Vivar.
He was a very learned and wise man, full of years, who
lived in seclusion with his family near the city of Vivar. On
more than one occasion he had been called to advise the
king about affairs of state. Yet his greatest pleasure was in
teaching his wisdom to his sons and watching them grow
into stalwart manhood.

The royal herald° found don Diego seated in his library
surrounded by books and maps and manuscripts. The old
scholar listened courteously to the herald's announcement,
glanced wistfully at his manuscripts, and then sighed. "You
may tell His Majesty that I have heard and will obey his command," he said. But when the herald had left, don Diego
muttered to himself, "And yet I prefer the company of
these manuscripts to the company of kings." It was just
at that moment that Rodrigo, don Diego's eldest son, burst
into the room. His eyes sparkled and his breath was quick.

He had been practicing swordplay and his tanned skin was beaded with sweat. "Pardon me, Father, I saw the king's herald ride by."

Don Diego looked up. Rodrigo was his favorite son and yet he was as different from his father as red wine is from white. His whole interest was in fighting. Archery, swordplay, lancing, riding—these were Rodrigo's favorite studies. And although the lad was only seventeen, yet his body was muscled and tall as a man's. "Indeed?" don Diego demanded severely. "And so you immediately left your practice to interrupt my studies?"

"Is there to be war, Father?" Rodrigo asked.

"Thanks be to God, no, there is not to be war, although I know you would like nothing better. Instead, there is to be a great Council of State. I must present myself before the king on the feast day of Saint John."

"Father, may I come?"

"No! Absolutely not. You have not been invited. You are not a noble, and I do not imagine that His Majesty requires the advice of a seventeen-year-old boy!"

Rodrigo blushed. "But the journey to the royal court is a long one, Father. You might meet bandits or Moors on the way. I could protect you."

Don Diego laughed. "It is true that I am an old man, but I am too poor to be molested by bandits, and there are no Moors between here and the royal court."

"But you might run into a raiding party, and besides—well, Father, if I do not ever meet the king, he will not know I exist, and I'll never be knighted!"

Don Diego shook his head patiently. "You are still too young to be knighted. As far as raiding parties are concerned, may I remind you that you have only your wooden practice sword, and we have only one horse? Perhaps you think I ought to walk while you ride *Pitiuso* to protect me from imaginary Moors with your wooden sword?"

"No, Father. I could ride behind you on *Pitiuso* and if we were attacked I would use your sword, *Tizone.*"

"Enough!" Don Diego raised his hand. "While you have

been babbling I have been thinking. I will indeed take you to the great Council."

"Thank you, Father."

"Silence! I will take you not for protection against ferocious Moors or to have you make a fool of yourself by asking the king to knight you. You shall accompany me to the royal court so that you may see for yourself what a tiresome thing it is. It will be an education for you. And may I remind you—"

Don Diego started to lecture Rodrigo in the principles of courtesy practiced at the court of Fernando I, but Rodrigo scarcely listened. In his excited imagination he had already saved his father from bandits and was about to lead the king's entire army in a great charge against the legions of the Moors.

Preparations were made. Rodrigo's mother made him a new cloak of crimson. Rodrigo himself polished *Pitiuso's* high-backed saddle and reins until they gleamed like ebony. He was so impatient for the journey to begin that he could not sleep at night, but would practice thrust and counter-thrust with his wooden sword until sunrise. Don Diego, meanwhile, busied himself in preparing a detailed history of Castille which he intended to present as a gift to King Fernando.

On the day of their departure, Rodrigo's mother, his younger brothers, Hernan and Bermudo, and the three old servants who had been with the family for many years came out to see them off. *Pitiuso,* although an old horse, held his head proudly and pawed impatiently at the ground. Rodrigo, his new cape clasped over his shoulders, kissed his mother farewell. Don Diego mounted *Pitiuso,* bade his wife good-by, cleared his throat and then made a lengthy speech during which he recounted most of the history of Spain and ended by commending° his family to the care of God. Then he motioned Rodrigo to mount behind him on *Pitiuso* and at long last they departed.

The journey from Vivar to the royal capital at Burgos was not a long one, but the lands they had to cross were rocky and barren and the roads were few and badly maintained. Because *Pitiuso* carried a double load, they could proceed no faster than the horse could walk. Don Diego passed the time instructing Rodrigo on the customs of the places they passed through. Rodrigo listened courteously, but his eyes were always roving to the distant mountains as if he expected a band of Moors to ride forth at any moment.

When evening came they stopped at a small inn by the side of the road near the city of Valladolid. While don Diego made arrangements for a room, Rodrigo took *Pitiuso* to a nearby well to water him. He found several soldiers with horses waiting at the well and they talked of various matters but especially of the endless wars against the Moors. Rodrigo listened and wished in his heart that he too were a veteran to speak of battles and sieges. While the soldiers were talking there suddenly came a cry from nearby, "Is there no Christian who will help me?"

Rodrigo and several of the soldiers rushed to find the voice. Soon they came upon a leper° who had sunk into a patch of quicksand. The leper was badly hurt and had already sunk in up to his waist.

"For the love of God," he cried piteously, "give me a hand to free me from this pit!"

But when the soldiers saw the terrible ravages° of leprosy on the man's face and arms they recoiled in horror.

But Rodrigo's heart was touched. Leaning over the quicksand he stretched out his arms, gripped the leper's hands and with a mighty pull drew him forth. It was then he saw that the man was almost naked and shivered desperately in the cold. Taking off his new cloak, he wrapped it around the leper's shoulders and said, "They will not allow you to stay at the inn, but if you wish you can sleep in the stables next to my horse *Pitiuso*. The straw is warm and I will bring you food."

"Thank you, my son," the leper answered. "It is not only by fighting that one gains heaven."

After seeing the leper safely to the stable, Rodrigo returned to the well to find *Pitiuso*. The soldiers drew away from him when he approached. "You may already be infected!" they cried. "You must be seeking death to touch a leper!"

Rodrigo shrugged. "Only what God wills may come to pass," he answered.

Then he gave water to *Pitiuso* and returned to the stable. He saw the leper sleeping on his cape, huddled in the straw. As he combed and groomed *Pitiuso* he decided that he would have to bring food secretly to the poor man for he feared that his father would react as the soldiers had.

A few hours later, after they had eaten, and while his father snored loudly on the bed next to him, Rodrigo arose, gathered together the bread and meat he had saved from his own meal and made his way to the stable. It was now past midnight. But when he arrived he found that the leper had disappeared. There was his cape, folded neatly beside *Pitiuso,* and there was the depression in the straw where the man had slept. But the leper himself had disappeared. Rodrigo was just about to return to the inn when he heard a voice behind him.

"Were you seeking me, Rodrigo?"

Rodrigo whirled and saw, standing at the stable entrance, a man dressed in an immaculate white tunic. A soft glow of light bathed the man's body although there was no moon that night. "Who are you?" Rodrigo asked in a trembling voice.

"Do not be afraid, Rodrigo. I am Saint Lazarus," the apparition° said. "It was I whom, for the love of God, you saved this day. In reward for your faith I am permitted to tell you that from this time forth you shall be invincible. Your fame will increase from day to day, and when you die it shall be with honor. As our Lord rescued me from the tomb, so has it been given to you to win a great victory even after you die." The apparition smiled, raised its hand in benediction and then vanished.

Rodrigo returned to the inn, but he slept not at all that night. As he thought of this strange happening he was certain of only one thing; he would never tell any living man of what had come to pass.

The next day passed in hot and dusty journeying. Don

Diego never ceased lecturing and Rodrigo's eyes were forever sharp for the distant cloud of dust that might announce bandits or Moors. Another night at another inn and still another day came and went while they made their way slowly beside the green banks of the *Rio Pisuerga*. It was late in the afternoon of the third day, when the sun glinted red on the distant peaks of the *Sierra Cantabria*, that *Pitiuso* suddenly reared and stopped short.

Within a minute Rodrigo had jumped down and was running toward a nearby outcropping of rock. There, behind the escarpment,° a nest of bandits might be waiting to fall upon them. Don Diego called after his son, but Rodrigo paid no heed. He climbed cautiously up the side of the escarpment and peered down. Then he stood up and laughed. His band of robbers was nothing more than a wild and starving horse, munching peacefully on the sparse grass in the shade of the rocks. He was a stallion, thin and uncombed, without a saddle. When Rodrigo approached, the horse allowed him to pat its neck. It was obviously not a wild horse, but one that had been abandoned or whose owner had met with misadventure.

By this time don Diego had ridden up on *Pitiuso*. "What a sorry-looking beast!" he exclaimed. "It has been alone for a long time."

"In that case it may as well be mine!" Rodrigo cried.

Don Diego laughed. "You would have to be a *babieca* indeed to want so forlorn a horse!" he said. By *babieca* he meant fool.

"So be it. I will have this horse and I shall call him *Babieca* and one day all the world will know of him!" Rodrigo ran his hands through the horse's tangled white mane.

"Well, it will be a rest for *Pitiuso*," don Diego admitted. "Take the horse if you will, but I fear that all the world will come to know of him as a joke."

Rodrigo spoke softly to the stallion and then quickly mounted. "You see, Father, he permits me to mount!"

"He simply hasn't the strength to run away. You will make a fine sight riding into the royal court on a horse like that!"

"By the time we arrive in Burgos, *Babieca* will look as well as *Pitiuso*."

And Rodrigo kept his word. That night he spent hours combing and grooming *Babieca* and each day and night for the rest of the journey he fed him prodigiously.° He even managed to buy an old cavalry saddle from a soldier at one of the inns and he polished it until it sparkled. By the time they arrived before the walls of Burgos, *Babieca* was a proud and well-groomed horse.

On the feast day of Saint John, Rodrigo accompanied his father to the great Hall of Justice in the royal palace. It seemed to him as they entered that he had plunged into a sea of color. The high stone walls of the hall were hung with brilliant tapestries. The fiery banners and pennants of Castille and Leon hung overhead from golden staffs. Ranks of soldiers in sparkling armor lined the hall with their lances raised, looking like a silver-tipped forest. So crowded was the hall with knights, counts, dukes, and peers, all wearing brilliantly colored capes and plumed helmets, that it seemed as if all the nobility of the kingdom were present. And that was very nearly true. Here were the tributary° kings of Navarre and Aragon, the Royal Princes Sancho, Alfonso and Garcia; there were the famous knights Arias Gonzalo, Peransules and Diego Lainez. And at the end of the hall Rodrigo could see King Fernando himself, seated upon a golden throne, the great jeweled sword of state resting across his knees while his bearded head inclined patiently to the long line of nobles who pressed forward to do him honor.

Rodrigo's eyes, sweeping this glittering pageant, suddenly came to rest on a nearby group of nobles. They clustered around a tall and powerful man who seemed to be speaking gravely. But it was not the men who caught Rodrigo's eye. It was the slim figure of a young girl standing next to them. Suddenly it seemed to Rodrigo that all the color and brilliance of the gathering faded into gray beside the jet-black brilliance of her hair and the soft luster of her cheeks. Rodrigo could not leave his father's side, but he could not take his eyes away from the beautiful young girl. As he accompanied don Diego through the ranks of courtiers toward the throne, the unknown beauty suddenly glanced up, as if aware that someone had been staring at her. When her glance fell upon Rodrigo her face paled and then her lips parted slightly in a smile. It was as if both Rodrigo and the girl had suddenly recognized each other as old friends — and much more.

"Father," Rodrigo whispered, "who is that girl?"

Don Diego followed Rodrigo's glance. "That is doña Jimena, the daughter of the Count of Lozano, who is the tall man standing beside her. And if the count notices you staring at her he will pay you his respects rather roughly, I fear."

The old man's words were interrupted suddenly by the shrill blasting of trumpets. Rodrigo found himself standing with his father in the front ranks of courtiers before the king. Fernando rose to his feet, looked slowly at the great throng and gently caressed his long white beard. Then he spoke.

"We, Fernando, King of Castille and Emperor of Leon, Overlord of Aragon and of Navarre, Tributary Lord of the Emirates of Toledo and Zaragoza, declare that a great Council of State is now convened. We thank you for your attendance upon our wishes and we beseech the blessing of Almighty God upon this Council that we may be led to just and righteous solutions of the problems which afflict our realm."

The king seated himself and once again the trumpets sounded.

Now a herald stepped forward and from a great roll of parchment called out the names of all those present. As each name was called a noble would come forward, bend his knee to King Fernando and offer up his sword for service. The king would speak a few words and return the sword, and the next name would ring through the huge hall. When Rodrigo saw the priceless jewels, costly furs, and golden weapons that the nobles presented as gifts to the king, he felt a sudden pang of shame that his father had brought only a parchment history of Castille.

"Don Diego de Vivar!"

Rodrigo found himself kneeling alongside his father before the king. The old scholar had presented his sword. The king gripped it firmly and handed it back. Then don Diego handed the king his parchment history. "Your Majesty, please accept this history of your Kingdom of Castille in testimony to the great love and esteem we bear you."

King Fernando accepted the book and smiled. "Don Diego, of all the gifts I have received this day, yours is the richest. You have given us the gift of your wisdom which is famous throughout our realm."

"Your Majesty does me honor!" don Diego replied proudly. "May I present to Your Majesty my eldest son, Rodrigo?"

The king's eyes turned to Rodrigo. "A fine young man, don Diego. He has the build of a warrior."

"I fear so, Your Majesty. He does not inherit my love of scholarship."

"Would you be a warrior, Rodrigo?" the king asked gravely.

"Yes, Your Majesty!" Rodrigo exclaimed. "I would be a knight to fight always in Your Majesty's cause!"

The king smiled. "You must prove yourself to be a knight." Then he frowned. "I fear there will soon be fighting enough in Castille."

Rodrigo hardly remembered how he and his father left that splendid hall. All that afternoon, while don Diego and some few of the king's closest advisors were gathered together in private council, Rodrigo spent his time in the royal stables, grooming *Pitiuso* and *Babieca,* while he pondered° two problems. How was he to prove himself so that the king would knight him, and how was he to go about making the acquaintance of the beautiful Jimena?

It was later in the day, while Rodrigo sat on a stone bench outside the stable entrance still pondering these matters, when don Diego appeared. The old scholar's face was hard and his eyes flashed fire. Rodrigo had never seen his father so enraged.

"Father, what has happened?"

Don Diego's lips were tightly clenched but at last he spoke as if tearing the words from his heart. "I have been publicly insulted, before the king!"

Rodrigo stepped back, his hands clenching as if seeking weapons. "Who? Why?" were the only words he spoke.

"We were assembled in private council," don Diego said slowly. "The question before us was whether the king should divide his realm among his three sons when he dies, as has been our custom. I spoke up for the more ancient Gothic rule that the entire kingdom be inherited by the eldest son since that is our only hope against the Moors. But the great nobles prefer three weak kings to one strong one. Their spokesman was the Count of Lozano."

"But that is no insult, Father—"

"Hear me! The king made no decision regarding the inheritance. He will do that later. But he appointed me tutor to his three sons. It is a great honor. He said that if there must be three kings in Castille, he would have them brought up in wisdom. But the Count of Lozano had hoped to be appointed Royal Tutor himself. He and the other great nobles hope thus to influence the princes. The argument grew heated, I fear." Don Diego's voice sank away.

"And then?"

"Then, Rodrigo, the Count of Lozano said that I could only instruct the princes in cowardice. He slapped me twice across the face! If I were but a few years younger—"

Don Diego fell silent and the silence grew intense. Rodrigo realized that he must now make the acquaintance of the beautiful Jimena as the enemy of her father. For he knew his duty clearly.

"Father, you instructed me, and you did not teach me cowardice. Give me your sword!"

Don Diego smiled gravely. "You speak as I hoped you would." He unbuckled his sword and handed it to Rodrigo. "Take this sword, Rodrigo. It is named *Tizone*, and in my youth it was accustomed to avenging° wrongs!"

Rodrigo took the sword, kissed his father on each cheek, and then hurried to saddle *Babieca*. When he led the horse forth he asked, "Where will I find the Count of Lozano now, Father?"

"He is quartered with his followers at the castle of Belares near the north gate of the city."

Rodrigo mounted and, without a backward look, spurred *Babieca* to a gallop.

It did not take him long to reach the castle of Belares. And as he rode into the great courtyard of the castle he saw the Count of Lozano, about to dismount from his horse.

"Who are you and what do you want?" the count demanded when he saw Rodrigo's warlike aspect.

"I am Rodrigo de Vivar. Do not dismount, count. I have come to take back the honor you stole from my father."

The count laughed. "Go away, young man! You are not even a knight, and yet you wish to cross swords with a man who is accustomed to victory! Depart while you may!"

"Then test me, count, to see whether I too can accustom myself to victory. Or do you only care to fight against the old and defenseless?"

"Leave me quickly, Rodrigo, before I lose my patience and give you the same blows I gave your father—or worse!"

"I see, count, that your patience makes you a coward!"

On hearing these words, the Count of Lozano, purple with rage, drew his sword and spurred his horse to charge against Rodrigo.

But Rodrigo had already guessed the count's intention. He parried° the count's sword with *Tizone* and made *Babieca* turn quickly. Then, before the count had time to recover from his first charge, Rodrigo was upon him. *Tizone* struck sparks of fire from the count's sword while *Babieca* reared, wheeled, and charged like a true war horse.

By this time many people had rushed from the castle to watch the fight and among them was Jimena. As she saw what was happening and recognized who battled against her father, her face paled and, as if some dreadful premonition° had come to her, she could only whisper over and over, "No, please, God. No—"

Rodrigo and the count continued to fight, their swords clashing tirelessly, their horses' mouths flecked with foam. The count's experience was clearly matched by Rodrigo's youth and anger.

But when Rodrigo noticed Jimena's pallid face among the onlookers, he paused for a moment. "Count," he cried, "beg my father's pardon and we shall put an end to this quarrel!"

"I ask no pardon of cowards and villains! If you are afraid then run away and tell your father he should be ashamed to have engendered° such a cowardly son!"

Hearing these insults, Rodrigo forgot Jimena and attacked with such fury that the count found himself barely able to ward off the flashing blows of *Tizone*.

Standing up in *Babieca's* stirrups, his eyes fiery, and *Tizone* flashing on high, Rodrigo appeared to be an avenging angel. Soon he gave the count such a blow that the count's sword clattered from his hand. But *Tizone* cleft downward through shield and helmet and the count fell from his horse mortally wounded.

A cry of horror went up from the crowd of onlookers. Jimena, who had been praying that the fight might somehow end peacefully, fell fainting into the arms of her maid. And just at that moment five royal heralds galloped into the castle courtyard. They saw quickly what had happened and rode over to Rodrigo.

"We had come, by His Majesty's command, to prevent what has already come to pass," one of them said. "Rodrigo de Vivar, you are ordered before the king!"

Rodrigo bowed his head, glanced for one anguished moment toward the portal° through which Jimena had been carried, and followed the heralds from the castle.

Rodrigo was brought into the king's presence in the great Hall of Justice. But now the hall was empty save for guards and don Diego, who stood next to the king's throne. Rodrigo knelt to the king and then knelt before his father and presented *Tizone*. "Take back your sword, Father. With it I return to you the honor of which you were robbed."

Don Diego placed his hands on Rodrigo's shoulders and raised him up. "You shall keep this sword, my son. He who defends the honor of a family should be its head!"

King Fernando had watched all this in silence. Stroking his long white beard and with the faintest trace of a smile on his lips, he now spoke. "Rodrigo de Vivar, you have proved yourself in the test of battle worthy of being knighted. Kneel before me!"

Rodrigo knelt before the king.

Fernando touched Rodrigo's right shoulder with his sword. "Rodrigo de Vivar, do you wish to be a knight?" he demanded.

"Yes, Sire, I do!"

The king touched Rodrigo's left shoulder with his sword. "Rodrigo de Vivar, do you wish to be a knight?"

"Yes, Sire, I do!"

"Then, in the name of God and Santiago, I make you a knight! Be brave and loyal!" Then the king raised Rodrigo to his feet and embraced him as a brother.

"Your Majesty does me great honor!" Rodrigo exclaimed. He could barely find words to express the tumult of emotions within him.

The king seated himself upon his throne. "That may be, Rodrigo," he said sternly. "But now we come to a grave matter. In killing the Count of Lozano, even to avenge an insult, you have committed a crime. The punishment for such a crime is banishment.° How say you?"

Rodrigo turned to his father. "Give me your benediction,° Father. I would not have it thought that my hand serves only to avenge insults. For this reason I shall go forth to do battle with the Moors!"

"You have proclaimed your own sentence, Rodrigo," the king said. "We hereby banish you from all of our realms until it is our pleasure to recall you. But we shall decide upon that only when we have proofs of your loyalty and valor."

"I have heard and will obey, Sire!"

And with his father's blessing and *Tizone* buckled to his side, Rodrigo hurried from the royal palace. He found *Babieca* waiting for him impatiently as if anxious to help his young master prove himself on the field of battle for his king.

So it was that Rodrigo de Vivar in one afternoon had avenged his family's honor, lost the love of doña Jimena,

been knighted by his king and banished from Castille.
Now he rode forth from the royal city of Burgos, one man
with but one sword, to do battle alone against the legions
of the Moors.

---

*Do especially Questions 16, 17, 61, 75, 89, 92, 103, 109, and
111. Consult the Prose Narrative Model on page 33.*

The Terrifying Adventures
of Don Quixote

MIGUEL DE CERVANTES   Translated by Samuel Putnam

In a village of La Mancha the name of which I have no
desire to recall, there lived not so long ago one of those
gentlemen who always have a lance in the rack, an ancient
buckler,° a skinny nag, and a greyhound for the chase. A
stew with more beef than mutton in it, chopped meat for
his evening meal, scraps for a Saturday, lentils° on Friday,
and a young pigeon as a special delicacy for Sunday, went
to account for three-quarters of his income. The rest of it
he laid out on a broadcloth greatcoat° and velvet stockings
for feast days, with slippers to match, while the other days of
the week he cut a figure in a suit of the finest homespun....

This gentleman of ours was close on to fifty, of a robust
constitution but with little flesh on his bones and a face
that was lean and gaunt. He was noted for his early rising,
being very fond of the hunt. They will try to tell you that
his surname° was Quijada or Quesada—there is some
difference of opinion among those who have written on
the subject—but according to the most likely conjectures
we are to understand that it was really Quejana. But all

this means very little so far as our story is concerned, providing that in the telling of it we do not depart one iota° from the truth.

You may know, then, that the aforesaid gentleman, on those occasions when he was at leisure, which was most of the year around, was in the habit of reading books of chivalry° with such pleasure and devotion as to lead him almost wholly to forget the life of a hunter and even the administration of his estate. So great was his curiosity and infatuation in this regard that he even sold many acres of tillable land in order to be able to buy and read the books that he loved, and he would carry home with him as many of them as he could obtain.

Of all those that he thus devoured none pleased him so well as the ones that had been composed by the famous Feliciano de Silva,[1] whose lucid prose style and involved conceits° were as precious to him as pearls; especially when he came to read those tales of love and amorous challenges that are to be met with in many places, such a passage as the following, for example: "The reason of the unreason that afflicts my reason, in such a manner weakens my reason that I with reason lament me of your comeliness." And he was similarly affected when his eyes fell upon such lines as these: "... the high Heaven of your divinity divinely fortifies you with the stars and renders you deserving of that desert your greatness doth deserve...."

In short, our gentleman became so immersed in his reading that he spent whole nights from sundown to sunup and his days from dawn to dusk in poring over his books, until, finally, from so little sleeping and so much reading, his brain dried up and he went completely out of his mind. He had filled his imagination with everything that he had read, with enchantments,° knightly encounters, battles, challenges, wounds, with tales of love and its torments, and all sorts of impossible things, and as a result had come to believe that all these fictitious happenings were true; they were more real to him than anything else in the world....

---

[1] A rather obscure Spanish author of romantic tales.

At last, when his wits were gone beyond repair, he came to conceive the strangest idea that ever occurred to any madman in this world. It now appeared to him fitting and necessary, in order to win a greater amount of honor for himself and serve his country at the same time, to become a knight-errant° and roam the world on horseback, in a suit of armor; he would go in quest of adventures, by way of putting into practice all that he had read in his books; he would right every manner of wrong, placing himself in situations of the greatest peril such as would redound to the eternal glory of his name. As a reward for his valor and the might of his arm, the poor fellow could already see himself crowned Emperor of Trebizond[2] at the very least; and so, carried away by the strange pleasure that he found in such thoughts as these, he at once set about putting his plan into effect.

The first thing he did was to burnish° up some old pieces of armor, left him by his great-grandfather, which for ages had lain in a corner, moldering and forgotten. He polished and adjusted them as best he could, and then he noticed that one very important thing was lacking: there was no closed helmet, but only a morion, or visorless headpiece, with turned up brim of the kind foot soldiers wore. His ingenuity,° however, enabled him to remedy this, and he proceeded to fashion out of cardboard a kind of half-helmet, which, when attached to the morion, gave the appearance of a whole one. True, when he went to see if it was strong enough to withstand a good slashing blow, he was somewhat disappointed; for when he drew his sword and gave it a couple of thrusts, he succeeded only in undoing a whole week's labor. The ease with which he had hewed it to bits disturbed him no little, and he decided to make it over. This time he placed a few strips of iron on the inside, and then, convinced that it was strong enough, refrained° from putting it to any further test; instead, he adopted it then and there as the finest helmet ever made.

After this, he went out to have a look at his nag; and

[2]A medieval empire around the Black Sea and on the Caucasus.

although the animal had more *cuartos*, or cracks, in its hoof than there are quarters in a real,[3] and more blemishes than Gonela's[4] steed which *tantum pellis et ossa fuit*,[5] it nonetheless looked to its master like a far better horse than Alexander's Bucephalus or the Babieca of the Cid.[6] He spent all of four days in trying to think up a name for his mount; for—so he told himself—seeing that it belonged to so famous and worthy a knight, there was no reason why it should not have a name of equal renown. The kind of name he wanted was one that would at once indicate what the nag had been before it came to belong to a knight-errant and what its present status was; for it stood to reason that, when the master's worldly condition changed, his horse also ought to have a famous, high-sounding appella-tion, one suited to the new order of things and the new profession that it was to follow.

After he in his memory and imagination had made up, struck out, and discarded many names, now adding to and now subtracting from the list, he finally hit upon "Rocinante," a name that impressed him as being sonorous and at the same time indicative of what the steed had been when it was but a hack,[7] whereas now it was nothing other than the first and foremost of all the hacks in the world.

Having found a name for his horse that pleased his fancy, he then desired to do as much for himself, and this re-quired another week, and by the end of that period he had made up his mind that he was henceforth to be known as Don Quixote,[8] which, as has been stated, has led the authors of this veracious° history to assume that his real name must undoubtedly have been Quijada, and not Quesada as others would have it. But remembering that

---

[3]An old Spanish coin. There are eight reales in a dollar.
[4]A jester in the service of Borso, Duke of Ferrara, a city in northern Italy.
[5]*tantum pellis et ossa fuit*—Was all skin and bones.
[6]ALEXANDER'S BUCEPHALUS OR THE BABIECA OF THE CID—Bucephalus was the war-horse of Alexander the Great; Babieca the horse of the Spanish hero, the Cid.
[7]An old, worn-out horse. The word *Rocinante* is from the Spanish word *rocín*, meaning a *hack*.
[8]DON QUIXOTE—Pronounced (*Sp.*) dôn ke hô'tə.

the valiant Amadis was not content to call himself that and nothing more, but added the name of his kingdom and fatherland that he might make it famous also, and thus came to take the name Amadis of Gaul, so our good knight chose to add his place of origin and become "Don Quixote de la Mancha"; for by this means, as he saw it, he was making very plain his lineage° and was conferring honor upon his country by taking its name as his own.

And so, having polished up his armor and made the morion over into a closed helmet, and having given himself and his horse a name, he naturally found but one thing lacking still: he must seek out a lady of whom he could become enamored;° for a knight-errant without a ladylove was like a tree without leaves or fruit, a body without a soul.

"If," he said to himself, "as a punishment for my sins or by a stroke of fortune I should come upon some giant hereabouts, a thing that very commonly happens to knights-errant, and if I should slay him in a hand-to-hand encounter or perhaps cut him in two, or, finally, if I should vanquish° and subdue him, would it not be well to have someone to whom I may send him as a present, in order that he, if he is living, may come in, fall upon his knees in front of my sweet lady, and say in a humble and submissive tone of voice, 'I, lady, am the giant Caraculiambro, lord of the island Malindrania, who has been overcome in single combat by that knight who never can be praised enough, Don Quixote de la Mancha, the same who sent me to present myself before your Grace that your Highness may dispose of me as you see fit'?"

Oh, how our good knight reveled° in this speech, and more than ever when he came to think of the name that he should give his lady! As the story goes, there was a very good-looking farm girl who lived near by, with whom he had once been smitten, although it is generally believed that she never knew or suspected it. Her name was Aldonza Lorenzo, and it seemed to him that she was the one upon whom he should bestow the title of mistress of his thoughts. For her he wished a name that should not be incongruous° with his own and that would convey the suggestion of a princess or a great lady; and, accordingly, he resolved to call her "Dulcinea⁹ del Toboso," she being a native of that place. A musical name to his ears, out of the ordinary and significant, like the others he had chosen for himself and his appurtenances.°

Having, then, made all these preparations, he did not wish to lose any time in putting his plan into effect, for he could not but blame himself for what the world was losing by his delay, so many were the wrongs that were to be righted, the grievances to be redressed,° the abuses to be done away with, and the duties to be performed. Accordingly, without informing anyone of his intention and without letting anyone see him, he set out one morning before daybreak on one of those very hot days in July. Donning all his armor, mounting Rocinante, adjusting his ill-contrived helmet, bracing his shield on his arm, and taking up his lance, he sallied forth by the back gate of his stable yard into the open countryside. It was with great contentment and joy that he saw how easily he had made a beginning toward the fulfillment of his desire. . . .

[*In his first adventure, after being dubbed a knight by an innkeeper who he imagines is the lord of a castle, Don Quixote was so badly beaten by a mule driver that he was put in bed and watched over by his niece, the curate, and the barber. It was several days before he was able to get out of bed.*]

After that he remained at home very tranquilly° for a couple of weeks, without giving sign of any desire to repeat his former madness. During that time he had the most pleasant conversations with his two old friends, the curate and the barber, on the point he had raised to the effect that what the world needed most was knights-errant and a revival of chivalry. The curate would occasionally contradict him and again would give in, for it was only by means of this artifice° that he could carry on a conversation with him at all.

⁹The sweet one.

In the meanwhile Don Quixote was bringing his powers of persuasion to bear upon a farmer who lived near by, a good man — if this title may be applied to one who is poor — but with very few wits in his head. The short of it is, by pleas and promises, he got the hapless rustic° to agree to ride forth with him and serve him as his squire.° Among other things, Don Quixote told him that he ought to be more than willing to go, because no telling what adventure might occur which would win them an island, and then he (the farmer) would be left to be the governor of it. As a result of these and other similar assurances, Sancho Panza forsook his wife and children and consented to take upon himself the duties of squire to his neighbor.

Next, Don Quixote set out to raise some money, and by selling this thing and pawning that and getting the worst of the bargain always, he finally scraped together a reasonable amount. He also asked a friend of his for the loan of a buckler and patched up his broken helmet as well as he could. He advised his squire, Sancho, of the day and hour when they were to take the road and told him to see to laying in a supply of those things that were most necessary, and, above all, not to forget the saddlebags. Sancho replied that he would see to all this and added that he was also thinking of taking along with him a very good ass that he had, as he was not much used to going on foot.

With regard to the ass, Don Quixote had to do a little thinking, trying to recall if any knight-errant had ever had a squire thus asininely° mounted. He could not think of any, but nevertheless he decided to take Sancho with the intention of providing him with a nobler steed as soon as occasion offered; he had but to appropriate the horse of the first discourteous knight he met. Having furnished himself with shirts and all the other things that the innkeeper had recommended, he and Panza rode forth one night unseen by anyone and without taking leave of wife and children, housekeeper or niece. They went so far that by the time morning came they were safe from discovery had a hunt been started for them.

Mounted on his ass, Sancho Panza rode along like a

patriarch,° with saddlebags and flask, his mind set upon becoming governor of that island that his master had promised him. Don Quixote determined to take the same route and road over the Campo de Montiel that he had followed on his first journey; but he was not so uncomfortable this time, for it was early morning and the sun's rays fell upon them slantingly and accordingly did not tire them too much.

"Look, Sir Knight-errant," said Sancho, "your Grace should not forget that island you promised me; for no matter how big it is, I'll be able to govern it right enough."

"I would have you know, friend Sancho Panza," replied Don Quixote, "that among the knights-errant of old it was a very common custom to make their squires governors of the islands or the kingdoms that they won, and I am resolved that in my case so pleasing a usage shall not fall into desuetude.° I even mean to go them one better; for they very often, perhaps most of the time, waited until their squires were old men who had had their fill of serving their masters during bad days and worse nights, whereupon they would give them the title of count, or marquis at most, of some valley or province more or less. But if you live and I live, it well may be that within a week I shall win some kingdom with others dependent upon it, and it will be the easiest thing in the world to crown you king of one of them. You need not marvel at this, for all sorts of unforeseen things happen to knights like me, and I may readily be able to give you even more than I have promised."

"In that case," said Sancho Panza, "if by one of those miracles of which your Grace was speaking I should become king, I would certainly send for Juana Gutiérrez, my old lady, to come and be my queen, and the young ones could be infantes."[10]

"There is no doubt about it," Don Quixote assured him.

"Well, I doubt it," said Sancho, "for I think that even if God were to rain kingdoms upon the earth, no crown would sit well on the head of Juana Gutiérrez, for I am

[10]Sons of a king of Spain, except the heir to the throne.

telling you, sir, as a queen she is not worth two mara-vedis.[11] She would do better as a countess, God help her."

"Leave everything to God, Sancho," said Don Quixote, "and he will give you whatever is most fitting; but I trust you will not be so pusillanimous° as to be content with anything less than the title of viceroy."

"That I will not," said Sancho Panza, "especially seeing that I have in your Grace so illustrious a master who can give me all that is suitable to me and all that I can manage."

At this point they caught sight of thirty or forty windmills which were standing on the plain there, and no sooner had Don Quixote laid eyes upon them than he turned to his squire and said, "Fortune is guiding our affairs better than we could have wished; for you see there before you, friend Sancho Panza, some thirty or more lawless giants with whom I mean to do battle. I shall deprive them of their lives, and with the spoils° from this encounter we shall begin to enrich ourselves; for this is righteous warfare, and it is a great service to God to remove so accursed a breed from the face of the earth."

"What giants?" said Sancho Panza.

"Those that you see there," replied his master, "those with the long arms some of which are as much as two leagues° in length."

"But look, your Grace, those are not giants but windmills, and what appear to be arms are their wings which, when whirled in the breeze, cause the millstone° to go."

"It is plain to be seen," said Don Quixote, "that you have had little experience in this matter of adventures. If you are afraid, go off to one side and say your prayers while I am engaging them in fierce, unequal combat."

Saying this, he gave spurs to his steed Rocinante, without paying any heed to Sancho's warning that these were truly windmills and not giants that he was riding forth to attack. Nor even when he was close upon them did he perceive what they really were, but shouted at the top of his lungs, "Do not seek to flee, cowards and vile creatures that you

---

[11]Spanish copper coins worth a small part of a real.

are, for it is but a single knight with whom you have to deal!"

At that moment a little wind came up and the big wings began turning.

"Though you flourish as many arms as did the giant Briareus,"[12] said Don Quixote when he perceived this, "you still shall have to answer to me."

He thereupon commended himself with all his heart to his lady Dulcinea, beseeching her to succor° him in this peril; and, being well covered with his shield and with his lance at rest, he bore down upon them at a full gallop and fell upon the first mill that stood in his way, giving a thrust at the wing, which was whirling at such a speed that his lance was broken into bits and both horse and horseman went rolling over the plain, very much battered indeed. Sancho upon his donkey came hurrying to his master's assistance as fast as he could, but when he reached the spot, the knight was unable to move, so great was the shock with which he and Rocinante had hit the ground.

"God help us!" exclaimed Sancho, "did I not tell your Grace to look well, that those were nothing but windmills, a fact which no one could fail to see unless he had other mills of the same sort in his head?"

"Be quiet, friend Sancho," said Don Quixote. "Such are the fortunes of war, which more than any other are subject to constant change. What is more, when I come to think of it, I am sure that this must be the work of that magician Frestón, the one who robbed me of my study and my books, and who has thus changed the giants into windmills in order to deprive me of the glory of overcoming them, so great is the enmity° that he bears me; but in the end his evil arts shall not prevail against this trusty sword of mine."

"May God's will be done," was Sancho Panza's response. And with the aid of his squire the knight was once more mounted on Rocinante, who stood there with one shoulder half out of joint. And so, speaking of the adventure that had

[12]In Greek mythology, a hundred-handed giant who fought with the Olympians against the Titans.

just befallen them, they continued along the Puerto Lápice highway; for there, Don Quixote said, they could not fail to find many and varied adventures, this being a much traveled thoroughfare. The only thing was, the knight was exceedingly downcast over the loss of his lance. . . .

The short of the matter is, they spent the night under some trees, from one of which Don Quixote tore off a withered bough to serve him as a lance, placing it in the lance head from which he had removed the broken one. He did not sleep all night long for thinking of his lady Dulcinea; for this was in accordance with what he had read in his books, of men of arms in the forest or desert places who kept a wakeful vigil, sustained by the memory of their ladies fair. Not so with Sancho, whose stomach was full, and not with chicory° water. He fell into a dreamless slumber, and had not his master called him, he would not have been awakened either by the rays of the sun in his face or by the many birds who greeted the coming of the new day with their merry song. . . .

Don Quixote did not wish any breakfast; for, as has been said, he was in the habit of nourishing himself on savorous° memories. They then set out once more along the road to Puerto Lápice, and around three in the afternoon they came in sight of the pass that bears that name.

"There," said Don Quixote as his eyes fell upon it, "we may plunge our arms up to the elbow in what are known as adventures. But I must warn you that even though you see me in the greatest peril in the world, you are not to lay hand upon your sword to defend me, unless it be that those who attack me are rabble° and men of low degree, in which case you may very well come to my aid; but if they be gentlemen, it is in no wise permitted by the laws of chivalry that you should assist me until you yourself shall have been dubbed a knight."

"Most certainly, sir," replied Sancho, "your Grace shall be very well obeyed in this; all the more so for the reason that I myself am of a peaceful disposition and not fond of meddling in the quarrels and feuds of others. However, when it comes to protecting my own person, I shall not take account of those laws of which you speak, seeing that all laws, human and divine, permit each one to defend himself whenever he is attacked."

"I am willing to grant you that," assented Don Quixote, "but in this matter of defending me against gentlemen you must restrain° your natural impulses."

"I promise you I shall do so," said Sancho. "I will observe this precept as I would the Sabbath day."

As they were conversing in this manner, there appeared in the road in front of them two friars° of the Order of St. Benedict, mounted upon dromedaries°—for the she-mules they rode were certainly no smaller than that. The friars wore travelers' spectacles and carried sunshades, and behind them came a coach accompanied by four or five men on horseback and a couple of muleteers on foot. In the coach, as was afterwards learned, was a lady of Biscay,[13] on her way to Seville[14] to bid farewell to her husband, who had been appointed to some high post in the Indies. The religious were not of her company although they were going by the same road.

The instant Don Quixote laid eyes upon them he turned to his squire. "Either I am mistaken or this is going to be the most famous adventure that ever was seen; for those black-clad figures that you behold must be, and without any doubt are, certain enchanters° who are bearing with them a captive princess in that coach, and I must do all I can to right this wrong."

"It will be worse than the windmills," declared Sancho. "Look you, sir, those are Benedictine friars and the coach must be that of some travelers. Mark well what I say and what I do, lest the devil lead you astray."

"I have already told you, Sancho," replied Don Quixote, "that you know little where the subject of adventures is concerned. What I am saying to you is the truth, as you shall now see."

[13]A northwest province in Spain.
[14]A southern Spanish city.

With this, he rode forward and took up a position in the middle of the road along which the friars were coming, and as soon as they appeared to be within earshot he cried out to them in a loud voice, "O devilish and monstrous beings, set free at once the highborn princesses whom you bear captive in that coach, or else prepare at once to meet your death as the just punishment of your evil deeds."

The friars drew rein and sat there in astonishment, marveling as much at Don Quixote's appearance as at the words he spoke. "Sir Knight," they answered him, "we are neither devilish nor monstrous but religious of the Order of St. Benedict who are merely going our way. We know nothing of those who are in that coach, nor of any captive princesses either."

"Soft words," said Don Quixote, "have no effect on me. I know you for what you are, lying rabble!" And without waiting for any further parley° he gave spur to Rocinante and, with lowered lance, bore down upon the first friar with such fury and intrepidity° that, had not the fellow tumbled from his mule of his own accord, he would have been hurled to the ground and either killed or badly wounded. The second religious, seeing how his companion had been treated, dug his legs into his she-mule's flanks and scurried away over the countryside faster than the wind.

Seeing the friar upon the ground, Sancho Panza slipped lightly from his mount and, falling upon him, began stripping him of his habit. The two mule drivers accompanying the religious thereupon came running up and asked Sancho why he was doing this. The latter replied that the friar's garments belonged to him as legitimate spoils° of the battle that his master Don Quixote had just won. The muleteers, however, were lads with no sense of humor, nor did they know what all this talk of spoils and battles was about; but, perceiving that Don Quixote had ridden off to one side to converse with those inside the coach, they pounced upon Sancho, threw him to the ground, and proceeded to pull out the hair of his beard and kick him to a pulp, after which they went off and left him stretched out there, bereft° at once of breath and sense.

Without losing any time, they then assisted the friar to remount. The good brother was trembling all over from fright, and there was not a speck of color in his face, but when he found himself in the saddle once more he quickly spurred his beast to where his companion, at some little distance, sat watching and waiting to see what the result of the encounter would be. Having no curiosity as to the final outcome of the fray,° the two of them now resumed their journey, making more signs of the cross than the devil would be able to carry upon his back.

Meanwhile Don Quixote, as we have said, was speaking to the lady in the coach.

"Your beauty, my lady, may now dispose of your person as best may please you, for the arrogance° of your abductors lies upon the ground, overthrown by this good arm of mine; and in order that you may not pine to know the name of your liberator, I may inform you that I am Don Quixote de la Mancha, knight-errant and adventurer and captive of the peerless and beauteous Doña Dulcinea del Toboso. In payment of the favor you have received from me, I ask nothing other than that you return to El Toboso and on my behalf pay your respects to this lady, telling her that it was I who set you free."

One of the squires accompanying those in the coach, a Biscayan, was listening to Don Quixote's words, and when he saw that the knight did not propose to let the coach proceed upon its way but was bent upon having it turn back to El Toboso, he promptly went up to him, seized his lance, and said to him in bad Castilian and worse Biscayan, "Go, *caballero*,[15] and bad luck go with you; for by the God that created me, if you do not let this coach pass, me kill you or me no Biscayan."

Don Quixote heard him attentively enough and answered him very mildly, "If you were a *caballero*, which you are

[15]A Spanish knight; a gentleman or horseman.

not, I should already have chastised° you, wretched creature, for your foolhardiness and your impudence."

"Me no *caballero?*" cried the Biscayan. "Me swear to
God, you lie like a Christian. If you will but lay aside
your lance and unsheath your sword, you will soon see that
you are carrying water to the cat! Biscayan on land, gentleman at sea, but a gentleman in spite of the devil, and you
lie if you say otherwise."

" ' "You shall see as to that presently," said Agrajes,' "
Don Quixote quoted.[16] He cast his lance to the earth, drew
his sword, and, taking his buckler on his arm, attacked
the Biscayan with intent to slay him. The latter, when he
saw his adversary approaching, would have liked to dismount from his mule, for she was one of the worthless sort
that are let for hire and he had no confidence in her; but
there was no time for this, and so he had no choice but to
draw his own sword in turn and make the best of it. However, he was near enough to the coach to be able to snatch
a cushion from it to serve him as a shield; and then they
fell upon each other as though they were mortal enemies.
The rest of those present sought to make peace between
them but did not succeed, for the Biscayan with his dis-
jointed phrases kept muttering that if they did not let him
finish the battle then he himself would have to kill his
mistress and anyone else who tried to stop him.

The lady inside the carriage, amazed by it all and trembling at what she saw, directed her coachman to drive on a
little way; and there from a distance she watched the deadly
combat, in the course of which the Biscayan came down
with a great blow on Don Quixote's shoulder, over the top
of the latter's shield, and had not the knight been clad in
armor, it would have split him to the waist.

Feeling the weight of this blow, Don Quixote cried out,
"O lady of my soul, Dulcinea, flower of beauty, succor° this
your champion who out of gratitude for your many favors
finds himself in so perilous° a plight!" To utter these words,
lay hold of his sword, cover himself with his buckler, and

[16]Don Quixote here quotes Agrajes, a particularly menacing character
appearing in *Amadis of Gaul;* the statement is meant to initiate a fray.

attack the Biscayan was but the work of a moment; for he was now resolved to risk everything upon a single stroke.

As he saw Don Quixote approaching with so dauntless a bearing, the Biscayan was well aware of his adversary's courage and forthwith determined to imitate the example thus set him. He kept himself protected with his cushion, but he was unable to get his she-mule to budge to one side or the other, for the beast, out of sheer exhaustion and being, moreover, unused to such childish play, was incapable of taking a single step. And so, then, as has been stated, Don Quixote was approaching the wary° Biscayan, his sword raised on high and with the firm resolve of cleaving his enemy in two; and the Biscayan was awaiting the knight in the same posture, cushion in front of him and with uplifted sword. All the bystanders were trembling with suspense at what would happen as a result of the terrible blows that were threatened, and the lady in the coach and her maids were making a thousand vows and offerings to all the images and shrines in Spain, praying that God would save them all and the lady's squire from this great peril that confronted them.

But the unfortunate part of the matter is that at this very point the author of the history breaks off and leaves the battle pending, excusing himself upon the ground that he has been unable to find anything else in writing concerning the exploits of Don Quixote beyond those already set forth. It is true, on the other hand, that the second author of this work could not bring himself to believe that so unusual a chronicle would have been consigned to oblivion, nor that the learned ones of La Mancha were possessed of so little curiosity as not to be able to discover in their archives or registry° offices certain papers that have to do with this famous knight. Being convinced of this, he did not despair of coming upon the end of this pleasing story, and Heaven favoring him he did find it, as shall be related in the second part. . . .[17]

---

[17]This is the end of Part I of a four-part division; it is a common device of romantic epics to break off the narration between parts.

...The second part, according to the translation, began as follows:

As the two valorous and enraged combatants stood there, swords upraised and poised on high, it seemed from their bold mien° as if they must surely be threatening heaven, earth, and hell itself. The first to let fall a blow was the choleric° Biscayan, and he came down with such force and fury that, had not his sword been deflected in mid-air, that single stroke would have sufficed to put an end to this fearful combat and to all our knight's adventures at the same time; but fortune, which was reserving him for greater things, turned aside his adversary's blade in such a manner that, even though it fell upon his left shoulder, it did him no other damage than to strip him completely of his armor on that side, carrying with it a good part of his helmet along with half an ear, the headpiece clattering to the ground with a dreadful din, leaving its wearer in a sorry state.

Heaven help me! Who could properly describe the rage that now entered the heart of our hero of La Mancha as he saw himself treated in this fashion? It may merely be said that he once more reared himself in the stirrups,° laid hold of his sword with both hands, and dealt the Biscayan such a blow, over the cushion and upon the head, that, even so good a defense proving useless, it was as if a mountain had fallen upon his enemy. The latter now began bleeding through the mouth, nose, and ears; he seemed about to fall from his mule, and would have fallen, no doubt, if he had not grasped the beast about the neck, but at that moment his feet slipped from the stirrups and his arms let go, and the mule, frightened by the terrible blow, began running across the plain, hurling its rider to the earth with a few quick plunges.

Don Quixote stood watching all this very calmly. When he saw his enemy fall, he leaped from his horse, ran over very nimbly, and thrust the point of his sword into the Biscayan's eyes, calling upon him at the same time to surrender or otherwise he would cut off his head. The Biscayan was so bewildered that he was unable to utter a single word in reply, and things would have gone badly with him, so blind was Don Quixote in his rage, if the ladies of the coach, who up to then had watched the struggle in dismay, had not come up to him at this point and begged him with many blandishments° to do them the very great favor of sparing their squire's life.

To which Don Quixote replied with much haughtiness° and dignity, "Most certainly, lovely ladies, I shall be very happy to do that which you ask of me, but upon one condition and understanding, and that is that this knight promise me that he will go to El Toboso and present himself in my behalf before Doña Dulcinea, in order that she may do with him as she may see fit."

Trembling and disconsolate,° the ladies did not pause to discuss Don Quixote's request, but without so much as inquiring who Dulcinea might be they promised him that the squire would fulfill that which was commanded of him.

"Very well, then, trusting in your word, I will do him no further harm, even though he has well deserved it."

By this time Sancho Panza had got to his feet, somewhat the worse for wear as the result of the treatment he had received from the friars' lads. He had been watching the battle attentively and praying God in his heart to give the victory to his master, Don Quixote, in order that he, Sancho, might gain some island where he could go to be governor as had been promised him. Seeing now that the combat was over and the knight was returning to mount Rocinante once more, he went up to hold the stirrup for him; but first he fell on his knees in front of him and, taking his hand, kissed it and said, "May your Grace be pleased, Señor Don Quixote, to grant me the governorship of that island which you have won in this deadly affray;° for however large it may be, I feel that I am indeed capable of governing it as well as any man in this world has ever done."

To which Don Quixote replied, "Be advised, brother Sancho, that this adventure and other similar ones have nothing to do with islands; they are affairs of the crossroads in which one gains nothing more than a broken head or an ear the less. Be patient, for there will be others which will not only make you a governor, but more than that."

Sancho thanked him very much and, kissing his hand again and the skirt of his cuirass,° he assisted him up on Rocinante's back, after which the squire bestraddled° his own mount and started jogging along behind his master, who was now going at a good clip. Without pausing for any further converse with those in the coach, the knight made for a near-by wood, with Sancho following as fast as his beast could trot; but Rocinante was making such speed that the ass and its rider were left behind, and it was necessary to call out to Don Quixote to pull up and wait for them. He did so, reining in Rocinante until the weary Sancho had drawn abreast of him.

"It strikes me, sir," said the squire as he reached his master's side, "that it would be better for us to take refuge in some church; for in view of the way you have treated that one with whom you were fighting, it would be small wonder if they did not lay the matter before the Holy Brotherhood and have us arrested; and faith, if they do that, we shall have to sweat a-plenty before we come out of jail."

"Be quiet," said Don Quixote. "And where have you ever seen, or read of, a knight being brought to justice no matter how many homicides° he might have committed?"

"I know nothing about omecils,"[18] replied Sancho, "nor ever in my life did I bear one to anybody; all I know is that the Holy Brotherhood has something to say about those who go around fighting on the highway, and I want nothing of it."

"Do not let it worry you," said Don Quixote, "for I will rescue you from the hands of the Chaldeans,[19] not to speak of the Brotherhood. But answer me upon your life: have you ever seen a more valorous° knight than I on all the known face of the earth? Have you ever read in the his-

[18]*omecillo* (meaning *ill will* or *grudge*) is used here as a play on words with *homecidico*.
[19]A native of Chaldea; here connoting magical powers.

tories of any other who had more mettle in the attack, more perseverance in sustaining it, more dexterity in wounding his enemy, or more skill in overthrowing him?"

"The truth is," said Sancho, "I have never read any history whatsoever, for I do not know how to read or write; but what I would wager is that in all the days of my life I have never served a more courageous master than your Grace; I only hope your courage is not paid for in the place that I have mentioned."

Do especially Questions 83, 84, 95, 110, 117, 133, and 146. Consult the Prose Narrative Model on page 33.

MIGUEL DE CERVANTES SAAVEDRA *1547-1616*

Although the son of a surgeon, Miguel de Cervantes Saavedra came from a poor Spanish family. A trip to the major cities of Italy as chamberlain of Cardinal Guilio Acquaviva, service as a soldier at the Battle of Lepanto, and five years as prisoner of the Turks provided Cervantes with a solid store of romantic inspiration. His most famous work, *Don Quixote,* was begun as a satire on chivalry. As it developed, however, *Don Quixote* became an extensive narrative showing in the two central characters, Don Quixote and Sancho Panza, "the realistic and the idealistic in mankind."

PROBLEM QUESTIONS

1. Choose several specific incidents from the *Don Quixote* selection and explain what aspects of society and human behavior Cervantes is satirizing.

2. For what reasons could Don Quixote be called laughable? For what reasons could he be called brave? Justify your answer in each case.

3. Discuss the similarities and differences between Achillês, hero of *The Iliad,* and Siegfried. Refer to the text to substantiate your answer.

4. According to the French epic, Roland's sword, *Durendal,* originally belonged to Hector of Troy. Compare both warriors

as to decisions made, attitudes toward inevitable death, concepts of honor. Contrast their attitudes toward religion and proper burial.

5. What specific incident reveals El Cid's feelings toward his fellow man?

6. A boy becomes a man when he is willing to accept responsibility for his actions. Discuss how this growth specifically relates to Rodrigo.

7. Compare the Greek concept of the afterlife, described in the selections from Homer, to the Kingdom of Heaven described in the New Testament selections in Unit One.

NINETEENTH-CENTURY SHORT STORIES

It is really not until the nineteenth century that the term *short story* can be accurately applied to the kind of prose fiction illustrated in this volume. This makes the short story a very recent form of literature when one considers that other forms such as poetry, drama, and essay had been written for many centuries before the short story as such came into being. But to understand clearly how the short story originated, it is necessary to go back to the first quarter of the eighteenth century.

During the early 1700's in Europe and particularly in England, an important transformation was taking place. A rising middle class was gaining stature, power, and influence. In short, it was having a profound effect on the ways of nations. This middle class demanded, among other things, entertainment. Some it could get from the theater, but it craved something more widespread, more accessible. Thus during this time a great demand for certain kinds of writing developed. The people of the middle class wanted adventure, suspense, intrigue in the form of *prose* which was easier to read than was poetry. They wanted, also, to read about people, things, and places about which they had some understanding, that is, the contemporary.

Because of this new demand, a most important thing happened to literature. It came down, so to speak, from the palace into the market place. No longer was literature written largely to please patronizing aristocrats. Now, because of improved methods of printing and more and wealthier consumers, literature became a salable item, a product to be peddled. In London, England, an area known as Grub Street became the home of hundreds of writers trying to produce and market their productions. Most of these writings were in story form.

Earlier forms of storytelling were long and episodic. They usually dealt with one character and his perilous adventures as he blundered in and out of countless hair-raising situations. These serialized stories suited the times well. They satisfied the desire for exciting entertainment, and they were perfect for the large number of periodicals, journals, and magazines which were springing up throughout England and continental Europe. During the eighteenth century these strung-together stories constituted a major form of preoccupation for thousands of readers both in Europe and America where they were soon introduced in the growing cities of the Northeast.

But because of their length and episodic nature, these popular works of the eighteenth century were not short stories as we know them today. During the hundred years that followed, attempts were made to refine the form. Some of the more successful ones were achieved by the American writer Washington Irving. His stories "Rip Van Winkle," and "The Legend of Sleepy Hollow" are among the most famous in American literature.

It was Edgar Allan Poe, however, who made the first important statements about the short story. Poe felt that the story should be written in complete form; that it need not be related to a previous or subsequent episode. He felt that a story should be of such a length as could be read at one "sitting." But, more important, Poe felt that the story should have a definite internal unity. It should, he felt, be developed so as to create a single effect, and that no part should be unrelated to the effect. A story should have a beginning, a middle, and an ending all its own, although the ending did not have to be one of finality or triumph — that is, a "they lived happily ever after" type. It was Poe who announced this necessity for integrity in the short story, and who required an author to center his work around one effect and thus allow it to stand on its own. As you read Poe's story in the following unit, try to decide for yourself whether he was successful in practicing his theory.

For several reasons the short story excited the interests of writers of the nineteenth century. One factor in the rise of short stories can be located in mid-century. More and more writers began to turn to realism as a style of expression. They worked hard at being objective, at building accurate, concise detail, at describing "life as it is." Furthermore, both in Europe and America, there was a growing feeling among writers that the small places, the seemingly insignificant, the "old home town" was an especially fitting subject for literature. In this increasingly popular regional-realistic tradition, the story became a major form of expression.

It might be said that the nineteenth century was also a time of great interest and speculation about the findings, the achievements, the method, and the potential impact of science on the lives of men. This became increasingly an age of analyses: analyses of the universe, of society, of man himself. Before the end of the century, hundreds of stories were being written on incidents representative of social custom and reform. They were the product of a highly self-conscious people. Also, more and more "case study" stories were being written as men explored deeper into the human personality in their short stories. Earlier the story had often been referred to as a "slice of life." Now it could be more accurately called a "slice of life for a purpose," and the purpose was to reveal more and more about the nature of man and his environment.

As the century progressed, two groups of writers could be identified: those who continued to produce the exaggerated, spectacular, fanciful story purely for the pleasure of their readers, and those who used the short story as a medium for the expression of serious considerations about human experience. It is in these latter stories that the *art* of the short story developed.

As you read and study the stories in this unit, you will see that they are written largely in a conventional prose style — that is, they begin at the beginning and move steadily forward to the end. Events are presented in sequence — in the order in which they occur. The focus of the action is external and does not occur in the minds of individual

characters; statements made by people can be clearly dis-
criminated from their inner thoughts and feelings. Keep
these characteristics in mind. They will help you to distinguish stories of the nineteenth century from those which
developed in the twentieth century.

The Piece of String

GUY DE MAUPASSANT

Along all the roads around Goderville the peasants and
their wives were coming toward the burgh because it was
market day. The men were proceeding with slow steps,
the whole body bent forward at each movement of their
long twisted legs, deformed by their hard work, by the
weight on the plow which, at the same time, raised the left
shoulder and swerved the figure, by the reaping of the
wheat which made the knees spread to make a firm "purchase," by all the slow and painful labors of the country.
Their blouses, blue, "stiff-starched," shining as if varnished,
ornamented with a little design in white at the neck and
wrists, puffed about their bony bodies, seemed like bal-
loons ready to carry them off. From each of them a head,
two arms, and two feet protruded.°

Some led a cow or a calf by a cord, and their wives,
walking behind the animal, whipped its haunches with a
leafy branch to hasten its progress. They carried large
baskets on their arms from which, in some cases, chickens
and, in others, ducks thrust out their heads. And they
walked with a quicker, livelier step than their husbands.
Their spare straight figures were wrapped in a scanty° little
shawl, pinned over their flat bosoms, and their heads were
enveloped in a white cloth glued to the hair and sur-
mounted° by a cap.

Then a wagon passed at the jerky trot of a nag, shaking

strangely, two men seated side by side and a woman in the bottom of the vehicle, the latter holding on to the sides to lessen the hard jolts.

In the public square of Goderville there was a crowd, a throng of human beings and animals mixed together. The horns of the cattle, the tall hats with long nap of the rich peasant, and the headgear of the peasant women rose above the surface of the assembly. And the clamorous, shrill, screaming voices made a continuous and savage din which sometimes was dominated by the robust lungs of some countryman's laugh, or the long lowing of a cow tied to the wall of a house.

All that smacked of the stable, the dairy and the dirt heap, hay and sweat, giving forth that unpleasant odor, human and animal, peculiar to the people of the field.

Maître Hauchecome, of Bréauté, had just arrived at Goderville, and he was directing his steps toward the public square, when he perceived upon the ground a little piece of string. Maître Hauchecome, economical like a true Norman,[1] thought that everything useful ought to be picked up, and he bent painfully, for he suffered from rheumatism. He took the bit of thin cord from the ground and began to roll it carefully when he noticed Maître Malandain, the harness-maker, on the threshold of his door, looking at him. They had heretofore had business together on the subject of a halter,° and they were on bad terms, being both good haters. Maître Hauchecome was seized with a sort of shame to be seen thus by his enemy, picking a bit of string out of the dirt. He concealed his "find" quickly under his blouse, then in his trousers' pocket; then he pretended to be still looking on the ground for something which he did not find, and he went toward the market, his head forward, bent double by his pains.

He was soon lost in the noisy and slowly moving crowd, which was busy with interminable bargainings. The peasants milked, went and came, perplexed, always in fear of being cheated, not daring to decide, watching the

[1] An inhabitant of Normandy, a region in the northwest section of France.

vender's eye, ever trying to find the trick in the man and the flaw in the beast.

The women, having placed their great baskets at their feet, had taken out the poultry which lay upon the ground, tied together by the feet, with terrified eyes and scarlet crests.

They heard offers, stated their prices with a dry air and impassive face, or perhaps, suddenly deciding on some proposed reduction, shouted to the customer who was slowly going away: "All right, Maître Authirne, I'll give it to you for that."

Then little by little the square was deserted, and the Angelus° ringing at noon, those who had stayed too long scattered to their shops.

At Jourdain's the great room was full of people eating, as the big court was full of vehicles of all kinds, carts, gigs, wagons, dump carts, yellow with dirt, mended and patched, raising their shafts to the sky like two arms, or perhaps with their shafts in the ground and their backs in the air.

Just opposite the diners seated at the table, the immense fireplace, filled with bright flames, cast a lively heat on the backs of the row on the right. Three spits° were turning on which were chickens, pigeons, and legs of mutton; and an appetizing odor of roast beef and gravy dripping over the nicely browned skin rose from the hearth, increased the jovialness, and made everybody's mouth water.

All the aristocracy° of the plow ate there, at Maître Jourdain's, tavern keeper and horse dealer, a rascal who had money.

The dishes were passed and emptied, as were the jugs of yellow cider. Everyone told his affairs, his purchases, and sales. They discussed the crops. The weather was favorable for the green things but not for the wheat.

Suddenly the drum beat in the court, before the house. Everybody rose except a few indifferent persons, and ran to the door, or to the windows, their mouths still full and napkins in their hands.

After the public crier° had ceased his drum-beating, he called out in a jerky voice, speaking his phrases irregularly:

"It is hereby made known to the inhabitants of Goderville, and in general to all persons present at the market, that there was lost this morning, on the road to Benzeville, between nine and ten o'clock, a black leather pocketbook containing five hundred francs° and some business papers. The finder is requested to return same with all haste to the mayor's office or to Maître Fortune Houlbreque of Manneville. There will be twenty francs reward."

Then the man went away. The heavy roll of the drum and the crier's voice were again heard at a distance.

Then they began to talk of this event, discussing the chances that Maître Houlbreque had of finding or not finding his pocketbook.

And the meal concluded. They were finishing their coffee when a chief of the gendarmes° appeared upon the threshold.

He inquired:

"Is Maître Hauchecome, of Bréauté, here?"

Maître Hauchecome, seated at the other end of the table, replied:

"Here I am."

And the officer resumed:

"Maître Hauchecome, will you have the goodness to accompany me to the mayor's office? The mayor would like to talk to you."

The peasant, surprised and disturbed, swallowed at a draught his tiny glass of brandy, rose, and, even more bent than in the morning, for the first steps after each rest were especially difficult, set out, repeating: "Here I am, here I am."

The mayor was awaiting him, seated on an armchair. He was the notary of the vicinity, a stout, serious man with pompous phrases.

"Maître Hauchecome," said he, "you were seen this morning to pick up, on the road to Benzeville, the pocketbook lost by Maître Houlbreque, of Manneville."

The countryman, astounded, looked at the mayor, already terrified by this suspicion resting on him without his knowing why.

"Me? Me? Me pick up the pocketbook?"

"Yes, you, yourself."

"Word of honor, I never heard of it."

"But you were seen."

"I was seen, me? Who says he saw me?"

"Monsieur Malandain, the harness-maker."

The old man remembered, understood, and flushed with anger.

"Ah, he saw me, the clodhopper, he saw me pick up this string, here, M'sieu' the Mayor." And rummaging in his pocket he drew out the little piece of string.

But the mayor, incredulous,° shook his head.

"You will not make me believe, Maître Hauchecome, that Monsieur Malandain, who is a man worthy of credence, mistook this cord for a pocketbook."

The peasant, furious, lifted his hand, spat at one side to attest his honor, repeating:

"It is nevertheless the truth of the good God, the sacred truth, M'sieu' the Mayor. I repeat it on my soul and my salvation."

The mayor resumed:

"After picking up the object, you stood like a stilt, looking a long while in the mud to see if any piece of money had fallen out."

The good old man choked with indignation and fear.

"How anyone can tell—how anyone can tell—such lies to take away an honest man's reputation! How can anyone—"

There was no use in his protesting; nobody believed him. He was confronted° with Monsieur Malandain, who repeated and maintained his affirmation. They abused each other for an hour. At his own request, Maître Hauchecome was searched; nothing was found on him.

Finally the mayor, very much perplexed, discharged him with the warning that he would consult the public prosecutor and ask for further orders.

The news had spread. As he left the mayor's office, the old man was surrounded and questioned with a serious or bantering curiosity, in which there was no indignation.

He began to tell the story of the string. No one believed him. They laughed at him.

He went along, stopping his friends, beginning endlessly his statement and his protestations, showing his pockets turned inside out, to prove that he had nothing.

They said: "Old rascal, get out!"

And he grew angry, becoming exasperated, hot, and distressed at not being believed, not knowing what to do and always repeating himself.

Night came. He must depart. He started on his way with three neighbors to whom he pointed out the place where he had picked up the bit of string; and all along the road he spoke of his adventure.

In the evening he took a turn in the village of Bréauté, in order to tell it to everybody. He only met with incredulity.

It made him ill at night.

The next day about one o'clock in the afternoon, Marius Paumelle, a hired man in the employ of Maître Breton, husbandman at Ymanville, returned the pocketbook and its contents belonging to Maître Houlbreque of Manneville.

This man claimed to have found the object in the road; but not knowing how to read, he had carried it to the house and had given it to his employer.

The news spread through the neighborhood. Maître Hauchecome was informed of it. He immediately went the circuit and began to recount his story completed by the happy climax. He was in triumph.

"What grieved me so much was not the thing itself, as the lying. There is nothing so shameful as to be placed under a cloud on account of a lie."

He talked of his adventure all day long, he told it on the highway to people who were passing by, in the wineshop to people who were drinking there, and to persons coming out of church the following Sunday. He stopped strangers to tell them about it. He was calm now, and yet something disturbed him without his knowing exactly what it was. People had the air of joking while they listened. They did not seem convinced. He seemed to feel that remarks were being made behind his back.

On Tuesday of the next week he went to the market at Goderville, urged solely by the necessity he felt of discussing the case.

Malandain, standing at his door, began to laugh on seeing him pass. Why?

He approached a farmer from Crequetot, who did not let him finish, and giving him a thump in the stomach said to his face:

"You big rascal."

Then he turned his back on him.

Maître Hauchecome was confused. Why was he called a big rascal?

When he was seated at the table in Jourdain's tavern he commenced to explain "the affair."

A horse dealer from Monvilliers called to him:

"Come, come, old sharper, that's an old trick; I know all about your piece of string!"

Hauchecome stammered:

"But since the pocketbook was found."

But the other man replied:

"Shut up, papa, there is one that finds, and there is one that reports. At any rate you are mixed with it."

The peasant stood choking. He understood. They accused him of having had the pocketbook returned by a confederate, by an accomplice.

He tried to protest. All the table began to laugh.

He could not finish his dinner and went away, in the midst of jeers.

He went home ashamed and indignant, choking with anger and confusion, and more dejected that he was capable with his Norman cunning of doing what they had accused him of, and even boasting of it as of a good turn. His innocence to him, in a confused way, was impossible to prove, as his sharpness was known. And he was stricken to the heart by the injustice of the suspicion.

Then he began to recount the adventures again, prolonging his history everyday, adding each time, new reasons, more energetic protestations, more solemn oaths which he imagined and prepared in his hours of solitude, his whole mind given up to the story of the string. He was believed so much the less as his defense was more complicated and his arguing more subtile.

"Those are lying excuses," they said behind his back.

He felt it, consumed his heart over it, and wore himself out with useless efforts. He wasted away before their very eyes.

The wags now made him tell about the string to amuse them, as they make a soldier who has been on a campaign tell about his battles. His mind, touched to the depth, began to weaken.

Toward the end of December he took to his bed.

He died in the first days of January, and in the delirium of his death struggles he kept claiming his innocence, reiterating:

"A piece of string, a piece of string—look—here it is, M'sieu' the Mayor."

GUY DE MAUPASSANT   *1850-1893*

Guy de Maupassant grew up and was educated in Normandy, France. His personal experiences among the rustic farmers of the Normandy countryside enabled him to write forcefully about the hardships and toil of peasants like Maître Hauchecome in "The Piece of String." After serving in the French Army during the Franco-Prussian War, De Maupassant entered the French civil service. Later he served a literary apprenticeship under Flaubert which helped him to achieve such literary success that by 1884 he was able to leave the civil service post and devote himself entirely to writing. During his most fruitful decade he wrote more than thirty volumes of short stories, plays, novels, and travel sketches. The last years of his life were tragic. Showing signs of mental illness, he took an extended sea voyage which helped his declining condition only temporarily. He attempted suicide in January of 1892, but was to live on in his broken condition for another year and a half, dying in Paris at the age of forty-three.

SHORT STORY MODEL

The Piece of String approached from the Seven Views of the *Dictionary of Questions*

FIRST VIEW

1. What is my first impression of the work as a total unit? I am depressed by this cynical tale of human folly and pettiness. De Maupassant paints a vivid and shocking picture of the ruin of a drab, pathetic personality.

SECOND VIEW

2. Under which literary type would I classify the work from a first reading? Why? An imaginative prose work, short and complete in itself, it is obviously a short story.

THIRD VIEW

11. What is the theme of the work? I can generalize the truth exemplified in this story and suggest these possible expressions of the theme: (1) Whoever attaches too much importance to a good reputation and tries too vehemently to defend himself will lose his reputation. (2) It is foolish to value the opinions or judgments of men since they are not always true. (3) It is foolish to let your well-being and happiness depend upon what others think of you since their opinion is often formed falsely by deceiving circumstances and by their own tendency to think the worst of others.

17. What of major importance happened to the central character? After picking up a piece of string, Maître Hauchecome, overcome with shame at being seen by his enemy, tries to hide this economical deed; he is subsequently accused of finding and hiding a pocketbook coincidentally lost there that same day. The more he protests his innocence, the less he is believed; and he soon dies, obsessed with vindicating himself.

18. Is it probable that the author wants me to extend my preceding statement to "all men"; or "every man in such a situation"? De Maupassant does not make Hauchecome essentially different from other men of his social class — at least, many men would be similar or act similarly in such a situation.

FOURTH VIEW

42. If the work is tragedy — drama or nondrama — can I construct a graph giving the exposition, rising action, climax, falling action, and catastrophe?

Exposition: On a market day, Maître Hauchecome, a thrifty Norman peasant, bends over to pick up a piece of string. Noticing that his enemy is watching him, in shame he hides the string and pretends to be looking for something.

Rising Action: By coincidence, a pocketbook is lost there that same day. The enemy informs the police of what he saw Hauchecome doing, and the police summon him for questioning.

Climax: Hauchecome's story about the string, which he tells in such an excited manner, seems ridiculous; and neither the police nor anyone at the market believes him.

Falling Action: When the pocketbook is returned, Hauchecome triumphantly retells his story, thinking he is cleared of suspicion. But he is only the more disbelieved and laughed at, for he is known to be a crafty man, and it is thought that he got someone else to return it for him. Aware that now his innocence is beyond proof but indignant at the injustice of it all, Hauchecome becomes obsessed with telling his story and wastes away trying to clear himself. The more he improves his arguments, the less he is believed.

Catastrophe: Worn out by his vain efforts, he dies, still protesting his innocence.

FIFTH VIEW

43. How in particular do the theme and its development give meaning to every part of the work? To answer this, I choose these questions:

73. Is the plot cluttered by excessive detail? Does the story tell itself, or does the author himself intrude to editorialize or moralize? The author has used the element of compression. There is just enough description of the place, people, situation, etc., to give a realistic, accurate, and vivid setting for the action. With this setting and the characters involved, the story tells itself, and the meaning of the story, its theme, is unfolded in the progress of the plot itself. The author does not moralize or make comments on the meaning of the plot. The moral is the story itself.

76. How is the setting integrated with the theme? From the opening sentence on, we are in a particular but everyday setting. We are with the French peasants, hard-working country folk, of a century ago. It is market day, and there is great bustle, confusion, and din. Though the peasants are merrier than usual, the atmosphere is not a gay and carefree one. There are overtones of tenseness and drabness. These overworked, struggling farmers are never relaxed or free from worry. They are suspicious, bitter, and pessimistic—afraid of being cheated, full of pettiness, prone to think the worst of others, glad to find a target for their crude, mocking humor. This setting ideally suits the theme envisioned by the author.

110. If the work is tragedy, what personality trait of the main character is the "tragic flaw" from which the catastrophe emerges?

Although Hauchecome is partly the victim of circumstances and environment, he causes his own downfall. His personality trait which constitutes his tragic flaw is the exaggerated value he places on the good opinion of others. He is extremely concerned with what others think of him. It is this pride which causes him to hide the string and pretend he is looking for something when he notices his enemy has been watching him—and as a result he is suspected of finding the purse. This same fear that others will not think well of him makes him overanxious to defend himself—which makes him appear all the more guilty. So the weakness of the main character—his desire for esteem—shatters his well-being and leads to the catastrophe.

117. Is it possible throughout the work to sympathize with the feelings of the central character? Hauchecome is not an especially admirable or lovable character. He is in no way heroic. But we do feel pity for him. After all, he is innocent of the act for which he is despised. From our own experience of being blamed for something we haven't done, we can understand and sympathize with his strong emotions. When he "grew angry, becoming exasperated, hot, and distressed at not being believed," we can't help feeling sorry for him, even though it is stated that "with his Norman cunning [he was capable] of doing what they had accused him of, and even boasting of it as a good turn." Exhausting himself in useless efforts to prove his innocence, Hauchecome becomes a pathetic figure.

SIXTH VIEW

146. How does my understanding of the present work contribute to an understanding of the politics, sociology, religion, etc., of the period? How does it contribute to further understanding of life in general? The story suggests what it might have been like to be a poor farmer in France at that time. It tells about some of the characteristics and values of the people of that nation, time, and class. More especially, though, the story gives further insights into life in general. Its meaning is not tied down to a particular place, period, or people. It portrays the folly human nature is capable of. It warns us of the fragile nature of reputation and advises us not to seek so worthless a goal. Our popularity and our reputation are determined by what other people think of us and say about us; and, as this story illustrates so well, people can often be mistaken in their opinions—especially because they are often inclined to think the worst of us.

SEVENTH VIEW

147. What is my final evaluation of the work? How does the work clarify, support, or contradict my own concept of what the

"Good Life" is? Like every good story, "The Piece of String" is limited; it does not attempt to explore every aspect of reality. But the story is so typically human, so representative of man's folly that it does clarify and confirm our beliefs about man. We know that men are often upset by circumstances, that they are often foolishly—and to their own destruction—anxious for popularity, fame, and good reputation.

The Black Cat

EDGAR ALLAN POE

For the most wild, yet most homely° narrative which I am about to pen, I neither expect nor solicit belief. Mad indeed would I be to expect it, in a case where my very senses reject their own evidence. Yet, mad am I not—and very surely do I not dream. But tomorrow I die, and today I would unburthen my soul. My immediate purpose is to place before the world, plainly, succinctly,° and without comment, a series of mere household events. In their consequences, these events have terrified—have tortured—have destroyed me. Yet I will not attempt to expound them. To me, they have presented little but Horror—to many they will seem less terrible than *barroques*.[1] Hereafter, perhaps, some intellect may be found which will reduce my phantasm to the commonplace—some intellect more calm, more logical, and far less excitable than my own, which will perceive, in the circumstances I detail with awe, nothing more than an ordinary succession of very natural causes and effects.

From my infancy I was noted for the docility° and humanity of my disposition. My tenderness of heart was even so conspicuous as to make me the jest of my companions. I was especially fond of animals, and was indulged° by my parents with a great variety of pets. With these I spent

---

[1] The *Baroque* style in writing is one in which much is made of detail, often fantastic detail, to produce mood or atmosphere. Poe's stories are perfect examples of this style.

most of my time, and never was so happy as when feeding and caressing them. This peculiarity of character grew with my growth, and, in my manhood, I derived from it one of my principal sources of pleasure. To those who have cherished an affection for a faithful and sagacious° dog, I need hardly be at the trouble of explaining the nature or the intensity of the gratification thus derivable. There is something in the unselfish and self-sacrificing love of a brute, which goes directly to the heart of him who has had frequent occasion to test the paltry friendship and gossamer° fidelity of mere *Man*.

I married early, and was happy to find in my wife a disposition not uncongenial with my own. Observing my partiality for domestic pets, she lost no opportunity of procuring those of the most agreeable kind. We had birds, gold fish, a fine dog, rabbits, a small monkey, and *a cat*.

This latter was a remarkably large and beautiful animal, entirely black, and sagacious to an astonishing degree. In speaking of his intelligence, my wife, who at heart was not a little tinctured° with superstition, made frequent allusion to the ancient popular notion, which regarded all black cats as witches in disguise. Not that she was ever *serious* upon this point — and I mention the matter at all for no better reason than that it happens, just now, to be remembered.

Pluto — this was the cat's name — was my favorite pet and playmate. I alone fed him, and he attended me wherever I went about the house. It was even with difficulty that I could prevent him from following me through the streets.

Our friendship lasted, in this manner, for several years, during which my general temperament and character — through the instrumentality of the Fiend Intemperance° — had (I blush to confess it) experienced a radical alteration for the worse. I grew, day by day, more moody, more irritable, more regardless of the feelings of others. I suffered[2] myself to use intemperate language to my wife. At length, I even offered her personal violence. My pets, of course, were made to feel the change in my disposition. I not only

[2]Allowed.

neglected, but ill-used them. For Pluto, however, I still retained sufficient regard to restrain me from maltreating him, as I made no scruple of maltreating the rabbits, the monkey, or even the dog, when by accident, or through affection, they came in my way. But my disease grew upon me—for what disease is like Alcohol!—and at length even Pluto, who was now becoming old, and consequently some-what peevish—even Pluto began to experience the effects of my ill temper.

One night, returning home, much intoxicated, from one of my haunts° about town, I fancied that the cat avoided my presence. I seized him; when, in his fright at my violence, he inflicted a slight wound upon my hand with his teeth. The fury of a demon instantly possessed me. I knew my-self no longer. My original soul seemed, at once, to take its flight from my body; and a more than fiendish malevolence,° gin-nurtured, thrilled every fiber of my frame. I took from my waistcoat-pocket a penknife, opened it, grasped the poor beast by the throat, and deliberately cut one of its eyes from the socket! I blush, I burn, I shudder, while I pen the damnable atrocity.

When reason returned with the morning—when I had slept off the fumes of the night's debauch°—I experienced a sentiment half of horror, half of remorse, for the crime of which I had been guilty; but it was, at best, a feeble and equivocal° feeling, and the soul remained untouched. I again plunged into excess, and soon drowned in wine all memory of the deed.

In the meantime the cat slowly recovered. The socket of the lost eye presented, it is true, a frightful appearance, but he no longer appeared to suffer any pain. He went about the house as usual, but, as might be expected, fled in extreme terror at my approach. I had so much of my old heart left, as to be at first grieved by this evident dislike on the part of a creature which had once so loved me. But this feeling soon gave place to irritation. And then came, as if to my final and irrevocable overthrow, the spirit of PER-VERSENESS.° Of this spirit philosophy takes no account. Yet I am not more sure that my soul lives, than I am that perverseness is one of the primitive impulses of the human heart—one of the indivisible primary faculties, or sentiments, which give direction to the character of Man. Who has not, a hundred times, found himself committing a vile or a silly action, for no other reason than because he knows he should *not?* Have we not a perpetual inclination, in the teeth of our best judgment, to violate that which is *Law,* merely because we understand it to be such? This spirit of perverseness, I say, came to my final overthrow. It was this unfathomable° longing of the soul *to vex itself*—to offer violence to its own nature—to do wrong for the wrong's sake only—that urged me to continue and finally to consummate° the injury I had inflicted upon the unoffending brute. One morning, in cold blood, I slipped a noose about its neck and hung it to the limb of a tree—hung it with the tears streaming from my eyes, and with the bitterest remorse at my heart—hung it *because* I knew that it had loved me, and *because* I felt it had given me no reason of offense; hung it *because* I knew that in so doing I was committing a sin—a deadly sin that would so jeopardize my immortal soul as to place it—if such a thing were possible—even beyond the reach of the infinite mercy of the Most Merciful and Most Terrible God.

On the night of the day on which this cruel deed was done, I was aroused from sleep by the cry of fire. The curtains of my bed were in flames. The whole house was blazing. It was with great difficulty that my wife, a servant, and myself, made our escape from the conflagration.° The destruction was complete. My entire worldly wealth was swallowed up, and I resigned myself thenceforward to despair.

I am above the weakness of seeking to establish a sequence of cause and effect, between the disaster and the atrocity. But I am detailing a chain of facts—and wish not to leave even a possible link imperfect. On the day succeeding the fire, I visited the ruins. The walls, with one exception, had fallen in. This exception was found in a compartment wall, not very thick, which stood about the middle of the house, and against which had rested the head of my bed. The plastering had here, in great measure, resisted the action of the fire — a fact which I attributed to its having been recently spread. About this wall a dense crowd were collected, and many persons seemed to be examining a particular portion of it with very minute° and eager attention. The words "strange!" "singular!" and other similar expressions, excited my curiosity. I approached and saw, as if graven in *bas-relief°* upon the white surface, the figure of a gigantic *cat*. The impression was given with an accuracy truly marvelous. There was a rope about the animal's neck.

When I first beheld this apparition — for I could scarcely regard it as less — my wonder and my terror were extreme. But at length reflection came to my aid. The cat, I remembered, had been hung in a garden adjacent° to the house. Upon the alarm of fire, this garden had been immediately filled by the crowd — by some one of whom the animal must have been cut from the tree and thrown, through an open window, into my chamber. This had probably been done with the view of arousing me from sleep. The falling of other walls had compressed the victim of my cruelty into the substance of the freshly-spread plaster; the lime of which, with the flames and the *ammonia°* from the carcass, had then accomplished the portraiture as I saw it.

Although I thus readily accounted to my reason, if not altogether to my conscience, for the startling fact just detailed, it did not the less fail to make a deep impression upon my fancy. For months I could not rid myself of the phantasm of the cat; and, during this period, there came back into my spirit a half-sentiment that seemed, but was not, remorse. I went so far as to regret the loss of the animal, and to look about me, among the vile haunts which I now habitually frequented,° for another pet of the same species, and of somewhat similar appearance, with which to supply its place.

One night as I sat, half stupified, in a den of more than infamy, my attention was suddenly drawn to some black object, reposing upon the head of one of the immense hogsheads° of Gin, or of Rum, which constituted the chief

furniture of the apartment. I had been looking steadily at
the top of this hogshead for some minutes, and what now
caused me surprise was the fact that I had not sooner
perceived the object thereupon. I approached it, and
touched it with my hand. It was a black cat—a very large
one—fully as large as Pluto, and closely resembling him
in every respect but one. Pluto had not a white hair upon
any portion of his body; but this cat had a large, although
indefinite splotch of white, covering nearly the whole
region of the breast.

Upon my touching him, he immediately arose, purred
loudly, rubbed against my hand, and appeared delighted
with my notice. This, then, was the very creature of which
I was in search. I at once offered to purchase it of the landlord; but this person made no claim to it—knew nothing of
it—had never seen it before.

I continued my caresses, and, when I prepared to go
home, the animal evinced a disposition to accompany me.
I permitted it to do so; occasionally stooping and patting
it as I proceeded. When it reached the house it domesti-
cated° itself at once, and became immediately a great
favorite with my wife.

For my own part, I soon found a dislike to it arising
within me. This was just the reverse of what I had antici-
pated; but—I know not how or why it was—its evident
fondness for myself rather disgusted and annoyed me. By
slow degrees, these feelings of disgust and annoyance
rose into the bitterness of hatred. I avoided the creature;
a certain sense of shame, and the remembrance of my
former deed of cruelty, preventing me from physically
abusing it. I did not, for some weeks, strike, or otherwise
violently ill use it; but gradually—very gradually—I came
to look upon it with unutterable loathing, and to flee
silently from its odious° presence, as from the breath of a
pestilence.

What added, no doubt, to my hatred of the beast, was the
discovery, on the morning after I brought it home, that, like
Pluto, it also had been deprived of one of its eyes. This
circumstance, however, only endeared° it to my wife, who,

as I have already said, possessed, in a high degree, that humanity of feeling which had once been my distinguishing trait, and the source of many of my simplest and purest pleasures.

With my aversion° to this cat, however, its partiality for myself seemed to increase. It followed my footsteps with a pertinacity° which it would be difficult to make the reader comprehend. Whenever I sat, it would crouch beneath my chair, or spring upon my knees, covering me with its loathsome caresses. If I arose to walk it would get between my feet and thus nearly throw me down, or, fastening its long sharp claws in my dress, clamber, in this manner, to my breast. At such times, although I longed to destroy it with a blow, I was yet withheld from so doing, partly by a memory of my former crime, but chiefly — let me confess it at once — by absolute *dread* of the beast.

This dread was not exactly a dread of physical evil — and yet I should be at a loss how otherwise to define it. I am almost ashamed to own — yes, even in this felon's° cell, I am almost ashamed to own — that the terror and horror with which the animal inspired me, had been heightened by one of the merest chimeras° it would be possible to conceive. My wife had called my attention, more than once, to the character of the mark of white hair, of which I have spoken, and which constituted the sole visible difference between the strange beast and the one I had destroyed. The reader will remember that this mark, although large, had been originally very indefinite; but, by slow degrees — degrees nearly imperceptible, and which for a long time my Reason struggled to reject as fanciful — it had, at length, assumed a rigorous distinctness of outline. It was now the representation of an object that I shudder to name — and for this, above all, I loathed, and dreaded, and would have rid myself of the monster *had I dared* — it was now, I say, the image of a hideous — of a ghastly thing — of the GALLOWS!° — oh, mournful and terrible engine of Horror and of Crime — of Agony and of Death!

And now was I indeed wretched beyond the wretchedness of mere Humanity. And *a brute beast* — whose fellow

I had contemptuously° destroyed—*a brute beast* to work out for *me*—for me a man, fashioned in the image of the High God—so much of insufferable woe! Alas! neither by day nor by night knew I the blessing of Rest any more! During the former the creature left me no moment alone; and, in the latter, I started, hourly, from dreams of unutterable fear, to find the hot breath of *the thing* upon my face, and its vast weight—an incarnate° Nightmare that I had no power to shake off—incumbent° eternally upon my *heart!*

Beneath the pressure of torments such as these, the feeble remnant of the good within me succumbed.° Evil thoughts became my sole intimates—the darkest and most evil of thoughts. The moodiness of my usual temper increased to hatred of all things and of all mankind; while, from the sudden, frequent, and ungovernable outbursts of a fury to which I now blindly abandoned myself, my uncomplaining wife, alas! was the most usual and the most patient of sufferers.

One day she accompanied me, upon some household errand, into the cellar of the old building which our poverty compelled us to inhabit. The cat followed me down the steep stairs, and, nearly throwing me headlong, exasperated me to madness. Uplifting an axe, and forgetting, in my wrath, the childish dread which had hitherto stayed my hand, I aimed a blow at the animal, which, of course, would have proved instantly fatal had it descended as I wished. But this blow was arrested by the hand of my wife. Goaded by the interference into a rage more than demoniacal,° I withdrew my arm from her grasp and buried the axe in her brain. She fell dead upon the spot without a groan.

This hideous murder accomplished, I set myself forthwith, and with entire deliberation, to the task of concealing the body. I knew that I could not remove it from the house, either by day or by night, without the risk of being observed by the neighbors. Many projects entered my mind. At one period I thought of cutting the corpse into minute fragments, and destroying them by fire. At another, I resolved to dig a grave for it in the floor of the cellar. Again, I deliberated about casting it in the well in the yard—about packing it in a box, as if merchandise, with the usual arrangements, and so getting a porter to take it from the house. Finally I hit upon what I considered a far better expedient than either of these. I determined to wall it up in the cellar—as the monks of the Middle Ages are recorded to have walled up their victims.

For a purpose such as this the cellar was well adapted. Its walls were loosely constructed, and had lately been plastered throughout with a rough plaster, which the dampness of the atmosphere had prevented from hardening. Moreover, in one of the walls was a projection, caused by a false chimney, or fireplace, that had been filled up, and made to resemble the rest of the cellar. I made no doubt that I could readily displace the bricks at this point, insert the corpse, and wall the whole up as before, so that no eye could detect anything suspicious.

And in this calculation I was not deceived. By means of a crowbar° I easily dislodged the bricks, and, having carefully deposited the body against the inner wall, I propped it in that position, while, with little trouble, I relaid the whole structure as it originally stood. Having procured mortar, sand, and hair, with every possible precaution, I prepared a plaster which could not be distinguished from the old, and with this I very carefully went over the new brick-work. When I had finished, I felt satisfied that all was right. The wall did not present the slightest appearance of having been disturbed. The rubbish on the floor was picked up with the minutest care. I looked around triumphantly, and said to myself—"Here at least, then, my labor has not been in vain."

My next step was to look for the beast which had been the cause of so much wretchedness; for I had, at length, firmly resolved to put it to death. Had I been able to meet with it, at the moment, there could have been no doubt of its fate; but it appeared that the crafty animal had been alarmed at the violence of my previous anger, and forebore° to present itself in my present mood. It is impossible to describe, or to imagine, the deep, the blissful sense of relief which the absence of the detested creature occasioned in my bosom. It did not make its appearance during the night—and thus for one night at least, since its introduction into the house, I soundly and tranquilly° slept; aye, *slept* even with the burden of murder upon my soul!

The second and the third day passed, and still my tormentor came not. Once again I breathed as a free man. The monster, in terror, had fled the premises forever! I should behold it no more! My happiness was supreme! The guilt of my dark deed disturbed me but little. Some few inquiries had been made, but these had been readily answered. Even a search had been instituted—but of course nothing was to be discovered. I looked upon my future felicity° as secured.

Upon the fourth day of the assassination, a party of the police came, very unexpectedly, into the house, and proceeded again to make rigorous investigation of the premises. Secure, however, in the inscrutability° of my place of concealment, I felt no embarrassment whatever. The officers bade me accompany them in their search. They left no nook or corner unexplored. At length, for the third or fourth time, they descended into the cellar. I quivered not in a muscle. My heart beat calmly as that of one who slumbers in innocence. I walked the cellar from end to end. I folded my arms upon my bosom, and roamed easily to and fro. The police were thoroughly satisfied and prepared to depart. The glee at my heart was too strong to be restrained. I burned to say if but one word, by way of triumph, and to render doubly sure their assurance of my guiltlessness.

"Gentlemen," I said at last, as the party ascended the steps, "I delight to have allayed your suspicions. I wish you all health, and a little more courtesy. By the bye, gentlemen, this—this is a very well-constructed house." (In the rabid desire to say something easily, I scarcely knew what I uttered at all.)—"I may say an *excellently* well-constructed house. These walls—are you going, gentlemen?—these walls are solidly put together"; and here, through the mere frenzy° of bravado, I rapped heavily with a cane which I held in my hand, upon that very portion of the brick-work behind which stood the corpse of the wife of my bosom.

But may God shield and deliver me from the fangs of the Arch-Fiend! No sooner had the reverberation° of my blows sunk into silence, than I was answered by a voice from within the tomb!—by a cry, at first muffled and broken, like the sobbing of a child, and then quickly swelling into one long, loud, and continuous scream, utterly anomalous° and inhuman—a howl—a wailing shriek, half of horror and half of triumph, such as might have arisen only out of hell, conjointly° from the throats of the damned in their agony and of the demons that exult in the damnation.

Of my own thoughts it is folly to speak. Swooning, I staggered to the opposite wall. For one instant the party upon the stairs remained motionless, through extremity of terror and of awe. In the next, a dozen stout arms were toiling at the wall. It fell bodily. The corpse, already greatly decayed and clotted with gore, stood erect before the eyes of the spectators. Upon its head, with red extended mouth and solitary eye of fire, sat the hideous beast whose craft had seduced° me into murder, and whose informing voice had consigned me to the hangman. I had walled the monster up within the tomb!

Do especially Questions 45, 46, 47, 48, 61, 81, 92, 117, and 154. Consult the Short Story Model on page 156.

EDGAR ALLAN POE   *1809-1849*

Edgar Allan Poe was adopted by a wealthy family in Richmond, Virginia, after the death of his parents. Following his graduation from a notable academy in England, he enrolled at the University of Virginia. In 1835 he moved to Richmond where he became assistant editor of the *Southern Literary Messenger* and married his cousin Virginia Clemm. Poe, his wife, and his mother-in-law, moved to New York in 1836. During this period he wrote many stories and articles for various magazines, worked on the New York *Mirror*, and edited the *Broadway Journal*. Because he believed strongly that a short story should produce a single, unified impression, Poe chose each word with great care in order to realize this effect.

The Outcasts of Poker Flat

BRET HARTE

As Mr. John Oakhurst, gambler, stepped into the main street of Poker Flat on the morning of the twenty-third of November, 1850, he was conscious of a change in its moral° atmosphere since the preceding night. Two or three men, conversing earnestly together, ceased as he approached, and exchanged significant glances. There was a Sabbath lull in the air, which, in a settlement unused to Sabbath influences, looked ominous.°

Mr. Oakhurst's calm, handsome face betrayed small concern in these indications. Whether he was conscious of any predisposing° cause was another question. "I reckon they're after somebody," he reflected; "likely it's me." He returned to his pocket the handkerchief with which he had been whipping away the red dust of Poker Flat from his neat boots, and quietly discharged his mind of any further conjecture.

In point of fact, Poker Flat was "after somebody." It had lately suffered the loss of several thousand dollars, two valuable horses, and a prominent citizen. It was experiencing a spasm of virtuous reaction quite as lawless and ungovernable as any of the acts that had provoked it. A secret committee had determined to rid the town of all improper persons. This was done permanently in regard to two men who were then hanging from the boughs of a sycamore in the gulch,° and temporarily in the banishment of certain other objectionable characters. I regret to say that some of these were ladies. It is but due to the sex, however, to state that their impropriety° was professional, and it was only in such easily established standards of evil that Poker Flat ventured to sit in judgment.

Mr. Oakhurst was right in supposing that he was included in this category. A few of the committee had urged hanging him as a possible example and a sure method of reimbursing° themselves from his pockets of the sums he had won from them. "It's agin justice," said Jim Wheeler, "to let

this yer young man from Roaring Camp—an entire stranger
—carry away our money." But a crude sentiment of equity°
residing in the breasts of those who had been fortunate
enough to win from Mr. Oakhurst overruled this narrower
local prejudice.

Mr. Oakhurst received his sentence with philosophic
calmness, none the less coolly that he was aware of the
hesitation of his judges. He was too much of a gambler not
to accept fate. With him life was at best an uncertain game,
and he recognized the usual percentage in favor of the
dealer.

A body of armed men accompanied the deported wickedness of Poker Flat to the outskirts of the settlement. Besides Mr. Oakhurst, who was known to be a coolly desperate
man, and for whose intimidation° the armed escort was
intended, the expatriated° party consisted of a young
woman familiarly known as "The Duchess"; another who
had won the title of "Mother Shipton"; and "Uncle Billy,"
a suspected sluice° robber and confirmed drunkard.

The cavalcade provoked no comments from the spectators, nor was any word uttered by the escort. Only when
the gulch which marked the uttermost limit of Poker Flat
was reached, the leader spoke briefly and to the point. The
exiles were forbidden to return at the peril of their lives.

As the escort disappeared, their pent-up feelings found
vent in a few hysterical tears from the Duchess, some bad
language from Mother Shipton, and a Parthian° volley of
expletives° from Uncle Billy. The philosophic Oakhurst
alone remained silent. He listened calmly to Mother
Shipton's desire to cut somebody's heart out, to the repeated statements of the Duchess that she would die in the
road, and to the alarming oaths that seemed to be bumped
out of Uncle Billy as he rode forward.

With the easy good humor characteristic of his class, he
insisted upon exchanging his own riding horse, "Five-
Spot," for the sorry mule which the Duchess rode. But
even this act did not draw the party into any closer sympathy. The young woman readjusted her somewhat
draggled° plumes with a feeble, faded coquetry;° Mother

Shipton eyed the possessor of "Five-Spot" with malevolence,° and Uncle Billy included the whole party in one
sweeping anathema.°

The road to Sandy Bar — a camp that, not having as yet
experienced the regenerating influences of Poker Flat,
consequently seemed to offer some invitation to the emigrants — lay over a steep mountain range. It was distant a
day's severe travel. In that advanced season the party
soon passed out of the moist, temperate regions of the foot-
hills into the dry, cold, bracing air of the Sierras. The trail
was narrow and difficult. At noon the Duchess, rolling out
of her saddle upon the ground, declared her intention of
going no farther, and the party halted.

The spot was singularly wild and impressive. A wooded
amphitheater, surrounded on three sides by precipitous
cliffs and naked granite, sloped gently toward the crest
of another precipice that overlooked the valley. It was,
undoubtedly, the most suitable spot for a camp, had camp-
ing been advisable. But Mr. Oakhurst knew that scarcely
half the journey to Sandy Bar was accomplished, and the
party were not equipped or provisioned for delay. This
fact he pointed out to his companions curtly, with a philosophic commentary on the folly of "throwing up their hand
before the game was played out."

But they were furnished with liquor, which in this
emergency stood them in place of food, fuel, rest, and
prescience.° In spite of his remonstrances, it was not
long before they were more or less under its influence.
Uncle Billy passed rapidly from a bellicose° state into one
of stupor, the Duchess became maudlin,° and Mother
Shipton snored. Mr. Oakhurst alone remained erect,
leaning against a rock, calmly surveying them.

Mr. Oakhurst did not drink. It interfered with a profession which required coolness, impassiveness, and
presence of mind, and, in his own language, he "couldn't
afford it." As he gazed at his recumbent fellow exiles, the
loneliness begotten of his pariah° trade, his habits of life,
his very vices, for the first time seriously oppressed him.
He bestirred himself in dusting his black clothes, washing

his hands and face, and other acts characteristic of his studiously neat habits, and for a moment forgot his annoyance.

The thought of deserting his weaker and more pitiable companions never perhaps occurred to him. Yet he could not help feeling the want of that excitement which, singularly enough, was most conducive° to that calm equanimity° for which he was notorious. He looked at the gloomy walls that rose a thousand feet sheer° above the circling pines around him, at the sky ominously clouded, at the valley below, already deepening into shadow; and, doing so, suddenly he heard his own name called.

A horseman slowly ascended the trail. In the fresh, open face of the newcomer Mr. Oakhurst recognized Tom Simson, otherwise known as "The Innocent," of Sandy Bar. He had met him some months before over a "little game," and had, with perfect equanimity, won the entire fortune—amounting to some forty dollars—of that guileless° youth. After the game was finished, Mr. Oakhurst drew the youthful speculator behind the door and thus addressed him: "Tommy, you're a good little man, but you can't gamble worth a cent. Don't try it over again." He then handed his money back, pushed him gently from the room, and so made a devoted slave of Tom Simson.

There was a remembrance of this in his boyish and enthusiastic greeting of Mr. Oakhurst. He had started, he said, to go to Poker Flat to seek his fortune. "Alone?" No, not exactly alone; in fact (a giggle), he had run away with Piney Woods. Didn't Mr. Oakhurst remember Piney? She used to wait on the table at the Temperance House? They had been engaged a long time, but old Jake Woods had objected, and so they had run away, and were going to Poker Flat to be married, and here they were. And they were tired out, and how lucky it was they had found a place to camp, and company.

All this the Innocent delivered rapidly, while Piney, a stout, comely° damsel of fifteen, emerged from behind the pine tree, where she had been blushing unseen, and rode to the side of her lover.

Mr. Oakhurst seldom troubled himself with sentiment, still less with propriety; but he had a vague idea that the situation was not fortunate. He retained, however, his presence of mind sufficiently to kick Uncle Billy, who was about to say something, and Uncle Billy was sober enough to recognize in Mr. Oakhurst's kick a superior power that would not bear trifling. He then endeavored to dissuade Tom Simson from delaying further, but in vain. He even pointed out the fact that there was no provision, nor means of making a camp. But, unluckily, the Innocent met this objection by assuring the party that he was provided with an extra mule loaded with provisions, and by the discovery of a rude attempt at a log house near the trail. "Piney can stay with Mrs. Oakhurst," said the Innocent, pointing to the Duchess, "and I can shift for myself."

Nothing but Mr. Oakhurst's admonishing foot saved Uncle Billy from bursting into a roar of laughter. As it was, he felt compelled to retire up the canyon° until he could recover his gravity. There he confided the joke to the tall pine trees, with many slaps of his leg, contortions of his face, and the usual profanity. But when he returned to the party, he found them seated by a fire—for the air had grown strangely chill and the sky overcast—in apparently amicable° conversation.

Piney was actually talking in an impulsive girlish fashion to the Duchess, who was listening with an interest and animation she had not shown for many days. The Innocent was holding forth, apparently with equal effect, to Mr. Oakhurst and Mother Shipton, who was actually relaxing into amiability.°

"Is this yer a d—d picnic?" said Uncle Billy, with inward scorn, as he surveyed the sylvan° group, the glancing firelight, and the tethered animals in the foreground. Suddenly an idea mingled with the alcoholic fumes that disturbed his brain. It was apparently of a jocular° nature, for he felt impelled to slap his leg again and cram his fist into his mouth.

As the shadows crept slowly up the mountain, a slight breeze rocked the tops of the pine trees and moaned through their long and gloomy aisles. The ruined cabin, patched and covered with pine boughs, was set apart for the ladies. As the lovers parted, they unaffectedly exchanged a kiss, so honest and sincere that it might have been heard above the swaying pines. The frail Duchess and the malevolent Mother Shipton were probably too stunned to remark upon this last evidence of simplicity, and so turned without a word to the hut. The fire was replenished, the men lay down before the door, and in a few minutes were asleep.

Mr. Oakhurst was a light sleeper. Toward morning he awoke benumbed and cold. As he stirred the dying fire, the wind, which was now blowing strongly, brought to his cheek that which caused the blood to leave it—snow!

He started to his feet with the intention of awakening the sleepers, for there was no time to lose. But turning to where Uncle Billy had been lying, he found him gone. A suspicion leaped to his brain, and a curse to his lips. He ran to the spot where the mules had been tethered—they were no longer there. The tracks were already rapidly disappearing in the snow.

The momentary excitement brought Mr. Oakhurst back to the fire with his usual calm. He did not waken the sleepers. The Innocent slumbered peacefully, with a smile on his good-humored, freckled face; the virgin Piney slept beside her frailer sisters as sweetly as though attended by celestial° guardians; and Mr. Oakhurst, drawing his blanket over his shoulders, stroked his mustaches and waited for the dawn. It came slowly in a whirling mist of snowflakes that dazzled and confused the eye. What could be seen of the landscape appeared magically changed. He looked over the valley, and summed up the present and future in two words, "Snowed in!"

A careful inventory of the provisions, which, fortunately for the party, had been stored within the hut, and so escaped the felonious° fingers of Uncle Billy, disclosed the fact that with care and prudence they might last ten days longer.

"That is," said Mr. Oakhurst *sotto voce*° to the Innocent,

"if you're willing to board us. If you ain't—and perhaps you'd better not—you can wait till Uncle Billy gets back with provisions." For some occult° reason, Mr. Oakhurst could not bring himself to disclose Uncle Billy's rascality, and so offered the hypothesis that he had wandered from the camp and had accidentally stampeded the animals. He dropped a warning to the Duchess and Mother Shipton, who of course knew the facts of their associate's defection.°

"They'll find out the truth about us *all* when they find out anything," he added significantly, "and there's no good frightening them now."

Tom Simson not only put all his worldly store at the disposal of Mr. Oakhurst, but seemed to enjoy the prospect of their enforced seclusion. "We'll have a good camp for a week, and then the snow'll melt, and we'll all go back together."

The cheerful gaiety of the young man and Mr. Oakhurst's calm infected the others. The Innocent, with the aid of pine boughs, extemporized° a thatch for the roofless cabin, and the Duchess directed Piney in the rearrangement of the interior with a taste and tact that opened the blue eyes of that provincial maiden to their fullest extent.

"I reckon now you're used to fine things at Poker Flat," said Piney.

The Duchess turned away sharply to conceal something that reddened her cheeks through their professional tint, and Mother Shipton requested Piney not to "chatter." But when Mr. Oakhurst returned from a weary search for the trail, he heard the sound of happy laughter echoed from the rocks. He stopped in some alarm, and his thoughts first naturally reverted to the whiskey, which he had prudently cached.° "And yet it don't somehow sound like whiskey," said the gambler. It was not until he caught sight of the blazing fire through the still blinding storm, and the group around it, that he settled to the conviction that it was "square fun."

Whether Mr. Oakhurst had cached his cards with the whiskey as something debarred° the free access of the com-

munity, I cannot say. It was certain that, in Mother Shipton's words, he "didn't say 'cards' once" during that
evening. Haply the time was beguiled by an accordion,
produced somewhat ostentatiously by Tom Simson from
his pack. Notwithstanding some difficulties attending the
manipulation° of this instrument, Piney Woods managed
to pluck several reluctant melodies from its keys, to an
accompaniment by the Innocent on a pair of bone casta-
nets.°

But the crowning festivity of the evening was reached
in a rude camp-meeting hymn, which the lovers, joining
hands, sang with great earnestness and vociferation.° I
fear that a certain defiant tone and Covenanters'° swing to
its chorus, rather than any devotional quality, caused it
speedily to infect the others, who at last joined in the
refrain:

> I'm proud to live in the service of the Lord,
> And I'm bound to die in His army.

The pines rocked, the storm eddied and whirled above the
miserable group, and the flames of their altar leaped
heavenward, as if in token of the vow.

At midnight the storm abated, the rolling clouds parted,
and the stars glittered keenly above the sleeping camp.
Mr. Oakhurst, whose professional habits had enabled him
to live on the smallest possible amount of sleep, in dividing
the watch with Tom Simson somehow managed to take
upon himself the greatest part of that duty. He excused
himself to the Innocent by saying that he had "often been
a week without sleep."

"Doing what?" asked Tom.

"Poker!" replied Oakhurst sententiously.° "When a man
gets a streak of luck he don't get tired. The luck gives in
first. Luck," continued the gambler reflectively, "is a mighty
queer thing. All you know about it for certain is that it's
bound to change. And it's finding out when it's going to
change that makes you. We've had a streak of bad luck
since we left Poker Flat—you come along, and slap you get

into it, too. If you can hold your cards right along you're all right. For," added the gambler, with cheerful irrelevance,°

> 'I'm proud to live in the service of the Lord,
> And I'm bound to die in His army.'"

The third day came, and the sun, looking through the white-curtained valley, saw the outcasts divide their slowly decreasing store of provisions for the morning meal. It was one of the peculiarities of that mountain climate that its rays diffused a kindly warmth over the wintry landscape, as if in regretful commiseration° of the past. But it revealed drift on drift of snow piled high around the hut—a hopeless, uncharted, trackless sea of white lying below the rocky shores to which the castaways still clung.

Through the marvelously clear air the smoke of the pastoral village of Poker Flat rose miles away. Mother Shipton saw it, and from a remote pinnacle° of her rocky fastness hurled in that direction a final malediction.° It was her last vituperative attempt, and perhaps for that reason was invested with a certain degree of sublimity.° It did her good, she privately informed the Duchess. "Just you go out there and cuss, and see."

She then set herself to the task of amusing "the child," as she and the Duchess were pleased to call Piney. Piney was no chicken, but it was a soothing and original theory of the pair thus to account for the fact that she didn't swear and wasn't improper.

When night crept up again through the gorges, the reedy notes of the accordion rose and fell in fitful spasms and long-drawn gasps by the flickering campfire. But music failed to fill entirely the aching void left by insufficient food, and a new diversion° was proposed by Piney—storytelling. Neither Mr. Oakhurst nor his female companions caring to relate their personal experiences, this plan would have failed too, but for the Innocent.

Some months before he had chanced upon a stray copy of Mr. Pope's ingenious° translation of *The Iliad*.[1] He now

[1]Alexander Pope (1688-1744), an English poet, translated Homer's *Iliad* into English verse.

proposed to narrate the principal incidents of that poem —
having thoroughly mastered the argument and fairly forgotten the words — in the current vernacular° of Sandy Bar.
And so for the rest of that night the Homeric demigods
again walked the earth. Trojan bully and wily Greek[2]
wrestled in the winds, and the great pines in the canyon
seemed to bow to the wrath of the son of Peleus.[3]

Mr. Oakhurst listened with quiet satisfaction. Most
especially was he interested in the fate of "Ash-heels,"
as the Innocent persisted in denominating° the "swift-
footed Achilles."

So, with small food and much of Homer and the accordion, a week passed over the heads of the outcasts. The
sun again forsook them, and again from leaden skies the
snowflakes were sifted over the land. Day by day closer
around them drew the snowy circle, until at last they looked
from their prison over drifted walls of dazzling white that
towered twenty feet above their heads. It became more
and more difficult to replenish their fires, even from the
fallen trees beside them, now half hidden in the drifts.
And yet no one complained.

The lovers turned from the dreary prospect and looked
into each other's eyes, and were happy. Mr. Oakhurst settled himself coolly to the losing game before him. The
Duchess, more cheerful than she had been, assumed the
care of Piney.

Only Mother Shipton — once the strongest of the party —
seemed to sicken and fade. At midnight on the tenth day
she called Oakhurst to her side. "I'm going," she said, in
a voice of querulous° weakness, "but don't say anything
about it. Don't waken the kids. Take the bundle from
under my head, and open it."

Mr. Oakhurst did so. It contained Mother Shipton's
rations for the last week, untouched. "Give 'em to the
child," she said, pointing to the sleeping Piney.

"You've starved yourself," said the gambler.

[2]TROJAN . . . GREEK — *The Iliad* is concerned with the last stages of the war
between the Trojans and the Greeks. The Greeks finally took Troy through
deception.
[3]Achillês, the hero of Homer's *Iliad*.

"That's what they call it," said the woman querulously, as she lay down again, and, turning her face to the wall, passed quietly away.

The accordion and the bones were put aside that day, and Homer was forgotten. When the body of Mother Shipton had been committed to the snow, Mr. Oakhurst took the Innocent aside, and showed him a pair of snowshoes, which he had fashioned from the old pack saddle.

"There's one chance in a hundred to save her yet," he said, pointing to Piney; "but it's there," he added, pointing toward Poker Flat. "If you can reach there in two days she's safe."

"And you?" asked Tom Simson.

"I'll stay here," was the curt reply.

The lovers parted with a long embrace. "You are not going, too?" said the Duchess, as she saw Mr. Oakhurst apparently waiting to accompany him.

"As far as the canyon," he replied. He turned suddenly and kissed the Duchess, leaving her pallid° face aflame, and her trembling limbs rigid with amazement.

Night came, but not Mr. Oakhurst. It brought the storm again and the whirling snow. Then the Duchess, feeding the fire, found that someone had quietly piled beside the hut enough fuel to last a few days longer. The tears rose to her eyes, but she hid them from Piney.

The women slept but little. In the morning, looking into each other's faces, they read their fate. Neither spoke, but Piney, accepting the position of the stronger, drew near and placed her arm around the Duchess' waist. They kept this attitude for the rest of the day. That night the storm reached its greatest fury, and, rending asunder the protecting vines, invaded the very hut.

Toward morning they found themselves unable to feed the fire, which gradually died away. As the embers slowly blackened, the Duchess crept closer to Piney, and broke the silence of many hours: "Piney, can you pray?"

"No, dear," said Piney simply.

The Duchess, without knowing exactly why, felt relieved, and, putting her head upon Piney's shoulder, spoke no more. And so reclining, the younger and purer pillowing the head of her soiled sister upon her virgin breast, they fell asleep.

The wind lulled as if it feared to waken them. Feathery drifts of snow, shaken from the long pine boughs, flew like white-winged birds, and settled about them as they slept. The moon through the rifted° clouds looked down upon what had been the camp. But all human stain, all trace of earthly travail,° was hidden beneath the spotless mantle mercifully flung from above.

They slept all that day and the next, nor did they waken when voices and footsteps broke the silence of the camp. And when pitying fingers brushed the snow from their wan faces, you could scarcely have told from the equal peace that dwelt upon them which was she that had sinned. Even the law of Poker Flat recognized this, and turned away, leaving them still locked in each other's arms.

But at the head of the gulch, on one of the largest pine trees, they found the deuce° of clubs pinned to the bark with a bowie knife. It bore the following, written in pencil in a firm hand:

BENEATH THIS TREE
LIES THE BODY
OF

JOHN OAKHURST,
WHO STRUCK A STREAK OF BAD LUCK
ON THE 23D OF NOVEMBER 1850,
AND
HANDED IN HIS CHECKS
ON THE 7TH DECEMBER, 1850.

And pulseless and cold, with a derringer° by his side and a bullet in his heart, though still calm as in life, beneath the snow lay he who was at once the strongest and yet the weakest of the outcasts of Poker Flat.

Do especially Questions 47, 48, 59, 75, 80, 83, 101, 117, and 154. Consult the Short Story Model on page 156.

BRET HARTE *1836-1902*

Francis Bret Harte was born in Albany, New York. At fifteen, he accompanied his mother to California. In 1868 he founded the *Overland Monthly,* in which was published his most celebrated poem, "Plain Language from Truthful James," as well as his most famous stories: "The Luck of Roaring Camp," "The Outcasts of Poker Flat," and "Tennessee's Partner." First master of the "local-color" story, he drew people as he saw them in rugged living conditions. Small-time gamblers, hard-handed prospectors, not-too-respectable women, road bandits—these are his characters, always in the setting of the gold fields. Bret Harte shows the murderer, the fallen woman, the outcast as essentially human in noble acts of sacrifice. He skillfully blends humor with pathos, achieving real insight into human actions.

An Occurrence at
Owl Creek Bridge

AMBROSE BIERCE

A man stood upon a railroad bridge in northern Alabama, looking down into the swift waters twenty feet below. The man's hands were behind his back, the wrists bound with a cord. A rope closely encircled his neck. It was attached to a stout cross-timber above his head, and the slack fell to the level of his knees. Some loose boards laid upon the sleepers[1] supporting the metals of the railway supplied a footing for him and his executioners—two private soldiers of the Federal army, directed by a sergeant who in civil life may have been a deputy° sheriff. At a short remove upon the same temporary platform was an officer in the uniform of his rank, armed. He was a captain. A sentinel° at each end of the bridge stood with his rifle in the position known as "support," that is to say, vertical in front of the left shoulder, the hammer resting on the forearm thrown straight across the chest—a formal and unnatural position, enforcing an erect carriage of the body. It did not appear

[1]Pieces of wood fastened next to the rails to hold them in place.

to be the duty of these two men to know what was occurring at the center of the bridge; they merely blockaded the two ends of the footplanking which traversed° it.

Beyond one of the sentinels nobody was in sight; the railroad ran straight away into a forest for a hundred yards, then, curving, was lost to view. Doubtless there was an outpost farther along. The other bank of the stream was open ground—a gentle acclivity° crowned with a stockade of vertical tree trunks, loopholed for rifles, with a single embrasure° through which protruded the muzzle of a brass cannon commanding the bridge. Midway up the slope between the bridge and fort were the spectators—a single company of infantry in line, at "parade rest," the butts of the rifles on the ground, the barrels inclining slightly backward against the right shoulder, the hands crossed upon the stock.° A lieutenant stood at the right of the line, the point of his sword upon the ground, his left hand resting upon his right. Excepting the group of four at the center of the bridge, not a man moved. The company faced the bridge, staring stonily, motionless. The sentinels, facing the banks of the stream, might have been statues to adorn the bridge. The captain stood with folded arms, silent, observing the work of his subordinates, but making no sign. Death is a dignitary who, when he comes announced, is to be received with formal manifestations of respect, even by those most familiar with him. In the code of military etiquette silence and fixity are forms of deference.°

The man who was engaged in being hanged was apparently about thirty-five years of age. He was a civilian, if one might judge from his habit, which was that of a planter. His features were good—a straight nose, firm mouth, broad forehead, from which his long dark hair was combed straight back, falling behind his ears to the collar of his well-fitting frock coat. He wore a mustache and pointed beard, but no whiskers; his eyes were large and dark gray, and had a kindly expression which one would hardly have expected in one whose neck was in the hemp.° Evidently this was no vulgar assassin. The liberal military code makes provision for hanging many kinds of persons, and gentlemen are not excluded.

The preparations being complete, the two private soldiers stepped aside and each drew away the plank upon which he had been standing. The sergeant turned to the captain, saluted, and placed himself immediately behind that officer, who in turn moved apart one pace. These movements left the condemned man and the sergeant standing on the two ends of the same plank, which spanned three of the cross-ties of the bridge. The end upon which the civilian stood almost, but not quite, reached a fourth. This plank had been held in place by the weight of the captain; it was now held by that of the sergeant. At a signal from the former the latter would step aside, the plank would tilt, and the condemned man go down between two ties. The arrangement commended itself to his judgment as simple and effective. His face had not been covered nor his eyes bandaged. He looked a moment at his "unsteadfast footing," then let his gaze wander to the swirling water of the stream racing madly beneath his feet. A piece of dancing driftwood caught his attention, and his eyes followed it down the current. How slowly it appeared to move! What a sluggish stream!

He closed his eyes in order to fix his last thoughts upon his wife and children. The water, touched to gold by the early sun, the brooding mists under the banks at some distance down the stream, the fort, the soldiers, the piece of drift—all had distracted him. And now he became conscious of a new disturbance. Striking through the thought of his dear ones was a sound which he could neither ignore nor understand, a sharp, distinct, metallic percussion° like the stroke of a blacksmith's hammer upon the anvil; it had the same ringing quality. He wondered what it was, and whether immeasurably distant or near by—it seemed both. Its recurrence was regular, but as slow as the tolling of a death knell.° He awaited each stroke with impatience and —he knew not why—apprehension. The intervals of silence grew progressively longer; the delays became maddening. With their greater infrequency the sounds increased in strength and sharpness. They hurt his ear like the thrust of a knife; he feared he would shriek. What he heard was the ticking of his watch.

He unclosed his eyes and saw again the water below him. "If I could free my hands," he thought, "I might throw off the noose and spring into the stream. By diving I could evade the bullets and, swimming vigorously, reach the bank, take to the woods, and get away home. My home, thank God, is as yet outside their lines; my wife and little ones are still beyond the invader's farthest advance."

As these thoughts, which have here to be set down in words, were flashed into the doomed man's brain rather than evolved from it, the captain nodded to the sergeant. The sergeant stepped aside.

Peyton Farquhar was a well-to-do planter, of an old and highly respected Alabama family. Being a slaveowner, and, like other slaveowners, a politician, he was naturally an original secessionist° and ardently devoted to the Southern cause. Circumstances of an imperious nature, which it is unnecessary to relate here, had prevented him from taking service with the gallant army that had fought the disastrous campaigns ending with the fall of Corinth, and he chafed° under the inglorious restraint, longing for the release of his energies, the larger life of the soldier, the opportunity for distinction. That opportunity, he felt, would come, as it comes to all in wartime. Meanwhile he did what he could. No service was too humble for him to perform in aid of the South, no adventure too perilous for him to undertake if consistent with the character of a civilian who was at heart a soldier, and who in good faith and without too much qualification assented to at least a part of the frankly villainous dictum° that all is fair in love and war.

One evening while Farquhar and his wife were sitting on a rustic bench near the entrance to his grounds, a gray-clad soldier rode up to the gate and asked for a drink of water. Mrs. Farquhar was only too happy to serve him with her own white hands. While she was fetching the water, her husband approached the dusty horseman and inquired eagerly for news from the front.

"The Yanks are repairing the railroads," said the man, "and are getting ready for another advance. They have reached the Owl Creek Bridge, put it in order, and built a stockade on the north bank. The commandant has issued an order, which is posted everywhere, declaring that any civilian caught interfering with the railroad, its bridges, tunnels, or trains, will be summarily° hanged. I saw the order."

"How far is it to the Owl Creek Bridge?" Farquhar asked.

"About thirty miles."

"Is there no force on this side the creek?"

"Only a picket post half a mile out, on the railroad, and a single sentinel at this end of the bridge."

"Suppose a man—a civilian and student of hanging— should elude the picket post and perhaps get the better of the sentinel," said Farquhar, smiling, "what could he accomplish?"

The soldier reflected. "I was there a month ago," he replied. "I observed that the flood of last winter had lodged a great quantity of driftwood against the wooden pier at this end of the bridge. It is now dry and would burn like tow."°

The lady had now brought the water, which the soldier drank. He thanked her ceremoniously, bowed to her husband, and rode away. An hour later, after nightfall, he repassed the plantation, going northward in the direction from which he had come. He was a Federal scout.

As Peyton Farquhar fell straight downward through the bridge, he lost consciousness and was as one already dead. From this state he was awakened—ages later, it seemed to him—by the pain of a sharp pressure upon his throat, followed by a sense of suffocation. Keen, poignant° agonies seemed to shoot from his neck downward through every fiber of his body and limbs. These pains seemed to flash along well-defined lines of ramification,° and to beat with an inconceivably rapid periodicity. They seemed like streams of pulsating fire, heating him to an intolerable temperature. As to his head, he was conscious of nothing but a feeling of fullness—of congestion. These sensations were unaccompanied by thought. The intellectual part of his nature was already effaced;° he had power only to feel, and feeling was torment. He was conscious of motion. Encompassed in a luminous° cloud, of which he was now merely the fiery heart, without material substance, he swung through unthinkable arcs of oscillation,° like a vast pendulum. Then all at once, with terrible suddenness, the light about him shot upward with the noise of a loud plash; a frightful roaring was in his ears, and all was cold and dark. The power of thought was restored; he knew that the rope had broken and he had fallen into the stream. There was no additional strangulation; the noose about his neck was already suffocating him, and kept the water from his lungs. To die of hanging at the bottom of a river—the idea seemed to him ludicrous. He opened his eyes in the darkness and saw above him a gleam of light, but how distant, how inaccessible! He was still sinking, for the light became fainter and fainter until it was a mere glimmer. Then it began to grow and brighten, and he knew that he was rising toward the surface—knew it with reluctance, for he was now very comfortable. "To be hanged and drowned," he thought, "that is not so bad; but I do not wish to be shot. No; I will not be shot; that is not fair."

He was not conscious of an effort, but a sharp pain in his wrists apprized him that he was trying to free his hands. He gave the struggle his attention, as an idler might observe the feat of a juggler, without interest in the outcome. What splendid effort—what magnificent, what superhuman strength! Ah, that was a fine endeavor! Bravo! The cord fell away; his arms parted and floated upward, the hands dimly seen on each side in the growing light. He watched them with a new interest as first one and then the other pounced upon the noose at his neck. They tore it away and thrust it fiercely aside, its undulations resembling those of a water snake. "Put it back! put it back!" He thought he shouted these words to his hands, for the undoing of the noose had been succeeded by the direst pang that he had yet experienced. His neck ached horribly; his brain was on fire; his heart, which had been fluttering faintly, gave a great leap, trying to force itself out at his mouth. His whole body was racked and wrenched with an insupportable anguish! But his disobedient hands gave no heed to the command. They beat the water vigorously with quick, downward strokes, forcing him to the surface. He felt his head emerge; his eyes were blinded by the sunlight; his chest expanded convulsively,° and with a supreme and crowning agony his lungs engulfed a great draught of air, which instantly he expelled in a shriek!

He was now in full possession of his physical senses. They were, indeed, preternaturally[2] keen and alert. Something in the awful disturbance of his organic system had so exalted and refined them that they made record of things never before perceived. He felt the ripples upon his face and heard their separate sounds as they struck. He looked at the forest on the bank of the stream, saw the individual trees, the leaves and the veining of each leaf—saw the very insects upon them: the locusts, the brilliant-bodied flies, the gray spiders stretching their webs from twig to twig. He noted the prismatic colors[3] in all the dewdrops upon a million blades of grass. The humming of the gnats that danced above the eddies° of the stream, the beating of the dragonflies' wings, the strokes of the water-spiders' legs, like oars which had lifted their boat—all these made audible music. A fish slid along beneath his eyes, and he heard the rush of its body parting the water.

He had come to the surface facing down the stream; in a moment the visible world seemed to wheel slowly round, himself the pivotal° point, and he saw the bridge, the fort, the soldiers upon the bridge, the captain, the sergeant, the two privates, his executioners. They were in silhouette against the blue sky. They shouted and gesticulated, pointing at him. The captain had drawn his pistol, but did not fire; the others were unarmed. Their movements were grotesque and horrible, their forms gigantic.

[2]With more than ordinary powers of sight and hearing.
[3]Rainbow colors seen when sunlight shines through a prism.

Suddenly he heard a sharp report, and something struck the water smartly within a few inches of his head, spattering his face with spray. He heard a second report, and saw one of the sentinels with his rifle at his shoulder, a light cloud of blue smoke rising from the muzzle. The man in the water saw the eye of the man on the bridge gazing into his own through the sights of the rifle. He observed that it was a gray eye, and remembered having read that gray eyes were keenest, and that all famous marksmen had them. Nevertheless, this one had missed.

A counter-swirl had caught Farquhar and turned him half round; he was again looking into the forest on the bank opposite the fort. The sound of a clear, high voice in a monotonous singsong now rang out behind him and came across the water with a distinctness that pierced and subdued all other sounds, even the beating of the ripples in his ears. Although no soldier, he had frequented camps enough to know the dread significance of that deliberate drawling, aspirated[4] chant; the lieutenant on shore was taking a part in the morning's work. How coldly and pitilessly—with what an even, calm intonation, presaging° and enforcing tranquillity in the men—with what accurately measured intervals fell those cruel words:

"Attention, company. . . Shoulder arms. . . Ready! . . . Aim! . . . Fire!"

Farquhar dived—dived as deeply as he could. The water roared in his ears like the voice of Niagara, yet he heard the dulled thunder of the volley and, rising again toward the surface, met shining bits of metal, singularly flattened, oscillating slowly downward. Some of them touched him on the face and hands, then fell away, continuing their descent. One lodged between his collar and neck; it was uncomfortably warm, and he snatched it out.

As he rose to the surface, gasping for breath, he saw that he had been a long time under water; he was perceptibly° farther downstream—nearer to safety! The soldiers had almost finished reloading; the metal ramrods flashed

[4]Said with harsh, throaty sounds, stressing the "s" and "h" in words.

all at once in the sunshine as they were drawn from the barrels, turned in the air, and thrust into their sockets. The two sentinels fired again, independently and ineffectually.

The hunted man saw all this over his shoulder; he was now swimming vigorously with the current. His brain was as energetic as his arms and legs; he thought with the rapidity of lightning.

"The officer," he reasoned, "will not make that martinet's° error a second time. It is as easy to dodge a volley as a single shot. He had probably already given the command to fire at will. God help me, I cannot dodge them all!"

An appalling plash within two yards of him was followed by a loud rushing sound, *diminuendo*,[5] which seemed to travel back through the air to the fort and died in an explosion which stirred the very river to its deeps! A rising sheet of water curved over him, fell down upon him, blinded him, strangled him! The cannon had taken a hand in the game. As he shook his head free from the commotion of the smitten water, he heard the deflected shot humming through the air ahead, and in an instant it was cracking and smashing the branches in the forest beyond.

"They will not do that again," he thought; "the next time they will use a charge of grape.[6] I must keep my eye upon the gun; the smoke will apprise me—the report arrives too late; it lags behind the missile. That is a good gun."

Suddenly he felt himself whirled round and round—spinning like a top. The water, the banks, the forest, the now distant bridge, fort, and men—all were commingled and blurred. Objects were represented by their colors only; circular horizontal streaks of color—that was all he saw. He had been caught in a vortex° and was being whirled on with a velocity of advance and gyration° that made him giddy and sick. In a few moments he was flung upon the gravel at the foot of the left bank of the stream—the southern bank—and behind a projecting point which concealed him from his enemies. The sudden arrest of his motion,

[5]With gradually lessening loudness.
[6]CHARGE OF GRAPE—A cluster of small iron balls shot in one charge from a cannon; much like buckshot from a shotgun.

the abrasion° of one of his hands on the gravel, restored him, and he wept with delight. He dug his fingers into the sand, threw it over himself in handfuls, and audibly blessed it. It looked like diamonds, rubies, emeralds; he could think of nothing beautiful which it did not resemble. The trees upon the bank were giant garden plants; he noted a definite order in their arrangement, inhaled the fragrance of their blooms. A strange, roseate light shone through the spaces among their trunks, and the wind made in their branches the music of Aeolian harps.[7] He had no wish to perfect his escape — was content to remain in that enchanting spot until retaken.

A whizz and rattle of grapeshot among the branches high above his head roused him from his dream. The baffled cannoneer had fired him a random farewell. He sprang to his feet, rushed up the sloping bank, and plunged into the forest.

All that day he traveled, laying his course by the rounding sun. The forest seemed interminable;° nowhere did he discover a break in it, not even a woodman's road. He had not known that he lived in so wild a region. There was something uncanny° in the revelation.

By nightfall he was fatigued, footsore, famishing. The thought of his wife and children urged him on. At last he found a road which led him in what he knew to be the right direction. It was as wide and straight as a city street, yet it seemed untraveled. No fields bordered it, no dwelling anywhere. Not so much as the barking of a dog suggested human habitation. The black bodies of the trees formed a straight wall on both sides, terminating on the horizon in a point, like a diagram in a lesson in perspective.[8] Overhead, as he looked up through this rift in the wood, shone great golden stars looking unfamiliar and grouped in strange constellations. He was sure they were arranged in some order which had a secret and malign significance. The wood on either side was full of singular noises, among

---

[7]A box fitted with tuned strings so that the wind makes music by blowing through the strings. Aeolus was the Greek god of the winds.
[8]The art of representing distance in drawing or painting.

which — once, twice, and again — he distinctly heard whispers in an unknown tongue.

His neck was in pain, and lifting his hand to it, he found it horribly swollen. He knew that it had a circle of black where the rope had bruised it. His eyes felt congested;° he could no longer close them. His tongue was swollen with thirst; he relieved its fever by thrusting it forward from between his teeth into the cold air. How softly the turf had carpeted the untraveled avenue! He could no longer feel the roadway beneath his feet!

Doubtless, despite his suffering, he had fallen asleep while walking, for now he sees another scene — perhaps he has merely recovered from a delirium.° He stands at the gate of his own home. All is as he left it, and all bright and beautiful in the morning sunshine. He must have traveled the entire night. As he pushes open the gate and passes up the wide white walk, he sees a flutter of female garments; his wife, looking fresh and cool and sweet, steps down from the veranda to meet him. At the bottom of the steps she stands waiting, with a smile of ineffable joy, an attitude of matchless grace and dignity. Ah, how beautiful she is! He springs forward with extended arms. As he is about to clasp her, he feels a stunning blow upon the back of the neck; a blinding white light blazes all about him with a sound like the shock of a cannon — then all is darkness and silence!

Peyton Farquhar was dead; his body, with a broken neck, swung gently from side to side beneath the timbers of the Owl Creek Bridge.

Do especially Questions 75, 84, 93, 94, 97, and 100. Consult the Short Story Model on page 156.

AMBROSE GWINETT BIERCE   1842-1914

We know approximately where Bierce was born: at a camp meeting in Meigs County near Chester, Ohio. But the exact time and place of his death are unknown, for during the Mexican revolution he disappeared into Mexico at the age of seventy-one and met a mysterious end. His education was obtained in a country school;

he had no formal college preparation. Yet Bierce shows in his style an amazing succinctness. In 1861 he joined the Union Army as a private, rose to be a lieutenant, and finally became a major before receiving his discharge, having been wounded twice in the fighting of Kennesaw Mountain. His stories about the Civil War, *Tales of Soldiers and Civilians,* show precision of plot and excellent descriptions of nature. After the war Bierce moved to California where he wrote for the Hearst *Sunday Examiner,* being the foremost critic of the time in California. Later he contributed to the New York *American* and *Cosmopolitan* magazines. Many of his stories about the West show a strong resemblance to Bret Harte's stories; he admits being influenced, too, by Poe. Among the many essays, criticisms, poems, and other works to be found in his twelve volumes of *Collected Works* which he published (1909-1912), his major contributions are his short stories.

The Last Class

(The Story of a Little Alsatian)

ALPHONSE DAUDET Translated by George Burnham Ives

I was very late for school that morning, and I was terribly afraid of being scolded, especially as Monsieur Hamel had told us that he should examine us on participles, and I did not know the first thing about them. For a moment I thought of staying away from school and wandering about the fields. It was such a warm, lovely day. I could hear the blackbirds whistling on the edge of the wood, and in the Rippert field, behind the sawmill, the Prussians going through their drill. All that was much more tempting to me than the rules concerning participles; but I had the strength to resist, and I ran as fast as I could to school.

As I passed the mayor's office, I saw that there were people gathered about the little board on which notices were posted. For two years all our bad news had come from that board—battles lost, conscriptions,° orders from head-quarters; and I thought without stopping:

"What can it be now?"

Then, as I ran across the square, Wachter the blacksmith, who stood there with his apprentice,° reading the placard, called out to me: "Don't hurry so, my boy; you'll get to your school soon enough!"

I thought that he was making fun of me, and I ran into Monsieur Hamel's little yard all out of breath.

Usually, at the beginning of school, there was a great uproar which could be heard in the street, desks opening and closing, lessons repeated aloud in unison,° with our ears stuffed in order to learn quicker, and the teacher's stout ruler beating on the desk:

"A little more quiet!"

I counted on all this noise to get to my bench unnoticed; but as it happened, that day everything was quiet, like a Sunday morning. Through the open window I saw my comrades already in their places, and Monsieur Hamel walking back and forth with the terrible iron ruler under his arm. I had to open the door and enter, in the midst of that perfect silence. You can imagine whether I blushed and whether I was afraid!

But no! Monsieur Hamel looked at me with no sign of anger and said very gently:

"Go at once to your seat, my little Frantz; we were going to begin without you."

I stepped over the bench and sat down at once at my desk. Not until then, when I had partly recovered from my fright, did I notice that our teacher had on his handsome blue coat, his plaited° ruff, and the black silk embroidered breeches,° which he wore only on days of inspection or of distribution of prizes. Moreover, there was something extraordinary, something solemn about the whole class. But what surprised me most was to see at the back of the room, on the benches which were usually empty, some people from the village sitting, as silent as we were; old Hauser with his three-cornered hat, the ex-mayor, the ex-postman, and others besides. They all seemed depressed; and Hauser had brought an old spelling-book with gnawed° edges, which he held wide-open on his knee, with his great spectacles askew.°

While I was wondering at all this, Monsieur Hamel had mounted his platform, and in the same gentle and serious voice with which he had welcomed me, he said to us:

"My children, this is the last time that I shall teach you. Orders have come from Berlin to teach nothing but German in the schools of Alsace and Lorraine.[1] The new teacher arrives tomorrow. This is the last class in French, so I beg you to be very attentive."

Those few words overwhelmed me. Ah! the villains! that was what they had posted at the mayor's office.

My last class in French!

And I barely knew how to write! So I should never learn! I must stop short where I was! How angry I was with myself because of the time I had wasted, the lessons I had missed, running about after nests, or sliding on the Saar![2] My books, which only a moment before I thought so tiresome, so heavy to carry—my grammar, my sacred history—seemed to me now like old friends, from whom I should be terribly grieved to part. And it was the same about Monsieur Hamel. The thought that he was going away, that I should never see him again, made me forget the punishments, the blows with the ruler.

Poor man! It was in honor of that last lesson that he had put on his fine Sunday clothes; and I understood now why those old fellows from the village were sitting at the end of the room. It seemed to mean that they regretted not having come oftener to the school. It was also a way of thanking our teacher for his forty years of faithful service, and of paying their respects to the fatherland which was vanishing.

I was at that point in my reflections when I heard my name called. It was my turn to recite. What would I not have given to be able to say from beginning to end that famous rule about participles, in a loud, distinct voice, without a slip! But I got mixed up at the first words, and I stood there swaying against my bench, with a full heart, afraid to raise my head. I heard Monsieur Hamel speaking to me:

"I will not scold you, my little Frantz; you must be punished enough; that is the way it goes; every day we say to ourselves: 'Pshaw! I have time enough. I will learn

[1]Two provinces in northeast France which have been disputed territory for many hundreds of years. In 1871, the time of this story, these two provinces again went to Germany.
[2]A European river flowing north from the Vosges Mountains in France to the Mosel River in Germany.

tomorrow.' And then you see what happens. Ah! it has
been the great misfortune of our Alsace always to postpone
its lessons until tomorrow. Now those people are entitled
to say to us: 'What! you claim to be French, and you can
neither speak nor write your language!' In all this, my poor
Frantz, you are not the guiltiest one. We all have our fair
share of reproaches° to address to ourselves.

"Your parents have not been careful enough to see that
you were educated. They preferred to send you to work in
the fields or in the factories, in order to have a few more
sous.° And have I nothing to reproach myself for? Have I
not often made you water my garden instead of studying?
And when I wanted to go fishing for trout, have I ever
hesitated to dismiss you?"

Then, passing from one thing to another, Monsieur
Hamel began to talk to us about the French language,
saying that it was the most beautiful language in the
world, the most clear, the most substantial;° that we must
always retain it among ourselves, and never forget it, because when a people falls into servitude, "so long as it
clings to its language, it is as if it held the key to its prison."
Then he took the grammar and read us our lesson. I was
amazed to see how readily I understood. Everything that
he said seemed so easy to me, so easy. I believed, too,
that I had never listened so closely, and that he, for his
part, had never been so patient with his explanations.
One would have said that, before going away, the poor man
desired to give us all his knowledge, to force it all into our
heads at a single blow.

When the lesson was at an end we passed to writing.
For that day Monsieur Hamel had prepared some entirely
new examples, on which was written in a fine, round hand:
"France, Alsace, France, Alsace." They were like little
flags, waving all about the class, hanging from the rods of
our desks. You should have seen how hard we all worked
and how silent it was! Nothing could be heard save the
grinding of the pens over the paper. At one time some
cockchafers[3] flew in; but no one paid any attention to them,

[3] Large European beetles.

not even the little fellows, who were struggling with their straight lines with a will and conscientious° application, as if even the lines were French. On the roof of the school-house pigeons cooed° in low tones, and I said to myself as I listened to them:

"I wonder if they are going to compel them to sing in German too!"

From time to time, when I raised my eyes from my paper, I saw Monsieur Hamel sitting motionless in his chair and staring at the objects about him as if he wished to carry away in his glance the whole of his little schoolhouse. Think of it! For forty years he had been there in the same place, with his yard in front of him and his class just as it was! But the benches and desks were polished and rubbed by use; the walnuts in the yard had grown, and the hop-vine° which he himself had planted now festooned the win-dows even to the roof. What a heart-rending thing it must have been for that poor man to leave all those things, and to hear his sister walking back and forth in the room overhead, packing their trunks! For they were to go away the next day — to leave the province forever.

However, he had the courage to keep the class to the end. After the writing, we had the lesson in history; then the little ones sang all together the *ba, be, bi, bo, bu.* Yonder, at the back of the room, old Hauser had put on his spec-tacles, and, holding his spelling-book in both hands, he spelled out the letters with them. I could see that he, too, was applying himself. His voice shook with emotion, and it was so funny to hear him that we all longed to laugh and to cry. Ah! I shall remember that last class.

Suddenly the church clock struck twelve, then the Angelus rang. At the same moment the bugles of the Prussians returning from drill blared under our windows. Monsieur Hamel rose, pale as death, from his chair. Never had he seemed to me so tall.

"My friends," he said, "my friends, I . . . I . . . ."

But something suffocated° him. He could not finish the sentence.

Thereupon he turned to the blackboard, took a piece of

chalk, and, bearing on with all his might, he wrote in the
largest letters he could:

"*Vive la France!*"[4]

Then he stood there, with his head resting against the
wall, and without speaking, he motioned to us with his
hand:

"That is all; go."

[4]Long live France!

> Do especially Questions 44, 45, 75, 112, 114, 116, and 146.
> Consult the Short Story Model on page 156.

ALPHONSE DAUDET   1840-1897

Alphonse Daudet produced a variety of literary works, including
novels, short stories, poems, biographies, and plays. Having
spent his youth in Provence, Daudet was forced by poverty at the
age of sixteen to go to work as a novice instructor. Perhaps this
hectic experience as a youthful teacher, which lasted only two
years, enabled him to appreciate the dedication and strength
of character of a man like Monsieur Hamel, the tragic figure in
"The Last Class." Following his brief teaching career, Daudet
joined his brother in Rome, intent upon a career of writing.

The Peasant Marey

FYODOR DOSTOEVSKY Translated by Constance Garnett

It was the second day in Easter week. The air was warm,
the sky was blue, the sun was high, warm, bright, but my
soul was very gloomy. I sauntered behind the prison barracks. I stared at the palings° of the stout prison fence,
counting them; but I had no inclination to count them,
though it was my habit to do so. This was the second day
of the "holidays" in the prison; the convicts were not taken
out to work, there were numbers of men drunk, loud abuse
and quarreling were springing up continually in every
corner. There were hideous, disgusting songs, and card-
parties installed beside the platform-beds.° Several of the

Reprinted with permission of The Macmillan Company from *An Honest Thief and
Other Stories* by Fyodor Dostoevsky. Translated by Constance Garnett. Printed in
Great Britain. Reprinted also by permission of William Heinemann Ltd.

convicts who had been sentenced by their comrades, for special violence, to be beaten till they were half dead, were lying on the platform-bed, covered with sheepskins till they should recover and come to themselves again; knives had already been drawn several times. For these two days of holiday all this had been torturing me till it made me ill. And indeed I could never endure without repulsion the noise and disorder of drunken people, and especially in this place. On these days even the prison officials did not look into the prison, made no searches, did not look for vodka, understanding that they must allow even these outcasts to enjoy themselves once a year, and that things would be even worse if they did not. At last a sudden fury flamed up in my heart. A political prisoner called M. met me; he looked at me gloomily, his eyes flashed and his lips quivered. *"Je hais ces brigands!"*[1] he hissed at me through his teeth, and walked on. I returned to the prison ward, though only a quarter of an hour before I had rushed out of it as though I were crazy, when six stalwart fellows had all together flung themselves upon the drunken Tatar Gazin to suppress him and had begun beating him; they beat him stupidly, a camel might have been killed by such blows, but they knew that this Hercules[2] was not easy to kill, and so they beat him without uneasiness. Now on returning I noticed on the bed in the furthest corner of the room Gazin lying unconscious, almost without sign of life. He lay covered with a sheepskin, and everyone walked round him, without speaking; though they confidently hoped that he would come to himself next morning, yet if luck was against him, maybe from a beating like that, the man would die. I made my way to my own place opposite the window with the iron grating, and lay on my back with my hands behind my head and my eyes shut. I liked to lie like that; a sleeping man is not molested, and meanwhile one can dream and think. But I could not dream, my heart was beating uneasily, and M.'s words, *"Je hais ces*

[1]"I hate these outlaws."
[2]In Greek mythology Hercules is the personification of physical strength and prowess.

brigands!" were echoing in my ears. But why describe my impressions? I sometimes dream even now of those times at night, and I have no dreams more agonizing.° Perhaps it will be noticed that even to this day I have scarcely once spoken in print of my life in prison. *The House of the Dead* I wrote fifteen years ago in the character of an imaginary person, a criminal who had killed his wife. I may add by the way that since then, very many persons have supposed, and even now maintain, that I was sent to penal° servitude for the murder of my wife.

Gradually I sank into forgetfulness and by degrees was lost in memories. During the whole course of my four years in prison I was continually recalling all my past, and seemed to live over again the whole of my life in recollection. These memories rose up of themselves, it was not often that I summoned them of my own will. Each would begin from some point, some little thing, at times unnoticed, and then by degrees there would rise up a complete picture, some vivid and complete impression. I used to analyze these impressions, give new features to what had happened long ago, and best of all, I used to correct it, correct it continually, that was my great amusement. On this occasion, I suddenly for some reason remembered an unnoticed moment in my early childhood when I was only nine years old—a moment which I should have thought I had utterly forgotten; but at that time I was particularly fond of memories of my early childhood. I remembered the month of August in our country house: a dry bright day but rather cold and windy; summer was waning° and soon we should have to go to Moscow to be bored all winter with French lessons, and I was so sorry to leave the country. I walked past the threshing-floor and, going down the ravine,° I went up to the dense thicket of bushes that covered the further side of the ravine as far as the copse.° And I plunged right into the midst of the bushes, and heard a peasant plowing alone on the clearing about thirty paces away. I knew that he was plowing up the steep hill and the horse was moving with effort, and from time to time the peasant's call "Come up!" floated upwards to me.

I knew almost all our peasants, but I did not know who it was plowing now, and, indeed, I did not care, I was absorbed in my own affairs. I was busy, too; I was breaking off switches from the nut trees to whip the frogs with. Nut sticks make such fine whips, but they do not last; while birch twigs are just the opposite. I was interested, too, in beetles and other insects; I used to collect them, some were very ornamental. I was very fond, too, of the little nimble red and yellow lizards with black spots on them, but I was afraid of snakes. Snakes, however, were much more rare than lizards. There were not many mushrooms there. To get mushrooms one had to go to the birch wood, and I was about to set off there. And there was nothing in the world that I loved so much as the wood with its mushrooms and wild berries, with its beetles and its birds, its hedgehogs° and squirrels, with its damp smell of dead leaves which I loved so much, and even as I write I smell the fragrance of our birch wood: these impressions will remain for my whole life. Suddenly in the midst of the profound stillness I heard a clear and distinct shout, "Wolf!" I shrieked and, beside myself with terror, calling out at the top of my voice, ran out into the clearing and straight to the peasant who was plowing.

It was our peasant Marey. I don't know if there is such a name, but everyone called him Marey—a thick-set, rather well-grown peasant of fifty, with a good many gray hairs in his dark brown, spreading beard. I knew him, but had scarcely ever happened to speak to him till then. He stopped his horse on hearing my cry, and when, breathless, I caught with one hand at his plow and with the other at his sleeve, he saw how frightened I was.

"There is a wolf!" I cried, panting.

He flung up his head, and could not help looking round for an instant, almost believing me.

"Where is the wolf?"

"A shout ... someone shouted: 'Wolf' ..." I faltered out.

"Nonsense, nonsense! A wolf? Why, it was your fancy!° How could there be a wolf?" he muttered, reassuring me. But I was trembling all over, and still kept tight hold of his smock° frock, and I must have been quite pale. He looked at me with an uneasy smile, evidently anxious and troubled over me.

"Why, you have had a fright, *aïe, aïe!*" He shook his head. "There, dear. . . . Come little one, *aïe!*"

He stretched out his hand, and all at once stroked my cheek.

"Come, come, there; Christ be with you! Cross yourself!"

But I did not cross myself. The corners of my mouth were twitching,° and I think that struck him particularly. He put out his thick, black-nailed, earth-stained finger and softly touched my twitching lips.

"*Aïe,* there, there," he said to me with a slow, almost motherly smile. "Dear, dear, what is the matter? There; come, come!"

I grasped at last that there was no wolf, and that the shout that I had heard was my fancy. Yet that shout had been so clear and distinct, but such shouts (not only about wolves) I had imagined once or twice before, and I was aware of that. (These hallucinations° passed away later as I grew older.)

"Well, I will go then," I said, looking at him timidly and inquiringly.

"Well, do, and I'll keep watch on you as you go. I won't let the wolf get you," he added, still smiling at me with the same motherly expression. "Well, Christ be with you! Come, run along then." And he made the sign of the cross over me and then over himself. I walked away, looking back almost at every tenth step. Marey stood still with his mare as I walked away, and looked after me and nodded to me every time I looked round. I must own I felt a little ashamed at having let him see me so frightened, but I was still very much afraid of the wolf as I walked away, until I reached the first barn halfway up the slope of the ravine; there my fright vanished completely, and all at once our yard-dog Volchok flew to meet me. With Volchok I felt quite safe, and I turned round to Marey for the last time; I could not see his face distinctly, but I felt that he was still nodding and smiling affectionately at me. I waved to him; he waved back at me and started his little mare. "Come up!" I heard his call in the distance again, and the little mare pulled at the plow again.

All this I recalled all at once, I don't know why, but with extraordinary minuteness of detail. I suddenly roused myself and sat up on the sleeping-platform, and, I remember, found myself still smiling quietly at my memories. I brooded° over them for another minute.

When I got home that day I told no one of my "adventure" with Marey. And indeed it was hardly an adventure. And in fact I soon forgot Marey. When I met him now and then afterwards, I never even spoke to him about the wolf or anything else; and all at once now, twenty years afterwards in Siberia, I remembered this meeting with such distinctness to the smallest detail. So it must have lain hidden in my soul, though I knew nothing of it, and rose suddenly to my memory when it was wanted; I remembered the soft motherly smile of the poor serf,° the way he signed me with the cross and shook his head. "There, there, you have had a fright, little one!" And I remembered particularly the thick earth-stained finger with which he softly and with timid tenderness touched my quivering lips. Of course anyone would have reassured a child, but something quite different seemed to have happened in that solitary° meeting; and if I had been his own son, he could not have looked at me with eyes shining with greater love. And what made him like that? He was our serf and I was his little master, after all. No one would know that he had been kind to me and reward him for it. Was he, perhaps, very fond of little children? Some people are. It was a solitary meeting in the deserted fields, and only God, perhaps, may have seen from above with what deep and humane° civilized feeling, and with what a delicate, almost feminine tenderness, the heart of a coarse, brutally ignorant Russian serf, who had as yet no expectation, no idea even of his freedom, may be filled. Was not this, perhaps, what Konstantin Aksakov[3]

[3]A Russian novelist of the early nineteenth century (1791-1859).

meant when he spoke of the high degree of culture of our peasantry?

And when I got down off the bed and looked around me, I remember I suddenly felt that I could look at these unhappy creatures with quite different eyes, and that suddenly by some miracle all hatred and anger had vanished utterly from my heart. I walked about, looking into the faces that I met. That shaven peasant, branded on his face as a criminal, bawling° his hoarse, drunken song, may be that very Marey; I cannot look into his heart.

I met M. again that evening. Poor fellow! he could have no memories of Russian peasants, and no other view of these people but: *"Je hais ces brigands!"* Yes, the Polish prisoners had more to bear than I.

Do especially Questions 20, 75, 103, 133, 146, and 149. Consult the Short Story Model on page 156.

An Honest Thief

FYODOR DOSTOEVSKY Translated by Constance Garnett

One morning, just as I was about to set off to my office, Agravena, my cook, washerwoman, and housekeeper, came in to me and, to my surprise, entered into conversation.

She had always been such a silent, simple creature that, except for her daily inquiry about dinner, she had not uttered a word for the last six years. I, at least, had heard nothing else from her.

"Here I have come in to have a word with you, sir," she began abruptly; "you really ought to let the little room."

"Which little room?"

"Why, the one next the kitchen, to be sure."

Reprinted with permission of The Macmillan Company from *An Honest Thief and Other Stories* by Fyodor Dostoevsky. Translated by Constance Garnett. Printed in Great Britain. Reprinted also by permission of William Heinemann Ltd.

"What for?"

"What for? Why, because folks do take in lodgers, to be sure."

"But who would take it?"

"Who would take it? Why, a lodger would take it, to be sure."

"But, my good woman, one could not put a bedstead in it; there wouldn't be room to move! Who could live in it?"

"Who wants to live there? As long as he has a place to sleep in. Why, he would live in the window."

"In what window?"

"In what window? As though you didn't know! The one in the passage, to be sure. He would sit there, sewing or doing anything else. Maybe he would sit on a chair, too. He's got a chair; and he has a table, too; he's got everything."

"Who is 'he,' then?"

"Oh, a good man, a man of experience. I will cook for him. And I'll ask him three roubles[1] a month for his board and lodging."

After prolonged efforts I succeeded at last in learning from Agravena that an elderly man had somehow managed to persuade her to admit him into the kitchen as a lodger and boarder. Any notion Agravena took into her head had to be carried out; if not, I knew she would give me no peace. When anything was not to her liking, she at once began to brood, and sank into a deep dejection that would last for a fortnight° or three weeks. During that period my dinners were spoiled, my linen was mislaid, my floors went unscrubbed; in short, I had a great deal to put up with. I had observed long ago that this inarticulate woman was incapable of conceiving a project, of originating an idea of her own. But if anything like a notion or a project was by some means put into her feeble brain, to prevent its being carried out meant, for a time, her moral assassination. And so, as I cared more for my peace of mind than for anything else, I forthwith consented.

[1]About seventy-five cents.

"Has he a passport[2] anyway, or something of the sort?"

"To be sure, he has. He is a good man, a man of experience; three roubles he's promised to pay."

The very next day the new lodger made his appearance in my modest bachelor quarters; but I was not put out by this, indeed I was inwardly pleased. I lead as a rule a very lonely hermit's existence. I have scarcely any friends; I hardly ever go anywhere. As I had spent ten years never coming out of my shell, I had, of course, grown used to solitude. But another ten or fifteen years or more of the same solitary existence, with the same Agravena, in the same bachelor quarters, was in truth a somewhat cheerless prospect. And therefore a new inmate, if well-behaved, was a heaven-sent blessing.

Agravena had spoken truly: my lodger was certainly a man of experience. From his passport it appeared that he was an old soldier, a fact which I should have known indeed from his face. An old soldier is easily recognized. Astafy Ivanovitch was a favorable specimen of his class. We got on very well together. What was best of all, Astafy Ivanovitch would sometimes tell a story, describing some incident in his own life. In the perpetual boredom of my existence such a storyteller was a veritable° treasure. One day he told me one of these stories. It made an impression on me. The following event was what led to it.

I was left alone in the flat; both Astafy and Agravena were out on business of their own. All of a sudden I heard from the inner room somebody—I fancied a stranger—come in; I went out; there actually was a stranger in the passage, a short fellow wearing no overcoat in spite of the cold autumn weather.

"What do you want?"

"Does a clerk called Alexandrov live here?"

"Nobody of that name here, brother. Good-bye."

"Why, the dvornik[3] told me it was here," said my visitor, cautiously retiring toward the door.

"Be off, be off, brother, get along."

[2] A passport was required of everyone, natives as well as foreigners.
[3] Lodge-keeper; concierge.

Next day after dinner, while Astafy Ivanovitch was fitting on a coat which he was altering for me, again someone came into the passage. I half opened the door.

Before my very eyes my yesterday's visitor, with perfect composure,° took my wadded greatcoat from the peg and, stuffing it under his arm, darted out of the flat. Agravena stood all the time staring at him, agape with astonishment and doing nothing for the protection of my property. Astafy Ivanovitch flew in pursuit of the thief and ten minutes later came back out of breath and empty-handed. He had vanished completely.

"Well, there's a piece of luck, Astafy Ivanovitch!"

"It's a good job your cloak is left! Or he would have put you in a plight, the thief!"

But the whole incident had so impressed Astafy Ivanovitch that I forgot the theft as I looked at him. He could not get over it. Every minute or two he would drop the work upon which he was engaged, and would describe over again how it had all happened, how he had been standing, how the greatcoat had been taken down before his very eyes, not a yard away, and how it had come to pass that he could not catch the thief. Then he would sit down to his work again, then leave it once more, and at last I saw him go down to the dvornik to tell him all about it, and to upbraid° him for letting such a thing happen in his domain. Then he came back again and began scolding Agravena. Then he sat down to his work again, and long afterwards he was still muttering to himself how it had all happened, how he stood there and I was here, how before our eyes, not a yard away, the thief took the coat off the peg, and so on. In short, though Astafy Ivanovitch understood his business, he was a terrible slow-coach and busybody.

"He's made fools of us, Astafy Ivanovitch," I said to him in the evening, as I gave him a glass of tea. I wanted to while away the time by recalling the story of the lost greatcoat, the frequent repetition of which, together with the great earnestness of the speaker, was beginning to become very amusing.

"Fools, indeed, sir! Even though it is no business of

mine, I am put out. It makes me angry though it is not my coat that was lost. To my thinking there is no vermin in the world worse than a thief. Another takes what you can spare, but a thief steals the work of your hands, the sweat of your brow, your time . . . Ugh, it's nasty! One can't speak of it! It's too vexing. How is it you don't feel the loss of your property, sir?"

"Yes, you are right, Astafy Ivanovitch, better if the thing had been burnt; it's annoying to let the thief have it, it's disagreeable."

"Disagreeable! I should think so! Yet, to be sure, there are thieves and thieves. And I have happened, sir, to come across an honest thief."

"An honest thief? But how can a thief be honest, Astafy Ivanovitch?"

"There you are right indeed, sir. How can a thief be honest? There are none such. I only meant to say that he was an honest man, sure enough, and yet he stole. I was simply sorry for him."

"Why, how was that, Astafy Ivanovitch?"

"It was about two years ago, sir. I had been nearly a year out of a place, and just before I lost my place I made the acquaintance of a poor lost creature. We got acquainted in a public-house. He was a drunkard, a vagrant,° a beggar, he had been in a situation of some sort, but from his drinking habits he had lost his work. Such a ne'er-do-well! God only knows what he had on! Often you wouldn't be sure if he'd a shirt under his coat; everything he could lay his hands upon he would drink away. But he was not one to quarrel; he was a quiet fellow. A soft, good-natured chap. And he'd never ask, he was ashamed; but you could see for yourself the poor fellow wanted a drink, and you would stand it for him. And so we got friendly, that's to say, he stuck to me . . . It was all one to me. And what a man he was, to be sure! Like a little dog he would follow me; wherever I went there he would be; and all that after our first meeting, and he as thin as a thread-paper! At first it was 'let me stay the night'; well, I let him stay.

"I looked at his passport, too; the man was all right.

"Well, the next day it was all the same story, and then the third day he came again and sat all day in the window and stayed the night. Well, thinks I, he is sticking to me; give him food and drink and shelter at night, too—here am I, a poor man, and a hanger-on to keep as well! And before he came to me, he used to go in the same way to a government clerk's; he attached himself to him; they were always drinking together; but he, through trouble of some sort, drank himself into the grave. My man was called Emelyan Ilyitch. I pondered and pondered what I was to do with him. To drive him away I was ashamed. I was sorry for him; such a pitiful, God-forsaken creature I never did set eyes on. And not a word said, either; he does not ask, but just sits there and looks into your eyes like a dog. To think what drinking will bring a man down to!

"I keep asking myself how I am to say to him: 'You must be moving, Emelyanoushka, there's nothing for you here, you've come to the wrong place. I shall soon not have a bite for myself, how am I to keep you too?'

"I sat and wondered what he'd do when I said that to him. And I seemed to see how he'd stare at me, if he were to hear me say that, how long he would sit and not understand a word of it. And when it did get home to him at last, how he would get up from the window, would take up his bundle—I can see it now, the red-check handkerchief full of holes, with God knows what wrapped up in it, which he had always with him, and then how he would set his shabby old coat to rights, so that it would look decent and keep him warm, so that no holes would be seen—he was a man of delicate feelings! And how he'd open the door and go out with tears in his eyes. Well, there's no letting a man go to ruin like that . . . One's sorry for him.

"And then, again, I think, how am I off myself? Wait a bit, Emelyanoushka, says I to myself, you've not long to feast with me: I shall soon be going away and then you will not find me.

"Well, sir, our family made a move; and Alexander Filimonovitch, my master (now desceased, God rest his soul!) said, 'I am thoroughly satisfied with you, Astafy Ivanovitch;

when we come back from the country we will take you on again.' I had been butler with them; a nice gentleman he was, but he died that same year. Well, after seeing him off, I took my belongings, what little money I had, and I thought I'd have a rest for a time, so I went to an old woman I knew, and I took a corner in her room. There was only one corner free in it. She had been a nurse, so now she had a pension and a room of her own. Well, now good-bye, Emelyanoushka, thinks I, you won't find me now, my boy.

"And what do you think, sir? I had gone out to see a man I knew, and when I came back in the evening, the first thing I saw was Emelyanoushka! There he was, sitting on my box and his checked bundle beside him; he was sitting in his ragged old coat, waiting for me. And to while away the time he had borrowed a church book from the old lady, and was holding it wrong side upwards. He'd scented° me out! My heart sank! Well, thinks I, there's no help for it— why didn't I turn him out at first? So I asked him straight off: 'Have you brought your passport, Emelyanoushka?'

"I sat down on the spot, sir, and began to ponder: will a vagabond like that be very much trouble to me? And on thinking it over it seemed he would not be much trouble. He must be fed, I thought. Well, a bit of bread in the morning, and to make it go down better I'll buy him an onion. At midday I should have to give him another bit of bread and an onion; and in the evening, onion again with kvass,[4] with some more bread if he wanted it. And if some cabbage soup were to come our way, then we should both have had our fill. I am no great eater myself, and a drinking man, as we all know, never eats; all he wants is herb-brandy or green vodka. He'll ruin me with his drinking, I thought, but then another idea came into my head, sir, and took great hold on me. So much so that if Emelyanoushka had gone away I should have felt that I had nothing to live for, I do believe . . . I determined on the spot to be a father and guardian to him. I'll keep him from ruin, I thought, I'll wean him from the glass! You wait a bit, thought I; very

[4] A Russian fermented drink like sour beer, made from rye, barley, or rye bread.

well, Emelyanoushka, you may stay, only you must behave yourself; you must obey orders.

"Well, thinks I to myself, I'll begin by training him to work of some sort, but not all at once, let him enjoy himself a little first, and I'll look round and find something you are fit for, Emelyanoushka. For every sort of work a man needs a special ability, you know, sir. And I began to watch him on the quiet; I soon saw Emelyanoushka was a desperate character. I began, sir, with a word of advice: I said this and that to him. 'Emelyanoushka,' said I, 'you ought to take a thought and mend your ways. Have done with drinking! Just look what rags you go about in: that old coat of yours, if I may make bold to say so, is fit for nothing but a sieve. A pretty state of things! It's time to draw the line, sure enough.' Emelyanoushka sat and listened to me with his head hanging down. Would you believe it, sir? It had come to such a pass with him, he'd lost his tongue through drink and could not speak a word of sense. Talk to him of cucumbers and he'd answer back about beans! He would listen and listen to me and then heave such a sigh. 'What are you sighing for, Emelyan Ilyitch?' I asked him.

"'Oh, nothing; don't you mind me, Astafy Ivanovitch. Do you know there were two women fighting in the street today, Astafy Ivanovitch? One upset the other woman's basket of cranberries by accident.'

"'Well, what of that?'

"'And the second one upset the other's cranberries on purpose and trampled them under foot, too.'

"'Well, and what of it, Emelyan Ilyitch?'

"'Why, nothing, Astafy Ivanovitch, I just mentioned it.'

"'"Nothing, I just mentioned it!"' Emelyanoushka, my boy, I thought, you've squandered and drunk away your brains!

"'And do you know, a gentleman dropped a money-note on the pavement in Gorohovy Street; no, it was Sadovy Street. And a peasant saw it and said, "That's my luck"; and at the same time another man saw it and said, "No, it's my bit of luck. I saw it before you did."'

"'Well, Emelyan Ilyitch?'

" 'And the fellows had a fight over it, Astafy Ivanovitch. But a policeman came up, took away the note, gave it back to the gentleman and threatened to take up both men.'

" 'Well, but what of that? What is there edifying about it, Emelyanoushka?'

" 'Why, nothing, to be sure. Folks laughed, Astafy Ivanovitch.'

" 'Ach, Emelyanoushka! What do the folks matter? You've sold your soul for a brass farthing! But do you know what I have to tell you, Emelyan Ilyitch?'

" 'What, Astafy Ivanovitch?'

" 'Take a job of some sort, that's what you must do. For the hundredth time I say to you, set to work, have some mercy on yourself!'

" 'What could I set to, Astafy Ivanovitch? I don't know what job I could set to, and there is no one who will take me on, Astafy Ivanovitch.'

" 'That's how you came to be turned off, Emelyanoushka, you drinking man!'

" 'And do you know Vlass, the waiter, was sent for to the office today, Astafy Ivanovitch?'

" 'Why did they send for him, Emelyanoushka?' I asked.

" 'I could not say why, Astafy Ivanovitch. I suppose they wanted him there, and that's why they sent for him.'

"A-ach, thought I, we are in a bad way, poor Emelyanoushka! The Lord is chastising us for our sins. Well, sir, what is one to do with such a man?

"But a cunning fellow he was, and no mistake. He'd listen and listen to me, but at last I suppose he got sick of it. As soon as he sees I am beginning to get angry, he'd pick up his old coat and out he'd slip and leave no trace. He'd wander about all day and come back at night drunk. Where he got the money from, the Lord only knows; I had no hand in that.

" 'No,' said I, 'Emelyan Ilyitch, you'll come to a bad end. Give over drinking, mind what I say now, give it up! Next time you come home in liquor, you can spend the night on the stairs. I won't let you in!'

"After hearing that threat, Emelyanoushka sat at home

that day and the next; but on the third he slipped off again.
I waited and waited; he didn't come back. Well, at last, I
don't mind owning, I was in a fright, and I felt for the man
too. What have I done to him? I thought. I've scared him
away. Where's the poor fellow gone to now? He'll get lost
maybe. Lord have mercy upon us!

"Night came on; he did not come. In the morning I went
out into the porch; I looked, and if he hadn't gone to sleep
in the porch! There he was with his head on the step, and
chilled to the marrow of his bones.

" 'What next, Emelyanoushka, God have mercy on you!
Where will you get to next?'

" 'Why, you were—sort of—angry with me, Astafy Ivanovitch, the other day; you were vexed and promised to put
me to sleep in the porch, so I didn't—sort of—venture to
come in, Astafy Ivanovitch, and so I lay down here . . .'

"I did feel angry, and sorry too.

" 'Surely you might undertake some other duty, Emelyanoushka, instead of lying here guarding the steps,' I said.

" 'Why, what other duty, Astafy Ivanovitch?'

" 'You lost soul'—I was in such a rage, I called him that—
'if you could but learn tailoring-work! Look at your old
rag of a coat! It's not enough to have it in tatters, here you
are sweeping the steps with it! You might take a needle and
boggle° up your rags, as decency demands. Ah, you
drunken man!'

"What do you think, sir? He actually did take a needle.
Of course I said it in jest, but he was so scared he set to
work. He took off his coat and began threading the needle.
I watched him; as you may well guess, his eyes were all
red and bleary, and his hands were all of a shake. He kept
shoving and shoving the thread and could not get it through
the eye of the needle; he kept screwing his eyes up and
wetting the thread and twisting it in his fingers—it was no
good! He gave it up and looked at me.

" 'Well,' said I, 'this is a nice way to treat me! If there
had been folks by to see, I don't know what I should have
done! Why, you simple fellow, I said it to you in joke, as
a reproach. Give over your nonsense. God bless you! Sit

quiet and don't put me to shame, don't sleep on my stairs
and make a laughing-stock of me.'

"'Why, what am I to do, Astafy Ivanovitch? I know very
well I am a drunkard and good for nothing! I can do nothing but vex you, my bene-benefactor°....'

"And at that his blue lips began all of a sudden to quiver,
and a tear ran down his white cheeks and trembled on his
stubbly chin, and then poor Emelyanoushka burst into a
regular flood of tears. Mercy on us! I felt as though a knife
were thrust into my heart! The sensitive creature! I'd never
have expected it! Who could have guessed it? No, Emelyanoushka, thought I, I shall give you up altogether. You
can go your way like the rubbish you are.

"Well, sir, why make a long story of it? And the whole
affair is so trifling; it's not worth wasting words upon. Why,
you, for instance, sir, would not have given a thought to it,
but I would have given a great deal — if I had a great deal
to give — that it never should have happened at all.

"I had a pair of riding breeches by me, sir, deuce take
them, fine, first-rate riding breeches they were, too, blue
with a check on it. They'd been ordered by a gentleman
from the country, but he would not have them after all; said
they were not full enough, so they were left on my hands.
It struck me they were worth something. At the second-
hand dealer's I ought to get five silver roubles for them, or
if not I could turn them into two pairs of trousers for Petersburg gentlemen and have a piece over for a waistcoat for
myself. Of course for poor people like us everything comes
in. And it happened just then that Emelyanoushka was
having a sad time of it. There he sat day after day; he did
not drink, not a drop passed his lips, but he sat and moped
like an owl. It was sad to see him — he just sat and brooded.
Well, thought I, either you've not got a copper to spend, my
lad, or else you're turning over a new leaf of yourself,
you've given it up, you've listened to reason. Well, sir,
that's how it was with us; and just then came a holiday. I
went to vespers;° when I came home I found Emelyanoushka sitting in the window, drunk and rocking to and fro.

"Ah! so that's what you've been up to, my lad! And I

went to get something out of my chest. And when I looked in, the breeches were not there . . . I rummaged here and there; they'd vanished. When I'd ransacked everywhere and saw they were not there, something seemed to stab me to the heart. I ran first to the old dame and began accusing her; of Emelyanoushka I'd not the faintest suspicion, though there was cause for it in his sitting there drunk.

" 'No,' said the old body, 'God be with you, my fine gentleman, what good are riding breeches to me? Am I going to wear such things? Why, a skirt I had I lost the other day through a fellow of your sort . . . I know nothing; I can tell you nothing about it,' she said.

" 'Who has been here, who has been in?' I asked.

" 'Why, nobody has been, my good sir,' says she; 'I've been here all the while; Emelyan Ilyitch went out and came back again; there he sits, ask him.'

" 'Emelyanoushka,' said I, 'have you taken those new riding breeches for anything; you remember the pair I made for that gentleman from the country?'

" 'No, Astafy Ivanovitch,' said he; 'I've not—sort of—touched them.'

"I was in a state! I hunted high and low for them—they were nowhere to be found. And Emelyanoushka sits there rocking himself to and fro. I was squatting on my heels facing him and bending over the chest, and all at once I stole a glance at him . . . Alack, I thought; my heart suddenly grew hot within me and I felt myself flushing up too. And suddenly Emelyanoushka looked at me.

" 'No, Astafy Ivanovitch,' said he, 'those riding breeches of yours, maybe, you are thinking, maybe, I took them, but I never touched them.'

" 'But what can have become of them, Emelyan Ilyitch?'

" 'No, Astafy Ivanovitch,' said he, 'I've never seen them.'

" 'Why, Emelyan Ilyitch, I suppose they've run off themselves, eh?'

" 'Maybe they have, Astafy Ivanovitch.'

"When I heard him say that, I got up at once, went up to him, lighted the lamp and sat down to work to my sewing. I was altering a waistcoat for a clerk who lived below us.

And wasn't there a burning pain and ache in my breast! I shouldn't have minded so much if I had put all the clothes I had in the fire. Emelyanoushka seemed to have an inkling of what a rage I was in. When a man is guilty, you know, sir, he scents trouble far off, like the birds of the air before a storm.

"'Do you know what, Astafy Ivanovitch,' Emelyanoushka began, and his poor old voice was shaking as he said the words, 'Antip Prohoritch, the apothecary, married the coachman's wife this morning, who died the other day—'

"I did give him a look, sir, a nasty look it was; Emelyanoushka understood it too. I saw him get up, go to the bed, and begin to rummage there for something. I waited— he was busy there a long time and kept muttering all the while, 'No, not there, where can the blessed things have got to?' I waited to see what he'd do; I saw him creep under the bed on all fours. I couldn't bear it any longer. 'What are you crawling about under the bed for, Emelyan Ilyitch?' said I.

"'Looking for the breeches, Astafy Ivanovitch. Maybe they've dropped down there somewhere.'

"'Why should you try to help a poor simple man like me,' said I, 'crawling on your knees for nothing, sir?'—I called him that in my vexation.°

"'Oh, never mind, Astafy Ivanovitch, I'll just look. They'll turn up, maybe, somewhere.'

"'H'm,' said I, 'look here, Emelyan Ilyitch!'

"'What is it, Astafy Ivanovitch?' said he.

"'Haven't you simply stolen them from me like a thief and a robber, in return for the bread and salt you've eaten here?' said I.

"I felt so angry, sir, at seeing him fooling about on his knees before me.

"'No, Astafy Ivanovitch.'

"And he stayed lying as he was on his face under the bed. A long time he lay there and then at last he crept out. I looked at him, and the man was as white as a sheet. He stood up, and sat down near me in the window and sat so for some ten minutes.

"'No, Astafy Ivanovitch,' he said, and all at once he stood up and came towards me, and I can see him now; he looked dreadful. 'No, Astafy Ivanovitch,' said he, 'I never— sort of—touched your breeches.'

"He was all of a shake, poking himself in the chest with a trembling finger, and his poor old voice shook so that I was frightened, sir, and sat as though I was rooted to the window-seat.

"'Well, Emelyan Ilyitch,' said I, 'as you will, forgive me if I, in my foolishness, have accused you unjustly. As for the breeches, let them go hang; we can live without them. We've still our hands, thank God; we need not go thieving or begging from some other poor man; we'll earn our bread.'

"Emelyanoushka heard me out and went on standing there before me. I looked up, and he had sat down. And there he sat all evening without stirring. At last I lay down to sleep. Emelyanoushka went on sitting in the same place. When I looked out in the morning, he was lying curled up in his old coat on the bare floor; he felt too crushed even to come to bed. Well, sir, I felt no more liking for the fellow from that day, in fact for the first few days I hated him. I felt, as one may say, as though my own son had robbed me, and done me a deadly hurt. Ach, thought I, Emelyanoushka, Emelyanoushka! And Emelyanoushka, sir, went on drinking for a whole fortnight without stopping. He was drunk all the time, and regularly besotted.° He went out in the morning and came back late at night, and for a whole fortnight I didn't get a word out of him. It was as though grief was gnawing at his heart, or as though he wanted to do for himself completely. At last he stopped; he must have come to the end of all he'd got, and then he sat in the window again. I remember he sat there without speaking for three days and three nights; all of a sudden I saw that he was crying. He was just sitting there, sir, and crying like anything; a perfect stream, as though he didn't know how his tears were flowing. And it's a sad thing, sir, to see a grownup man and an old man, too, crying from woe and grief.

"'What's the matter, Emelyanoushka?' said I.

"He began to tremble so that he shook all over. I spoke to him for the first time since that evening.

"'Nothing, Astafy Ivanovitch.'

"'God be with you, Emelyanoushka, what's lost is lost. Why are you moping° about like this?' I felt sorry for him.

"'Oh, nothing, Astafy Ivanovitch, it's no matter. I want to find some work to do, Astafy Ivanovitch.'

"'And what sort of work, pray, Emelyanoushka?'

"'Why, any sort; perhaps I could find a situation such as I used to have. I've been already to ask Fedosay Ivanitch. I don't like to be a burden on you, Astafy Ivanovitch. If I can find a situation, Astafy Ivanovitch, then I'll pay you it all back, and make you a return for all your hospitality.'

"'Enough, Emelyanoushka, enough; let bygones be bygones—and no more to be said about it. Let us go on as we used to do before.'

"'No, Astafy Ivanovitch, you, maybe, think—but I never touched your riding breeches.'

"'Well, have it your own way, God be with you, Emelyanoushka.'

"'No, Astafy Ivanovitch, I can't go on living with you, that's clear. You must excuse me, Astafy Ivanovitch.'

"'Why, God bless you, Emelyan Ilyitch, who's offending you and driving you out of the place—am I doing it?'

"'No, it's not the proper thing for me to live with you like this, Astafy Ivanovitch. I'd better be going.'

"He was so hurt, it seemed, he stuck to his point. I looked at him, and sure enough, up he got and pulled his old coat over his shoulders.

"'But where are you going, Emelyan Ilyitch? Listen to reason: what are you about? Where are you off to?'

"'No, good-bye, Astafy Ivanovitch, don't keep me now'—and he was blubbering again—'I'd better be going. You're not the same now.'

"'Not the same as what? I am the same. But you'll be lost by yourself like a poor helpless babe, Emelyan Ilyitch.'

"'No, Astafy Ivanovitch, when you go out now, you look at your chest and it makes me cry to see it, Astafy Ivanovitch. You'd better let me go, Astafy Ivanovitch, and forgive me all the trouble I've given you while I've been living with you.'

"Well, sir, the man went away. I waited for a day; I expected he'd be back in the evening—no. Next day no sign of him, nor the third day either. I began to get frightened; I was so worried, I couldn't drink, I couldn't eat, I couldn't sleep. The fellow had quite disarmed me. On the fourth day I went out to look for him; I peeped into all the taverns, to inquire for him—but no, Emelyanoushka was lost. 'Have you managed to keep yourself alive, Emelyanoushka?' I wondered. 'Perhaps he is lying dead under some hedge, poor drunkard, like a sodden° log.' I went home more dead than alive. Next day I went out to look for him again. And I kept cursing myself that I'd been such a fool as to let the man go off by himself. On the fifth day it was a holiday—in the early morning I heard the door creak. I looked up and there was my Emelyanoushka coming in. His face was blue and his hair was covered with dirt as though he'd been sleeping in the street; he was as thin as a match. He took off his old coat, sat down on the chest, and looked at me. I was delighted to see him, but I felt overtaken in some sin, as true as I am here, sir, I'd have died like a dog before I'd have come back. But Emelyanoushka did come back. And a sad thing it was, sure enough, to see a man sunk so low. I began to look after him, to talk kindly to him, to comfort him.

"'Well, Emelyanoushka,' said I, 'I am glad you've come back. Had you been away much longer I should have gone to look for you in the taverns again today. Are you hungry?'

"'No, Astafy Ivanovitch.'

"'Come, now, aren't you really? Here, brother, is some cabbage soup left over from yesterday; there was meat in it; it is good stuff. And here is some bread and onion. Come, eat it, it'll do you no harm.'

"I made him eat it, and I saw at once that the man had not tasted food for maybe three days—he was as hungry as a wolf. So it was hunger that had driven him to me. My heart was melted looking at the poor fellow. 'Let me run to the tavern,' thought I, 'I'll get something to ease his heart, and then we'll make an end of it. I've no more anger in my heart against you, Emelyanoushka!' I brought him some vodka. 'Here, Emelyan Ilyitch, let us have a drink for the holiday. Like a drink? And it will do you good.' He held out his hand, held it out greedily; he was just taking it, and then he stopped himself. But a minute after, I saw him take it, and lift it to his mouth, spilling it on his sleeve. But though he got it to his lips, he set it down on the table again.

"'What is it, Emelyanoushka?'

"'Nothing, Astafy Ivanovitch, I — sort of — '

"'Won't you drink it?'

"'Well, Astafy Ivanovitch, I'm not — sort of — going to drink any more, Astafy Ivanovitch.'

"'Do you mean you've given it up altogether, Emelyanoushka, or are you only not going to drink today?'

"He did not answer. A minute later I saw him rest his head on his hand.

"'What's the matter, Emelyanoushka, are you ill?'

"'Why, yes, Astafy Ivanovitch, I don't feel well.'

"I took him and laid him down on the bed. I saw that he really was ill: his head was burning hot and he was shivering with fever. I sat by him all day; towards night he was worse. I mixed him some oil and onion and kvass and bread broken up.

"'Come, eat some of this,' said I, 'and perhaps you'll be better.' He shook his head. 'No,' said he, 'I won't have any dinner today, Astafy Ivanovitch.'

"I made some tea for him; I quite flustered our old woman — he was no better. Well, thinks I, it's a bad outlook! The third morning I went for a medical gentleman. There was one I knew living close by, Kostopravov by name. I'd made his acquaintance when I was in service with the Bosomyagins; he'd attended me. The doctor came and looked at him. 'He's in a bad way,' said he, 'it was no use sending for me. But if you like I can give him a powder.' Well, I didn't give him a powder. I thought that's just the doctor's little game; and then the fifth day came.

"He lay, sir, dying before my eyes. I sat in the window with my work in my hands. The old woman was heating the stove. We were all silent. My heart was simply breaking over him, the good-for-nothing fellow; I felt as if it were a son of my own I was losing. I knew that Emelyanoushka was looking at me. I'd seen the man all the day long making up his mind to say something and not daring to.

"At last I looked up at him; I saw such misery in the poor fellow's eyes. He had kept them fixed on me, but when he saw that I was looking at him, he looked down at once.

"'Astafy Ivanovitch.'

"'What is it, Emelyanoushka?'

"'If you were to take my old coat to a second-hand dealer's, how much do you think they'd give you for it, Astafy Ivanovitch?'

"'There's no knowing how much they'd give. Maybe they would give me a rouble for it, Emelyan Ilyitch.'

"But if I had taken it, they wouldn't have given a farthing⁵ for it, but would have laughed in my face for bringing such a trumpery° thing. I simply said that to comfort the poor fellow, knowing the simpleton he was.

"'But I was thinking, Astafy Ivanovitch, they might give you three roubles for it; it's made of cloth, Astafy Ivanovitch. How could they give only one rouble for a cloth coat?'

"'I don't know, Emelyan Ilyitch,' said I, 'if you are thinking of taking it you should certainly ask three roubles to begin with.'

"Emelyanoushka was silent for a time, and then he addressed me again—

"'Astafy Ivanovitch.'

"'What is it, Emelyanoushka?' I asked.

"'Sell my coat when I die, and don't bury me in it. I can lie as well without it; and it's a thing of some value—it might come in useful.'

"I can't tell you how it made my heart ache to hear him. I saw that the death agony was coming on him. We were

⁵Something less than a penny.

silent again for a bit. So an hour passed by. I looked at him again: he was still staring at me, and when he met my eyes he looked down again.

"'Do you want some water to drink, Emelyan Ilyitch?' I asked.

"'Give me some, God bless you, Astafy Ivanovitch.'

"I gave him a drink.

"'Thank you, Astafy Ivanovitch,' said he.

"'Is there anything else you would like, Emelyanoushka?'

"'No, Astafy Ivanovitch, there's nothing I want, but I—sort—of—'

"'What?'

"'I only—'

"'What is it, Emelyanoushka?'

"'Those riding breeches—it was—sort of—I who took them—Astafy Ivanovitch.'

"'Well, God forgive you, Emelyanoushka,' said I, 'you poor, sorrowful creature. Depart in peace!'

"And I was choking myself, sir, and the tears were in my eyes. I turned aside for a moment.

"'Astafy Ivanovitch—'

"I saw Emelyanoushka wanted to tell me something; he was trying to sit up, trying to speak, and mumbling something. He flushed red all over suddenly, looked at me ... then I saw him turn white again, whiter and whiter, and he seemed to sink away all in a minute. His head fell back, he drew one breath, and gave up his soul to God."

Do especially Questions 11, 20, 45, 73, 83, 84, 90, 91, 96, 99, 102, 109, 112, 113, 116, 148, and 150. Consult the Short Story Model on page 156.

FYODOR MIKHAILOVICH DOSTOEVSKY   *1821-1881*

At an early age Dostoevsky became familiar with suffering and death, for he lived with his family on the grounds of Mariinsky Hospital for the poor where his father was a physician. In 1837 he entered St. Petersburg School for Military Engineering, but found his four years there very depressing. He gave up his job as draftsman in 1844 and devoted himself entirely to writing.

Dostoevsky's first novel, *Poor Folk*, gained for him considerable recognition. Suffering from epilepsy all his life, Dostoevsky no doubt faced the most dramatic episode in his life in 1849 when, being arrested on the charge of belonging to a secret organization of young radical socialists, he was brought before a firing squad with nineteen friends. Only at the last minute was the sentence of capital punishment commuted to imprisonment in Siberia. In *Notes from the House of the Dead* he recounts his horrible experiences during the four years he was imprisoned. Upon leaving the "House of the Dead," he went to serve five years in the army. Finally after nine years, he returned to St. Petersburg and resumed his writing. Editing monthly magazines and writing novels, Fyodor worked under unending pressure, for he constantly needed money. In 1868 he fled to Germany to escape the bill collectors. During this period his second wife, Anna, who had once been his stenographer, helped him through a severe crisis in which he took to gambling. Returning to St. Petersburg in 1871, Dostoevsky wrote *Crime and Punishment* (1866), *The Idiot* (1869), *The Possessed* (1871), and *The Brothers Karamazov* (1880). Fyodor Dostoevsky constantly raises profound questions in his psychological probings. He shows us that the same man is capable of both the most sublime virtue and the most degrading crimes.

How Much Land Does a Man Need?

LEO TOLSTOY Translated by Louise and Aylmer Maude

An elder sister came to visit her younger sister in the country. The elder was married to a tradesman in town, the younger to a peasant in the village. As the sisters sat over their tea talking, the elder began to boast of the advantages of town life: saying how comfortably they lived there, how well they dressed, what fine clothes her children wore, what good things they ate and drank, and how she went to the theater, promenades,° and entertainments.

"How Much Land Does a Man Need?" from *Twenty-three Tales* by Leo Tolstoy, translated by A. Maude. Reprinted by permission of Oxford University Press, London.

The younger sister was piqued,° and in turn disparaged°
the life of a tradesman, and stood up for that of a peasant.

"I would not change my way of life for yours," she said.
"We may live roughly, but at least we are free from anxiety.
You live in better style than we do, but though you often
earn more than you need, you are very likely to lose all
you have. You know the proverb, 'Loss and gain are
brothers twain.' It often happens that people who are
wealthy one day are begging their bread the next. Our
way is safer. Though a peasant's life is not a fat one, it is a
long one. We shall never grow rich, but we shall always
have enough to eat."

The elder sister said sneeringly:°

"Enough? Yes, if you like to share with the pigs and the
calves! What do you know of elegance or manners! However much your good man may slave, you will die as you
are living—on a dung-heap—and your children the same."

"Well, what of that?" replied the younger. "Of course
our work is rough and coarse. But, on the other hand, it is
sure, and we need not bow to anyone. But you, in your
towns, are surrounded by temptations; today all may be
right, but tomorrow the Evil One may tempt your husband
with cards, wine, or women, and all will go to ruin. Don't
such things happen often enough?"

Pahom, the master of the house, was lying on the top of
the stove[1] and he listened to the women's chatter.

"It is perfectly true," thought he. "Busy as we are from
childhood tilling Mother Earth, we peasants have no time
to let any nonsense settle in our heads. Our only trouble
is that we haven't land enough. If I had plenty of land, I
shouldn't fear the Devil himself!"

The women finished their tea, chatted a while about
dress, and then cleared away the tea things and lay down
to sleep.

But the Devil had been sitting behind the stove, and had
heard all that was said. He was pleased that the peasant's
wife had led her husband into boasting, and that he had

[1] A large stove built of brick was used in most peasant homes. Its wide
flat top made a warm place for the master of the house to sleep.

said that if he had plenty of land he would not fear the Devil himself.

"All right," thought the Devil. "We will have a tussle.° I'll give you land enough; and by means of that land I will get you into my power."

Close to the village there lived a lady, a small landowner who had an estate of about three hundred acres. She had always lived on good terms with the peasants until she engaged as her steward° an old soldier, who took to burdening the people with fines. However careful Pahom tried to be, it happened again and again that now a horse of his got among the lady's oats, now a cow strayed into her garden, now his calves found their way into her meadows — and he always had to pay a fine.

Pahom paid up, but grumbled, and going home in a temper, was rough with his family. All through that summer, Pahom had much trouble because of this steward, and he was even glad when winter came and the cattle had to be stabled. Though he grudged the fodder° when they could no longer graze on the pasture land, at least he was free from anxiety about them.

In the winter the news got about that the lady was going to sell her land and that the keeper of the inn on the highroad was bargaining for it. When the peasants heard this they were very much alarmed.

"Well," thought they, "if the innkeeper gets the land, he will worry us with fines worse than the lady's steward. We all depend on that estate."

So the peasants went on behalf of their commune,[2] and asked the lady not to sell the land to the innkeeper, offering her a better price for it themselves. The lady agreed to let them have it. Then the peasants tried to arrange for the commune to buy the whole estate, so that it might be held by them all in common. They met twice to discuss it, but could not settle the matter; the Evil One sowed discord among them and they could not agree. So they decided to

[2]A small unit of government in Russia in which the people share common property in the village.

buy the land individually, each according to his means; and the lady agreed to this plan as she had to the other.

Presently Pahom heard that a neighbor of his was buying fifty acres, and that the lady had consented to accept one half in cash and to wait a year for the other half. Pahom felt envious.

"Look at that," thought he, "the land is all being sold, and I shall get none of it." So he spoke to his wife.

"Other people are buying," said he, "and we must also buy twenty acres or so. Life is becoming impossible. That steward is simply crushing us with his fines."

So they put their heads together and considered how they could manage to buy it. They had one hundred roubles[3] laid by. They sold a colt and one half of their bees, hired out one of their sons as a laborer and took his wages in advance; borrowed the rest from a brother-in-law, and so scraped together half the purchase money.

Having done this, Pahom chose out a farm of forty acres, some of it wooded, and went to the lady to bargain for it. They came to an agreement, and he shook hands with her upon it and paid her a deposit in advance. Then they went to town and signed the deeds; he paying half the price down, and undertaking to pay the remainder within two years.

So now Pahom had land of his own. He borrowed seed, and sowed it on the land he had bought. The harvest was a good one, and within a year he had managed to pay off his debts both to the lady and to his brother-in-law. So he became a landowner, plowing and sowing his own land, making hay on his own land, cutting his own trees, and feeding his cattle on his own pasture. When he went out to plow his fields, or to look at his growing corn, or at his grass meadows, his heart would fill with joy. The grass that grew and the flowers that bloomed there seemed to him unlike any that grew elsewhere. Formerly, when he had passed by that land, it had appeared the same as any other land, but now it seemed quite different.

[3]A *ruble* is a Russian coin worth about twenty-five cents.

So Pahom was well contented, and everything would have been right if the neighboring peasants would only not have trespassed on his cornfields and meadows. He appealed to them most civilly, but they still went on: now the communal herdsmen° would let the village cows stray into his meadows, the horses from the night pasture would get among his corn. Pahom turned them out again and again, and forgave their owners, and for a long time he forbore° to prosecute° anyone. But at last he lost patience and complained to the District Court. He knew it was the peasants' want of land, and no evil intent on their part, that caused the trouble, but he thought:

"I cannot go on overlooking it or they will destroy all I have. They must be taught a lesson."

So he had them up, gave them one lesson, and then another, and two or three of the peasants were fined. After a time Pahom's neighbors began to bear him a grudge for this, and would now and then let their cattle onto his land on purpose. One peasant even got into Pahom's wood at night and cut down five young lime° trees for their bark. Pahom passing through the wood one day noticed something white. He came nearer and saw the stripped trunks lying on the ground, and close by stood the stumps where the trees had been. Pahom was furious.

"If he had only cut one here and there it would have been bad enough," thought Pahom, "but the rascal has actually cut down a whole clump. If I could only find out who did this, I would pay him out."

He racked his brains as to who it could be. Finally he decided: "It must be Semyon—no one else could have done it." So he went to Semyon's homestead to have a look round, but he found nothing, and only had an angry scene. However, he now felt more certain than ever that Semyon had done it, and he lodged a complaint. Semyon was summoned. The case was tried, and retried, and at the end of it all Semyon was acquitted, there being no evidence against him. Pahom felt still more aggrieved,° and let his anger loose upon the elder and the judges.

"You let thieves grease your palms," said he. "If you

were honest folk yourselves you would not let a thief go free."

So Pahom quarreled with the judges and with his neighbors. Threats to burn his buildings began to be uttered. So though Pahom had more land, his place in the commune was much worse than before.

About this time a rumor got about that many people were moving to new parts.

"There's no need for me to leave my land," thought Pahom. "But some of the others might leave our village and then there would be more room for us. I would take over their land myself and make my estate a bit bigger. I could then live more at ease. As it is, I am still too cramped to be comfortable."

One day Pahom was sitting at home when a peasant, passing through the village, happened to call in. He was allowed to stay the night, and supper was given him. Pahom had a talk with this peasant and asked him where he came from. The stranger answered that he came from beyond the Volga,[4] where he had been working. One word led to another, and the man went on to say that many people were settling in those parts. He told how some people from his village had settled there. They had joined the commune, and had had twenty-five acres per man granted them. The land was so good, he said, that the rye sown on it grew as high as a horse, and so thick that five cuts of a sickle made a sheaf.° One peasant, he said, had brought nothing with him but his bare hands, and now he had six horses and two cows of his own.

Pahom's heart kindled with desire. He thought:

"Why should I suffer in this narrow hole, if one can live so well elsewhere? I will sell my land and my homestead here, and with the money I will start afresh over there and get everything new. In this crowded place one is always having trouble. But I must first go and find out all about it myself."

Towards summer he got ready and started. He went

[4] A river in Russia, the longest in Europe.

down the Volga on a steamer to Samara, then walked
another three hundred miles on foot, and at last reached
the place. It was just as the stranger had said. The peasants had plenty of land: every man had twenty-five acres of
communal land given him for his use, and anyone who had
money could buy, besides, at a rouble an acre as much
good freehold° land as he wanted.

Having found out all he wished to know, Pahom returned home as autumn came on, and began selling off his
belongings. He sold his land at a profit, sold his homestead
and all his cattle, and withdrew from membership of the
commune. He only waited till the spring, and then started
with his family for the new settlement.

As soon as Pahom and his family reached their new
abode, he applied for admission into the commune of a
large village. He stood treat to the elders and obtained the
necessary documents. Five shares of communal land were
given him for his own and his sons' use: that is to say—one
hundred and twenty-five acres (not all together, but in
different fields) besides the use of the communal pasture.
Pahom put up the buildings he needed, and bought cattle.
Of the communal land alone he had three times as much as
at his former home, and the land was good cornland. He
was ten times better off than he had been. He had plenty
of arable° land and pasturage, and could keep as many head
of cattle as he liked.

At first, in the bustle of building and settling down,
Pahom was pleased with it all, but when he got used to it
he began to think that even here he had not enough land.
The first year, he sowed wheat on his share of the communal land and had a good crop. He wanted to go on
sowing wheat, but had not enough communal land for the
purpose, and what he had already used was not available;
for in those parts wheat is only sown on virgin° soil or on
fallow° land. It is sown for one or two years, and then the
land lies fallow till it is again overgrown with prairie grass.
There were many who wanted such land and there was not
enough for all; so that people quarreled about it. Those

who were better off wanted it for growing wheat, and those who were poor wanted it to let to dealers, so that they might raise money to pay their taxes. Pahom wanted to sow more wheat, so he rented land from a dealer for a year. He sowed much wheat and had a fine crop, but the land was too far from the village—the wheat had to be carted more than ten miles. After a time Pahom noticed that some peasant-dealers were living on separate farms and were growing wealthy; and he thought:

"If I were to buy some freehold land and have a homestead on it, it would be a different thing altogether. Then it would all be nice and compact."

The question of buying freehold land recurred to him again and again.

He went on in the same way for three years, renting land and sowing wheat. The seasons turned out well and the crops were good, so that he began to lay money by. He might have gone on living contentedly, but he grew tired of having to rent other people's land every year, and having to scramble for it. Wherever there was good land to be had, the peasants would rush for it and it was taken up at once, so that unless you were sharp about it you got none. It happened in the third year that he and a dealer together rented a piece of pasture land from some peasants; and they had already plowed it up, when there was some dispute and the peasants went to law about it, and things fell out so that the labor was all lost.

"If it were my own land," thought Pahom, "I should be independent, and there would not be all this unpleasantness."

So Pahom began looking out for land which he could buy; and he came across a peasant who had bought thirteen hundred acres, but having got into difficulties was willing to sell again cheap. Pahom bargained and haggled° with him, and at last they settled the price at fifteen hundred roubles, part in cash and part to be paid later. They had all but clinched the matter when a passing dealer happened to stop at Pahom's one day to get a feed for his horses. He drank tea with Pahom and they had a talk. The dealer said that he was just returning from the land of the Bashkirs,[5] far away, where he had bought thirteen thousand acres of land, all for a thousand roubles. Pahom questioned him further, and the tradesman said:

"All one need do is to make friends with the chiefs. I gave away about one hundred roubles' worth of silk robes and carpets, besides a case of tea, and I gave wine to those who would drink it; and I got the land for less than a kopeck[6] an acre." And he showed Pahom the title deeds, saying:

"The land lies near a river, and the whole prairie is virgin soil."

Pahom plied° him with questions, and the tradesman said:

"There is more land there than you could cover if you walked a year, and it all belongs to the Bashkirs. They are as simple as sheep, and land can be got almost for nothing."

"There now," thought Pahom, "with my one thousand roubles, why should I get only thirteen hundred acres, and saddle myself with a debt besides? If I take it out there, I can get more than ten times as much for the money."

Pahom inquired how to get to the place, and as soon as the tradesman had left him, he prepared to go there himself. He left his wife to look after the homestead, and started on his journey, taking his man with him. They stopped at a town on their way and bought a case of tea, some wine, and other presents, as the tradesman had advised. On and on they went until they had gone more than three hundred miles, and on the seventh day they came to a place where the Bashkirs had pitched their tents. It was all just as the tradesman had said. The people lived on the steppes,[7] by a river, in felt-covered tents. They neither tilled the ground, nor ate bread. Their cattle and horses grazed in herds on the steppe. The colts were tethered° behind the tents, and the mares were driven to

[5]A tribe of Finnish and Turkish descent living in the Ural Mountains.
[6]A Russian coin worth about one-half a cent.
[7]Extensive plains in Russia.

them twice a day. The mares were milked, and from the milk kumiss[8] was made. It was the women who prepared kumiss, and they also made cheese. As far as the men were concerned, drinking kumiss and eating mutton, and playing on their pipes, was all they cared about. They were all stout and merry, and all the summer long they never thought of doing any work. They were quite ignorant, and knew no Russian, but were good-natured enough.

As soon as they saw Pahom, they came out of their tents and gathered round their visitor. An interpreter was found, and Pahom told them he had come about some land. The Bashkirs seemed very glad; they took Pahom and led him into one of the best tents, where they made him sit on some down° cushions placed on a carpet, while they sat round him. They gave him some tea and kumiss, and had a sheep killed, and gave him mutton to eat. Pahom took presents out of his cart and distributed them among the Bashkirs, and divided the tea amongst them. The Bashkirs were delighted. They talked a great deal among themselves, and then told the interpreter to translate.

"They wish to tell you," said the interpreter, "that they like you, and that it is our custom to do all we can to please a guest and repay him for his gifts. You have given us presents, now tell us which of the things we possess please you best, that we may present them to you."

"What pleases me best here," answered Pahom, "is your land. Our land is crowded and the soil is exhausted; but you have plenty of land and it is good land. I never saw the like of it."

The interpreter translated. The Bashkirs talked among themselves for a while. Pahom could not understand what they were saying, but saw that they were much amused and that they shouted and laughed. Then they were silent and looked at Pahom while the interpreter said:

"They wish me to tell you that in return for your presents they will gladly give you as much land as you want. You have only to point it out with your hand and it is yours."

[8]A beverage.

The Bashkirs talked again for a while and began to dispute. Pahom asked what they were disputing about, and the interpreter told him that some of them thought they ought to ask their Chief about the land and not act in his absence, while others thought there was no need to wait for his return.

While the Bashkirs were disputing, a man in a large fox-fur cap appeared on the scene. They all became silent and rose to their feet. The interpreter said, "This is our Chief himself."

Pahom immediately fetched the best dressing gown and five pounds of tea, and offered these to the Chief. The Chief accepted them, and seated himself in the place of honor. The Bashkirs at once began telling him something. The Chief listened for a while, then made a sign with his head for them to be silent, and addressing himself to Pahom, said in Russian:

"Well, let it be so. Choose whatever piece of land you like; we have plenty of it."

"How can I take as much as I like?" thought Pahom. "I must get a deed to make it secure, or else they may say, 'It is yours,' and afterwards may take it away again."

"Thank you for your kind words," he said aloud. "You have much land, and I only want a little. But I should like to be sure which bit is mine. Could it not be measured and made over to me? Life and death are in God's hands. You good people give it to me, but your children might wish to take it away again."

"You are quite right," said the Chief. "We will make it over to you."

"I heard that a dealer had been here," continued Pahom, "and that you gave him a little land, too, and signed title deeds to that effect. I should like to have it done in the same way."

The Chief understood.

"Yes," replied he, "that can be done quite easily. We have a scribe, and we will go to town with you and have the deed properly sealed."

"And what will be the price?" asked Pahom.

"Our price is always the same: one thousand roubles a day."

Pahom did not understand.

"A day? What measure is that? How many acres would that be?"

"We do not know how to reckon it out," said the Chief. "We sell it by the day. As much as you can go round on your feet in a day is yours, and the price is one thousand roubles a day."

Pahom was surprised.

"But in a day you can get round a large tract of land," he said.

The Chief laughed.

"It will all be yours," said he. "But there is one condition: If you don't return on the same day to the spot whence you started, your money is lost."

"But how am I to mark the way that I have gone?"

"Why, we shall go to any spot you like, and stay there. You must start from that spot and make your round, taking a spade with you. Wherever you think necessary, make a mark. At every turning, dig a hole and pile up the turf; then afterwards we will go round with a plow from hole to hole. You may make as large a circuit° as you please, but before the sun sets you must return to the place you started from. All the land you cover will be yours."

Pahom was delighted. It was decided to start early next morning. They talked awhile, and after drinking some more kumiss and eating some more mutton, they had tea again, and then the night came on. They gave Pahom a feather bed to sleep on, and the Bashkirs dispersed for the night, promising to assemble the next morning at daybreak and ride out before sunrise to the appointed spot.

Pahom lay on the feather bed, but could not sleep. He kept thinking about the land.

"What a large tract I will mark off!" thought he. "I can easily do thirty-five miles in a day. The days are long now, and within a circuit of thirty-five miles what a lot of land there will be! I will sell the poorer land, or let it to peas-

ants, but I'll pick out the best and farm it. I will buy two
ox teams, and hire two more laborers. About a hundred and
fifty acres shall be plowland, and I will pasture cattle on
the rest."

Pahom lay awake all night, and dozed off only just before
dawn. Hardly were his eyes closed when he had a dream.
He thought he was lying in that same tent and heard somebody chuckling outside. He wondered who it could be, and
rose and went out, and he saw the Bashkir Chief sitting in
front of the tent holding his sides and rolling about with
laughter. Going nearer to the Chief, Pahom asked: "What
are you laughing at?" But he saw that it was no longer the
Chief, but the dealer who had recently stopped at his house
and had told him about the land. Just as Pahom was going
to ask, "Have you been here long?" he saw that it was not
the dealer, but the peasant who had come up from the
Volga, long ago, to Pahom's old home. Then he saw that
it was not the peasant either, but the Devil himself with
hoofs and horns, sitting there and chuckling, and before
him lay a man barefoot, prostrate on the ground, with only
trousers and shirt on. And Pahom dreamt that he looked
more attentively to see what sort of a man it was that was
lying there, and he saw that the man was dead, and that it
was himself! He awoke horror-struck.

"What things one does dream," thought he.

Looking round he saw through the open door that the
dawn was breaking. "It's time to wake them up," thought
he. "We ought to be starting."

He got up, roused his man (who was sleeping in his cart),
bade him harness; and went to call the Bashkirs.

"It's time to go to the steppe to measure the land," he
said.

The Bashkirs rose and assembled, and the Chief came
too. Then they began drinking kumiss again, and offered
Pahom some tea, but he would not wait.

"If we are to go, let us go. It is high time," said he.

The Bashkirs got ready and they all started: some mounted
on horses, and some in carts. Pahom drove in his own small

cart with his servant and took a spade with him. When they reached the steppe, the morning red was beginning to kindle. They ascended a hillock° (called by the Bashkirs a *shikhan*) and dismounting from their carts and their horses, gathered in one spot. The Chief came up to Pahom and stretching out his arm towards the plain:

"See," said he, "all this, as far as your eye can reach, is ours. You may have any part of it you like."

Pahom's eyes glistened: it was all virgin soil, as flat as the palm of your hand, as black as the seed of a poppy, and in the hollows different kinds of grasses grew breast-high.

The Chief took off his fox-fur cap, placed it on the ground, and said:

"This will be the mark. Start from here, and return here again. All the land you go round shall be yours."

Pahom took out his money and put it on the cap. Then he took off his outer coat, remaining in his sleeveless undercoat. He unfastened his girdle and tied it tight below his stomach, put a little bag of bread into the breast of his coat, and tying a flask of water to his girdle,° he drew up the tops of his boots, took the spade from the man, and stood ready to start. He considered for some moments which way he had better go—it was tempting everywhere.

"No matter," he concluded, "I will go towards the rising sun."

He turned his face to the east, stretched himself, and waited for the sun to appear above the rim.

"I must lose no time," he thought, "and it is easier walking while it is still cool."

The sun's rays had hardly flashed above the horizon, before Pahom, carrying the spade over his shoulder, went down into the steppe.

Pahom started walking neither slowly nor quickly. After having gone a thousand yards he stopped, dug a hole, and placed pieces of turf one on another to make it more visible. Then he went on; and now that he had walked off his stiffness he quickened his pace. After a while he dug another hole.

Pahom looked back. The hillock could be distinctly seen in the sunlight, with the people on it, and the glittering tires of the cart wheels. At a rough guess Pahom concluded that he had walked three miles. It was growing warmer; he took off his undercoat, flung it across his shoulder, and went on again. It had grown quite warm now; he looked at the sun, it was time to think of breakfast.

"The first shift is done, but there are four in a day, and it is too soon yet to turn. But I will just take off my boots," said he to himself.

He sat down, took off his boots, stuck them into his girdle, and went on. It was easy walking now.

"I will go on for another three miles," thought he, "and then turn to the left. This spot is so fine, that it would be a pity to lose it. The further one goes, the better the land seems."

He went straight on for a while, and when he looked round, the hillock was scarcely visible and the people on it looked like black ants, and he could just see something glistening there in the sun.

"Ah," thought Pahom, "I have gone far enough in this direction, it is time to turn. Besides I am in a regular sweat, and very thirsty."

He stopped, dug a large hole, and heaped up pieces of turf. Next he untied his flask, had a drink, and then turned sharply to the left. He went on and on; the grass was high, and it was very hot.

Pahom began to grow tired: he looked at the sun and saw that it was noon.

"Well," he thought, "I must have a rest."

He sat down, and ate some bread and drank some water; but he did not lie down, thinking that if he did he might fall asleep. After sitting a little while, he went on again. At first he walked easily: the food had strengthened him; but it had become terribly hot and he felt sleepy, still he went on, thinking: "An hour to suffer, a lifetime to live."

He went a long way in this direction also, and was about to turn to the left again, when he perceived a damp hollow: "It would be a pity to leave that out," he thought. "Flax would do well there." So he went on past the hollow, and dug a hole on the other side of it before he turned the corner. Pahom looked towards the hillock. The heat made the air hazy: it seemed to be quivering, and through the haze the people on the hillock could scarcely be seen.

"Ah!" thought Pahom, "I have made the sides too long; I must make this one shorter." And he went along the third side, stepping faster. He looked at the sun: it was nearly halfway to the horizon, and he had not yet done two miles of the third side of the square. He was still ten miles from the goal.

"No," he thought, "though it will make my land lopsided, I must hurry back in a straight line now. I might go too far, and as it is I have a great deal of land."

So Pahom hurriedly dug a hole, and turned straight towards the hillock.

Pahom went straight towards the hillock, but he now walked with difficulty. He was done up with the heat, his bare feet were cut and bruised, and his legs began to fail. He longed to rest, but it was impossible if he meant to get back before sunset. The sun waits for no man, and it was sinking lower and lower.

"Oh, dear," he thought, "if only I have not blundered trying for too much! What if I am too late?"

He looked towards the hillock and at the sun. He was still far from his goal, and the sun was already near the rim.

Pahom walked on and on; it was very hard walking but he went quicker and quicker. He pressed on, but was still far from the place. He began running, threw away his coat, his boots, his flask, and his cap, and kept only the spade which he used as a support.

"What shall I do?" he thought again. "I have grasped too much and ruined the whole affair. I can't get there before the sun sets."

And this fear made him still more breathless. Pahom went on running; his soaking shirt and trousers stuck to him and his mouth was parched.° His breast was working like a blacksmith's bellows, his heart was beating like a hammer, and his legs were giving way as if they did not belong to him. Pahom was seized with terror lest he should die of the strain.

Though afraid of death, he could not stop. "After having run all that way they will call me a fool if I stop now," thought he. And he ran on and on, and drew near and heard the Bashkirs yelling and shouting to him, and their cries inflamed his heart still more. He gathered his last strength and ran on.

The sun was close to the rim, and, cloaked in mist, looked large, and red as blood. Now, yes now, it was about to set! The sun was quite low, but he was also quite near his aim. Pahom could already see the people on the hillock waving their arms to hurry him up. He could see the fox-fur cap on the ground and the money on it, and the Chief sitting on the ground holding his sides. And Pahom remembered his dream.

"There is plenty of land," thought he, "but will God let me live on it? I have lost my life, I have lost my life! I shall never reach that spot!"

Pahom looked at the sun, which had reached the earth: one side of it had already disappeared. With all his remaining strength he rushed on, bending his body forward so that his legs could hardly follow fast enough to keep him from falling. Just as he reached the hillock it suddenly grew dark. He looked up—the sun had already set! He gave a cry: "All my labor has been in vain," thought he, and was about to stop, but he heard the Bashkirs still shouting, and remembered that though to him, from below, the sun seemed to have set, they on the hillock could still see it. He took a long breath and ran up the hillock. It was still light there. He reached the top and saw the cap. Before it sat the Chief laughing and holding his sides. Again Pahom remembered his dream, and he uttered a cry: his legs gave way beneath him, he fell forward and reached the cap with his hands.

"Ah, that's a fine fellow!" exclaimed the Chief. "He has gained much land!"

Pahom's servant came running up and tried to raise him,

but he saw that blood was flowing from his mouth. Pahom was dead!

The Bashkirs clicked their tongues to show their pity.

His servant picked up the spade and dug a grave long enough for Pahom to lie in, and buried him in it. Six feet from his head to his heels was all he needed.

Do especially Questions 17, 18, 21, 42, 107, 110, 150, and 157. Consult the Short Story Model on page 156.

God Sees the Truth, but Waits

LEO TOLSTOY
Translated by Arthur Mendel and Barbara Makanowitzky

In the town of Vladimir there lived a young merchant named Aksenov. He owned two shops and his own house. A handsome fellow with fair curly hair, he was the life of the party and the first to strike up a song. When he was younger, Aksenov used to drink a lot, and when he had drunk too much would get into brawls; but since his marriage, he had given up drinking except for occasional lapses.

One summer day, Aksenov had to travel to a fair at Nizhni. When he began to say good-by to his family, his wife said to him:

"Ivan Dmitrievich, don't go today. I had a bad dream about you."

Aksenov chuckled and said:

"Are you afraid that I'll go off on a binge° at the fair?"

"I don't know myself what I fear, but it was such a strange

thing that I dreamed—you had come back from another town and had taken off your hat, and I saw that your hair had gone completely gray."

Aksenov laughed.

"That means there'll be profits! You'll see, I'll have good fortune and bring you rich gifts."

Then he said good-by and left.

When he had gone half the way, he met a merchant friend of his and they stopped for the night. They drank tea together and went to sleep in adjoining rooms. Aksenov did not like to sleep long. He awoke in the middle of the night and, since it was easier to travel while it was still cool he woke the coachman and told him to harness the horses. Then he went to the soot-covered cabin of the inn-keeper, paid his bill, and left.

After he had gone forty versts,[1] he stopped again, fed the horses, and rested on the front porch of the inn. At dinner time, he went out onto the back porch, asked for a samovar,[2] took a guitar and began to play. Suddenly a troika[3] with ringing bells drove up to the inn. An official and two soldiers got out of the carriage. The official went up to Aksenov and asked him who he was and where he was from. Aksenov told him what he wanted to know and asked if he would like to join him for tea. But the official continued to question him: "Where did you sleep last night? Were you alone or with a merchant? Did you see the merchant in the morning? Why did you leave the inn so early?" Askenov wondered why he was being asked these things. He told him all that had occurred, then added, "But why are you questioning me like this? I'm not some kind of thief or bandit. I am traveling on my own business, and there's nothing for you to question me about."

Then the official called a soldier and said:

"I am the district police officer, and I am asking you these questions because the merchant you stayed with last night has been found with his throat cut. Show me your things. Search him!"

[1] About twenty-seven miles.
[2] A metal urn with an internal tube for heating water in making tea.
[3] A vehicle drawn by a team of three horses abreast.

They went into the cabin, took out his suitcase and bag, untied them and began to search. Suddenly, the officer pulled out a knife from the bag and shouted:

"Whose knife is this?"

Aksenov looked. He saw that they had found a knife covered with blood in his bag, and he was frightened.

"And why is there blood on the knife?"

Aksenov wanted to answer, but could not speak.

"I ... I don't know ... I ... knife ... I, not mine ..."

Then the officer said:

"In the morning they found a merchant with his throat cut. There is no one besides you who could have done it. The cabin was locked from the inside, and no one except you had been inside. You have in your bag a knife covered with blood, and, in fact, guilt is written all over your face. Now tell us, how did you kill him and how much money did you steal?"

Aksenov swore that he did not do it, that he had not seen the merchant since they had drunk tea together, that the only money he had was his own eight thousand rubles,[4] that the knife was not his. But his voice broke, his face was pale, and he shook with fear as though he were guilty.

The officer called a soldier and told him to bind Aksenov and take him out to a cart. When they bound his feet and lifted him onto the cart, Aksenov crossed himself and began to cry. They took away his bags and money and sent him to jail in a nearby town. Inquiries were made in Vladimir to find out what sort of man Aksenov was. All the merchants and inhabitants of Vladimir noted that when he was younger Aksenov drank and caroused,° but that he was a good man.

Then he was brought to trial and charged with the murder of a merchant from Riazan and the theft of twenty thousand rubles.

His wife was grief-stricken and did not know what to think. Her children were young: one was still at the breast. She took them all and went to the town where her husband

[4]About $2,000.

was imprisoned. At first they refused to let her in, but she implored the prison authorities, and they took her to her husband. When she saw him in prison clothes, chained, and with thieves, she collapsed and for a long time remained unconscious. Then she placed her children about her, sat beside him, and began to tell him about things at home and to ask about all that had happened to him. He told her everything.

"And what now?" she asked.

"We must petition the Tsar. They cannot let an innocent man perish!"

His wife said that she had already sent a petition to the Tsar but that it had not been allowed to reach him.

Aksenov was silent and only grew more despondent.°

"It wasn't for nothing that, you remember, I dreamed of your turning gray," his wife said. "Look, you are already beginning to gray from grief. You should not have gone."

She began to run her fingers through his hair and said:

"Vanya, my dearest one, tell your wife the truth; didn't you do it?"

"And you too suspect me?" He covered his face with his hands and wept. A guard came in then and said that his wife and children had to leave. Aksenov said good-by to his family for the last time.

When his wife had left, Aksenov began to think about all that had been said. When he recalled that his wife too had suspected him and that she had asked if he killed the merchant, he said to himself:

"Clearly, only God can know the truth, and one must turn to God alone and from God alone await mercy." From that time on Aksenov ceased sending petitions, ceased hoping, and only prayed to God. He was sentenced to flogging and hard labor. The sentence was carried out. They flogged him with a knout,° and when the knout wounds had closed, they herded him along with other convicts to Siberia.

For twenty-six years Aksenov lived in Siberian servitude. The hair of his head turned as white as snow and his beard grew long, thin, and gray. All his joyfulness vanished.

He grew hunched, moved along quietly, spoke little, never laughed, and often prayed to God.

While in prison Aksenov learned to make boots. With the money he earned he bought *The Lives of the Saints* and read it when there was light enough in the prison. On holidays he went to the prison church where he read the Gospels and, since his voice was still good, sang in the choir. The prison officials liked Aksenov for his humility, and his fellow prisoners respected him and called him "Grandpa" and "Godly one." When there were any petitions concerning prison conditions, the other prisoners always sent Aksenov to present them to the officials; and when quarrels arose among them, the prisoners always went to him to judge the case.

No one from Aksenov's home wrote him, and he did not even know if his wife and children were still alive.

One day they brought some new convicts to the prison. In the evening all the old convicts gathered around the new ones and began to ask them what town or village they were from and why they had been exiled. Aksenov also sat down on one of the long, elevated shelf-bunks near the new inmates and dejectedly listened to what they said.

One of the new convicts was a tall, robust old man of about sixty with a clipped, gray beard. He was telling of his arrest.

"So, fellows, I was sent here for no reason at all. I unharnessed a horse from a coachman's sleigh. They grabbed me. 'Thief,' they said. I told them that I had only wanted to get where I was going faster and that I had let the horse go. In fact, the coachman was a friend of mine. 'All right?' I asked. 'No, you stole the horse,' they said. Now, I have stolen things, but they didn't know what or where. I've done things that should have landed me here long ago, although they never caught me. But there's no justice at all in their driving me here this time. Lies! I've been in Siberia before, although I didn't stay long."

"Where are you from?" one of the convicts asked.

"Our family comes from Vladimir, local tradespeople. My name is Makar, Makar Semenovich, in full."

Aksenov raised his head and asked:

"Semenych, have you ever heard anything about the Aksenov merchants in Vladimir? Are they alive?"

"Who hasn't heard of them! Rich merchants, although their father is in Siberia, a sinner like ourselves, no doubt. And you, Grandpa, what are you in for?"

Aksenov did not like to talk about his own misfortune. He sighed and said:

"For my sins I have spent these twenty-six years in hard labor."

"And what sort of sins?" Makar Semenov asked.

"Those worth this punishment," Aksenov said, and he wanted to say no more about it. But the other prisoners told the newcomer why Aksenov had been sent to Siberia. They told him how someone had killed a merchant and had planted a knife on Aksenov and that for this Aksenov had been falsely convicted.

When Makar Semenov heard this and looked at Aksenov, he slapped his knees with his hands and said:

"Well, that's something! That's really something! How you've aged, Grandpa!"

They asked him why he was so surprised and where he had seen Aksenov, but Makar Semenov did not answer and only said:

"It's a miracle, lads, the way people meet."

At these words Aksenov began to wonder if this man knew something about the murder of the merchant, and he asked:

"Have you heard of this affair before, Semenych, or have you seen me before?"

"Of course I've heard about it! News travels quickly. But it happened long ago, and you forget what you've heard."

"Did you ever hear, perhaps, who killed the merchant?" Aksenov then asked.

Makar Semenov laughed and said:

"The one whose knife they found in your bag probably did it. And if someone did plant a knife on you, well, a man's not a thief until he's caught, you know. But how could anyone have put a knife in your bag? Wasn't it right by your head? You would have heard something."

As soon as Aksenov heard these words he realized that it was this very man who had killed the merchant. He got up and walked off. All that night he could not fall asleep, but lay deeply depressed. He recalled the past. He saw his wife as she had been on that last day when he left for the fair. It was as though she stood there alive before him. He saw her face and her eyes. He heard her voice speak to him and laugh. He saw his children as they were then, little ones, one in a little coat, the other at the breast. And he remembered how he himself had been then — young and gay. He recalled how he had sat on the porch at the inn where they arrested him, how he had played the guitar and how happy he had been. And he remembered the place they had whipped him, the executioner, the crowd gathered around, the chains, the convicts, the whole twenty-six years of prison life: and he remembered his age. So great a gloom came upon him that he wanted to kill himself.

"And all because of that scoundrel!" Aksenov thought.

He felt such fury toward Makar Semenov that he wanted to revenge himself even though it cost him his own life. He prayed all night, but could not calm down. The next day he did not go near Makar Semenov and did not look at him.

This went on for two weeks. Aksenov could not sleep nights and he was so forlorn he did not know where to turn.

One night while he was walking about the prison barracks he noticed handfuls of dirt being thrown from beneath one of the long shelf-bunks shared by the prisoners. He stopped to look. Suddenly, Makar Semenov jumped out from under the bunk and with a frightened expression looked at Aksenov. Aksenov wanted to move on in order not to face him, but Makar grabbed his arm and told him how he had been digging a passage beneath the wall and carrying dirt out in his boot tops and how he had been scattering the dirt in the street when the prisoners were sent off to work.

"Just be quiet about this, old fellow, and I'll take you

along. If you talk, they'll whip me. But I won't let you get away—I'll kill you."

Looking at the scoundrel, Aksenov shook with rage. He jerked his arm away and said:

"There's no reason for me to leave here, and there's no need to kill me—you killed me long ago. And whether or not I tell about you depends on how God directs my soul."

The next day as they were leading the convicts off to work, a guard noticed Makar Semenov scattering dirt. They searched the barracks and found the hole. The warden came to the barracks and asked all of them: "Who dug this hole?" They all denied doing it. Those who knew the truth did not betray Makar Semenov because they knew that he would be whipped half to death. Then the warden turned to Aksenov. He knew that Aksenov was an honorable man and said:

"Old man, you are truthful—tell me before God, who did this?"

Makar Semenov stood as though nothing had happened, looking at the warden, but not turning to look at Aksenov. Aksenov's lips and hands trembled and for a long time he could not speak. He thought to himself: "Why should I protect him, why should I forgive him when he has ruined my life? Let him pay for my torments. But if I tell, they'll flog him. And what if I have been wrong about him? In any case will things be any easier for me?"

The warden asked him again:

"Well, old man, tell the truth, who dug the hole?"

Aksenov glanced at Makar Semenov and said:

"I cannot tell, your excellency. God has not directed me to do so. I will not tell. It is in your power to do what you want with me."

No matter how hard the warden tried to persuade him, Aksenov said nothing more. So, they did not discover who had dug the hole.

The next night, as Aksenov lay on his bed and had just about fallen asleep, he heard someone come up to him and sit on the bunk at his feet. He looked in the dark and recognized Makar.

"What more do you want of me? What are you doing here?" he asked.

Makar Semenov was silent. Aksenov raised himself and said:

"What do you want? Get out of here or I'll call the guard."

Makar Semenov bent close to Aksenov and in a whisper said:

"Ivan Dmitrich, forgive me!"

"For what shall I forgive you?"

"I killed the merchant and planted the knife on you. I wanted to kill you too, but I heard noises outside. I slipped the knife into your bag and climbed out the window."

Aksenov was silent and did not know what to say. Makar Semenov dropped from the bunk, bowed to the ground and said:

"Ivan Dmitrich, forgive me. For God's sake, forgive me. I'll confess that I killed the merchant. They'll pardon you, and you can go home."

"It's easy for you to talk," Aksenov said, "but how I have suffered! Where can I go now? . . . My wife is dead, my children have forgotten me. There's no place for me."

Makar Semenov did not rise, but beat his head on the ground and said:

"Ivan Dmitrich, forgive! When they whipped me with a knout it was easier for me than it is now to look at you . . . But you pitied me before when you didn't betray me. Forgive me for Christ's sake! Forgive this accursed wretch." And he began to sob.

When Aksenov heard Makar Semenov weeping, he began to cry himself and said:

"God will forgive you. Perhaps I am a hundred times worse than you."

Suddenly, his soul grew calm. He ceased to yearn for his home and he no longer wanted to leave prison, but only thought of his final hour.

In spite of what Aksenov had said, Makar Semenov confessed his guilt. When they issued the order permitting Aksenov to return home, he was already dead.

> *Do especially Questions 16-20, 47, 75, 89, 95, 102, 103, 106, 107, 108, 111, 146, 149, and 157. Consult the Short Story Model on page 156.*

LEO TOLSTOY *1828-1910*

Count Leo Nikolayevich Tolstoy was born into a wealthy, land-owning Russian family. His early education was private; later he attended the University of Kazan, which he left before completing his degree. He then joined the army in the Caucasus, and while there he spent much time among the primitive Cossack settlers. Already he was making his reputation as an author with his autobiographical sketches *Childhood, Boyhood,* and *Youth,* and three Sevastopol stories characterized by stark realism. Upon leaving the army, he returned to Moscow and the family estate. But in 1857 and again in 1860 he traveled to Europe where he was disillusioned by the increasing spirit of materialism that was swallowing up Western culture. In 1862 he married Sophia Andreyevna Behrs. Very soon after his marriage, 1863, he completed his well-known novel *War and Peace.* Through his own literary efforts and his intense personal search for an ultimate meaning of life, Tolstoy decided to pattern his life according to the teaching of the Gospel. The single precept of his new faith, taken from the Sermon on the Mount, was the law of brotherly love, which man finds in his own conscience. In an effort to live out his personal moral convictions, Tolstoy rid himself of all personal possessions. However, his practical-minded wife objected when he proposed to divide up the estate among the peasants. Disagreement followed, and finally Leo fled his home. During the flight the eighty-two-year-old author caught pneumonia and died in a small railroad station in Astapovo.

The Slanderer

ANTON CHEKHOV Translated by Herman Bernstein

Sergey Kapitonich Akhineyev, the teacher of calligraphy,° gave his daughter Natalya in marriage to the teacher of history and geography, Ivan Petrovich Loshadinikh. The

"The Slanderer" by Anton Chekhov, from *Greatest Short Stories*, translated by Herman Bernstein, published by P. F. Collier.

wedding feast went on swimmingly. They sang, played, and danced in the parlor. Waiters, hired for the occasion from the club, bustled about hither and thither like madmen, in black frock coats and soiled white neckties. A loud noise of voices smote the air. From the outside people looked in at the windows — their social standing gave them no right to enter.

Just at midnight the host, Akhineyev, made his way to the kitchen to see whether everything was ready for the supper. The kitchen was filled with smoke from the floor to the ceiling; the smoke reeked with the odors of geese, ducks, and many other things. Victuals° and beverages were scattered about on two tables in artistic disorder. Marfa, the cook, a stout, red-faced woman, was busying herself near the loaded tables.

"Show me the sturgeon,° dear," said Akhineyev, rubbing his hands and licking his lips. "What a fine odor! I could just devour the whole kitchen! Well, let me see the sturgeon!"

Marfa walked up to one of the benches and carefully lifted a greasy newspaper. Beneath that paper, in a huge dish, lay a big fat sturgeon, amid capers,° olives, and carrots. Akhineyev glanced at the sturgeon and heaved a sigh of relief. His face became radiant, his eyes rolled. He bent down, and, smacking his lips, gave vent° to a sound like a creaking wheel. He stood a while, then snapped his fingers for pleasure, and smacked his lips once more.

"Bah! The sound of a hearty kiss. Whom have you been kissing there, Marfushka?" someone's voice was heard from the adjoining room, and soon the closely cropped head of Vankin, the assistant school instructor, appeared in the doorway. "Whom have you been kissing here? A-a-ah! Very good! Sergey Kapitonich! A fine old man indeed! With the female sex tête-à-tête!"°

"I wasn't kissing at all," said Akhineyev, confused; "who told you, you fool? I only — smacked my lips on account of — in consideration of my pleasure — at the sight of the fish."

"Tell that to someone else, not to me!" exclaimed Vankin,

whose face expanded into a broad smile as he disappeared behind the door. Akhineyev blushed.

"The devil knows what may be the outcome of this!" he thought. "He'll go about tale-bearing now, the rascal. He'll disgrace me before the whole town, the brute!"

Akhineyev entered the parlor timidly and cast furtive° glances to see what Vankin was doing. Vankin stood near the piano and, deftly° bending down, whispered something to the inspector's sister-in-law, who was laughing.

"That's about me!" thought Akhineyev. "About me, the devil take him! She believes him, she's laughing. My God! No, that mustn't be left like that. No. I'll have to fix it so that no one shall believe him. I'll speak to all of them, and he'll remain a foolish gossip in the end."

Akhineyev scratched his head, and, still confused, walked up to Padekoi.

"I was in the kitchen a little while ago, arranging things there for the supper," he said to the Frenchman. "You like fish, I know, and I have a sturgeon just so big. About two yards. Ha, ha, ha! Yes, by the way, I have almost forgotten. There was a real anecdote° about that sturgeon in the kitchen. I entered the kitchen a little while ago and wanted to examine the food. I glanced at the sturgeon and for pleasure, I smacked my lips—it was so piquant!° And just at the moment the fool Vankin entered and says—ha, ha, ha—and says: 'A-a! A-a-ah! You have been kissing here?'— with Marfa; just think of it—with the cook! What a piece of invention, that blockhead. The woman is ugly, she looks like a monkey, and he says we were kissing. What a queer fellow!"

"Who's a queer fellow?" asked Tarantulov, as he approached them.

"I refer to Vankin. I went out into the kitchen—"

The story of Marfa and the sturgeon was repeated.

"That makes me laugh. What a queer fellow he is. In my opinion it is more pleasant to kiss the dog than to kiss Marfa," added Akhineyev, and, turning around, he noticed Mzda.

"We have been speaking about Vankin," he said to him.

"What a queer fellow. He entered the kitchen and noticed me standing beside Marfa, and immediately he began to invent different stories. 'What?' he says, 'you have been kissing each other!' He was drunk, so he must have been dreaming. 'And I,' I said, 'I would rather kiss a duck than kiss Marfa. And I have a wife,' said I, 'you fool.' He made me appear ridiculous."

"Who made you appear ridiculous?" inquired the teacher of religion, addressing Akhineyev.

"Vankin. I was standing in the kitchen, you know, and looking at the sturgeon—" And so forth. In about half an hour all the guests knew the story about Vankin and the sturgeon.

"Now let him tell," thought Akhineyev, rubbing his hands. "Let him do it. He'll start to tell them, and they'll cut him short: 'Don't talk nonsense, you fool! We know all about it.'"

And Akhineyev felt so much appeased° that, for joy, he drank four glasses of brandy over and above his fill. Having escorted his daughter to her room, he went to his own and soon slept the sleep of an innocent child, and on the following day he no longer remembered the story of the sturgeon. But, alas! Man proposes and God disposes. The evil tongue does its wicked work, and even Akhineyev's cunning did not do him any good. One week later, on a Wednesday, after the third lesson, when Akhineyev stood in the teachers' room and discussed the vicious° inclinations of the pupil Visyekin, the director approached him, and, beckoning to him, called him aside.

"See here, Sergey Kapitonich," said the director. "Pardon me. It isn't my affair, yet I must make it clear to you, nevertheless. It is my duty—You see, rumors are on foot that you are on intimate terms with that woman—with your cook—It isn't my affair, but—You may be on intimate terms with her, you may kiss her—You may do whatever you like, but, please, don't do it so openly! I beg of you. Don't forget that you are a pedagogue."°

Akhineyev stood as though frozen and petrified.° Like

one stung by a swarm of bees and scalded with boiling water, he went home. On his way it seemed to him as though the whole town stared at him as at one besmeared with tar—At home new troubles awaited him.

"Why don't you eat anything?" asked his wife at their dinner. "What are you thinking about? Are you thinking about Cupid,[1] eh? You are longing for Marfushka. I know everything already, you Mahomet.[2] Kind people have opened my eyes, you barbarian!"

And she slapped him on the cheek.

He rose from the table, and staggering, without cap or coat, directed his footsteps toward Vankin. The latter was at home.

"You rascal!" he said to Vankin. "Why have you covered me with mud before the whole world? Why have you slandered me?"

"How; what slander? What are you inventing?"

"And who told everybody that I was kissing Marfa? Not you, perhaps? Not you, you murderer?"

Vankin began to blink his eyes, and all the fibers° of his face began to quiver. He lifted his eyes toward the image and ejaculated:

"May God punish me, may I lose my eyesight and die, if I said even a single word about you to anyone! May I have neither house nor home!"

Vankin's sincerity admitted of no doubt. It was evident that it was not he who had gossiped.

"But who was it? Who?" Akhineyev asked himself, going over in his mind all his acquaintances, and striking his chest. "Who was it?"

[1]In Roman mythology, the god of love. He is usually pictured as a naked, winged boy with bow and arrow.

[2]In substance Sergey's wife is calling her husband something less than a Christian.

Do especially Questions 11, 43, 89, 102, 110, 147, and 157. Consult the Short Story Model on page 156.

ANTON CHEKHOV *1860-1904*

Anton Pavlovich Chekhov was born in Taganrog on the Sea of
Azov. When Anton was in his teens, his father fled to Moscow
to avoid large debts, thus leaving the boy to shift for himself.
After finishing school in his native town, the young Chekhov went
to Moscow where he began his medical studies. In order to pay
for his training, he began to write short anecdotal pieces which
when published became quite popular. Soon writing became his
main occupation and his first book, *Motley Stories* (1886), gained
him considerable stature. A collection, *In the Twilight* (1888),
which followed, was widely recognized, and his long story "The
Steppe" consolidated his claim to recognition as a leading Russian fictionist. In the same year, he completed *Ivanov*, his first
play. In the sixteen years that followed, Chekhov produced a
steady stream of stories as well as a number of plays, the most
famous of which were *The Sea Gull, The Three Sisters,* and *The
Cherry Orchard.* Chekhov died prematurely, at the age of forty-
four, after a lingering illness of tuberculosis. Even at this early
age, he ranked as one of Russia's most renowned and versatile
writers.

The Brothers

BJÖRNSTJERNE BJÖRNSON Translated by Anders Orbeck

The schoolmaster's name was Baard, and he had a brother
named Anders. They thought a great deal of each other,
enlisted together, lived together in town, went through the
war together, served in the same company, and both rose
to the rank of corporal. When they came home from the
war, people said they were two fine stalwart° fellows.

Then their father died. He left much personal property,
which it was difficult to divide, and therefore they said to
each other that they would not let this come between them,
but would put the property up at auction, that each might

"The Brothers" by Björnstjerne Björnson, translated by Anders Orbeck, from *Told
in Norway.* Reprinted by permission of The American-Scandinavian Foundation.

buy what he wanted, and both share the proceeds. And it was so done.

But the father had owned a large gold watch, which had come to be known far and wide, for it was the only gold watch people in those parts had ever seen. When this watch was put up, there were many wealthy men who wanted it, but when both brothers began to bid, all the others desisted.° Now Baard expected that Anders would let him have it, and Anders expected the same of Baard. They bid in turn, each trying the other out, and as they bid they looked hard at each other. When the watch had gone up to twenty dollars, Baard began to feel that this was not kind of his brother, and bid over him until he almost reached thirty. When Anders did not withdraw even then, Baard felt that Anders no longer remembered how good he had often been to him, and that he was furthermore the elder of the two; and the watch went over thirty. Anders still kept on. Baard then raised the price to forty dollars with one bound, and no longer looked at his brother. It grew very still in the auction room; only the bailiff° repeated the figures quietly. Anders thought, as he stood there, that if Baard could afford to go to forty dollars, so could he, and if Baard begrudged° him the watch, he might as well take it, and bid over him. This to Baard seemed the greatest disgrace that had ever befallen him; and bid fifty dollars in a low voice. There were many people there, and Anders said to himself that he would not let his brother mock him before them all, and again raised the bid. Baard burst out laughing.

"One hundred dollars and my brotherhood into the bargain," he said, as he turned on his heel, and left the room.

A little later, as he stood saddling the horse he had just bought at the auction, a man came out to him.

"The watch is yours; Anders gave in."

The instant he heard the news, there welled up in him a sense of remorse; he thought of his brother and not of the watch. The saddle was already in place, but he paused, his hand on his horse, uncertain whether to mount. Many people came out, Anders among them, and when he saw his brother, with horse saddled, ready to leave, he little knew what Baard was turning over in his mind.

"Thanks for the watch, Baard!" he shouted over to him. "You shall never see the day when your brother shall tread on your heels!"

"Nor you the day I shall darken your doors again!" Baard answered, his face pale, as he swung himself on his horse.

After that day neither of them ever set foot in the home where they had both lived with their father.

Anders married into a crofter's° family not long afterward, but he did not invite Baard to the wedding. Nor did Baard go to the church. The first year he was married, Anders lost his only cow. It was found dead one morning on the north side of the house, where it had been tethered,° and no one could explain what it had died of. Other misfortunes befell him, and he fared from bad to worse. But the heaviest blow came when his hayloft and all it contained burned down one night in the dead of winter. No one knew how the fire had started.

"This has been done by someone who wishes me ill," Anders said, and all that night he wept. He became a poor man, and he lost all inclination to work.

The evening after the fire, Baard appeared at his brother's house. Anders lay on his bed, but sprang up as Baard entered.

"What do you want here?" he asked, then stopped short, and stood staring fixedly at his brother.

Baard waited a little before he answered.

"I want to help you, Anders; you're in a bad way."

"I'm faring° no worse than you wished me to fare! Go— else I'm not sure I can master myself."

"You're mistaken, Anders; I regret—"

"Go, Baard, or God have mercy on us both!"

Baard drew back a step.

"If you want the watch," he said in a trembling voice, "you can have it."

"Go, Baard!" shrieked his brother, and Baard, unwilling to stay any longer, left.

In the meanwhile Baard had fared thus. As soon as he heard of his brother's misfortunes, he had suffered a change of heart, but pride held him back. He felt urged to go to church, and there he vowed many a good resolve, but he lacked strength to carry them out. He frequently went so far that he could see the house, but either someone was just coming out, or there were strangers there, or Anders stood chopping wood outside—there was always something in the way.

But one Sunday, late in the winter, he again went to church, and that Sunday Anders, too, was there. Baard saw him. He had grown pale and thin, and he wore the same clothes he had worn when the brothers were together, although now they were old and patched. All through the service Anders looked steadily at the minister. To Baard it seemed that he was kind and gentle, and he recalled their childhood days, and what a good boy Anders had been. That day Baard even went to communion, and he made a solemn vow to God that he would make up with his brother, come what might. This resolution swept through his soul as he drank the wine, and when he arose he felt an impulse to go over and take a seat beside him, but there was someone in the way, and Anders did not look up. After the service there was still something in the way; there were too many people about; Anders' wife was with him, and her he did not know. He decided it would be better to seek Anders in his home and have a quiet talk with him.

When evening came, he set out. He went right up to the door. Then he paused, and as he stood there listening, he heard his name mentioned; it was the wife speaking.

"He went to communion this morning," she was saying. "I am sure he was thinking of you."

"No, it wasn't of me he was thinking," Anders replied. "I know him; he thinks only of himself."

For a long time nothing was said, and Baard sweat, as he stood there, although it was a cold night. The wife inside was busy with a kettle; the fire on the hearth crackled and hissed; a child cried now and then, and Anders rocked it. At length the wife spoke again.

"I believe you are both thinking of each other though you won't admit it."

"Let us talk of something else," Anders answered.

After a little he got up to go out. Baard had to hide in the woodshed; but then Anders, too, came to the shed to get an armful of wood. From where he stood in the corner Baard could see him clearly. He had taken off his thread-bare Sunday clothes, and put on his uniform, just like Baard's own. These they had promised each other never to wear, but to pass on as heirlooms° to their children. Anders' was now patched and worn out, so that his strong, well-built frame seemed bundled in rags, while at the same time Baard could hear the gold watch ticking in his own pocket. Anders went over to the brushwood, but instead of bending down immediately to gather up his load, he leaned back against a pile of wood, and looked up at the sky glimmering brightly with stars. Then he sighed heavily and muttered to himself, "Well — well — well — oh Lord, oh Lord!"

As long as he lived, Baard never forgot those words. He wanted to step forward then, but his brother coughed, and it seemed so difficult. No more was needed to hold him back. Anders took his armful of fagots,° and as he went out, brushed past Baard so close that the twigs struck him in the face.

For fully ten minutes more he stood rooted to the spot, and it is doubtful how much longer he might have stayed had not a chill, on top of the emotional stress, seized him, and set him shivering through and through. Then he went out. He frankly confessed to himself that he was too cowardly to enter now; wherefore he conceived another plan. From an ash barrel, which stood in the corner he had just left, he selected some bits of charcoal, found a pitch-pine splinter, went up into the hayloft, closed the door, and struck a light. When he had lit the torch he searched about for the peg on which Anders hung his lantern when he came out early in the morning to thresh.° Baard then took his gold watch and hung it on the peg, put out his light, and left. He felt so relieved in his mind that he raced over the snow like a youngster.

The day following he heard that the hayloft had burned down during the night. Presumably sparks had flown from the torch he had used while hanging up the watch.

This so overwhelmed Baard that all that day he kept to himself as though he were ill, brought out his hymnbook, and sang until the people in the house thought something was wrong with him. But in the evening he went out. It was bright moonlight. He went over to his brother's place, dug around in the charred ruins of the fire, and found, sure enough, a little lump of melted gold—all that remained of the watch.

It was with this in his hand that he had gone in to his brother, anxious to explain everything, and to sue for peace. But how he fared that evening has already been told.

A little girl had seen him digging in the ashes; some boys, on their way to a dance, had observed him go down toward his brother's the Sunday evening in question; and the people where he lived explained how strangely he had acted on the Monday following. And inasmuch as everyone knew that he and his brother were bitter enemies, these details were reported to the authorities, and an inquiry instituted. No one could prove anything against him, yet suspicion hovered around him. He could now less than ever approach his brother.

Anders had thought of Baard when the hayloft burned, but had said nothing. When he had seen him enter his house, the following evening, pale and strange, he had forthwith thought: He is smitten° with remorse, but for such a terrible outrage against his brother there can be no forgiveness. Since then he heard how people had seen Baard go down toward his home the evening of the fire, and although nothing was brought to light at the inquiry, he felt convinced that his brother was the guilty one.

They met at the hearing, Baard in his good clothes, Anders in his worn-out rags. Baard looked at his brother as he entered, and Anders was conscious, in his inmost heart, of an anxious pleading in his eyes. He doesn't want me to say anything, thought Anders; and when he was asked whether he suspected his brother of the deed he answered loudly and decisively, "No!"

Anders took to drinking heavily after that day, and it was not long before he was in a bad way. Even worse, however, fared Baard, although he did not drink; he was so changed that people hardly knew him.

Then late one evening a poor woman entered the little room Baard rented and asked him to come with her. He recognized her; it was his brother's wife. Baard understood at once what her errand was, turned deathly pale, dressed himself, and followed her without a word. A pale glimmer shone from Anders' window, now flickering, now vanishing, and this light they followed, for there was no path across the snow. When Baard again stood in the doorway, he was met with a strange odor which almost made him ill. They went in. A little child sat eating charcoal over by the hearth, its face all black, but it looked up and laughed and showed its white teeth. It was his brother's child.

Over on the bed, with all sorts of clothes over him, lay Anders, pale, emaciated,° his forehead high and smooth, and stared at his brother with hollow eyes. Baard's knees trembled. He sat down at the foot of the bed and burst into uncontrollable weeping. The sick man looked at him intently and said nothing. At length he asked his wife to go out, but Baard motioned for her to remain. And then the two brothers began to talk to each other. They explained everything, from the day they bid for the watch down through the years to this day when they finally met again. Baard ended by taking out the lump of gold, which he always carried about him, and it came to light in the course of their talk that never for one single day in all these years had they been really happy.

Anders did not say much, for he had little strength, but Baard watched by the bedside as long as Anders was ill.

"Now I am perfectly well," Anders said one morning, on awakening. "Now, brother, we shall live together always, just as in the old days, and never leave each other."

But that day he died.

The widow and the child Baard took home with him, and they were henceforth well taken care of. But what the brothers had talked of at the bedside came out through the walls and the night, and became generally known to all the people in the valley. Baard grew to be the most highly respected man among them. They all honored him as one who had had a great sorrow and had found peace again, or as one who had returned after a long absence. And Baard grew in strength of mind by reason of all their friendliness. He became a godly man, and wishing to be of some use, as he said, the old corporal turned schoolmaster. What he impressed upon the children, first and last, was love, and himself he practiced it till the children came to love him as a playmate and a father.

Do especially Questions 14, 17, 18, 19, 20, 75, and 99. Consult the Short Story Model on page 156.

BJÖRNSTJERNE BJÖRNSON   1832-1910

Björnstjerne Björnson, tall, erect, with a crop of blond hair and a booming voice, was himself the perfect model for his Viking heroes. One of the most prolific writers Norway has produced, Björnson was journalist, critic, dramatist, short-story writer, and novelist; but most important of all, he was a patriot. A Nobel prize winner in 1903, he was primarily interested in the unification of his native Norway, and it is fitting that one of his poems has become the Norwegian national anthem. Björnson's early plays portrayed the agricultural-yeoman class of Norway; his later dramatic works proved to be revolutionary forerunners of Ibsen's social drama.

PROBLEM QUESTIONS

1. In many of his stories, Poe emphasized the elements of mystery and horror. How are these evident in "The Black Cat"?

2. Upon what narrative devices or elements does the story by Ambrose Bierce depend for its effect?

3. Why does Bret Harte say at the end of "The Outcasts of Poker Flat" that his central character, the gambler, was "the strongest yet the weakest" of the outcasts?

4. Describe the mental and emotional changes in the narrator in "The Peasant Marey." What causes these changes? What was the author's purpose in writing the story?

5. Draw some comparisons and contrasts between the narrators of "The Peasant Marey" and "An Honest Thief." How does each narrator reveal his own character in the telling of the story? In what way was the thief "honest"? Compare the morality of the thief with that of the prisoners in "The Peasant Marey."

6. What is the most significant theme of "The Slanderer"? What makes this theme so unusual, and what can be learned from it? Compare the character of Akineyev in "The Slanderer" with that of Maître Hauchecome in "The Piece of String."

7. Where are the emotions of love, hate, and misunderstanding to be found in "The Brothers"? Which emotion seems to you to be most powerfully portrayed?

8. Which of the stories in this unit show best the trend in the nineteenth century toward the development of the "regional-realistic" story? Which of them might be considered "case studies" of human personality? How do all of the stories show the development of the short story as an *artistic* form differing from the medieval prose narratives which preceded them?

9. What passages and instances in the two Tolstoy stories create and heighten suspense?

TWENTIETH-CENTURY SHORT STORIES

By the beginning of the twentieth century, the short story had become clearly established as an important medium of expression in literature. It was still a popular form with readers, and attracted the talents of large numbers of serious creative artists. Writers were no longer making use of excerpts from lengthy, episodic works. The short story could stand on its own.

The modern short story can actually be found in two distinctly different types. The first of these is a direct descendant from that which was once written in Grub Street. We can arbitrarily term it the "popular" short story. Popular stories are written in great numbers for the general reading public. They can be found in the thousands of magazines which appear in drug stores, passenger terminals, or newsstands throughout our country. These stories do not pretend to represent great artistic achievement. They are usually based on exciting adventures or center around domestic problems. They are conventional, often contrived, and are concerned, for the most part, with matters of contemporary significance. For our purposes they are not important because they do not aim at making significant statements about the lives of men and therefore are not to be studied as an art form.

The second kind of short story to be found in our century can be called the "artistic" story. The writer's purpose in such stories is to convey through his narrative certain basic truths or propositions about human experience. These stories are, like the popular ones, most often set in contemporary surroundings, but the ideas found within them are usually those of universal significance. Furthermore, the artistic stories of the twentieth century are characteristically *experimental* in style, and in this respect they are distinctly different from their nineteenth-century counterparts.

Most stories written in the nineteenth century were what could be termed "plot" stories. The emphasis in these earlier selections was generally on some movement, some clearly perceived physical action. The fundamental conflict was most often very evident and the sequence of events was chronologically clear. Short-story writers of our times have changed the emphasis from plot to analysis of character, and it is in this area that short fictional works of this century are most clearly experimental. It is on the thoughts, the emotions, the inner nature of the individual that most modern writers of short stories like to dwell, and for this reason, the plots of many stories are underplayed and sometimes difficult to follow.

Since the mind and emotions of man are usually complicated and often inconsistent, today's writers of short stories have been able to take a great variety of *positions* in developing their works. They can, for instance, portray the mind of the disturbed person who does not view life in an orderly fashion. The result of this kind of picture can be one of total confusion and lack of recognizable pattern, or simply lack of plot. Other writers, also intensely interested in psychological aspects, develop analyses of the person who is in a state of great joy, fear, or anger. The outside world never appears in its "normal" condition to a person who is experiencing intense emotion, thus the stories of such people are often unusual in both theme and structure.

The kinds of interests just described account for the fact that many twentieth-century stories tend to shift in time and place—to make use of the "flashback"—in their narratives and are thus rather hard for the unwary reader to follow and, more important, "make sense" of. The writer of the short story cannot and does not attempt to develop the complete picture of the character he is attempting to analyze. A novelist may furnish a thorough description of the inner life of one or more of his characters; a short story writer chooses not to employ the time or space to develop his characters exhaustively. What he generally does is to focus on one or two incidents which have occurred to his major character and then dwell on the way or ways in which the character has reacted to them. Thus the reader is left to speculate as to the degree to which this reaction is representative of the character's overall attitude toward life. In Miss Gordimer's story, the last in this volume, the incident described is seemingly trivial, and the reaction of the character involved is underdescribed, but it is necessary to weigh this reaction carefully in judging the nature of the main character and the life she must lead from the point at which the story ends.

Another consistent device used in analytic modern short stories is what James Joyce, the famous twentieth-century Irish writer, has called an "epiphany." In such stories, the focus of the entire work is on the sudden, unexpected, and frequently shattering realization of something by the central figure in the work. It may be a new insight into his own character or into that of someone who is close to him, but it comes as a jolt (usually both to the character and the reader), and the implication is almost invariably present that this revelation will have a profound effect on the life of the character who has experienced it. Once again, look for this technique in Miss Gordimer's story. Like so many other twentieth-century stories, it is present in very sparse detail.

With all the unusual approaches to describing human experience which can be found in the modern short story, it is important to remember that the form, like poetry, must be read *slowly* and *carefully*. Every detail must be considered for its possible contribution to a total effect. In the stories that follow you will find unusual time sequences, emphasis on the inner nature of people, complicated beginnings, unexpected realizations within characters, and endings which have no finality and tend to leave you hanging in midair. Most of all, you will find that a great deal is left unsaid. And if the stories are truly to be studied, *you must make these inferences.* Remember that the incidents in the stories, regardless of their seeming lack of dramatic quality or underdevelopment by the writer, will almost without exception contain something which represents symbolically a fundamental notion about the ways of man.

The Rat Trap

SELMA LAGERLÖF

Once upon a time there was a man who went around selling small rat traps of wire. He made them himself at odd moments, from material he got by begging in the stores or at the big farms. But even so, the business was not especially profitable, so he had to resort to both begging and petty° thievery to keep body and soul together. Even so, his clothes were in rags, his cheeks were sunken, and hunger gleamed in his eyes.

No one can imagine how sad and monotonous life can appear to such a vagabond,° who plods along the road, left to his own meditations. But one day this man had fallen into a line of thought which really seemed to him entertaining. He had naturally been thinking of his rat traps when suddenly he was struck by the idea that the whole world about him — the whole world with its lands and seas, its cities and villages — was nothing but a big rat trap. It had never existed for any other purpose than to set baits° for people. It offered riches and joys, shelter and food, heat and clothing, exactly as the rat trap offered cheese and pork, and as soon as anyone let himself be tempted to touch the bait, it closed in on him, and then everything came to an end.

The world had, of course, never been very kind to him, so it gave him unwonted joy to think ill of it in this way.

It became a cherished pastime of his, during many dreary ploddings, to think of people he knew who had let themselves be caught in the dangerous snare, and of others who were still circling around the bait.

One dark evening as he was trudging along the road he caught sight of a little gray cottage by the roadside, and he knocked on the door to ask shelter for the night. Nor was he refused. Instead of the sour faces which ordinarily met him, the owner, who was an old man without wife or child, was happy to get someone to talk to in his loneliness. Immediately he put the porridge° pot on the fire and gave him supper; then he carved off such a big slice from his tobacco roll that it was enough both for the stranger's pipe and his own. Finally he got out an old pack of cards and played "mjölis" with his guest until bedtime.

The old man was just as generous with his confidence as with his porridge and tobacco. The guest was informed at once that in his days of prosperity his host had been a crofter at Ramsjö Ironworks and had worked on the land. Now that he was no longer able to do day labor, it was his cow which supported him. Yes, that bossy was extraordinary. She could give milk for the creamery every day, and last month he had received all of thirty kroner[1] in payment.

The stranger must have seemed incredulous, for the old man got up and went to the window, took down a leather pouch which hung on a nail in the very window frame, and picked out three wrinkled ten-kroner bills. These he held up before the eyes of his guest, nodding knowingly, and then stuffed them back into the pouch.

The next day both men got up in good season. The crofter was in a hurry to milk his cow, and the other man probably thought he should not stay in bed when the head of the house had gotten up. They left the cottage at the same time. The crofter locked the door and put the key in his pocket. The man with the rat traps said good-by and thank you, and thereupon each went his own way.

But half an hour later the rat-trap peddler stood again

[1]The plural form of the word *krona*. The krona is the monetary unit of Sweden. In 1950 each krona was worth about nineteen cents.

before the door. He did not try to get in, however. He only went up to the window, smashed a pane, stuck in his hand, and got hold of the pouch with the thirty kroner. He took the money and thrust it into his own pocket. Then he hung the leather pouch very carefully back in its place and went away.

As he walked along with the money in his pocket he felt quite pleased with his smartness. He realized, of course, that at first he dared not continue on the public highway, but must turn off the road, into the woods. During the first hours this caused him no difficulty. Later in the day it became worse, for it was a big and confusing forest which he had gotten into. He tried, to be sure, to walk in a definite direction, but the paths twisted back and forth so strangely! He walked and walked, without coming to the end of the wood, and finally he realized that he had only been walking around in the same part of the forest. All at once he recalled his thoughts about the world and the rat trap. Now his own turn had come. He had let himself be fooled by a bait and had been caught. The whole forest, with its trunks and branches, its thickets and fallen logs, closed in upon him like an impenetrable° prison from which he could never escape.

It was late in December. Darkness was already descending over the forest. This increased the danger, and increased also his gloom and despair. Finally he saw no way out, and he sank down on the ground, tired to death, thinking that his last moment had come. But just as he laid his head on the ground, he heard a sound—a hard, regular thumping. There was no doubt as to what that was. He raised himself. "Those are the hammer strokes from an iron mill," he thought. "There must be people near by." He summoned all his strength, got up, and staggered in the direction of the sound.

The Ramsjö Ironworks, which are now closed down, were, not so long ago, a large plant, with smelter,° rolling mill,° and forge.° In the summertime long lines of heavily loaded barges and scows° slid down the canal which led to a large inland lake, and in the wintertime the roads near the mill were black from all the coal dust which sifted down from the big charcoal crates.

During one of the long dark evenings just before Christmas, the master smith and his helper sat in the dark forge near the furnace waiting for the pig iron,° which had been put in the fire, to be ready to put on the anvil. Every now and then one of them got up to stir the glowing mass with a long iron bar, returning in a few moments, dripping with perspiration, though, as was the custom, he wore nothing but a long shirt and a pair of wooden shoes.

All the time there were many sounds to be heard in the forge. The big bellows groaned and the burning coal cracked. The fire boy shoveled charcoal into the maw° of the furnace with a great deal of clatter. Outside roared the waterfall, and a sharp north wind whipped the rain against the brick-tiled roof.

It was probably on account of all this noise that the blacksmiths did not notice that a man had opened the gate and entered the forge, until he stood close up to the furnace.

Surely it was nothing unusual for poor vagabonds without any better shelter for the night to be attracted to the forge by the glow of light which escaped through the sooty panes, and to come in to warm themselves in front of the fire. The blacksmiths glanced only casually and indifferently at the intruder. He looked the way people of his type usually did, with a long beard, dirty, ragged, and with a bunch of rat traps dangling on his chest.

He asked permission to stay, and the master blacksmith nodded a haughty consent without honoring him with a single word.

The tramp did not say anything, either. He had not come there to talk but only to warm himself and sleep.

In those days the Ramsjö iron mill was owned by a very prominent ironmaster whose greatest ambition was to ship out good iron to the market. He watched both night and day to see that the work was done as well as possible, and at this very moment he came into the forge on one of his nightly rounds of inspection.

Naturally the first thing he saw was the tall ragamuffin°

who had eased his way so close to the furnace that steam rose from his wet rags. The ironmaster did not follow the example of the blacksmiths, who had hardly deigned to look at the stranger. He walked close up to him, looked him over very carefully, then tore off his slouch hat to get a better view of his face.

"But of course it is you, Nils Olof!" he said. "How you do look!"

The man with the rat traps had never before seen the ironmaster of Ramsjö and did not even know what his name was. But it occurred to him that if the fine gentleman thought he was an old acquaintance, he might perhaps throw him a couple of kroner. Therefore he did not want to undeceive him all at once.

"Yes, God knows things have gone downhill with me," he said.

"You should not have resigned from the regiment," said the ironmaster. "That was a mistake. If only I had still been in the service at the time, it never would have happened. Well, now of course you will come home with me."

To go along up to the manor house and be received by the owner like an old regimental comrade—that, however, did not please the tramp.

"No, I couldn't think of it!" he said, looking quite alarmed.

He thought of the thirty kroner. To go up to the manor house would be like throwing himself voluntarily into the lions' den. He only wanted a chance to sleep here in the forge and then sneak away as inconspicuously° as possible.

The ironmaster assumed that he felt embarrassed because of his miserable clothing.

"Please don't think that I have such a fine home that you cannot show yourself there," he said. "Elizabeth is dead, as you may already have heard. My boys are abroad, and there is no one at home except my oldest daughter and myself. We were just saying that it was too bad we didn't have any company for Christmas. Now come along with me and help us make the Christmas food disappear a little faster."

But the stranger said no, and no, and again no, and the ironmaster saw that he must give in.

"It looks as though Captain von Stahle prefers to stay with you tonight, Stjernström," he said to the master blacksmith, and turned on his heel.

But he laughed to himself as he went away, and the blacksmith, who knew him, understood very well that he had not said his last word.

It was not more than half an hour before they heard the sound of carriage wheels outside the forge, and a new guest came in, but this time it was not the ironmaster. He had sent his daughter, apparently hoping that she would have better powers of persuasion than he himself.

She entered, followed by a valet,° carrying on his arm a big fur coat. She was not at all pretty, but seemed modest and quite shy. In the forge everything was just as it had been earlier in the evening. The master blacksmith and his apprentice still sat on their bench, and iron and charcoal still glowed in the furnace. The stranger had stretched himself out on the floor and lay with a piece of pig iron under his head and his hat pulled down over his eyes. As soon as the young girl caught sight of him, she went up and lifted his hat. The man was evidently used to sleeping with one eye open. He jumped up abruptly and seemed to be quite frightened.

"My name is Edla Willmansson," said the young girl. "My father came home and said that you wanted to sleep here in the forge tonight, and then I asked permission to come and bring you home to us. I am so sorry, Captain, that you are having such a hard time."

She looked at him compassionately with her heavy eyes, and then she noticed that the man was afraid. "Either he has stolen something or else he has escaped from jail," she thought, and added quickly, "You may be sure, Captain, that you will be allowed to leave us just as freely as you came. Only please stay with us over Christmas Eve."

She said this in such a friendly manner that the rat-trap peddler must have felt confidence in her.

"It would never have occurred to me that you would

bother with me yourself, miss," he said. "I will come at once."

He accepted the fur coat which the valet handed him with a deep bow, threw it over his rags, and followed the young lady out to the carriage, without granting the astonished blacksmiths so much as a glance.

But while he was riding up to the manor house he had evil forebodings.°

"Why the devil did I take that fellow's money?" he thought. "Now I am sitting in the trap and will never get out of it."

The next day was Christmas Eve, and when the ironmaster came into the dining room for breakfast he probably thought with satisfaction of his old regimental comrade whom he had run across so unexpectedly.

"First of all we must see to it that he gets a little flesh on his bones," he said to his daughter, who was busy at the table. "And then we must see that he gets something else to do than to run around the country selling rat traps."

"It is queer that things have gone downhill with him as badly as that," said the daughter. "Last night I did not think there was anything about him to show that he had once been an educated man."

"You must have patience, my little girl," said the father. "As soon as he gets clean and dressed up, you will see something different. Last night he was naturally embarrassed. The tramp manners will fall away from him with the tramp clothes."

Just as he said this the door opened and the stranger entered. Yes, now he was truly clean and well dressed. The valet had bathed him, cut his hair, and shaved him. Moreover, he was dressed in a good-looking suit of clothes which belonged to the ironmaster. He wore a white shirt and a starched collar and whole shoes.

But although his guest was now so well groomed, the ironmaster did not seem pleased. He looked at him with puckered° brow, and it was easy to understand that when he had seen the strange fellow in the uncertain reflection from the furnace he might have made a mistake, but that now, when he stood there in broad daylight, it was impossible to mistake him for an old acquaintance.

"What does this mean?" he thundered.

The stranger made no attempt to dissimulate.° He saw at once that the splendor had come to an end.

"It is not my fault, sir," he said. "I never pretended to be anything but a poor trader, and I pleaded and begged to be allowed to stay in the forge. But no harm has been done. At worst I can put on my rags again and go away."

"Well," said the ironmaster, hesitating a little, "it was not quite honest, either. You must admit that, and I should not be surprised if the sheriff would like to have something to say in the matter."

The tramp took a step forward and struck the table with his fist.

"Now I am going to tell you, Mr. Ironmaster, how things are," he said. "This whole world is nothing but a big rat trap. All the good things that are offered you are nothing but cheese rinds° and bits of pork, set out to drag a poor fellow into trouble. And if the sheriff comes now and locks me up for this, then you, Mr. Ironmaster, must remember that a day may come when you yourself may want to get a big piece of pork, and then you will get caught in the trap."

The ironmaster began to laugh.

"That was not so badly said, my good fellow. Perhaps we should let the sheriff alone on Christmas Eve. But now get out of here as fast as you can."

But just as the man was opening the door, the daughter said, "I think he ought to stay with us today. I don't want him to go." And with that she went and closed the door.

"What in the world are you doing?" said the father.

The daughter stood there quite embarrassed and hardly knew what to answer. That morning she had felt so happy when she thought how homelike and Christmassy she was going to make things for the poor hungry wretch. She could not get away from the idea all at once, and that was why she had interceded for the vagabond.

"I am thinking of this stranger here," said the young

girl. "He walks and walks the whole year long, and there is probably not a single place in the whole country where he is welcome and can feel at home. Wherever he turns he is chased away. Always he is afraid of being arrested and cross-examined. I should like to have him enjoy a day of peace with us here—just one in the whole year."

The ironmaster mumbled something in his beard. He could not bring himself to oppose her.

"It was all a mistake, of course," she continued. "But anyway I don't think we ought to chase away a human being whom we have asked to come here, and to whom we have promised Christmas cheer."

"You do preach worse than a parson," said the iron-master. "I only hope you won't have to regret this."

The young girl took the stranger by the hand and led him up to the table.

"Now sit down and eat," she said, for she could see that her father had given in.

The man with the rat traps said not a word; he only sat down and helped himself to the food. Time after time he looked at the young girl who had interceded for him. Why had she done it? What could the crazy idea be?

After that, Christmas Eve at Ramsjö passed just as it always had. The stranger did not cause any trouble because he did nothing but sleep. The whole forenoon he lay on the sofa in one of the guest rooms and slept at one stretch. At noon they woke him up so that he could have his share of the good Christmas fare, but after that he slept again. It seemed as though for many years he had not been able to sleep as quietly and safely as here at Ramsjö.

In the evening, when the Christmas tree was lighted, they woke him up again, and he stood for a while in the drawing room, blinking as though the candlelight hurt him, but after that he disappeared again. Two hours later he was aroused once more. He then had to go down into the dining room and eat the Christmas fish and porridge.

As soon as they got up from the table he went around to each one present and said thank you and good night, but when he came to the young girl she gave him to understand that it was her father's intention that the suit which he wore was to be a Christmas present—he did not have to return it; and if he wanted to spend next Christmas Eve in a place where he could rest in peace, and be sure that no evil would befall him, he would be welcomed back again.

The man with the rat traps did not answer anything to this. He only stared at the young girl in boundless amazement.

The next morning the ironmaster and his daughter got up in good season to go to the early Christmas service. Their guest was still asleep, and they did not disturb him.

When, at about ten o'clock, they drove back from church, the young girl sat and hung her head even more dejectedly° than usual. At church she had learned that one of the old crofters of the ironworks had been robbed by a man who went around selling rat traps.

"Yes, that was a fine fellow you let into the house," said her father. "I only wonder how many silver spoons are left in the cupboard by this time."

The wagon had hardly stopped at the front steps when the ironmaster asked the valet whether the stranger was still there. He added that he had heard at church that the man was a thief. The valet answered that the fellow had gone and that he had not taken anything with him at all. On the contrary, he had left behind a little package which Miss Willmansson was to be kind enough to accept as a Christmas present.

The young girl opened the package, which was so badly done up that the contents came into view at once. She gave a little cry of joy. She found a small rat trap, and in it lay three wrinkled ten-kroner notes. But that was not all. In the rat trap lay also a letter written in large, jagged characters:

"HONORED AND NOBLE MISS:

"Since you have been so nice to me all day long, as if I was a captain, I want to be nice to you, in return, as if I was a real captain, for I do not want you to be embarrassed at this Christmas season by a thief; but you can give back the money to the old man on the roadside, who has the money pouch hanging on the window frame as a bait for poor wanderers.

"The rat trap is a Christmas present from a rat who would have been caught in this world's rat trap if he had not been raised to captain, because in that way he got power to clear himself.

"Written with friendship and high regard,

CAPTAIN VON STAHLE"

Do especially Questions 11, 81, 85, 91, 113, and 114. Consult the Short Story Model on page 156.

SELMA LAGERLÖF   *1858-1940*

The first woman to receive the Nobel prize for literature (1909), Selma Lagerlöf came to love agrarian Sweden as a young child when, because of poor health, she took to reading Swedish folklore. Although her works departed from the contemporary pattern of scientific realism, Lagerlöf's romantic novels, tales, and legends (such as "The Rat Trap") were widely read and enjoyed.

The Cabuliwallah

SIR RABINDRANATH TAGORE

My five-year-old daughter Mini cannot live without chattering. I really believe that in all her life she has not wasted a minute in silence. Her mother is often vexed at this, and would stop her prattle,° but I would not. To see Mini quiet is unnatural, and I cannot bear it long. And so my own talk with her is always lively.

One morning, for instance, when I was in the midst of the seventeenth chapter of my new novel, my little Mini stole into the room, and putting her hand into mine, said, "Father! Ramdayal the doorkeeper calls a crow a krow! He doesn't know anything, does he?"

Before I could explain the differences of language in the world, she was embarked on the full tide of another subject. "What do you think, Father? Bhola says there is an elephant in the clouds, blowing water out of his trunk, and that is why it rains!"

And then, darting off anew, while I sat still making ready some reply to this last saying, "Father! what relation is Mother to you?"

"My dear little sister in the law!"[1] I murmured involuntarily to myself, but with a grave face contrived° to answer, "Go and play with Bhola, Mini! I am busy!"

The window of my room overlooks the road. The child had seated herself at my feet near my table, and was playing softly, drumming on her knees. I was hard at work on my seventeenth chapter, where Protrap Singh, the hero, had just caught Kanchanlata, the heroine, in his arms and was about to escape with her by the third-story window of the castle, when all of a sudden Mini left her play and ran to the window crying, "A Cabuliwallah[2], a Cabuliwallah!" Sure enough in the street below was a Cabuliwallah, passing slowly along. He wore the loose soiled clothing of his people, with a tall turban;° there was a bag on his back, and he carried boxes of grapes in his hand.

I cannot tell what were my daughter's feelings at the sight of this man, but she began to call him loudly. "Ah!" I thought, "he will come in, and my seventeenth chapter will never be finished!" At which exact moment the Cabuliwallah turned and looked up at the child. When she

[1] In India a wife is thought of as a legal sister to her husband.
[2] A native of Kabul, a province on the northwest border of India. Kabul is in the country of Afghanistan.

saw this, overcome by terror, she fled to her mother's protection and disappeared. She had a blind belief that inside the bag which the big man carried there were perhaps two or three other children like herself. The peddler meanwhile entered my doorway and greeted me with a smiling face.

So precarious° was the position of my hero and my heroine that my first impulse was to stop and buy something, since the man had been called. I made some small purchases and a conversation began about Abdurrahman, the Russians, the English, and the Frontier Policy.

As he was about to leave, he asked: "And where is the little girl, sir?"

— And I, thinking that Mini must get rid of her false fear, had her brought out.

She stood by my chair and looked at the Cabuliwallah and his bag. He offered her nuts and raisins, but she would not be tempted, and only clung the closer to me, with all her doubts increased.

This was their first meeting.

One morning, however, not many days later, as I was leaving the house, I was startled to find Mini, seated on a bench near the door, laughing and talking, with the great Cabuliwallah at her feet. In all her life, it appeared, my small daughter had never found so patient a listener, save her father. And already the corner of her little *sari*° was stuffed with almonds and raisins, the gift of her visitor. "Why did you give her those?" I said, and taking out an eight-anna[3] bit, I handed it to him. The man accepted the money without demur° and slipped it into his pocket.

Alas, on my return an hour later I found the unfortunate coin had made twice its own worth of trouble! For the Cabuliwallah had given it to Mini, and her mother catching sight of the bright round object, had pounced on the child with, "Where did you get that eight-anna bit?"

"The Cabuliwallah gave it to me," said Mini cheerfully.

[3]An eight-anna bit is worth approximately ten cents in American currency.

"The Cabuliwallah gave it to you!" cried her mother, much shocked. "Oh, Mini! how could you take it from him?"

I, entering at the moment, saved her from impending° disaster and proceeded to make my own inquiries.

It was not the first or second time, I found, that the two had met. The Cabuliwallah had overcome the child's first terror by a judicious° bribery of nuts and almonds, and the two were now great friends.

They had many quaint jokes, which afforded them much amusement. Seated in front of him, looking down on his gigantic frame in all her tiny dignity, Mini would ripple her face with laughter and begin, "O Cabuliwallah, Cabuliwallah, what have you got in your bag?"

And he would reply in the nasal accents of the mountaineer, "An elephant!" Not much cause for merriment, perhaps; but how they both enjoyed the witticism! And for me, this child's talk with a grown-up man had always in it something strangely fascinating.

Then the Cabuliwallah, not to be behindhand, would take his turn, "Well, little one, and when are you going to the father-in-law's house?"[4]

Now most small Bengali[5] maidens have heard long ago about the father-in-law's house; but we, being a little new-fangled, had kept these things from our child, and Mini at this question must have been a trifle bewildered. But she would not show it, and with ready tact replied: "Are *you* going there?"

Among men of the Cabuliwallah's class, however, it is well known that the words *father-in-law's house* have a double meaning. It is a euphemism° for *jail*, the place where we are well cared for at no expense to ourselves. In this sense would the sturdy peddler take my daughter's question. "Ah," he would say, shaking his fist at an invisible policeman, "I will thrash my father-in-law!" Hearing

[4]Traditionally, Hindu girls were married young and went to live with their husband's parents.
[5]A native of Bengal, a province in northeast India.

this and picturing the poor discomfited° relative, Mini would go off into peals of laughter in which her formidable friend would join.

These were autumn mornings, the very time of year when kings of old went forth to conquest; and I, never stirring from my little corner in Calcutta, would let my mind wander over the whole world. At the very name of another country my heart would go out to it, and at the sight of a foreigner in the streets I would fall to weaving a network of dreams — the mountains, the glens, and the forests of his distant home, with his cottage in its setting and the free and independent life of far-away wilds. Perhaps the scenes of travel conjure themselves up before me and pass and repass in my imagination all the more vividly because I lead such a vegetable existence that a call to travel would fall upon me like a thunderbolt. In the presence of this Cabuliwallah I was immediately transported to the foot of arid° mountain peaks, with narrow little defiles° twisting in and out among their towering heights. I could see the string of camels bearing the merchandise, and the company of turbaned merchants, carrying some of their queer old firearms, and some of their spears, journeying downward toward the plains. I could see — but at some such point Mini's mother would intervene, imploring me to "beware of that man."

Mini's mother is unfortunately a very timid lady. Whenever she hears a noise in the street or sees people coming toward the house, she always jumps to the conclusion that they are either thieves or drunkards or snakes or tigers or malaria or cockroaches or caterpillars or an English sailor. Even after all these years of experience, she is not able to overcome her terror. So she was full of doubts about the Cabuliwallah and used to beg me to keep a watchful eye on him.

I tried to laugh her fear gently away, but then she would turn round on me seriously and ask me solemn questions.

Were children never kidnaped?

Was it, then, not true that there was slavery in Kabul?

Was it so very absurd that this big man should be able to carry off a tiny child?

I urged that, though not impossible, it was highly improbable. But this was not enough, and her dread persisted. As it was indefinite, however, it did not seem right to forbid the man the house, and the intimacy went on unchecked.

Once a year in the middle of January, Rahmun, the Cabuliwallah, was in the habit of returning to his country, and as the time approached he would be very busy, going from house to house collecting his debts. This year, however, he could always find time to come to see Mini. It would have seemed to an outsider that there was some conspiracy° between the two, for when he could not come in the morning, he would appear in the evening.

Even to me it was a little startling now and then, in the corner of a dark room, suddenly to surprise this tall, loose-garmented, much-bebagged man; but when Mini would run in smiling, with her "O! Cabuliwallah! Cabuliwallah!" and the two friends, so far apart in age, would subside into their old laughter and their old jokes, I felt reassured.

One morning, a few days before he had made up his mind to go, I was correcting my proof sheets° in my study. It was chilly weather. Through the window the rays of the sun touched my feet, and the slight warmth was very welcome. It was almost eight o'clock, and the early pedestrians were returning home, with their heads covered. All at once I heard an uproar in the street, and looking out, saw Rahmun being led away bound between two policemen, and behind them a crowd of curious boys. There were bloodstains on the clothes of the Cabuliwallah, and one of the policemen carried a knife. Hurrying out, I stopped them and inquired what it all meant. Partly from one, partly from another, I gathered that a certain neighbor had owed the peddler something for a Rampuri[6] shawl, but had falsely denied having bought it, and that in the course of the quarrel Rahmun had struck him. Now in the heat of his excite-

[6]From Rampur, a province in north central India.

ment, the prisoner began calling his enemy all sorts of names, when suddenly in a verandah of my house appeared my little Mini, with her usual exclamation: "O Cabuli-wallah! Cabuliwallah!" Rahmun's face lighted up as he turned to her. He had no bag under his arm today, so she could not discuss the elephant with him. She at once there-fore proceeded to the next question, "Are you going to the father-in-law's house?" Rahmun laughed and said, "Just where I am going, little one!" Then seeing the reply did not amuse the child, he held up his fettered hands. "Ah," he said, "I would have thrashed that old father-in-law, but my hands are bound!"

On a charge of murderous assault° Rahmun was sen-tenced to some years' imprisonment.

Time passed away, and he was not remembered. The accustomed work in the accustomed place was ours, and the thought of the once free mountaineer spending his years in prison seldom or never occurred to us. Even my light-hearted Mini, I am ashamed to say, forgot her old friend. New companions filled her life. As she grew older she spent more of her time with girls. So much time indeed did she spend with them that she came no more, as she used to do, to her father's room. I was scarcely on speaking terms with her.

Years had passed away. It was once more autumn and we had made arrangements for our Mini's marriage. It was to take place during the Puja holidays.[7] With Durga returning to Kailas, the light of our home was to depart to her hus-band's house and leave her father's in the shadow.

The morning was bright. After the rains there was a sense of ablution° in the air, and the sun-rays looked like pure gold. So bright were they that they gave a beautiful radi-ance even to the sordid brick walls of our Calcutta lanes. Since early dawn today the wedding pipes° had been sounding, and at each beat my own heart throbbed. The wail of the tune, Bhairavi, seemed to intensify my pain at

[7]Hindu religious holidays in the fall of the year.

the approaching separation. My Mini was to be married tonight.

From early morning, noise and bustle had pervaded the house. In the courtyard the canopy had to be slung on its bamboo poles; the chandeliers° with their tinkling sound must be hung in each room and verandah. There was no end of hurry and excitement. I was sitting in my study, looking through the accounts, when someone entered, saluting respectfully, and stood before me. It was Rahmun the Cabuliwallah. At first I did not recognize him. He had no bag, nor the long hair, nor the same vigor that he used to have. But he smiled, and I knew him again.

"When did you come, Rahmun?" I asked him.

"Last evening," he said, "I was released from jail."

The words struck harsh upon my ears. I had never before talked with one who had wounded his fellow, and my heart shrank within itself when I realized this, for I felt that the day would have been better-omened° had he not turned up.

"There are ceremonies going on," I said, "and I am busy. Could you perhaps come another day?"

At once he turned to go, but as he reached the door he hesitated and said, "May I not see the little one, sir, for a moment?" It was his belief that Mini was still the same. He had pictured her running to him as she used, calling "O Cabuliwallah! Cabuliwallah!" He had imagined, too, that they would laugh and talk together, just as of old. In fact, in memory of former days he had brought, carefully wrapped up in paper, a few almonds and raisins and grapes, obtained somehow from a countryman, for his own little fund was dispersed.°

I said again, "There is a ceremony in the house and you will not be able to see anyone today."

The man's face fell. He looked wistfully at me for a moment, said "Good morning," and went out.

I felt a little sorry and would have called him back, but I found he was returning of his own accord. He came close up to me holding out his offerings and said, "I brought these few things, sir, for the little one. Will you give them to her?"

I took them and was going to pay him, but he caught my hand and said, "You are very kind, sir! Keep me in your recollection. Do not offer me money!—You have a little girl; I, too, have one like her in my own home. I think of her and bring fruits to your child, not to make a profit for myself."

Saying this, he put his hand inside his big loose robe and brought out a small and dirty piece of paper. With great care he unfolded this and smoothed it out with both hands on my table. It bore the impression of a little hand. Not a photograph. Not a drawing. The impression of an ink-smeared hand laid flat on the paper. This touch of his own little daughter had been always on his heart as he had come year after year to Calcutta to sell his wares in the streets.

Tears came to my eyes. I forgot that he was a poor Kabuli fruit seller, while I was . . . but no, what was I more than he? He also was a father.

That impression of the hand of his little *Parbati*[8] in her distant mountain home reminded me of my own little Mini.

I sent for Mini immediately from the inner apartment. Many difficulties were raised, but I would not listen. Clad in the red silk of her wedding day, with the sandal paste[9] on her forehead, and adorned as a young bride, Mini came and stood bashfully before me.

The Cabuliwallah looked a little staggered at the apparition. He could not revive their old friendship. At last he smiled and said, "Little one, are you going to your father-in-law's house?"

But Mini now understood the meaning of the word "father-in-law," and she could not reply to him as of old. She flushed up at the question and stood before him with her bridelike face turned down.

I remembered the day when the Cabuliwallah and my Mini had first met, and I felt sad. When she had gone, Rahmun heaved a deep sigh and sat down on the floor. The

[8]A Hindu term of affection meaning daughter.
[9]A caste mark made of oil extracted from the sandalwood tree.

idea had suddenly come to him that his daughter, too, must have grown in this long time and that he would have to make friends with her anew. Assuredly he would not find her as he used to know her. And besides, what might not have happened to her in these eight years?

The marriage pipes sounded and the mild autumn sun streamed round us. But Rahmun sat in the little Calcutta lane and saw before him the barren° mountains of Afghanistan.

I took out a bank note and gave it to him, saying, "Go back to your own daughter, Rahmun, in your own country, and may the happiness of your meeting bring good fortune to my child!"

Having° made this present, I had to curtail° some of the festivities. I could not have the electric lights I had intended nor the military band, and the ladies of the house were despondent° at it. But to me the wedding feast was all the brighter for the thought that in a distant land a long-lost father met again with his only child.

Do especially Questions 11, 81, 85, 91, 113, and 114. Consult the Short Story Model on page 156.

SIR RABINDRANATH TAGORE   *1861-1941*

Educated by tutors in his native India, Tagore came to England in 1878 where he attended lectures at University College, London. He went back to India, fully intending to return to England and study law; but an accident, taken as an omen by his father, prevented his further formal education. Talented both in music and literature from youth, Tagore's first published works appeared in 1876 in a magazine called *Sprouting Knowledge.* Sir Rabindranath — Tagore is actually not a name, but a title of nobility — wrote over one hundred thousand lines of poetry and translated into English many of his own works, as well as the works of other Indian authors. While lecturing in the United States in 1913, he won the Nobel prize for literature. He was knighted in 1915 and received honorary degrees from four Indian universities. After lecturing at Oxford he made an extensive tour of Germany, Denmark, Russia, the United States, and Persia. Some of Tagore's works available in English are *The Crescent Moon, The Home and the World,* and *The Religion of Man.*

Quality

JOHN GALSWORTHY

I knew him from the days of my extreme youth, because he
made my father's boots;° inhabiting with his elder brother
two little shops let into one, in a small bystreet—now no
more, but then most fashionably placed in the West End.

That tenement[1] had a certain quiet distinction; there
was no sign upon its face that he made for any of the Royal
Family[2]—merely his own German name of Gessler Brothers,
and in the window a few pairs of boots. I remember that it
always troubled me to account for those unvarying boots
in the window, for he made only what was ordered, reaching nothing down,[3] and it seemed so inconceivable that
what he made could ever have failed to fit. Had he bought
them to put there? That, too, seemed inconceivable. He
would never have tolerated in his house leather on which
he had not worked himself. Besides, they were too beautiful—the pair of pumps, so inexpressibly slim, the patent
leathers with cloth tops, making water come into one's
mouth, the tall brown riding boots with marvelous sooty
glow, as if, though new, they had been worn a hundred
years. Those pairs could only have been made by one who
saw before him the Soul of Boot—so truly were they
prototypes[4] incarnating the very spirit of all footgear.
These thoughts, of course, came to me later, though even
when I was promoted to him, at the age of perhaps four-
teen, some inkling° haunted me of the dignity of himself
and brother. For to make boots—such boots as he made—

[1]In the sense used here, rented property.
[2]English shopkeepers who had sold something to a member of the royal
family, no matter how long ago, mentioned this fact in their advertising.
The shoemaker in this story refuses to put up such a sign.
[3]REACHING NOTHING DOWN—That is, from a shelf. Gessler kept no stock
of ready-made shoes.
[4]Models; patterns.

seemed to me then, and still seems to me, mysterious and wonderful.

I remember well my shy remark, one day, while stretching out to him my youthful foot:

"Isn't it awfully hard to do, Mr. Gessler?"

And his answer, given with a sudden smile out of the sardonic[5] redness of his beard: "Id is an Ardt!"

Himself, he was a little as if made from leather, with his yellow crinkly face, and crinkly reddish hair and beard, and neat folds slanting down his cheeks to the corners of his mouth, and his guttural[6] and one-toned voice, for leather is a sardonic substance, and stiff and slow of purpose. And that was the character of his face, save that his eyes, which were gray-blue, had in them the simple gravity of one secretly possessed by the Ideal. His elder brother was so very like him—though watery, paler in every way, with a great industry—that sometimes in early days I was not quite sure of him until the interview was over. Then I knew that it was he, if the words, "I will ask my brudder," had not been spoken; and that, if they had, it was his elder brother.

When one grew old and wild and ran up bills, one somehow never ran them up with Gessler Brothers. It would not have seemed becoming to go in there and stretch out one's foot to that blue iron-spectacled glance, owing him for more than—say—two pairs, just the comfortable reassurance° that one was still his client.

For it was not possible to go to him very often—his boots lasted terribly, having something beyond the temporary—some, as it were, essence of boot stitched into them.

One went in, not as into most shops, in the mood of: "Please serve me, and let me go!" but restfully, as one enters a church; and, sitting on the single wooden chair, waited—for there was never anybody there. Soon, over the top edge of that sort of well—rather dark, and smelling soothingly of leather—which formed the shop, there would

[5]Scornful with the scorn of a perfectionist who is impatient with those who spare themselves.
[6]Harsh; throaty.

be seen his face, or that of his elder brother, peering down. A guttural sound, and the tip-tap of bast[7] slippers beating the narrow wooden stairs, and he would stand before one without coat, a little bent, in leather apron, with sleeves turned back, blinking—as if awakened from some dream of boots, or like an owl surprised in daylight and annoyed at this interruption.

And I would say: "How do you do, Mr. Gessler? Could you make me a pair of Russia leather boots?"

Without a word he would leave me, retiring whence he came, or into the other portion of the shop, and I would continue to rest in the wooden chair, inhaling the incense of his trade. Soon he would come back, holding in his thin, veined hand a piece of gold-brown leather. With eyes fixed on it, he would remark: "What a beaudiful biece!" When I, too, had admired it, he would speak again. "When do you wand dem?" And I would answer: "Oh! As soon as you conveniently can." And he would say: "Tomorrow fordnighd?"[8] Or if he were his elder brother: "I will ask my brudder!"

Then I would murmur: "Thank you! Good morning, Mr. Gessler." "Goot morning!" he would reply, still looking at the leather in his hand. And as I moved to the door, I would hear the tip-tap of his bast slippers restoring him, up the stairs, to his dream of boots. But if it were some new kind of footgear that he had not yet made me, then indeed he would observe ceremony—divesting me of my boot and holding it long in his hand, looking at it with eyes at once critical and loving, as if recalling the glow with which he had created it, and rebuking° the way in which one had disorganized this masterpiece. Then, placing my foot on a piece of paper, he would two or three times tickle the outer edges with a pencil and pass his nervous fingers over my toes, feeling himself into the heart of my requirements.

I cannot forget that day on which I had occasion to say to him: "Mr. Gessler, that last pair of town walking boots creaked, you know."

[7]Rope or fiber.
[8]FORDNIGHD: Fortnight, that is, two weeks.

He looked at me for a time without replying, as if expecting me to withdraw or qualify the statement, then said:

"Id shouldn'd 'ave greaked."

"It did, I'm afraid."

"You goddem wed before dey found demselves?"

"I don't think so."

At that he lowered his eyes, as if hunting for memory of those boots, and I felt sorry I had mentioned this grave thing.

"Zend dem back!" he said; "I will look at dem."

A feeling of compassion for my creaking boots surged up in me, so well could I imagine the sorrowful long curiosity of regard which he would bend on them.

"Zome boods," he said slowly, "are bad from birdt.[9] If I can do noding wid dem, I dake dem off your bill."

Once (once only) I went absent-mindedly into his shop in a pair of boots bought in an emergency at some large firm's. He took my order without showing me any leather, and I could feel his eyes penetrating the inferior integument[10] of my foot. At last he said:

"Dose are nod my boods."

The tone was not one of anger, nor of sorrow, not even of contempt, but there was in it something quiet that froze the blood. He put his hand down and pressed a finger on the place where the left boot, endeavoring to be fashionable, was not quite comfortable.

"Id 'urds you dere," he said. "Dose big virms[11] 'ave no self-respect. Drash!" And then, as if something had given way within him, he spoke long and bitterly. It was the only time I ever heard him discuss the conditions and hardships of his trade.

"Dey ged id all," he said, "dey ged id by adverdisement, nod by work. Dey dake id away from us, who lofe our boods. Id gomes to this—bresently I haf no work. Every year id gets less—you will see." And looking at his lined face I saw things I had never noticed before, bitter things

[9]Birth.
[10]Covering.
[11]Firms.

and bitter struggle—and what a lot of gray hairs there seemed suddenly in his red beard!

As best I could, I explained the circumstances of the purchase of those ill-omened° boots. But his face and voice made so deep an impression that during the next few minutes I ordered many pairs. Nemesis fell![12] They lasted more terribly than ever. And I was not able conscientiously to go to him for nearly two years.

When at last I went I was surprised to find that outside one of the two little windows of his shop another name was painted, also that of a bootmaker—making, of course, for the Royal Family. The old familiar boots, no longer in dignified isolation, were huddled in the single window. Inside, the now contracted well of the one little shop was more scented and darker than ever. And it was longer than usual, too, before a face peered down, and the tip-tap of the bast slippers began. At last he stood before me, and, gazing through those rusty iron spectacles, said:

"Mr. ——, isn'd it?"

"Ah! Mr. Gessler," I stammered, "but your boots are really *too* good, you know! See, these are quite decent still!" And I stretched out to him my foot. He looked at it.

"Yes," he said, "beoble do nod wand good boods, id seems."

To get away from his reproachful eyes and voice I hastily remarked: "What have you done to your shop?"

He answered quietly: "Id was too exbensif. Do you wand some boods?"

I ordered three pairs, though I had only wanted two, and quickly left. I had, I do not know quite what feeling of being part, in his mind, of a conspiracy against him; or not perhaps so much against him as against his idea of boot. One does not, I suppose, care to feel like that; for it was again many months before my next visit to his shop, paid I remember, with the feeling: "Oh! well, I can't leave the old boy—so here goes! Perhaps it'll be his elder brother!"

---

[12]The ancient Greeks believed that the goddess Nemesis pursued, and struck down, mortals who had committed crimes or who were overconfident of success.

For his elder brother, I knew, had not character enough to reproach me, even dumbly.

And, to my relief, in the shop there did appear to be his elder brother, handling a piece of leather.

"Well, Mr. Gessler," I said, "how are you?"

He came close, and peered at me.

"I am breddy well," he said slowly, "but my elder brudder is dead."

And I saw that it was indeed himself — but how aged and wan! And never before had I heard him mention his brother. Much shocked, I murmured: "Oh! I am sorry!"

"Yes," he answered, "he was a good man, he made a good bood; but he is dead." And he touched the top of his head, where the hair had suddenly gone as thin as it had been on that of his poor brother, to indicate, I suppose, the cause of death. "He could nod ged over losing de oder shop. Do you wand any boods?" And he held up the leather in his hand: "Id's a beaudiful biece."

I ordered several pairs. It was very long before they came — but they were better than ever. One simply could not wear them out. And soon after that I went abroad.

It was over a year before I was again in London. And the first shop I went to was my old friend's. I had left a man of sixty, I came back to one of seventy-five, pinched and worn and tremulous,° who genuinely, this time, did not at first know me.

"Oh! Mr. Gessler," I said, sick at heart; "how splendid your boots are! See, I've been wearing this pair nearly all the time I've been abroad; and they're not half worn out, are they?"

He looked long at my boots — a pair of Russia leather, and his face seemed to regain steadiness. Putting his hand on my instep, he said:

"Do dey vid you here? I 'ad drouble wid dat bair, I remember." I assured him that they had fitted beautifully.

"Do you wand any boods?" he said. "I can make dem quickly; id is a slack dime."

I answered: "Please, please! I want boots all around — every kind!"

"I will make a vresh model. Your food must be bigger."
And with utter slowness, he traced round my foot, and felt
my toes, only once looking up to say:

"Did I dell you my brudder was dead?"

To watch him was painful, so feeble had he grown; I was
glad to get away.

I had given those boots up, when one evening they came.
Opening the parcel, I set the four pairs out in a row. Then
one by one I tried them on. There was no doubt about it.
In shape and fit, in finish and quality of leather, they were
the best he had ever made me. And in the mouth of one
of the town walking boots I found his bill. The amount was
the same as usual, but it gave me quite a shock. He had
never before sent it in till quarter day.[13] I flew down-
stairs, and wrote a check, and posted it at once with my
own hand.

A week later, passing the little street, I thought I would
go in and tell him how splendidly the new boots fitted.
But when I came to where his shop had been, his name was
gone. Still there, in the window, were the slim pumps, the
patent leathers with cloth tops, the sooty riding boots.

I went in, very much disturbed. In the two little shops —
again made into one — was a young man with an English
face.

"Mr. Gessler in?" I said.

He gave me a strange, ingratiating look.

"No, sir," he said, "no. But we can attend to anything
with pleasure. We've taken the shop over. You've seen our
name, no doubt, next door. We make for some very good
people."

"Yes, yes," I said, "but Mr. Gessler?"

"Oh!" he answered; "dead."

"Dead! But I only received these boots from him last
Wednesday week."

"Ah!" he said; "a shockin' go. Poor old man starved 'imself."

"Good God!"

"Slow starvation, the doctor called it! You see he went to

[13]The day when quarterly payments become due.

work in such a way! Would keep the shop on; wouldn't have a soul touch his boots except himself. When he got an order, it took him such a time. People won't wait. He lost everybody. And there he'd sit, goin' on and on—I will say that for him—not a man in London made a better boot! But look at the competition! He never advertised! Would 'ave the best leather, too, and do it all 'imself. Well, there it is. What could you expect with his ideas?"

"But starvation—"

"That may be a bit flowery, as the sayin' is—but I know myself he was sittin' over his boots day and night, to the very last. You see I used to watch him. Never gave 'imself time to eat; never had a penny in the house. All went in rent and leather. How he lived so long I don't know. He regular let his fire go out. He was a character. But he made good boots."

"Yes," I said, "he made good boots."

And I turned and went out quickly, for I did not want that youth to know that I could hardly see.

Do especially Questions 11, 102, 106, 107, 108, and 147. Consult the Short Story Model on page 156.

JOHN GALSWORTHY *1867-1933*

Even though as a student at Harrow and Oxford John Galsworthy showed little interest in writing, he later turned to a literary career at the suggestion and encouragement of Ada Galsworthy, the wife of his cousin Arthur. In his younger years he tried law like his father, but, in special need of money, soon set out on a series of extensive journeys to such far-flung places as Canada and the Fijis. On one of these trips he met and encouraged Joseph Conrad, chief officer of the *Torrens*, to continue writing. After composing several novels, essays, and sketches, Galsworthy turned in 1906 to dramatizing social problems in plays. For example, there were *The Silver Box*, treating of the unequal quality of justice given to different classes of society; *Strife*, which was concerned with industrial problems; and *Justice*, an account of deplorable prison conditions. In "Quality" he points out how the industrial revolution has destroyed the noble virtue of craftsmanship. In addition to receiving honorary degrees from Cambridge and five other English universities, Galsworthy was honored with the Nobel prize for literature in 1932, less than a year before his death.

War

LUIGI PIRANDELLO

The passengers who had left Rome by the night express had had to stop until dawn at the small station of Fabriano in order to continue their journey by the small old-fashioned "local" joining the main line with Sulmona.

At dawn, in a stuffy and smoky second-class carriage in which five people had already spent the night, a bulky woman in deep mourning was hoisted in—almost like a shapeless bundle. Behind her—puffing and moaning, followed her husband—a tiny man, thin and weakly, his face death-white, his eyes small and bright and looking shy and uneasy.

Having at last taken a seat he politely thanked the passengers who had helped his wife and who had made room for her; then he turned round to the woman trying to pull down the collar of her coat and politely inquired:

"Are you all right, dear?"

The wife, instead of answering, pulled up her collar again to her eyes, so as to hide her face.

"Nasty world," muttered the husband with a sad smile.

And he felt it his duty to explain to his traveling companions that the poor woman was to be pitied, for the war was taking away from her her only son, a boy of twenty to whom both had devoted their entire life, even breaking up their home at Sulmona to follow him to Rome, where he had to go as a student, then allowing him to volunteer for war with an assurance, however, that at least for six months he would not be sent to the front and now, all of a sudden, receiving a wire saying that he was due to leave in three days' time and asking them to go and see him off.

The woman under the big coat was twisting and wriggling, at times growling like a wild animal, feeling certain that all those explanations would not have aroused even a shadow of sympathy from those people who—most likely—

were in the same plight° as herself. One of them, who had
been listening with particular attention, said:

"You should thank God that your son is only leaving now
for the front. Mine has been sent there the first day of the
war. He has already come back twice wounded and been
sent back again to the front."

"What about me? I have two sons and three nephews at
the front," said another passenger.

"Maybe, but in our case it is our *only* son," ventured the
husband.

"What difference can it make? You may spoil your only
son with excessive attentions, but you cannot love him
more than you would all your other children if you had
any. Paternal° love is not like bread that can be broken
into pieces and split amongst the children in equal shares.
A father gives *all* his love to each one of his children without discrimination,° whether it be one or ten, and if I am
suffering now for my two sons, I am not suffering half for
each of them but double . . ."

"True . . . true . . ." sighed the embarrassed husband,
"but suppose (of course we all hope it will never be your
case) a father has two sons at the front and he loses one of
them, there is still one left to console him . . . while . . ."

"Yes," answered the other, getting cross, "a son left to
console him but also a son left for whom he must survive,
while in the case of the father of an only son, if the son
dies the father can die too and put an end to his distress.
Which of the two positions is the worse? Don't you see
how my case would be worse than yours?"

"Nonsense," interrupted another traveler, a fat, red-
faced man with bloodshot eyes of the palest gray.

He was panting. From his bulging eyes seemed to spurt
inner violence of an uncontrolled vitality° which his
weakened body could hardly contain.

"Nonsense," he repeated, trying to cover his mouth with
his hand so as to hide the two missing front teeth. "Nonsense. Do we give life to our children for our own benefit?"

The other travelers stared at him in distress. The one
who had had his son at the front since the first day of the

war sighed: "You are right. Our children do not belong to us, they belong to the Country. . . ."

"Bosh," retorted the fat traveler. "Do we think of the Country when we give life to our children? Our sons are born because . . . well, because they must be born and when they come to life they take our own life with them. This is the truth. We belong to them but they never belong to us. And when they reach twenty they are exactly what we were at their age. We too had a father and mother, but there were so many other things as well . . . girls, cigarettes, illusions,° new ties . . . and the Country, of course, whose call we would have answered—when we were twenty—even if father and mother had said no. Now, at our age, the love of our Country is still great, of course, but stronger than it is the love for our children. Is there any one of us here who wouldn't gladly take his son's place at the front if he could?"

There was a silence all round, everybody nodding as to approve.

"Why then," continued the fat man, "shouldn't we consider the feelings of our children when they are twenty? Isn't it natural that at their age they should consider the love for their Country (I am speaking of decent boys, of course) even greater than the love for us? Isn't it natural that it should be so, as after all they must look upon us as upon old boys who cannot move any more and must stay at home? If Country exists, if Country is a natural necessity, like bread, of which each of us must eat in order not to die of hunger, somebody must go to defend it. And our sons go, when they are twenty, and they don't want tears, because if they die, they die inflamed and happy (I am speaking, of course, of decent boys). Now, if one dies young and happy, without having the ugly sides of life, the boredom of it, the pettiness,° the bitterness of disillusion . . . what more can we ask for him? Everyone should stop crying; everyone should laugh, as I do . . . or at least thank God—as I do—because my son, before dying, sent me a message saying that he was dying satisfied at having ended his life in the best way he could have wished. That is why, as you see, I do not even wear mourning. . . ."

He shook his light fawn° coat as to show it; his livid° lip over his missing teeth was trembling, his eyes were watery and motionless, and soon after he ended with a shrill laugh which might well have been a sob.

"Quite so . . . quite so . . ." agreed the others.

The woman who, bundled in a corner under her coat, had been sitting and listening had—for the last three months— tried to find in the words of her husband and her friends something to console her in her deep sorrow, something that might show her how a mother should resign herself to send her son not even to death but to a probably dangerous life. Yet not a word had she found amongst the many which had been said . . . and her grief had been greater in seeing that nobody—as she thought—could share her feelings.

But now the words of the traveler amazed and almost stunned her. She suddenly realized that it wasn't the others who were wrong and could not understand her but herself who could not rise up to the same height of those fathers and mothers willing to resign themselves, without crying, not only to the departure of their sons but even to their death.

She lifted her head, she bent over from her corner trying to listen with great attention to the details which the fat man was giving to his companions about the way his son had fallen as a hero, for his King and his Country, happy and without regrets. It seemed to her that she had stumbled into a world she had never dreamt of, a world so far unknown to her, and she was so pleased to hear everyone joining in congratulating that brave father who could so stoically° speak of his child's death.

Then suddenly, just as if she had heard nothing of what had been said and almost as if waking up from a dream, she turned to the old man, asking him:

"Then . . . is your son really dead?"

Everybody stared at her. The old man, too, turned to look at her, fixing his great, bulging, horribly watery light gray eyes, deep in her face. For some little time he tried to answer, but words failed him. He looked and looked at her, almost as if only then—at that silly, incongruous° question—he had suddenly realized at last that his son was really dead—gone forever—forever. His face contracted, became horribly distorted,° then he snatched in haste a handkerchief from his pocket and, to the amazement of everyone, broke into harrowing,° heart-rending, uncontrollable sobs.

Do especially Questions 45, 46, 47, 96, 102, 103, 106, and 107. Consult the Short Story Model on page 156.

LUIGI PIRANDELLO   *1867-1936*

Luigi Pirandello's deep interest in human motivation characterized almost all of his literary work. Educated at the University of Rome as well as the University of Bonn, Pirandello, who brought the impressionistic movement to the Italian stage, won the Nobel prize for literature in 1934. In his plays Pirandello rejected the poetic language used by his predecessors, preferring, instead, the language of everyday life. No doubt the conditions of his own life prompted Pirandello's investigations of mental states. Born in a backward area of Italy, where violence was common and where a man was forced to defend his rights personally, he was troubled as a boy to see the rich receive special religious privileges. In 1894 he married Antonietta Portulano; and they were able to live comfortably, helped by an allowance which Antonietta received from her father. However, when a flood closed her father's sulphur mines and the allowance stopped, poverty provoked Pirandello's wife to insanity. But the author refused to commit her to an institution, and struggled to maintain her and their three children on the small salary which he received as an instructor in a teachers' college. Not until after World War I did recognition come to Pirandello, his first major success being the play *Six Characters in Search of an Author* (1921). His popularity rose steadily, resulting in the considerable influence which he has produced upon subsequent Italian drama.

The Quiet Man

MAURICE WALSH

Shawn Kelvin, a blithe° young lad of twenty, went to the
States to seek his fortune. And fifteen years thereafter he
returned to his native Kerry, his blitheness sobered and his
youth dried to the core, and whether he had made his
fortune or whether he had not, no one could be knowing
for certain. For he was a quiet man, not given to talking
about himself and the things he had done. A quiet man,
under middle size, with strong shoulders and deep-set
blue eyes below brows darker than his dark hair—that was
Shawn Kelvin. One shoulder had a trick of hunching
slightly higher than the other, and some folks said that came
from a habit he had of shielding his eyes in the glare of an
open-hearth furnace[1] in a place called Pittsburgh, while
others said it used to be a way he had of guarding his chin
that time he was a sort of sparring-partner° punching bag
at a boxing camp.

Shawn Kelvin came home and found that he was the last
of the Kelvins, and that the farm of his forefathers had
added its few acres to the ranch of Big Liam O'Grady, of
Moyvalla. Shawn took no action to recover his land, though
O'Grady had got it meanly. He had had enough of fighting,
and all he wanted now was peace. He quietly went amongst
the old and kindly friends and quietly looked about him
for the place and peace he wanted; and when the time
came, quietly produced the money for a neat, handy, small
farm on the first warm shoulder of Knockanore Hill below
the rolling curves of heather.° It was not a big place but
it was in good heart, and it got all the sun that was going;
and, best of all, it suited Shawn to the tiptop notch of
contentment; for it held the peace that tuned to his quiet-

[1]A type of furnace used in making steel. Because of its open construction,
it requires workers to withstand great heat.

ness, and it commanded the widest view in all Ireland—
vale and mountain and the lifting green plain of the Atlantic
Sea.

There, in a four-roomed, lime-washed, thatched° cottage,
Shawn made his life, and, though his friends hinted his
needs and obligations, no thought came to him of bringing
a wife into the place. Yet Fate[2] had the thought and the
dream in her loom for him. One middling imitation of a
man he had to do chores for him, an ex-navy pensioner
handy enough about house and byre,° but with no relish
for the sustained work of the field—and, indeed, as long as
he kept house and byre shipshape, he found Shawn an
easy master.

Shawn himself was no drudge toiler. He knew all about
drudgery and the way it wears out a man's soul. He plowed
a little and sowed a little, and at the end of a furrow he
would lean on the handles of the cultivator, wipe his brow,
if it needed wiping, and lose himself for whole minutes in
the great green curve of the sea out there beyond the high
black portals of Shannon mouth. And sometimes of an
evening he would see, under the glory of the sky, the faint
smoke smudge of an American liner. Then he would smile
to himself—a pitying smile—thinking of the poor devils,
with dreams of fortune luring them, going out to sweat in
Ironville, or to stand in a breadline. All these things were
behind Shawn forever.[3]

Market days he would go down and across to Listowel
town, seven miles, to do his bartering; and in the long
evenings, slowly slipping into the endless summer gloam-
ing,° his friends used to climb the winding lane to see him.
Only the real friends came that long road, and they were
welcome—fighting men who had been out in the "Sixteen";[4] Matt Tobin the thresher, the schoolmaster, the

[2]One or more of the three Roman goddesses (Clotho, Lachesis, and
Atropos) who control life of the human being. It is Clotho who spins the
thread of life in her loom.
[3]Shawn was in the United States during the depression of the 1930's and
has no illusions about the conditions of the immigrant to this country.
[4]A reference to the army of Irish volunteers which rebelled in 1916
against English rule.

young curate°—men like that. A stone jar of malt whisky
would appear on the table, and there would be a haze of
smoke and a maze of warm, friendly disagreements.

"Shawn, old son," one of them might hint, "aren't you
sometimes terrible lonely?"

"Never!" might retort Shawn derisively.° "Why?"

"Nothing but the daylight and the wind and the sun
setting with the wrath o' God."

"Just that! Well?"

"But after stirring times beyond in the States—"

"Ay! Tell me, fine man, have you ever seen a furnace in
full blast?"

"A great sight."

"Great surely! But if I could jump you into a steel
foundry this minute, you would be sure that God had
judged you faithfully into the very hob° of hell."

And then they would laugh and have another small one
from the stone jar.

And on Sundays Shawn used to go to church, three miles
down to the gray chapel above the black cliffs of Doon Bay.
There Fate laid her lure for him.

Sitting quietly on his wooden bench or kneeling on the
dusty footboard, he would fix his steadfast, deep-set eyes
on the vestmented celebrant and say his prayers slowly, or
go into that strange trance, beyond dreams and visions,
where the soul is almost at one with the unknowable.

But after a time, Shawn's eyes no longer fixed themselves
on the celebrant. They went no farther than two seats
ahead. A girl sat there, Sunday after Sunday she sat in front
of him, and Sunday after Sunday his first casual admiration grew warmer.

She had a white nape° to her neck and short red hair
above it, and Shawn liked the color and wave of that flame.
And he liked the set of her shoulders and the way the white
neck had of leaning a little forward and she at her prayers—
or her dreams°. And the service over, Shawn used to stay
in his seat so that he might get one quick but sure look at
her face as she passed out. And he liked her face, too—the
wide-set gray eyes, cheekbones firmly curved, clean-

molded lips, austere yet sensitive. And he smiled pityingly at himself that one of her name should make his pulses stir—for she was an O'Grady.

One person, only, in the crowded chapel noted Shawn's look and the thought behind the look. Not the girl. Her brother, Big Liam O'Grady of Moyvalla, the very man who as good as stole the Kelvin acres. And that man smiled to himself, too—the ugly, contemptuous° smile that was his by nature—and, after another habit he had, he tucked away his bit of knowledge in his mind corner against a day when it might come in useful for his own purposes.

The girl's name was Ellen—Ellen O'Grady. But in truth she was no longer a girl. She was past her first youth into that second one that has no definite ending. She might be thirty—she was no less—but there was not a lad in the countryside would say she was past her prime. The poise of her and the firm set of her bones below clean skin saved her from the fading of mere prettiness. Though she had been sought in marriage more than once, she had accepted no one, or rather, had not been allowed to encourage anyone. Her brother saw to that.

Big Liam O'Grady was a great raw-boned, sandy-haired man, with the strength of an ox and a heart no bigger than a sour apple. An overbearing man given to berserk° rages. Though he was a churchgoer by habit, the true god of that man was Money—red gold, shining silver, dull copper— the trinity that he worshiped in degree. He and his sister Ellen lived on the big ranch farm of Moyvalla, and Ellen was his housekeeper and maid of all work. She was a careful housekeeper, a good cook, a notable baker, and she demanded no wage. All that suited Big Liam splendidly, and so she remained single—a wasted woman.

Big Liam himself was not a marrying man. There were not many spinsters with a dowry° big enough to tempt him, and the few there were had acquired expensive tastes —a convent education, the deplorable art of hitting jazz out of a piano, the damnable vice of cigarette smoking, the purse-emptying craze for motor cars—such things.

But in due time, the dowry and the place—with a woman

tied to them—came under his nose, and Big Liam was no longer tardy. His neighbor, James Carey, died in March and left his fine farm and all on it to his widow, a youngish woman without children, a woman with a hard name for saving pennies. Big Liam looked once at Kathy Carey and looked many times at her broad acres. Both pleased him. He took the steps required by tradition. In the very first week of the following Shrovetide,[5] he sent an accredited emissary° to open formal negotiations, and that emissary came back within the hour.

"My soul," said he, "but she is the quick one! I hadn't ten words out of me when she was down my throat. 'I am in no hurry,' says she, 'to come wife to a house with another woman at the fire corner. When Ellen is in a place of her own, I will listen to what Liam O'Grady has to say.'"

"She will, I say!" Big Liam stopped him. "She will so."

There, now, was the right time to recall Shawn Kelvin and the look in his eyes. Big Liam's mind corner promptly delivered up its memory. He smiled knowingly and contemptuously.° Shawn Kelvin daring to cast sheep's eyes at an O'Grady! The undersized chicken heart, who took the loss of the Kelvin acres lying down! The little Yankee runt hidden away on the shelf of Knockanore! But what of it? The required dowry would be conveniently small, and the girl would never go hungry, anyway. There was Big Liam O'Grady, far descended from many chieftains.

The very next market day at Listowel he sought out Shawn Kelvin and placed a huge, sandy-haired hand on the shoulder that hunched to meet it.

"Shawn Kelvin, a word with you! Come and have a drink."

Shawn hesitated. "Very well," he said then. He did not care for O'Grady, but he would hurt no man's feelings.

They went across to Sullivan's bar and had a drink, and Shawn paid for it. And Big Liam came directly to his subject—almost patronizingly,° as if he were conferring a favor.

[5]The three days (Sunday, Monday, and Tuesday) preceding Ash Wednesday. Here the word probably means Lent itself.

"I want to see Ellen settled in a place of her own," said he.

Shawn's heart lifted into his throat and stayed there. But that steadfast face with the steadfast eyes gave no sign and, moreover, he could not say a word with his heart where it was.

"Your place is small," went on the big man, "but it is handy, and no load of debt on it, as I hear. Not much of a dowry ever came to Knockanore, and not much of a dowry can I be giving with Ellen. Say two hundred pounds° at the end of harvest, if prices improve. What do you say, Shawn Kelvin?"

Shawn swallowed his heart, and his voice came slow and cool: "What does Ellen say?"

"I haven't asked her," said Big Liam. "But what would she say, blast it?"

"Whatever she says, she will say it herself, not you, Big Liam."

But what could Ellen say? She looked within her own heart and found it empty; she looked at the granite crag° of her brother's face and contemplated herself a slowly withering spinster at his fire corner; she looked up at the swell of Knockanore Hill and saw the white cottage among the green small fields below the warm brown of the heather. Oh, but the sun would shine up there in the lengthening spring day and pleasant breezes blow in sultry summer; and finally she looked at Shawn Kelvin, that firmly built, small man with the clean face and the lustrous eyes below steadfast brow. She said a prayer to her God and sank head and shoulders in a resignation more pitiful than tears, more proud than the pride of chieftains. Romance? Welladay!

Shawn was far from satisfied with that resigned acceptance, but then was not the time to press for a warmer one. He knew the brother's wizened° soul, guessed at the girl's clean one, and saw that she was doomed beyond hope to a fireside sordidly° bought for her. Let it be his own fireside then. There were many worse ones—and God was good.

Ellen O'Grady married Shawn Kelvin. One small statement; and it holds the risk of tragedy, the chance of happiness, the probability of mere endurance—choices wide as the world.

But Big Liam O'Grady, for all his resolute promptness, did not win Kathy Carey to wife. She, foolishly enough, took to husband her own cattleman, a gay night rambler, who gave her the devil's own time and a share of happiness in the bygoing. For the first time, Big Liam discovered how mordant° the wit of his neighbors could be, and to contempt for Shawn Kelvin he now added an unreasoning dislike.

Shawn Kelvin had got his precious, red-haired woman under his own roof now. He had no illusions about her feelings for him. On himself, and on himself only, lay the task of molding her into a wife and lover. Darkly, deeply, subtly, away out of sight, with gentleness, with restraint, with a consideration beyond kenning,° that molding must be done, and she that was being molded must never know. He hardly knew, himself.

First he turned his attention to material things. He hired a small servant maid to help her with the housework. Then he acquired a rubber-tired tub cart and a half-bred gelding° with a knee action. And on market days, husband and wife used to bowl down to Listowel, do their selling and their buying, and bowl smoothly home again, their groceries in the well of the cart and a bundle of second-hand American magazines on the seat at Ellen's side. And in the nights, before the year turned, with the wind from the plains of the Atlantic keening° above the chimney, they would sit at either side of the flaming peat° fire, and he would read aloud strange and almost unbelievable things out of the high-colored magazines. Stories, sometimes, wholly unbelievable.

Ellen would sit and listen and smile, and go on with her knitting or her sewing; and after a time it was sewing she was at mostly—small things. And when the reading was done, they would sit and talk quietly in their own quiet way. For they were both quiet. Woman though she was, she got Shawn to do most of the talking. It could be that she, too, was probing and seeking, unwrapping the man's soul to feel the texture thereof, surveying the marvel of his life as he spread it diffidently° before her. He had a patient, slow, vivid way of picturing for her the things he had seen and felt. He made her see the glare of molten metal, lambent° yet searing, made her feel the sucking heat, made her hear the clang; she could see the roped square under the dazzle of the hooded arcs with the curling smoke layer above it, understand the explosive restraint of the game, thrill when he showed her how to stiffen wrist for the final devastating right hook. And often enough the stories were humorous, and Ellen would chuckle, or stare, or throw back her red, lovely curls in laughter. It was grand to make her laugh.

Shawn's friends, in some hesitation at first, came in ones and twos up the slope to see them. But Ellen welcomed them with her smile that was shy and, at the same time, frank, and her table was loaded for them with scones° and crumpets° and cream cakes and heather honey; and at the right time it was she herself that brought forth the decanter of whisky — no longer the half-empty stone jar — and the polished glasses. Shawn was proud as sin of her. She would sit then and listen to their discussions and be for-ever surprised at the knowledgeable man her husband was — the way he would discuss war and politics and the making of songs, the turn of speech that summed up a man or a situation. And sometimes she would put in a word or two and he listened too, and they would look to see if her smile commended° them, and be a little chastened by the wisdom of that smile — the age-old smile of the matriarch° from whom they were all descended. In no time at all, Matt Tobin the thresher, who used to think, "Poor old Shawn! Lucky she was to get him," would whisper to the schoolmaster: "Herrin's alive! That fellow's luck would astonish nations."

Women, in the outside world, begin by loving their husbands; and then, if Fate is kind, they grow to admire them; and, if Fate is not unkind, may descend no lower than liking and enduring. And there is the end of lawful romance. Look now at Ellen O'Grady. She came up to the shelf of Knockanore and in her heart was only a nucleus° of fear in a great emptiness, and that nucleus might grow into horror and disgust. But, glory of God, she, for reason piled on reason, presently found herself admiring Shawn Kelvin; and with or without reason, a quiet liking came to her for this quiet man who was so gentle and considerate; and then, one great heart-stirring dark o'night, she found herself fallen head and heels in love with her own husband. There is the sort of love that endures, but the road to it is a mighty chancy one.

A woman, loving her husband, may or may not be proud of him, but she will fight like a tiger if anyone, barring herself, belittles him. And there was one man that belittled Shawn Kelvin. Her brother, Big Liam O'Grady. At fair or market or chapel that dour° giant deigned not to hide his contempt and dislike. Ellen knew why. He had lost a wife and farm; he had lost in herself a frugally cheap house-keeper; he had been made the butt of a sly humor; and for these mishaps, in some twisted way, he blamed Shawn. But—and there came in the contempt—the little Yankee runt, who dared say nothing about the lost Kelvin acres, would not now have the gall or guts to demand the dowry that was due. Lucky the hound to steal an O'Grady to hungry Knockanore! Let him be satisfied with that luck!

One evening before a market day, Ellen spoke to her husband: "Has Big Liam paid you my dowry yet, Shawn?"

"Sure there's no hurry, girl," said Shawn.

"Have you ever asked him?"

"I have not. I am not looking for your dowry, Ellen."

"And Big Liam could never understand that." Her voice firmed. "You will ask him tomorrow."

"Very well so, *agrah*,"⁶ agreed Shawn easily.

And the next day, in that quiet diffident way of his, he asked Big Liam. But Big Liam was brusque° and blunt. He had no loose money and Kelvin would have to wait till he had. "Ask me again, Shawneen,"⁷ he finished, his

⁶If that is the way it has to be. The word indicates reluctance.
⁷The suffix *een* denotes a patronizing attitude when used of an adult.

face in a mocking smile, and turning on his heel, he plowed his great shoulders through the crowded market.

His voice had been carelessly loud and people had heard. They laughed and talked amongst themselves. "Begogs! The devil's own boy, Big Liam! What a pup to sell! Stealing the land and keeping a grip on the fortune! Ay, and a dangerous fellow, mind you, the same Big Liam! He would smash little Shawn at the wind of a word. And devil the bit his Yankee sparring tricks would help him!"

A friend of Shawn's, Matt Tobin the thresher, heard that and lifted his voice: "I would like to be there the day Shawn Kelvin loses his temper."

"A bad day for poor Shawn!"

"It might then," said Matt Tobin, "but I would come from the other end of Kerry to see the badness that would be in it for someone."

Shawn had moved away with his wife, not heeding° or not hearing.

"You see, Ellen?" he said in some discomfort. "The times are hard on the big ranchers, and we don't need the money, anyway."

"Do you think Big Liam does?" Her voice had a cut in it. "He could buy you and all Knockanore and be only on the fringe of his hoard. You will ask him again."

"But, girl dear, I never wanted a dowry with you."

She liked him to say that, but far better would she like to win for him the respect and admiration that was his due. She must do that now at all costs. Shawn, drawing back now, would be the butt of his fellow men.

"You foolish lad! Big Liam would never understand your feelings, with money at stake." She smiled and a pang went through Shawn's breast. For the smile was the smile of an O'Grady, and he could not be sure whether the contempt in it was for himself or for her brother.

Shawn asked Big Liam again, unhappy in his asking, but also dimly comprehending his woman's object. And Shawn asked again a third time. The issue was become a famous one now. Men talked about it, and women too. Bets were made on it. At fair or market, if Shawn was seen approaching Big Liam, men edged closer and women edged away. Some day the big fellow would grow tired of being asked, and in one of his terrible rages half kill the little lad as he had half killed other men. A great shame! Here and there, a man advised Shawn to give up asking and put the matter in a lawyer's hands. "I couldn't do that," was Shawn's only answer. Strangely enough, none of these prudent advisers were amongst Shawn's close friends. His friends frowned and said little, but they were always about, and always amongst them was Matt Tobin.

The day at last came when Big Liam grew tired of being asked. That was the big October cattle fair at Listowel, and he had sold twenty head of fat, Polled° Angus beeves at a good price. He was a hard dealer and it was late in the day before he settled at his own figure, so that the banks were closed and he was not able to make a lodgment.° He had, then, a great roll of bills in an inner vest pocket when he saw Shawn and Ellen coming across to where he was bargaining with Matt Tobin for a week's threshing. Besides, the day being dank,° he had had a drink or two more than was good for him and the whisky had loosened his tongue and whatever he had of discretion. By the powers! —it was time and past time to deal once and for all with this little gadfly° of a fellow, to show him up before the whole market. He strode to meet Shawn, and people got out of his savage way and edged in behind to lose nothing of this dangerous game.

He caught Shawn by the hunched shoulder—a rending° grip—and bent down to grin in his face.

"What is it, little fellow? Don't be ashamed to ask!"

Matt Tobin was probably the only one there to notice the ease with which Shawn wrenched his shoulder free, and Matt Tobin's eyes brightened. But Shawn did nothing further and said no word. His deep-set eyes gazed steadily at the big man.

The big man showed his teeth mockingly. "Go on, you whelp!° What do you want?"

"You know, O'Grady."

"I do. Listen, Shawneen!" Again he brought his hand-clap on the little man's shoulder. "Listen, Shawneen! If I had a dowry to give my sister, 'tis not a little shrimp like you would get her!"

His great hand gripped and he flung Shawn backwards as if he were only the image of a man filled with chaff.°

Shawn went backwards, but he did not fall. He gathered himself like a spring, feet under him, arms half-raised, head forward into hunched shoulder. But as quickly as the spring coiled,° as quickly it slackened, and he turned away to his wife. She was there facing him, tense and keen, her face pale and set, and a gleam of the race in her eyes.

"Woman, woman!" he said in his deep voice. "Why would you and I shame ourselves like this?"

"Shame!" she cried. "Will you let him shame you now?"

"But your own brother, Ellen—before them all?"

"And he cheating you—"

"Glory to God!" His voice was distressed. "What is his dirty money to me? Are you an O'Grady, after all?"

That stung her and she stung him back in one final effort. She placed a hand below her breast and looked *close*° into his face. Her voice was low and bitter, and only he heard: "I am an O'Grady. It is a great pity that the father of this my son is a Kelvin and a coward."

The bosses° of Shawn Kelvin's cheekbones were like hard marble, but his voice was as soft as a dove's.

"Is that the way of it? Let us be going home then, in the name of God!"

He took her arm, but she shook his hand off; nevertheless, she walked at his side, head up, through the people that made way for them. Her brother mocked them with his great, laughing bellow.

"That fixes the pair of them!" he cried, brushed a man who laughed with him out of his way, and strode off through the fair.

There was talk then—plenty of it. "Murder, but Shawn had a narrow squeak that time! Did you see the way he flung him? I wager he'll give Big Liam a wide road after this. And he by way of being a boxer! That's a pound you owe me, Matt Tobin."

"I'll pay it," said Matt Tobin, and that is all he said. He stood widelegged, looking at the ground, his hand ruefully° rubbing the back of his head and dismay and gloom on his face. His friend had failed him in the face of the people.

Shawn and Ellen went home in their tub cart and had not a single word or glance for each other on the road. And all that evening, at table or fireside, a heart-sickening silence held them in its grip. And all that night they lay side by side, still and mute. There was only one subject that possessed them and on that they dared speak no longer. They slept little, Ellen, her heart desolate, lay on her side, staring into the dark, grieving for what she had said and unable to unsay it. Shawn, on his back, contemplated things with a cold clarity. He realized that he was at the fork of life and that a finger pointed unmistakably. He must risk the very shattering of all happiness, he must do a thing so final and decisive that, once done, it could never again be questioned. Before morning, he came to his decision, and it was bitter as gall. He cursed himself. "Oh, you fool! You might have known that you should never have taken an O'Grady without breaking the O'Gradys."

He got up early in the morning at his usual hour and went out, as usual, to his morning chores — rebedding and fod-dering° the cattle, rubbing down the half-bred, helping the servant maid with the milk in the creaming pans — and, as usual, he came in to his breakfast, and ate it unhungrily and silently, which was not usual. But, thereafter he again went out to the stable, harnessed his gelding and hitched him to the tub cart. Then he returned to the kitchen and spoke for the first time.

"Ellen, will you come with me down to see your brother?"

She hesitated, her hands thrown wide in a helpless, hopeless gesture. "Little use you going to see my brother, Shawn. 'Tis I should go and — and not come back."

"Don't blame me now or later, Ellen. It has been put on me and the thing I am going to do is the only thing to be done. Will you come?"

"Very well," she agreed tonelessly. "I will be ready in a minute."

And they went the four miles down into the vale to the big farmhouse of Moyvalla. They drove into the great square of cobbled yard and found it empty.

On one side of the square was the long, low, lime-washed dwelling house; on the other, fifty yards away, the two-storied line of steadings° with a wide arch in the middle; and through the arch came the purr and zoom of a threshing machine. Shawn tied the half-bred to the wheel of a farm cart and, with Ellen, approached the house.

A slattern° servant girl leaned over the kitchen half-door and pointed through the arch. The master was out beyond in the haggard—the rickyard°—and would she run across for him?

"Never mind, *achara*,"[8] said Shawn, "I'll get him.... Ellen, will you go in and wait?"

"No," said Ellen, "I'll come with you." She knew her brother.

As they went through the arch, the purr and zoom grew louder and, turning the corner, they walked into the midst of activity. A long double row of cone-pointed cornstacks stretched across the yard and, between them, Matt Tobin's portable threshing machine was busy. The smooth-flying, eight-foot driving wheel made a sleepy purr and the black driving belt ran with a sag and heave to the red-painted thresher. Up there on the platform, bare-armed men were feeding the flying drum with loosened sheaves, their hands moving in a rhythmic sway. As the toothed drum bit at the corn sheaves it made an angry snarl that changed and slowed into a satisfied zoom. The wide conveying belt was carrying the golden straw up a steep incline to where other men were building a long rick;° still more men were attending to the corn shoots, shoulders bending under the weight of the sacks as they ambled° across to the granary.° Matt Tobin himself bent at the face of his engine, feeding the fire box with sods of hard black peat. There were not less

[8]Literally "dear one." A term often used with female servants.

than two score° men about the place, for, as was the custom, all Big Liam's friends and neighbors were giving him a hand with the threshing—"the day in harvest."

Big Liam came round the flank of the engine and swore. He was in his shirt sleeves, and his great forearms were covered with sandy hair.

"Look who's here!"

He was in the worst of tempers this morning. The stale dregs° of yesterday's whisky were still with him, and he was in the humor that, as they say, would make a dog bite its father. He took two slow strides and halted, feet apart and head truculently° forward.

"What is it this time?" he shouted. That was the un-Irish welcome he gave his sister and her husband.

Shawn and Ellen came forward steadily, and, as they came, Matt Tobin slowly throttled down his engine. Big Liam heard the change of pitch and looked angrily over his shoulder.

"What do you mean, Tobin? Get on with the work!"

"Big Liam, this is my engine, and if you don't like it, you can leave it!" And at that he drove the throttle shut and the purr of the flywheel slowly sank.

"We will see in a minute," threatened Big Liam, and turned to the two now near at hand.

"What is it?" he growled.

"A private word with you. I won't keep you long." Shawn was calm and cold.

"You will not—on a busy morning," sneered the big man. "There is no need for private words between me and Shawn Kelvin."

"There is need," urged Shawn. "It will be best for us all if you hear what I have to say in your own house."

"Or here on my own land. Out with it! I don't care who hears!"

Shawn looked round him. Up on the thresher, up on the straw rick, men leaned idle on fork handles and looked down at him; from here and there about the stackyard, men moved in to see, as it might be, what had caused the stoppage, but only really interested in the two brothers-in-law. He was in the midst of Clan O'Grady, for they were mostly O'Grady men—big, strong, blond men, rough, confident, proud of their breed. Matt Tobin was the only man he could call a friend. Many of the others were not unfriendly, but all had contempt in their eyes, or, what was worse, pity. Very well! Since he had to prove himself it was fitting that he do it here amongst the O'Grady men.

Shawn brought his eyes back to Big Liam—deep, steadfast eyes that did not waver. "O'Grady," said he—and he no longer hid his contempt—"you set a great store by money."

"No harm in that. You do it yourself, Shawneen."

"Take it so! I will play that game with you, as long as you like. You would bargain your sister and cheat; I will sell my soul. Listen, you big brute! You owe me two hundred pounds. Will you pay it?" There was an iron quality in his voice that was somehow awesome. The big man, about to start forward overbearingly,° restrained himself to a brutal playfulness.

"I will pay it when I am ready."

"Today."

"No; nor tomorrow."

"Right. If you break your bargain, I break mine."

"What's that?" shouted Big Liam.

"If you keep your two hundred pounds, you keep your sister."

"What is it?" shouted Big Liam again, his voice breaking in astonishment. "What is that you say?"

"You heard me. Here is your sister Ellen. Keep her!"

He was completely astounded out of his truculence.° "You can't do that!"

"It is done," said Shawn.

Ellen O'Grady had been quiet as a statue at Shawn's side, but now, slow like doom, she faced him. She leaned forward and looked into his eyes and saw the pain behind the strength.

"To the mother of your son, Shawn Kelvin?" she whispered that gently to him.

His voice came cold as a stone out of a stone face: "In
the face of God. Let Him judge me."

"I know—I know!" That was all she said, and walked
quietly across to where Matt Tobin stood at the face of his
engine.

Matt Tobin placed his hand on her arm. "Give him time,
acolleen,"[9] he whispered urgently. "Give him his own
time. He's slow, but he's deadly as a tiger when he moves."

Big Liam was no fool. He knew exactly how far he could
go. There was no use, at this juncture, in crushing the runt
under a great fist. There was some force in the little fellow
that defied dragooning.° Whatever people might think of
Kelvin, public opinion would be dead against himself.
Worse, his inward vision saw eyes leering° in derision,
mouths open in laughter. The scandal on his name would
not be bounded by the four seas of Erin. He must change
his stance while he had time. These thoughts passed
through his mind while he thudded the ground three times
with ironshod heel. Now he threw up his head and bel-
lowed his laugh.

"You fool! I was only making fun of you. What are your
dirty few pounds to the likes of me? Stay where you are."

He turned, strode furiously away, and disappeared
through the arch.

Shawn Kelvin was left alone in that wide ring of men.
The hands had come down off the ricks and thresher to see
closer. Now they moved back and aside, looked at one
another, lifted eyebrows, looked at Shawn Kelvin, frowned
and shook their heads. They knew Big Liam. They knew
that, yielding up the money, his savagery would break out
into something little short of killing. They waited, most of
them, to prevent that savagery going too far.

Shawn Kelvin did not look at anyone. He stood still as a
rock, his hands deep in his pockets, one shoulder hunched
forward, his eyes on the ground and his face strangely calm.

[9]Literally "my dear girl." A term of genuine affection addressed to someone very much admired.

He seemed the least perturbed man there. Matt Tobin held Ellen's arm in a steadying grip and whispered in her ear: "God is good, I tell you."

Big Liam was back in two minutes. He strode straight to Shawn and halted within a pace of him.

"Look, Shawneen!" In his raised hand was a crumpled bundle of greasy bank notes. "Here is your money. Take it, and then see what will happen to you. Take it!" He thrust it into Shawn's hand. "Count it. Make sure you have it all—and then I will kick you out of this haggard—and look"—he thrust forward a hairy fist—"if ever I see your face again, I will drive that through it. Count it, you spawn!"°

Shawn did not count it. Instead he crumpled it into a ball in his strong fingers. Then he turned on his heel and walked, with surprising slowness, to the face of the engine. He gestured with one hand to Matt Tobin, but it was Ellen, quick as a flash, who obeyed the gesture. Though the hot bar scorched her hand, she jerked open the door of the fire box and the leaping peat flames whispered out at her. And forthwith, Shawn Kelvin, with one easy sweep, threw the crumpled ball of notes into the heart of the flame. The whisper lifted one tone and one scrap of burned paper floated out of the funnel top. That was all the fuss the fire made of its work.

But there was fuss enough outside.

Big Liam O'Grady gave one mighty shout. No, it was more an anguished scream than a shout:

"My money! My good money!"

He gave two furious bounds forward, his great arms raised to crush and kill. But his hands never touched the small man.

"You dumb ox!" said Shawn Kelvin between his teeth. That strong, hunched shoulder moved a little, but no one there could follow the terrific drive of that hooked right arm. The smack of bone on bone was sharp as whip crack, and Big Liam stopped dead, went back on his heel, swayed a moment and staggered back three paces.

"Now and forever! Man of Kelvins!" roared Matt Tobin.

But Big Liam was a man of iron. That blow should have laid him on his back—blows like it had tied men to the ground for the full count. But Big Liam only shook his head, grunted like a boar, and drove in at the little man. And the little man, instead of circling away, drove in at him, compact of power.

The men of the O'Gradys saw then an exhibition that they had not knowledge enough to appreciate fully. Thousands had paid as much as ten dollars each to see the great Tiger Kelvin in action, his footwork, his timing, his hitting; and never was his action more devastating than now. He was a thunderbolt on two feet and the big man a glutton.

Big Liam never touched Shawn with clenched fist. He did not know how. Shawn, actually forty pounds lighter, drove him by sheer hitting across the yard.

Men for the first time saw a two-hundred-pound man knocked clean off his feet by a body blow. They saw for the first time the deadly restraint and explosion of skill.

Shawn set out to demolish his enemy in the briefest space of time, and it took him five minutes to do it. Five, six, eight times he knocked the big man down, and the big man came again, staggering, slavering,° raving, vainly trying to rend and smash. But at last he stood swaying and clawing helplessly, and Shawn finished him with his terrible double hit—left below the breastbone and right under the jaw.

Big Liam lifted on his toes and fell flat on his back. He did not even kick as he lay.

Shawn did not waste a glance at the fallen giant. He swung full circle on the O'Grady men and his voice of iron challenged them:

"I am Shawn Kelvin, of Knockanore Hill. Is there an O'Grady amongst you thinks himself a better man? Come then."

No man came.

He swung around then and walked straight to his wife. He halted before her.

His face was still of stone, but his voice quivered and had in it all the dramatic force of the Celt:

"Mother of my son, will you come home with me?"

She lifted to the appeal, voice and eye:

"Is it so you ask me, Shawn Kelvin?"

His face of stone quivered at last. "As my wife only— Ellen Kelvin!"

"Very well, heart's treasure." She caught his arm in both of hers. "Let us be going home."

"In the name of God," he finished for her.

And she went with him, proud as the morning, out of that place. But a woman, she would have the last word.

"Mother of God!" she cried. "The trouble I had to make a man of him!"

"God Almighty did that for him before you were born," said Matt Tobin softly.

Do especially Questions 41, 74, 83, 84, 86, 95, 96, 106, 109, and 111. Consult the Short Story Model on page 156.

MAURICE WALSH 1879-1964

The author of the short story "The Quiet Man," which became one of the most successful motion pictures of 1952, Maurice Walsh received his education at St. Michael's College, Listowell. He first visited Dublin to take a civil service examination. "I didn't want to pass!" he admitted. "I wanted to go out and fight for the Boers, but had a loyalty to my mother. I did that exam so recklessly, so debonairly, that I was in the first two hundred, and the next thing I knew I was pitchforked into the Customs Excise Service." His work with the Customs Service took Walsh to England, Scotland, and Wales. During the Civil War in Ireland, he lived in Dublin, and except for "sniping" was forced to spend most of his time indoors. Soon bored by reading, he tried writing, his casual effort resulting in *The Key Above the Door* which sold some hundred thousand copies. In most of the novels and short stories that have followed, Walsh writes of his native Kerry, the beautiful mountain country of southwestern Ireland. Written mainly to entertain, Walsh's romantic tales are often saved from sentimentality by touches of Gaelic humor.

The Apple Tree

KATHERINE MANSFIELD

There were two orchards belonging to the old house. One, that we called the "wild" orchard, lay beyond the vegetable garden; it was planted with bitter cherries and damsons° and transparent yellow plums. For some reason it lay under a cloud; we never played there, we did not even trouble to pick up the fallen fruit; and there, every Monday morning, to the round open space in the middle, the servant girl and the washerwoman carried the wet linen—grandmother's nightdresses, father's striped shirts, the hired man's cotton trousers, and the servant girl's "dreadfully vulgar" salmon-pink flannelette drawers jigged and slapped in horrid familiarity.

But the other orchard, far away and hidden from the house, lay at the foot of a little hill and stretched right over to the edge of the paddocks°—to the clumps of wattles° bobbing yellow in the bright sun and the blue gums with their streaming sickle-shaped leaves. There, under the fruit trees, the grass grew so thick and coarse that it tangled and knotted in your shoes as you walked, and even on the hottest day it was damp to touch when you stooped and parted it this way and that looking for windfalls—the apples marked with a bird's beak, the big bruised pears, the quinces,° so good to eat with a pinch of salt, but so delicious to smell that you could not bite for sniffing. . . .

One year the orchard had its Forbidden Tree.[1] It was an apple tree discovered by Father and a friend during an after-dinner prowl° one Sunday afternoon.

"Great Scott!" said the friend, lighting upon it with every appearance of admiring astonishment: "Isn't that a —— ?" And a rich, splendid name settled like an unknown bird upon the little tree.

[1]Reminiscent of the Tree of Knowledge in the Garden of Eden from which Adam and Eve were forbidden to eat.

"Yes, I believe it is," said Father lightly. He knew nothing whatever about the names of fruit trees.

"Great Scott!" said the friend again: "They're wonderful apples. Nothing like 'em—and you're going to have a tiptop crop. Marvellous apples! You can't beat 'em!"

"No, they're very fine—very fine," said Father carelessly, but looking upon the tree with new and lively interest.

"They're rare—they're very rare. Hardly ever see 'em in England nowadays," said the visitor and set a seal on Father's delight. For Father was a self-made man and the price he had to pay for everything was so huge and so painful that nothing rang so sweet to him as to hear his purchase praised. He was young and sensitive still. He still wondered whether in the deepest sense he got his money's worth. He still had hours when he walked up and down in the moonlight half deciding to "chuck this confounded rushing to the office every day—and clear out—clear out once and for all." And now to discover that he'd a valuable apple tree thrown in with the orchard—an apple tree that this Johnny from England positively envied!

"Don't touch that tree! Do you hear me, children!" said he, bland and firm; and when the guest had gone, with quite another voice and manner:

"If I catch either of you touching those apples you shall not only go to bed—you shall each have a good sound whipping!" Which merely added to its magnificence.

Every Sunday morning after church Father, with Bogey and me tailing after, walked through the flower garden, down the violet path, past the lace-bark tree, past the white rose and syringa bushes, and down the hill to the orchard. The apple tree—like the Virgin Mary—seemed to have been miraculously warned of its high honour, standing apart from its fellows, bending a little under its rich clusters, fluttering its polished leaves, important and exquisite° before Father's awful eye. His heart swelled to the sight— we knew his heart swelled. He put his hands behind his back and screwed up his eyes in the way he had. There it stood—the accidental thing—the thing that no one had been aware of when the hard bargain was driven. It hadn't been counted in, hadn't in a way been paid for. If the house had been burned to the ground at that time it would have meant less to him than the destruction of his tree. And how we played up to him, Bogey and I, Bogey with his scratched knees pressed together, his hands behind his back, too, and a round cap on his head with *H. M. S. Thunderbolt*[2] printed across it.

The apples turned from pale green to yellow; then they had deep pink stripes painted on them, and then the pink melted all over the yellow, reddened, and spread into a fine clear crimson.

At last the day came when Father took out of his waist-coat pocket a little pearl pen-knife. He reached up. Very slowly and very carefully he picked two apples growing on a bough.

"By Jove! They're warm," cried Father in amazement. "They're wonderful apples! Tip-top! Marvellous!" he echoed. He rolled them over in his hands.

"Look at that!" he said. "Not a spot—not a blemish!" And he walked through the orchard with Bogey and me stumbling after, to a tree stump under the wattles. We sat, one on either side of Father. He laid one apple down, opened the pearl pen-knife and neatly and beautifully cut the other in half.

"By Jove! Look at that!" he exclaimed.

"Father!" we cried, dutiful but really enthusiastic, too. For the lovely red colour had bitten right through the white flesh of the apple; it was pink to the shiny black pips° lying so justly in their scaly pods. It looked as though the apple had been dipped in wine.

"Never seen *that* before," said Father. "You won't find an apple like that in a hurry!" He put it to his nose and pronounced an unfamiliar word. "Bouquet!° What a bouquet!" And then he handed to Bogey one half, to me the other.

"Don't *bolt* it!" said he. It was agony to give even so

---

[2]*His Majesty's Ship Thunderbolt.*

much away. I knew it, while I took mine humbly and humbly Bogey took his.

Then he divided the second with the same neat beautiful little cut of the pearl knife.

I kept my eyes on Bogey. Together we took a bite. Our mouths were full of a floury stuff, a hard, faintly bitter skin — a horrible taste of something dry. . . .

"Well?" asked Father, very jovial. He had cut his two halves into quarters and was taking out the little pods. "Well?"

Bogey and I stared at each other, chewing desperately. In that second of chewing and swallowing a long silent conversation passed between us — and a strange meaning smile. We swallowed. We edged near Father, just touching him.

"Perfect!" we lied. "Perfect — Father. Simply lovely!"

But it was no use. Father spat his out and never went near the apple tree again.

Do especially Questions 44, 76, 81, 90, 96, and 148. Consult the Short Story Model on page 156.

KATHERINE MANSFIELD   *1888-1923*

Born in Wellington, New Zealand, of a colonial family, Katherine Mansfield Beauchamp went to London in 1903 to be educated at Queen's College, Harley Street. Always suffering from poor health and nervousness, she traveled widely on the Continent, writing as much as her frail condition would allow. She concentrated mainly on short stories, although she did write poetry. The sensitive, withdrawn short-story writer departed from the traditional British stress on plot, emphasizing instead mood and character development. Her stories were in the impressionistic manner of Chekhov. In 1911 she and her husband, J. Middleton Murry, edited *Rhythm,* a magazine of the arts meant as an outlet for budding talent. Her last years were filled with futile journeys to various places in an attempt to find relief for the lung condition which finally took her life in Fontainebleau, France. After her death, J. Middleton Murry edited her *Journal* and *Letters,* two works of Katherine Mansfield's personal revelations of her art and intentions.

The Sculptor's Funeral

WILLA CATHER

A group of the townspeople stood on the station siding of a little Kansas town, awaiting the coming of the night train, which was already twenty minutes overdue. The snow had fallen thick over everything; in the pale starlight the line of bluffs across the wide, white meadows south of the town made soft, smoke-coloured curves against the clear sky. The men on the siding stood first on one foot and then on the other, their hands thrust deep into their trousers pockets, their overcoats open, their shoulders screwed up with the cold; and they glanced from time to time toward the southeast, where the railroad track wound along the river shore. They conversed in low tones and moved about restlessly, seeming uncertain as to what was expected of them. There was but one of the company who looked as if he knew exactly why he was there, and he kept conspicuously° apart; walking to the far end of the platform, returning to the station door, then pacing up the track again, his chin sunk in the high collar of his overcoat, his burly shoulders drooping forward, his gait heavy and dogged. Presently he was approached by a tall, spare, grizzled man clad in a faded Grand Army suit, who shuffled out from the group and advanced with a certain deference,° craning his neck forward until his back made the angle of a jack-knife three-quarters open.

"I reckon she's a-goin' to be pretty late agin tonight, Jim," he remarked in a squeaky falsetto.° "S'pose it's the snow?"

"I don't know," responded the other man with a shade of annoyance, speaking from out an astonishing cataract of red beard that grew fiercely and thickly in all directions.

The spare man shifted the quill toothpick he was chewing to the other side of his mouth. "It ain't likely that anybody from the East will come with the corpse, I s'pose," he went on reflectively.

"I don't know," responded the other, more curtly than before.

"It's too bad he didn't belong to some lodge or other. I like an order funeral myself. They seem more appropriate for people of some reputation," the spare man continued, with an ingratiating concession in his shrill voice, as he carefully placed his toothpick in his vest pocket. He always carried the flag at the G. A. R.[1] funerals in the town.

The heavy man turned on his heel, without replying, and walked up the siding. The spare man rejoined the uneasy group. "Jim's ez full ez a tick, ez ushel," he commented commiseratingly.°

Just then a distant whistle sounded, and there was a shuffling of feet on the platform. A number of lanky boys, of all ages, appeared as suddenly and slimily as eels wakened by the crack of thunder; some came from the waiting-room, where they had been warming themselves by the red stove, or half asleep on the slat benches; others uncoiled themselves from baggage trucks or slid out of express wagons. Two clambered down from the driver's seat of a hearse that stood backed up against the siding. They straightened their stooping shoulders and lifted their heads, and a flash of momentary animation kindled their dull eyes at that cold, vibrant° scream, the world-wide call for men. It stirred them like the note of a trumpet; just as it had often stirred the man who was coming home tonight, in his boyhood.

The night express shot, red as a rocket, from out the eastward marsh lands and wound along the river shore under the long lines of shivering poplars that sentinelled° the meadows, the escaping steam hanging in gray masses against the pale sky and blotting out the Milky Way. In a moment the red glare from the headlight streamed up the snow-covered track before the siding and glittered on the wet, black rails. The burly man with the dishevelled red beard walked swiftly up the platform toward the approach-

[1]Grand Army of the Republic, an organization of Civil War veterans.

ing train, uncovering his head as he went. The group of men behind him hesitated, glanced questioningly at one another, and awkwardly followed his example. The train stopped, and the crowd shuffled up to the express car just as the door was thrown open, the man in the G. A. R. suit thrusting his head forward with curiosity. The express messenger appeared in the doorway, accompanied by a young man in a long ulster° and travelling cap.

"Are Mr. Merrick's friends here?" inquired the young man.

The group on the platform swayed uneasily. Philip Phelps, the banker, responded with dignity: "We have come to take charge of the body. Mr. Merrick's father is very feeble and can't be about."

"Send the agent out here," growled the express messenger, "and tell the operator to lend a hand."

The coffin was got out of its rough-box and down on the snowy platform. The townspeople drew back enough to make room for it and then formed a close semicircle about it, looking curiously at the palm leaf which lay across the black cover. No one said anything. The baggage man stood by his truck, waiting to get at the trunks. The engine panted heavily, and the fireman dodged in and out among the wheels with his yellow torch and long oil-can, snapping the spindle boxes.° The young Bostonian, one of the dead sculptor's pupils who had come with the body, looked about him helplessly. He turned to the banker, the only one of that black, uneasy, stoop-shouldered group who seemed enough of an individual to be addressed.

"None of Mr. Merrick's brothers are here?" he asked uncertainly.

The man with the red beard for the first time stepped up and joined the others. "No, they have not come yet; the family is scattered. The body will be taken directly to the house." He stooped and took hold of one of the handles of the coffin.

"Take the long hill road up, Thompson, it will be easier on the horses," called the liveryman° as the undertaker snapped the door of the hearse and prepared to mount to the driver's seat.

Laird, the red-bearded lawyer, turned again to the stranger: "We didn't know whether there would be anyone with him or not," he explained. "It's a long walk, so you'd better go up in the hack." He pointed to a single battered conveyance, but the young man replied stiffly: "Thank you, but I think I will go up with the hearse. If you don't object," turning to the undertaker, "I'll ride with you."

They clambered up over the wheels and drove off in the starlight up the long, white hill toward the town. The lamps in the still village were shining from under the low, snow-burdened roofs; and beyond, on every side, the plains reached out into emptiness, peaceful and wide as the soft sky itself, and wrapped in a tangible,° white silence.

When the hearse backed up to a wooden sidewalk before a naked, weather-beaten frame house, the same composite, ill-defined group that had stood upon the station siding was huddled about the gate. The front yard was an icy swamp, and a couple of warped planks, extending from the sidewalk to the door, made a sort of rickety° footbridge. The gate hung on one hinge, and was opened wide with difficulty. Steavens, the young stranger, noticed that something black was tied to the knob of the front door.

The grating sound made by the casket, as it was drawn from the hearse, was answered by a scream from the house; the front door was wrenched open, and a tall, corpulent° woman rushed out bareheaded into the snow and flung herself upon the coffin, shrieking: "My boy, my boy! And this is how you've come home to me!"

As Steavens turned away and closed his eyes with a shudder of unutterable repulsion, another woman, also tall, but flat and angular, dressed entirely in black, darted out of the house and caught Mrs. Merrick by the shoulders, crying sharply: "Come, come, Mother; you mustn't go on like this!" Her tone changed to one of obsequious° solemnity as she turned to the banker: "The parlour is ready, Mr. Phelps."

The bearers carried the coffin along the narrow boards, while the undertaker ran ahead with the coffin-rests. They bore it into a large, unheated room that smelled of dampness and disuse and furniture polish, and set it down under a hanging lamp ornamented with jingling glass prisms° and before a "Rogers group"² of John Alden and Priscilla,³ wreathed with smilax.° Henry Steavens stared about him with the sickening conviction that there had been a mistake, and that he had somehow arrived at the wrong destination. He looked at the clover-green Brussels,° the fat plush upholstery, among the handpainted china placques° and panels and vases, for some mark of identification—for something that might once conceivably have belonged to Harvey Merrick. It was not until he recognized his friend in the crayon portrait of a little boy in kilts° and curls, hanging above the piano, that he felt willing to let any of these people approach the coffin.

"Take the lid off, Mr. Thompson; let me see my boy's face," wailed the elderly woman between her sobs. This time Steavens looked fearfully, almost beseechingly into her face, red and swollen under its masses of strong, black, shiny hair. He flushed, dropped his eyes, and then, almost incredulously,° looked again. There was a kind of power about her face—a kind of brutal handsomeness, even; but it was scarred and furrowed by violence, and so coloured and coarsened by fiercer passions that grief seemed never to have laid a gentle finger there. The long nose was distended and knobbed at the end, and there were deep lines on either side of it; her heavy, black brows almost met across her forehead, her teeth were large and square, and set far apart—teeth that could tear. She filled the room; the men were obliterated,° seemed tossed about like twigs in an angry water, and even Steavens felt himself being drawn into the whirlpool.

The daughter—the tall, raw-boned woman in crêpe, with a mourning comb in her hair which curiously lengthened her long face—sat stiffly upon the sofa, her hands, conspicuous for their large knuckles, folded in her lap, her mouth and eyes drawn down, solemnly awaiting the opening of the coffin. Near the door stood a mulatto° woman, evidently

²Small figures by the American sculptor, John Rogers.
³Characters in Longfellow's poem, *The Courtship of Miles Standish.*

a servant in the house, with a timid bearing and an emaciated° face pitifully sad and gentle. She was weeping silently, the corner of her calico apron lifted to her eyes, occasionally suppressing a long, quivering sob. Steavens walked over and stood beside her.

Feeble steps were heard on the stairs, and an old man, tall and frail, odorous of pipe smoke, with shaggy, unkempt gray hair and a dingy beard, tobacco stained about the mouth, entered uncertainly. He went slowly up to the coffin and stood rolling a blue cotton handkerchief between his hands, seeming so pained and embarrassed by his wife's orgy of grief that he had no consciousness of anything else.

"There, there, Annie, dear, don't take on so," he quavered timidly, putting out a shaking hand and awkwardly patting her elbow. She turned and sank upon his shoulder with such violence that he tottered a little. He did not even glance toward the coffin, but continued to look at her with a dull, frightened, appealing expression, as a spaniel looks at the whip. His sunken cheeks slowly reddened and burned with miserable shame. When his wife rushed from the room, her daughter strode after her with set lips. The servant stole up to the coffin, bent over it for a moment, and then slipped away to the kitchen, leaving Steavens, the lawyer, and the father to themselves. The old man stood looking down at his dead son's face. The sculptor's splendid head seemed even more noble in its rigid stillness than in life. The dark hair had crept down upon the wide forehead; the face seemed strangely long, but in it there was not that repose we expect to find in the faces of the dead. The brows were so drawn that there were two deep lines above the beaked nose, and the chin was thrust forward defiantly.° It was as though the strain of life had been so sharp and bitter that death could not at once relax the tension and smooth the countenance into perfect peace — as though he were still guarding something precious, which might even yet be wrested from him.

The old man's lips were working under his stained beard. He turned to the lawyer with timid deference:° "Phelps and the rest are comin' back to set up with Harve, ain't they?" he asked. "Thank 'ee, Jim, thank 'ee." He brushed the hair back gently from his son's forehead. "He was a good boy, Jim; always a good boy. He was ez gentle ez a child and the kindest of 'em all—only we didn't none of us ever understand him." The tears trickled slowly down his beard and dropped upon the sculptor's coat.

"Martin, Martin! Oh, Martin! come here," his wife wailed from the top of the stairs. The old man started timorously: "Yes, Annie, I'm coming." He turned away, hesitated, stood for a moment in miserable indecision; then reached back and patted the dead man's hair softly, and stumbled from the room.

"Poor old man, I didn't think he had any tears left. Seems as if his eyes would have gone dry long ago. At his age nothing cuts very deep," remarked the lawyer.

Something in his tone made Steavens glance up. While the mother had been in the room, the young man had scarcely seen anyone else; but now, from the moment he first glanced into Jim Laird's florid° face and blood-shot eyes, he knew that he had found what he had been heart-sick at not finding before—the feeling, the understanding, that must exist in someone, even here.

The man was red as his beard, with features swollen and blurred by dissipation, and a hot, blazing blue eye. His face was strained—that of a man who is controlling himself with difficulty—and he kept plucking at his beard with a sort of fierce resentment. Steavens, sitting by the window, watched him turn down the glaring lamp, still its jangling pendants° with an angry gesture, and then stand with his hands locked behind him, staring down into the master's face. He could not help wondering what link there had been between the porcelain vessel and so sooty a lump of potter's clay.

From the kitchen an uproar was sounding; when the dining-room door opened, the import of it was clear. The mother was abusing the maid for having forgotten to make the dressing for the chicken salad which had been prepared for the watchers. Steavens had never heard anything in the least like it; it was injured, emotional, dramatic abuse, unique and masterly in its excruciating° cruelty, as violent and unrestrained as had been her grief of twenty minutes before. With a shudder of disgust the lawyer went into the dining room and closed the door into the kitchen.

"Poor Roxy's getting it now," he remarked when he came back. "The Merricks took her out of the poor-house years ago; and if her loyalty would let her, I guess the poor old thing could tell tales that would curdle your blood. She's the mulatto woman who was standing in here a while ago, with her apron to her eyes. The old woman is a fury; there never was anybody like her. She made Harvey's life a hell for him when he lived at home; he was so sick ashamed of it. I never could see how he kept himself sweet."

"He was wonderful," said Steavens slowly, "wonderful; but until tonight I have never known how wonderful."

"That is the eternal wonder of it, anyway; that it can come even from such a dung heap as this," the lawyer cried, with a sweeping gesture which seemed to indicate much more than the four walls within which they stood.

"I think I'll see whether I can get a little air. The room is so close I am beginning to feel rather faint," murmured Steavens, struggling with one of the windows. The sash was stuck, however, and would not yield, so he sat down dejectedly° and began pulling at his collar. The lawyer came over, loosened the sash with one blow of his big red fist and sent the window up a few inches. Steavens thanked him, but the nausea which had been gradually climbing into his throat for the last half hour left him with but one desire—a desperate feeling that he must get away from this place with what was left of Harvey Merrick. Oh, he comprehended well enough now the quiet bitterness of the smile that he had seen so often on his master's lips!

Once when Merrick returned from a visit home, he brought with him a singularly feeling and suggestive bas-relief[4] of a thin, faded old woman, sitting and sewing something pinned to her knee; while a full-lipped, full-blooded little urchin, his trousers held up by a single gallows,[5]

[4]Sculpture in which the figures stand out but slightly from the background.
[5]Suspenders for the trousers.

stood beside her, impatiently twitching her gown to call her attention to a butterfly he had caught. Steavens, impressed by the tender and delicate modelling of the thin, tired face, had asked him if it were his mother. He remembered the dull flush that had burned up in the sculptor's face.

.The lawyer was sitting in a rocking-chair beside the coffin, his head thrown back and his eyes closed. Steavens looked at him earnestly, puzzled at the line of the chin, and wondering why a man should conceal a feature of such distinction under that disfiguring shock of beard. Suddenly, as though he felt the young sculptor's keen glance, Jim Laird opened his eyes.

"Was he always a good deal of an oyster?" he asked abruptly. "He was terribly shy as a boy."

"Yes, he was an oyster, since you put it so," rejoined Steavens. "Although he could be very fond of people, he always gave one the impression of being detached. He disliked violent emotion; he was reflective, and rather distrustful of himself—except, of course, as regarded his work. He was sure enough there. He distrusted men pretty thoroughly and women even more, yet somehow without believing ill of them. He was determined, indeed, to believe the best; but he seemed afraid to investigate."

"A burnt dog dreads the fire," said the lawyer grimly, and closed his eyes.

Steavens went on and on, reconstructing that whole miserable boyhood. All this raw, biting ugliness had been the portion of the man whose mind was to become an exhaustless gallery of beautiful impressions—so sensitive that the mere shadow of a poplar leaf flickering against a sunny wall would be etched° and held there forever. Surely, if ever a man had the magic word in his finger tips, it was Merrick. Whatever he touched, he revealed its holiest secret; liberated it from enchantment and restored it to its pristine° loveliness. Upon whatever he had come in contact with, he had left a beautiful record of the experience—a sort of ethereal° signature; a scent, a sound, a colour that was his own.

Steavens understood now the real tragedy of his master's life; neither love nor wine, as many had conjectured, but a blow which had fallen earlier had cut deeper than anything else could have done—a shame not his, and yet so unescapably his, to hide in his heart from his very boyhood. And without—the frontier warfare; the yearning of a boy, cast ashore upon a desert of newness and ugliness and sordidness, for all that is chastened° and old, and noble with traditions.

At eleven o'clock the tall, flat woman in black announced that the watchers were arriving, and asked them to "step into the dining room." As Steavens rose, the lawyer said dryly: "You go on—it'll be a good experience for you. I'm not equal to that crowd tonight; I've had twenty years of them."

As Steavens closed the door after him he glanced back at the lawyer, sitting by the coffin in the dim light, with his chin resting on his hand.

The same misty group that had stood before the door of the express car shuffled into the dining room. In the light of the kerosene lamp they separated and became individuals. The minister, a pale, feeble-looking man with white hair and blond chin-whiskers, took his seat beside a small side table and placed his Bible upon it. The Grand Army man sat down behind the stove and tilted his chair back comfortably against the wall, fishing his quill toothpick from his waistcoat pocket. The two bankers, Phelps and Elder, sat off in a corner behind the dinner-table, where they could finish their discussion of the new usury° law and its effect on chattel security loans.[6] The real estate agent, an old man with a smiling, hypocritical° face, soon joined them. The coal and lumber dealer and the cattle shipper sat on opposite sides of the hard-coal burner, their feet on the nickel-work. Steavens took a book from his pocket and began to read. The talk around him ranged through various topics of local interest while the house was quieting down. When it was clear that the members of the family were in

[6]CHATTEL SECURITY LOANS—Loans made on personal property as security.

bed, the Grand Army man hitched his shoulders and, untangling his long legs, caught his heels on the rounds of his chair.

"S'pose there'll be a will, Phelps?" he queried in his weak falsetto.

The banker laughed disagreeably, and began trimming his nails with a pearl-handled pocket-knife.

"There'll scarcely be any need for one, will there?" he queried in his turn.

The restless Grand Army man shifted his position again, getting his knees still nearer his chin. "Why, the ole man says Harve's done right well lately," he chirped.

The other banker spoke up. "I reckon he means by that Harve ain't asked him to mortgage any more farms lately, so as he could go on with his education."

"Seems like my mind don't reach back to a time when Harve wasn't bein' edycated," tittered the Grand Army man.

There was a general chuckle. The minister took out his handkerchief and blew his nose sonorously.° Banker Phelps closed his knife with a snap. "It's too bad the old man's sons didn't turn out better," he remarked with reflective authority. "They never hung together. He spent money enough on Harve to stock a dozen cattle-farms, and he might as well have poured it into Sand Creek. If Harve had stayed at home and helped nurse what little they had, and gone into stock on the old man's bottom farm, they might all have been well fixed. But the old man had to trust everything to tenants and was cheated right and left."

"Harve never could have handled stock none," interposed the cattleman. "He hadn't it in him to be sharp. Do you remember when he bought Sander's mules for eight-year olds, when everybody in town knew that Sander's father-in-law give 'em to his wife for a wedding present eighteen years before, an' they was full-grown mules then?"

The company laughed discreetly, and the Grand Army man rubbed his knees with a spasm° of childish delight.

"Harve never was much account for anything practical, and he shore was never fond of work," began the coal and lumber dealer. "I mind the last time he was home; the day he left, when the old man was out to the barn helpin' his hand hitch up to take Harve to the train, and Cal Moots was patchin' up the fence; Harve, he come out on the step and sings out, in his lady-like voice: 'Cal Moots, Cal Moots! please come cord° my trunk.'"

"That's Harve for you," approved the Grand Army man. "I kin hear him howlin' yet, when he was a big feller in long pants and his mother used to whale him with a rawhide in the barn for lettin' the cows git foundered° in the cornfield when he was drivin' 'em home from pasture. He killed a cow of mine that-a-way onct—a pure Jersey and the best milker I had, an' the ole man had to put up for her. Harve, he was watchin' the sun set acrost the marshes when the anamile got away."

"Where the old man made his mistake was in sending the boy East to school," said Phelps, stroking his goatee° and speaking in a deliberate, judicial tone. "There was where he got his head full of nonsense. What Harve needed, of all people, was a course in some first-class Kansas City business college."

The letters were swimming before Steavens' eyes. Was it possible that these men did not understand, that the palm on the coffin meant nothing to them? The very name of their town would have remained forever buried in the postal guide had it not been now and again mentioned in the world in connection with Harvey Merrick's. He remembered what his master had said to him on the day of his death, after the congestion of both lungs had shut off any probability of recovery, and the sculptor had asked his pupil to send his body home. "It's not a pleasant place to be lying while the world is moving and doing and better-ing," he had said with a feeble smile, "but it rather seems as though we ought to go back to the place we came from, in the end. The townspeople will come in for a look at me; and after they have had their say, I shan't have much to fear from the judgment of God!"

The cattleman took up the comment. "Forty's young for a Merrick to cash in; they usually hang on pretty well. Probably he helped it along with whiskey."

"His mother's people were not long-lived, and Harvey never had a robust constitution," said the minister mildly. He would have liked to say more. He had been the boy's Sunday-school teacher, and had been fond of him; but he felt that he was not in a position to speak. His own sons had turned out badly, and it was not a year since one of them had made his last trip home in the express car, shot in a gambling-house in the Black Hills.

"Nevertheless, there is no disputin' that Harve frequently looked upon the wine when it was red, also variegated,° and it shore made an oncommon fool of him," moralized the cattleman.

Just then the door leading into the parlour rattled loudly and everyone started involuntarily, looking relieved when only Jim Laird came out. The Grand Army man ducked his head when he saw the spark in his blue, blood-shot eye. They were all afraid of Jim; he was a drunkard, but he could twist the law to suit his client's needs as no other man in all western Kansas could do, and there were many who tried. The lawyer closed the door behind him, leaned back against it and folded his arms, cocking his head a little to one side. When he assumed this attitude in the courtroom, ears were always pricked up, as it usually foretold a flood of withering sarcasm.

"I've been with you gentlemen before," he began in a dry, even tone, "when you've sat by the coffins of boys born and raised in this town; and, if I remember rightly, you were never any too well satisfied when you checked them up. What's the matter, anyhow? Why is it that reputable young men are as scarce as millionaires in Sand City? It might almost seem to a stranger that there was some way something the matter with your progressive town. Why did Ruben Sayer, the brightest young lawyer you ever turned out, after he had come home from the university as straight as a die,° take to drinking and forge a check and shoot himself? Why did Bill Merrit's son die of the shakes in a saloon in Omaha? Why was Mr. Thomas' son, here, shot in a gambling-house? Why did young Adams burn his mill to beat the insurance companies and go to the pen?"

The lawyer paused and unfolded his arms, laying one

clenched fist quietly on the table. "I'll tell you why. Because you drummed nothing but money and knavery into their ears from the time they wore knickerbockers; because you carped° away at them as you've been carping here tonight, holding our friends Phelps and Elder up to them for their models, as our grandfathers held up George Washington and John Adams. But the boys were young, and raw at the business you put them to, and how could they match coppers with such artists as Phelps and Elder? You wanted them to be successful rascals; they were only unsuccessful ones — that's all the difference. There was only one boy ever raised in this borderland between ruffianism and civilization who didn't come to grief, and you hated Harvey Merrick more for winning out than you hated all the other boys who got under the wheels. Lord, Lord, how you did hate him! Phelps, here, is fond of saying that he could buy and sell us all out any time he's a mind to; but he knew Harve wouldn't have given a tinker's° damn for his bank and all his cattle farms put together; and a lack of appreciation, that way, goes hard with Phelps.

"Old Nimrod thinks Harve drank too much; and this from such as Nimrod and me!

"Brother Elder says Harve was too free with the old man's money — fell short in filial consideration, maybe. Well, we can all remember the very tone in which brother Elder swore his own father was a liar, in the county court; and we all know that the old man came out of that partnership with his son as bare as a sheared lamb. But maybe I'm getting personal, and I'd better be driving ahead at what I want to say."

The lawyer paused a moment, squared his heavy shoulders, and went on: "Harvey Merrick and I went to school together, back East. We were dead in earnest, and we wanted you all to be proud of us some day. We meant to be great men. Even I, and I haven't lost my sense of humour, gentlemen, I meant to be a great man. I came back here to practice, and I found you didn't in the least want me to be a great man. You wanted me to be a shrewd lawyer — oh, yes! Our veteran here wanted me to get him an increase of pension, because he had dyspepsia;° Phelps wanted a new county survey that would put the widow Wilson's little bottom farm inside his south line; Elder wanted to lend money at five per cent a month, and get it collected; and Stark here wanted to wheedle old women up in Vermont into investing their annuities° in real-estate mortgages that are not worth the paper they are written on. Oh, you needed me hard enough, and you'll go on needing me!

"Well, I came back here and became the damned shyster° you wanted me to be. You pretend to have some sort of respect for me; and yet you'll stand up and throw mud at Harvey Merrick, whose soul you couldn't dirty and whose hands you couldn't tie. Oh, you're a discriminating lot of Christians! There have been times when the sight of Harvey's name in some Eastern paper has made me hang my head like a whipped dog; and, again, times when I liked to think of him off there in the world, away from all this hog-wallow, climbing the big, clean up-grade he'd set for himself.

"And we? Now that we've fought and lied and sweated and stolen, and hated as only the disappointed strugglers in a bitter, dead little Western town know how to do, what have we got to show for it? Harvey Merrick wouldn't have given one sunset over your marshes for all you've got put together, and you know it. It's not for me to say why, in the inscrutable° wisdom of God, a genius should ever have been called from this place of hatred and bitter waters; but I want this Boston man to know that the drivel he's been hearing here tonight is the only tribute any truly great man could have from such a lot of sick, side-tracked, burnt-dog, land-poor sharks as the here-present financiers of Sand City—upon which town may God have mercy!"

The lawyer thrust out his hand to Steavens as he passed him, caught up his overcoat in the hall, and had left the house before the Grand Army man had had time to lift his ducked head and crane his long neck about at his fellows.

Next day Jim Laird was drunk and unable to attend the funeral services. Steavens called twice at his office, but was compelled to start East without seeing him. He had a presentiment° that he would hear from him again, and left

his address on the lawyer's table; but if Laird found it, he
never acknowledged it. The thing in him that Harvey
Merrick had loved must have gone underground with
Harvey Merrick's coffin; for it never spoke again, and Jim
got the cold he died of driving across the Colorado mountains to defend one of Phelps's sons who had got into
trouble out there by cutting government timber.

Do especially Questions 11, 76, 77, 79, 80, 86, 102, and 111.
Consult the Short Story Model on page 156.

WILLA SIBERT CATHER   1873-1947

Although Willa Cather was born in Virginia, she moved to
Nebraska early in her life, and it was there that she found the
setting for her most notable writing. During her teens, she lived
among Czech, Scandinavian, and German farmers who had
migrated to the Nebraska plains. It was during these years
particularly that she developed her sharp insight into the life of
impoverished midwesterners. At the same time, she was gaining
from her neighbors an understanding of the traditions and culture
of Europe.

   After graduation from college (1895), Miss Cather spent some
time working on a small magazine and teaching high school
English in Pittsburgh. During those years she published several
short stories in *McClure's Magazine,* and eventually accepted a
position as editor of that journal. The publication of *O Pioneers*
(1913) was her first notable success as a novelist. It was followed
by such significant longer works as *My Antonia* (1918), and the
Pulitzer Prize winning novel *One of Ours* (1922) in which her
picture of a Nebraska farm boy in World War I displayed her
perceptions both of Europe and the American rural Midwest.

The Cricket Boy

P'U SUNG-LING Retold by Lin Yutang

When Kiti, a boy of eleven, came home with his father after
a day's fruitless search for crickets, he had a most wonderful
feeling—the discovery of his father as a play companion.
Kiti was an extremely impressionable child. Once, when
he was five, his father held a stick to punish him for some-

"The Cricket Boy" by P'u Sung-Ling from *Famous Chinese Short Stories* published
by The John Day Company. © 1948, 1951, 1952 by Lin Yutang. Reprinted by permission of The John Day Company, Inc., publisher.

thing, and Kiti's face turned so pale with fright that his father let the stick drop out of his hand. He had always had a great fear of his father, a taciturn° man of forty-five.

He was small for his age, about the size of other children of nine or ten, and the jacket which his mother had made for him a year ago, thinking he would grow up quickly, still seemed ample and long. His slim, childish figure was accentuated by a disproportionately large head and a pair of big, black, playful eyes and plump round cheeks. He jumped and skipped, rather than walked normally, and he was still very much a child in his emotions. When his brother was Kiti's age, he was already a great help to his mother, but not Kiti. Now, the brother was dead and his only sister was married into a family in another town. Kiti was perhaps pampered° by his mother, a sad but strongly built woman, who could be made to smile only by Kiti's unusual pranks and wiles. He still retained many childish ways in his looks and smiles, and in the intense joys and sorrows of childhood.

Kiti loved crickets as only boys can love, and, with a child's keen enthusiasm and poetic imagination, he found in the beauty and delicacy of the insect something utterly perfect, noble, and strong. He admired the cricket's complicated mandibles° and thought that no animal of a larger size in this world had such a lacquered,° armored body and legs. He thought that if an animal the size of a dog or pig had such a beautiful outfit—no, there was no comparable animal. Crickets had been his passion since his early childhood. Like all village children, he had played with them and had come to know the worth of a cricket by the sound of its creak, the size and angle of its legs, and the proportion and shape of its head and body. There was a northern window in his room, adjoining a back garden, and as he lay in bed listening to the song of the crickets, it seemed to him the most pleasing music in the world. It represented to him all that was good and strong and beautiful in this world. Confucius and Mencius[1] he learned quickly from his teacher, who was now his own father, and forgot just

[1]Chinese sages of the sixth and fourth centuries before Christ.

as quickly; but this song of the crickets he understood and remembered. He had heaped a pile of bricks and stones under the window for the purpose of attracting them. No grown-up seemed to understand this—certainly not his cold and severe father—but today for the first time, he had come out with Kiti and run over the mountainside to look for a champion fighter.

There had been a memorable incident when Kiti was six. He had brought a cricket to the classroom, and the teacher discovered it and crushed it. Kiti was so furious that when the teacher turned his back, Kiti leaped from his chair, saddled on his back and pummeled° the teacher with all the strength of his small fists, to the amusement of the students, until the teacher had to shake him down.

That afternoon, he had watched his father silently making a hand net with a bamboo handle for catching crickets. When the net was made, his father had said to him, "Kiti, bring that bamboo° box. We will go to the southern hills." It was beneath the scholar's dignity to announce that he was going to catch crickets.

But Kiti understood. He went out with his father and felt as if he were on a New Year holiday. It was like an answer to a child's prayer. He had gone out to catch crickets, but had never had the luxury of a proper net. Furthermore, he had never been allowed to go to the southern hills, about a mile and a half away, where he knew there were plenty of crickets.

It was July and the day was hot. The father and child, net in hand, ran all over the foothill slopes, making their way through thickets, jumping over ditches, turning over and peeping under stones, listening for that most important sound, the clear, metallic° chirp of a good champion. They had found no worthy champion, but they had found each other as companions. That was a wonderful new sensation for Kiti. He had seen his father's eyes shine when they heard a clear, sharp note, and heard him curse under his breath when they lost one in the underbrush. On their way back, his father was still uttering sighs of regret over missing the beautiful one. For the first time, his father had become human, and he loved his father then.

His father had not bothered to explain why he suddenly took an interest in crickets, and Kiti, though secretly delighted, saw no reason to ask. But when they got home he saw his mother standing at the door, waiting for them to return for supper.

"Did you catch any?" asked his mother anxiously.

"No!" The father's reply was solemn and heavy with disappointment.

Kiti wondered greatly about it. That night he asked his mother, when they were alone, "Tell me, Mother, does Father love crickets, too? I thought I was the only one."

"No, he does not. He has to do it."

"Why? For whom?"

"For the emperor. Your father is the head of the village. He received an order from the magistrate to catch a good fighter. Who dares disobey the emperor?"

"I do not understand." Kiti was still more puzzled.

"Nor do I. But your father has to catch a good one within the next ten days, or he will lose his job and be fined. We are too poor to pay, and he may have to go to jail if he fails."

Kiti gave up trying to understand and asked no more questions. He only knew that it was something of terrible importance.

At this time, there was a great craze for cricket fights among the ladies of the court, with heavy betting going on, and culminating° in the annual mid-autumn championship contests. It was perhaps an old tradition at the court, for the last premier of the Sung Dynasty[2] was known to have been watching his cricket fights when the armies of Genghis Khan[3] marched into the capital. The district of Hwayin where Mr. Cheng lived was not known for producing the best fighters, but a year ago, an alert magistrate of the pro-

[2]The Sung Dynasty ruled China from A.D. 960-1127; it was noted for promoting literature, philosophy, and art.
[3]The Mongol conqueror of China, and other countries, in the twelfth century.

vince had obtained a good champion and sent it to the court. A prince had written a letter to the governor of the province asking him to send more champions for the annual mid-autumn contest, and the governor had issued an order to all his magistrates to send their choicest selections from the districts to him. What had been a private request from a prince had become an edict° of the emperor, as far as the common people were concerned. The price of good crickets skyrocketed and one magistrate was known to have offered as much as a hundred dollars for a good champion. Cricket fights had also become a popular pastime among the local people, and those who had champions were reluctant° to part with them for any price.

Some heads of villages had taken the occasion to extort money from the people to buy crickets for the emperor, calling it the "crickets' levy." Mr. Cheng could have collected one or two hundred dollars from the villagers, pocketed half of it, and with the other half bought a cricket from the town. He, however, would do nothing of the kind. If it was his duty to submit a champion, he would go and catch it himself.

Kiti shared his father's anxiety and felt important because his child's pastime had now become a dignified, grown-up affair. He watched his father's expression, as they were taking a rest in the cool shade. His father took out his pipe, lighted it, and his eyebrows danced a little as he puffed. He seemed to want to say something but paused and puffed away at his pipe, opened his mouth and then stopped to puff again. Finally, he said with an almost guilty expression on his face, "Kiti, you can catch a good champion for me. It is worth a lot of money."

"How, Father?"

"You see, son, there is a national championship at the imperial palace on mid-autumn festival. The winner will be awarded a big prize by the emperor."

"Really—by the emperor himself?" exclaimed Kiti. "Does the emperor love crickets, too?"

"Yes," replied the father reluctantly, as if a shameful confession had been forced from his lips.

"Hey, Father, we might catch a good fighter and win the national championship!" Kiti was greatly excited. "Will you be able to see the emperor?"

"No, I will send the cricket through the magistrate, and then through the governor, if it is good enough. It has got to be good. There is a big award in silver for the champion owner."

"Father, we will catch one, and we will be rich!"

It was difficult to repress the child's enthusiasm. But the father, having told him an important secret, looked serious once more. They got up and continued the search. Kiti now felt it was his responsibility to catch a champion fighter for his father, and for his mother as well because he had often heard her complain about being poor.

"I will catch one and fight and fight till we win," said the child.

The father was now glad that Kiti knew so much about crickets and was able to help him. For three days, they could not find a champion, but on the fourth day, they had a streak of good luck. They had gone over the top of the hill and descended on the farther side where there was a deep thicket and heavy underbrush. Far down the slope was an ancient tomb site. The outline of the tomb, some fifty feet across, was clearly visible. Kiti suggested going down to the tomb where they might catch some good crickets, especially because the sand there was reddish yellow. They followed a small brook and reached the site where a great many stone slabs lay about, showing the outlines of the ancient tomb. Their hope was justified. The crickets were singing on that July afternoon, not a few, but dozens of them in concert. Kiti's senses were sharpened. A frog suddenly leaped from the grass under his feet and disappeared into a hole, from which sprang out a big, beautiful insect, hopping away in long, powerful strides. The big cricket disappeared into an underground hole protected by stone slabs. The father and son crouched down and listened with bated° breath to the rich, resonant° chirp. Kiti took a long blade of grass and tried to stir the insect out of the hole, but it stopped its singing. They were sure now that the prize champion was in that hole, but the crack was too small even for the child's small hands to reach down through it. The father tried to smoke it out without success. Then Kiti went to fetch some water to pour down the hole, while the father held the net in readiness outside the entrance.

In a few seconds, the cricket sprang neatly into their net. He was a beauty, of the kind called "blackneck," with wide jaws, slender body, and powerful legs bent at a high angle. His whole body was of a fine and deep reddish-brown lacquer finish. Their labor was rewarded.

They returned home happily and placed their prize in an earthen jar on a table in the father's room, carefully covered with a sheet of copper wire netting. Mr. Cheng would take it to town the next day to present it to the magistrate. He instructed his wife to guard it carefully against neighbors' cats, and he went out to get some chestnut meat[4] to feed it. Nobody was to touch it while he was away.

Kiti was excited beyond measure. He could not help coming into the room to listen to the insect's chirp and stare at it in sheer joy.

Then a tragedy happened. There was for a time no noise whatever in the jar. Kiti tapped it and still there was no sign of a movement. The cricket was apparently gone. He could not see into the dark jar, so he took it near the window and removed the wire net slowly to look when out hopped the cricket and landed on a book shelf. Kiti was desperate. He closed the window quickly and started to chase the insect around the room. In his excitement he neglected to use the net, and by the time he had caught the cricket under his palm, he had crushed its neck and broken one of its legs.

Kiti was pale with terror. His mouth was dry and he was without tears. He had destroyed what had promised to be a national champion.

"You accumulated debt of ten generations!" scolded his mother. "You are going to die! When your father returns, I do not know what he will do to you!"

[4]The edible part of the chestnut.

Kiti's face was deathly white. He finally broke into sobs and ran away from the house.

At supper time Kiti still had not returned. His father was enraged and mortified,° and threatened to give him a sound thrashing when he returned. The parents thought that he was hiding away, afraid to return, but believed that he would come home when he was hungry.

Toward ten o'clock, there was still no sign of Kiti, and the anger of the parents had turned into anxiety for him. They went out with a lantern into the night to search for him; and toward midnight they found Kiti's body at the bottom of a well.

When the child was brought out, he was apparently lifeless. There was a big wound on his head, but a trickle of fresh blood was still oozing from a cut on his forehead. It was a shallow well, but his whole body was drenched. They dried him and bandaged him, laying him on the bed, and were glad to find that his heart was still beating. Only a feeble breath indicated that the child was still alive. The shock was apparently so great that Kiti remained unconscious for a whole day, hovering between life and death. That evening they heard him mumbling in his sleep, "I have killed the champion—the blackneck, the blackneck!"

The next morning, Kiti could take some soup, but he was a changed child. All life seemed to have gone out of him. He could not recognize his father and mother. His sister, hearing of the incident, came to visit him, and he made no sign of recognition. An old doctor told them that he had been badly frightened and that his illness was too deep to be cured by medicines. The only coherent° words Kiti said were, "I have killed him!"

Happy that Kiti was at least alive, and hopeful of an eventual recovery, Mr. Cheng remembered that he had still four more days in which to catch another fighter. He had a faint hope that could he catch a good one and show it to Kiti, it might help to cure him. After all, there were plenty of crickets in the ancient tomb site. He slept lightly and at dawn he heard a chirp in his house. He got up and traced the sound to the kitchen, where he saw a small cricket resting high up on the wall.

A strange thing now happened. As the father stood looking at it, he thought how small and probably useless it was for such a loud chirp. But with three loud chirps the little one hopped down onto his sleeve, as if asking to be caught.

The father captured it and examined it slowly. It had a long neck and a plum-flower design on its wings. It might be a good fighter, but it was so small. He would not dare to offer it to the magistrate.

A neighboring young man had a local champion which had won every bout° in the village. He had put a high price on it, but he had found no buyer, so he brought it to Mr. Cheng's house, intending to sell it to him.

When Mr. Cheng suggested a match, the young man took a look at the little cricket and covered his mouth in laughter. The two insects were placed inside a cage, and Cheng felt ashamed of his cricket and wanted to withdraw. The young man insisted on a fight to show his insect's prowess,° and Cheng, thinking it would be no great sacrifice if the little one should be killed or maimed,° yielded. The two insects now stood facing each other inside a basin. The little one stood still while the big one opened its fangs and glowered as if eager for combat. The young man teased the little one with a pig's bristle to provoke it, but it remained unmoved. Again he prodded it, repeatedly, and suddenly the little fellow sprang into action, and the two insects fell at each other. In an instant, they saw the small cricket tilt its tail, raise its feelers,° and with a powerful leap, sink its jaws into the opponent's neck. The young man quickly lifted the cage and called the fight off in the hope of saving his pet. The little cricket raised its head and chirped triumphantly.

Cheng was greatly pleased and amazed, but while he was admiring his new find, along with his family, a male cricket came along unnoticed by them, and pecked at the prize. The little cricket hopped away, chased by the male, and in immediate reach of its claws. Cheng thought all was lost. Then he saw the male shaking its head repeatedly, and observed that the little cricket had perched safely on the male's neck and was harassing° it from that position. They were all astounded and delighted.

Now confident of the little cricket's fighting power, Cheng decided to present it to the magistrate, telling him the story. The magistrate was far from impressed and was very skeptical, but he gave the insect a trial. The cricket won every fight over others collected in his office. He tried it again on a male, and the little "plum-flower-wing" repeated his tactic of landing on the male's neck, to everybody's astonishment. Satisfied with the district champion, the magistrate put it in a copper-wire cage and sent it to the governor. It was already the last day of July, and he dispatched it on horseback.

The father waited and hoped; one cricket had brought on his son's illness, another one might cure him. Then he heard that the little cricket had become the provincial champion, and his hopes went higher. It would take probably a month before he heard the results of the national championship match.

"Huh!" said Kiti's mother to her husband when she was told of the little cricket's fighting tactics. "Is it not just like Kiti riding on the teacher's back and pommeling him from behind?"

Kiti did not recover from his shock. Most of the time he was asleep and his mother had to force food down his mouth with a spoon. The first few days, his muscles twitched° and he perspired heavily. The doctor came again and after hearing the symptoms announced that Kiti had burst his gall bladder in fright, and said that his *yang-yin*[5] system of internal secretions had turned backwards. His three spiritual and seven animal spirits had been frightened away. It would take a long and slow cure to restore his vitality.

After three days, Kiti suffered another fit of paroxysms.° Then his head seemed clearer for a day—it was the last day of July, his mother remembered clearly—and he could even

[5]The male-female, bright-dark, positive-negative, beneficent-malevolent principles present in a human being. The balance of these principles brings health.

smile when he said to his mother, "I have won!" His eyes stared vacantly.

"You have what?"

"I have won."

"Won what?"

"I do not know. I must win." He seemed to be still in a delirium.°

Then his spirit left him again, and he fell into a profound coma° for half a month.

At dawn, on the morning of August the eighteenth, Kiti's mother heard him calling, "Mother, I am hungry!"

It was the first time Kiti had called his mother since the incident. She jumped out of bed, called her husband, and they went in together to see their boy.

"Mother, I am hungry."

"My darling child, you are well again!" The mother wiped her eyes with the hem of her jacket.

"How are you feeling?" asked the father.

"I am feeling fine, Father."

"You have slept a long time."

"Have I? How long?"

"About three weeks. You scared us."

"Was it that long? I did not know anything. Father, I did not mean to hurt that champion. I was trying to capture him for you." Kiti's voice was perfectly normal, and he spoke as if the incident had happened only a day ago.

"Do not worry, Kiti," said the father. "While you were ill, I caught a better champion. He was small, but a terribly good fighter. The magistrate accepted it and sent it to the governor. I hear that he has won every fight."

"Then you have forgiven me?"

"Of course I have. Do not worry, son. That plucky little fighter may be a national champion yet. Now put your mind at rest, and soon you will be able to get up."

The family was happy once more. Kiti had a good appetite and only complained that his thighs were sore.

"That is very strange," said his mother.

"I feel, Mother, as if I had run and jumped hundreds of miles."

His mother massaged his legs, while Kiti kept on saying that his thighs were stiff.

In a day, Kiti was able to get up and walk a few steps. On the third day after his recovery, father, mother, and the boy were sitting by the lamp after supper, eating chestnuts.

"This is like the chestnut meat I had at the palace," Kiti remarked casually.

"Where?"

"At the imperial palace," Kiti replied, not knowing how strange his words must have sounded in his parents' ears.

"You must have been dreaming."

"No, Mother, I was there. Now I remember. All the ladies were dressed in red and blue and gold, when I came out of my golden cage."

"Did you dream that when you were ill?"

"No, it was true. Believe me, Mother, I was there."

"What did you see?"

"There were men with long beards and there was one I thought must be the emperor. They had come to see me. I only thought of Father and said to myself that I must win. When I was let out of the cage, I saw a big fellow. He had very long feelers and I got frightened, until the fight started. Night after night, I fought with only one idea that I must win for Father. On the last night, I met a redhead. He was fearful to look at. I was not afraid any more. I went at him, but when he came at me, I leaped away. I was in perfect form and felt very light and alert. I tore at his tail and bit off one of his front legs. He got mad and came at me with open fangs. I thought I was done for, but I bit him somewhere. Then he became confused. I saw his eye was bleeding. I sprang on his neck and finished him."

Kiti told all this so realistically that his parents listened in silence, knowing that he was perfectly sincere in describing what he had seen in his dreams.

"And you have won the national championship?" asked the father.

"I think I did. I wanted to so much. I only thought of you, Father."

The parents did not know whether to believe his story or

not. The child was not lying, they knew. They would wait and see.

The little cricket, sent in a golden cage by the imperial system, had reached the capital just one day before the contests began. The governor was risking a great deal in submitting such a small cricket to the prince. If the insect gave a good account of itself, well and good, but if it failed, he stood a chance of being ridiculed for being in his dotage.° He trembled at the thought. The official document of three thousand words accompanying the cricket was something unusual, both apologetic and bombastic° at the same time.

"My friend is mad," said the prince, after reading his letter.

"Why not give it a trial?" remarked his wife, the emperor's daughter.

The plucky little fighter fought with supercricket powers. As far as they could see, he had shown no fear when put in a basin opposite the other provincial champions.

After the first night in which he felled a champion almost twice his size, the little plum-flower-wing was regarded as a marvel and became the talk of the court.

Night after night, the little one won. It was true that he had the advantage of lightness and agility. While no champion could get at him, he always harassed the big fellows by his lightning attacks and bit the opponent here and there before he came in with deadly accuracy for a crushing bit. His accomplishments seemed incredible.

The contests lasted five nights from August fourteenth to August eighteenth. On the last night he became the champion. The next morning, the little champion had completely disappeared from his cage.

When the news reached Kiti's family, the father wept, and they were all overjoyed. The father put on his best gown and took Kiti along to the magistrate. He was told that he would be made an honorary member of the district college with monthly stipends for his support.

The family fortunes turned, and Kiti eventually was able

to go to college. Kiti not only felt embarrassed to have his story told, but he stopped watching cricket fights altogether. He could not stand it.

Later he became a *hanlin*[6] and was able to support his parents in ease and comfort in their old age. Mr. Cheng, now a proud grandfather, never tired of telling the story of his son, which grew better and better every time, and he always ended with the words, "There are many ways of showing filial° piety. When one's heart is good, the spirits of heaven and earth will show mercy to them that love their parents."

[6]In China, a member of the Han Lin Yuan, sometimes called the Imperial Academy. The position was one of very high literary and official honor under the old system.

Do especially Questions 74, 87, 90, 95, and 117. Consult the Short Story Model on page 156.

P'Ú SUNG-LING   *1640-1715*

In 1931 the only work of P'u Sung-Ling that was at all well known was *Chih-i* or *Strange Stories from a Chinese Studio.* Then in 1932 *Marriage As Retribution* was published and established as the work of P'u. In 1936 all his other writings were published under the title *Collected Works.* Most of his stories used one of three basic themes: jealous wives, hen-pecked husbands, or wicked mothers-in-law. The remarkable characteristic of P'u Sung-Ling's stories is that he developed these basic themes in three different literary forms: the short tale, romances in prose and verse, and long epic novels. His tales were an improvement over the tales of earlier Chinese authors because he gave his ghosts, fairies, and flower spirits a touch of humanity; and he showed more invention. Although P'u became a salaried licentiate° in 1685 and a senior licentiate in 1710, he never reached the *chu-jen* degree, which he worked for until he was past sixty. Therefore, unable to enter government service, he humbled himself to serve as secretary to his friends who had been able to pass the examinations for government service; and he taught in the family schools of the wealthy families of the locality. During his lifetime his tales were circulated in manuscript form; and not until 1766, fifty years after his death, were they published. Immediately they became the most highly respected collection read by the literate Chinese.

The Ruby

CORRADO ALVARO

The daily papers had recorded one of those news items that keep a town in a buzz of excitement for a whole day and finally make a circuit of the world. A ruby as big as a hazelnut, a famous stone, bearing a famous name, and said to be of enormous value, had disappeared. An Indian prince, on a visit to a North American city, had been wearing this jewel as an ornament. He had suddenly become aware of his loss after a journey he had made in a taxi that had set him down—incognito—at a hotel in the suburbs, for he had managed to evade the attention of both his private bodyguard and the police. The flying-squad was mobilized, the entire city awoke the following morning to a knowledge of the loss, and right up to midday hundreds of people cherished the hope of finding the celebrated stone in their own street. One of those waves of optimism and excitement had fallen on the town; the kind of feeling you get when the opulence of one individual enriches everybody else's hopes. The prince had not been very forthcoming in his statement to the police, but it ruled out any possibility that the lady accompanying him could have been responsible for the loss. They were not, therefore, to try and locate her. The taxi-driver came forward to testify that he had driven the Indian wearing his precious turban, and stated that he had deposited him and the lady in front of a hotel in the suburbs. The lady was a European, and the only thing that distinguished her was a magnificent diamond, the size of a pea, which she wore in her left nostril after the manner of certain wealthy Indians. This detail distracted the attention of the public for a while from the missing ruby and whetted their curiosity still more. The driver, after making a thorough search of the interior of the vehicle, checked up on the "fares" he had driven during

"The Ruby" by Corrado Alvaro, from *Modern Italian Stories*, translated by W. J. Strachan, published by Eyre and Spottiswoode (Publishers), Ltd. Reprinted by permission of Gerda Andrew.

the early hours of the morning in question; they had been a businessman, a foreigner whom he had taken down to the port and who was evidently sailing for Europe, and a woman. The foreigner, recognizable as an Italian, had emerged from one of the houses where emigrants lived in a colony; he had been wearing a pair of trousers of generous width such as are popular with emigrants, rough, thick-soled shoes of a type nowadays seen only among people of that social class, and a hard hat set above a thin, clean-shaven face, seamed with wrinkles. His luggage consisted of a heavy suitcase secured with stout cord and one other weighty box which appeared to be made of steel. He had embarked that same day, but any suspicion that might have alighted on him was immediately dispelled when it was realized that he had behaved as though he was riding in a taxi for the first time in his life. He had not managed to close the door properly and had hugged the front window all the time, possibly so as to avoid being suddenly jerked backward into the road, and he had gazed at the streets with the air of one who is leaving a town perhaps forever. The driver reserved his attention rather for the man who, on leaving the suburban hotel, had taken the taxi immediately after the prince and had given orders to be driven to the Italian workmen's quarter, at which point his place had been taken by the foreigner. The fare in question, of whom he had given a description and who must have been a local resident, was searched for in vain. Furthermore the fact that he had failed to answer the appeal published in the newspapers, offering a large reward, was a logical proof that it was not he who had got hold of the famous gem. However, since the missing stone was world-famed and easily recognizable, it was hoped that one day or other it would come to light.

The emigrant, meantime, was on his way home to a country town in Southern Italy after five years' absence and was ignorant of all this stir. He had with him the most unusual collections of odds and ends — even for an emigrant. A suitcase, made of artificial leather which he thought was real, contained his blue overalls, pressed and cleaned, twelve fountain-pens which he intended to sell to the people of the district, forgetting that most of them were herdsmen and not more than half a dozen of the inhabitants could put pen to paper. In addition, he had some crested table services, a pair of hair-clippers which he had used on his fellow-workers, a metal object whose function completely mystified him — it had the form of a pistol, but did not fire — twelve squares of American cloth and some novelties to impress and amuse his wife, son, and friends. The heavy part of his luggage was the somewhat battered steel strong-box; the lock was operated by a combination, the six-letter name, *Annina*. By way of ready cash he took a thousand dollars, which included three hundred to be paid back later to those from whom he had borrowed it for the voyage. In his waistcoat pocket he carried a lump of red crystal; it was many-faceted and as large as a walnut. He had come across it by chance in the taxi that had taken him down to the harbor, but he had no idea what it was for. His fingers had felt it behind the seat-cushions. He kept it as a lucky charm for the future; perhaps he would have it attached to his watch-chain as a pendant. It seemed odd that it had no hole bored through it. It could not, therefore, be one of those large stones which city ladies have on their necklaces.

The various objects one picks up just before leaving a foreign country are apt to acquire an extraordinary souvenir-value, giving one, as it were, a foretaste of distance and nostalgia. It was just such an affection that our emigrant felt for this lump of crystal, so cool to the touch, as translucent and clear as sugar candy.

He had established a small trade with all these different acquisitions. The strong-box, now fixed against the wall, the counter for his transactions, fountain-pens in a box, crested table services, squares of American cloth on which were depicted the Statue of Liberty and angels in the corners bearing the portraits of the founders of American Independence, each square embroidered with white and blue stars — five long years he had patiently built up his collection against his eventual return; selecting whatever would seem most of a novelty to the folk in a region like his own, though he might have taken his choice from the shabby second-hand goods that come from heaven knows where and go the rounds among the emigrant population.

So he who had started life as a day-laborer had now become a dealer in various wares. It had been the strong-box that had set him on that train of thought; he had taken to shopkeeping for no other reason. He had felt almost rich because all the money he had in his pockets was in foreign currency and would turn into a larger number of coins when he exchanged them. Mental calculations connected with this engrossed him at all sorts of odd moments. He felt a childish delight every time he fingered the red crystal in his pocket. He began to regard it as a kind of talisman. It became one of those useless objects we cherish all our lives and never have the strength of mind to get rid of, so that in the end they become part of ourselves and even family heirlooms. Whereas important things that we watch over or hide away disappear, objects of the kind referred to never get lost, and our minds hark back to them at intervals. A few days later, for example, the crystal reminded our emigrant of the day when he had embarked for home, the interior of the taxi, the streets which seemed to roll slowly up like a piece of drop-scenery at the end of a play and become distant memories.

He set up his shop in the upper part of the country-town inhabited by peasants and herdsmen. A fortnight after his arrival he had furnished the ground floor of a peasant's cottage with a long counter and shelves, where the blue packets of flour-paste and the blue muslin for housewives found a place, and on one side of the shop stood a cask of wine on a couple of trestles, and an earthenware jar of oil. The strong-box had been fixed against the wall, and he felt a great sense of pride when he opened it in the presence of his customers. In it reposed his account-ledger and the notebook containing a list of all the goods sold on tick that were to be paid at harvest-time or after the animal fairs. Gradually his business got to look like any other business; it acquired its own peculiar smell, there were chalk-marks made on the wall by his wife—who could not write—recording goods supplied on credit. His young son, however, who attended school, and was now beginning to be able to write customers' names in the register, sometimes took a turn in the shop and managed it quite expertly on hot afternoons when all trade had ceased except that in iced drinks for gentlemen recovering from their afternoon siesta.

Slowly, his wife's narrow, American-style slippers acquired more and more creases and she herself the complacent, meticulous air of a shopkeeper's wife. The supply of new material which her husband had brought home had finally ended up among the shop-soiled goods, and only the hard hat, looking almost new, was still left in the wardrobe. The squares of American cloth had been distributed as presents among the important customers; as for the fountain-pens, no one had wanted them. Someone had handled them roughly and the fragments still lay in the box. The shopkeeper, who was a boy at heart, often imagined that the pen nibs were of pure gold and he cherished them as a small boy cherishes tinfoil-wrapping off chocolates. He also hung onto an old newspaper printed in English. He had refused to part with it even when he was short of wrapping paper. Sometimes he would scrutinize it carefully and the advertisement illustrations would recall to him the people who smoked gold-tipped cigarettes, the street-boys, the gramophones, in fact all the life he had seen in the central parts of the city on the rare occasions of his visits there. As for the lump of crystal, he remembered it one day and gave it to his son who was celebrating his birthday with his friends. At that time, boys played a game which consisted in knocking down and conquering castles made of hazel-nuts by throwing a heavier one at it; the usual procedure was to select a larger nut, make a small hole in it, patiently scrape out the kernel, then fill it with small lead pellets. The crystal missile was just the thing, it was heavy enough to carry to the mark. Another of the boys used a glass marble of the kind extracted from lemonade bottles, which had the advantage of being round. The shopkeeper's son claimed that his was more

beautiful because it came from America and because it
was red. He cherished it in the way that boys do who never
lose objects of that kind. As his father contemplated this
curiosity which had become his child's plaything, his mind
would often dwell on the illusions he had once entertained
in the days when he traveled about the world, and the
world seemed to be filled with valuable things that had
been lost which the lucky ones found. That was why he
had always felt with his fingers under mattresses of berths
on steamers, behind leather cushions on buses and coaches,
according to where he happened to be. But he had never
found anything. Yes; there had been one occasion. He had
found five dollars in the street. It had been raining that
day, he remembered.

> *Do especially Questions 4, 11, 17, 75, 76, 89, 90, 93, 95, 102,*
> *114, and 116. Consult the Short Story Model on page 156.*

CORRADO ALVARO   *1895-1955*

Although Alvaro lived most of his life in Rome, the memory and
influence of his birthplace in southern Italy strongly affected all
of his fiction. Thus, in "The Ruby" he shows the sure touch of
one who understands the Italian emigrant to America and knows
in detail "the country town in Southern Italy" to which he returns.
In addition to being one of Italy's best fiction writers, Alvaro was
also highly respected as an editor and journalist.

Under Cover of Darkness

SHEN T'SUNG-WEN Translated by Y. Chia-Hua and Robert Payne

The bamboo raft, nimbly° manned by the two men, glided
quietly downstream. The raftsmen had passed unseen
through the river patrols, and were now only two miles
from their destination, but suddenly the raft ran aground on

"Under Cover of Darkness" by Shen T'Sung-Wen, translated by Y. Chia-Hua and
Robert Payne, from *Contemporary Chinese Short Stories*. Reprinted by permission
of Royle Publications, Ltd.

a wild bank overgrown with rushes and reeds, and while the raft remained still and unmoving, they heard the murmuring of the water and the rustling of the wind through the reeds.

Lu-Yi, an officer of the signal corps of the guerrilla° troops, began to blame the younger man, hoarsely. "What's the matter?" he asked. "Are you possessed by devils? You think it's funny, don't you? But if we are stranded here, they will soon find us out, and we shall be shot to pieces by their guns."

The boy who had been crouching on the raft stood up slowly, but still he made no sound. There was a faint shimmering light on the dark surface of the river, and in the water there lay the reflection of two men standing on a raft, a reflection which was upside-down. Silently the boy walked to the other end of the raft.

"Well, we have run aground. I guess we have caught in something!" It was the voice of a very young boy.

He went up to the older man, and still leaning against the oar which he held in one hand, he took over the bamboo pole and tried to push it hither and thither in the marshy water. They were at a bend in the river where the water was shallow, but from the murmur of the water it was clear that the river ran swift round the bend; and there was no reason why the rafts should remain still, unless something had caught hold of the bamboo raft from underneath.

Their spirits were tried. Lu-Yi began to grumble again, impatiently. "There's two miles to go," he said. "It's a desperately° dangerous area. There might be enemy patrols at any moment...."

The boy seemed to have no feeling for fear or sorrow. He silently listened to the older man, and then untied the automatic pistol and bullet-case from his belt, rolled up his trousers, and gently slid into the water. He found a foothold and stooped down to push the raft with both hands. They heard the long, low squeak of the bamboos, but the raft did not move, and seemed, indeed, to be constrained° by unseen hands.

Lu-Yi was still impatient. "Be careful," he murmured. "I know you are strong, but be careful. Better take off your clothes and feel with your hands underneath the bamboos. There seem to be devils and ghosts there...."

"Yes," the boy answered, with a little giggle. "Devils and ghosts. But let me try...."

He began to move slowly in the water, stretching his hands under the bamboos. Touching the ropes and knots which joined the raft together, he stooped down, his arms and shoulders buried under the cold water, and his chin kissing the rippling surface of the river. Meanwhile his feet sank in mud to the knees, and it took an effort to pull them up again. He was still feeling among the knots and ropes when he felt something hard and round striking against his fingers. He realized then that it was a millstone° entangled among ropes and clothes. He reached out his hands and felt the cold wetness of a human body. "A body!" he shouted out in mingled alarm and delight, for now at last he knew what was obstructing the raft. "A body!" he exclaimed. "It's the funniest thing...."

"Well, what is it?"

He did not answer. He ran his fingers over the body and touched the hair, the face, and then the arms. It was bound to the millstone with heavy ropes, which had somewhat curled round the bamboos.

"Even with a millstone round its neck, this body prevents us from moving," the boy laughed silently.

"Then take it away," the other commanded, and he was more impatient than ever when he heard the crowing of the first cocks in the distance. "The body of a good-for-nothing," he added contemptuously. "No good when he was alive, and no good when he was dead," he murmured softly.

The boy was still wading round the raft, trying to disentangle the rope. Lu-Yi drew his knife from his belt and tapped it against the side of the raft. "Boy, come here," he said. "Take the knife and cut the rope in two. If the devil doesn't loosen his hold, cut his hand off. Hurry up! We're in terrible danger, and we have to get to the army."

The boy, amused by the expression "loosen his hold," wondered at his companion's impatience.

There was a muffled noise of a knife stirring up the water and the raft began to turn a little. A little while later he went to the stern of the raft and put his shoulder against it. He began to push hard, but he only succeeded in lifting the raft a little above the level of the water. The raft kept turning, but did not move forward. It was difficult to manage the knife under water, and perhaps in the end they would have to take the raft to pieces and then join the bamboos up again. But there was no time. Besides, less than a mile downstream, they knew there was a pontoon° bridge held by the enemy. Lu-Yi could no longer restrain his impatience. He began to curse the boy for his light-heartedness and slowness, and promised to write a report on his negligence, inefficiency,° and lack of responsibility. The boy remained calm, unmoved.

"Well, then, we had better walk instead of wasting our time on the river," he said, in a perfectly matter-of-fact voice. "Otherwise we won't get there before dawn."

"There are traps laid for us all over the hills and valley," the other answered. "The devils are ready with their ropes and millstones round our necks before dawn."

"Fears can't stop us," the boy replied. "There's no other way."

At last the older man was convinced. They carried the two bullet-cases and the rest of their equipment onto the embankment, groping and stumbling in the dark. Then they sat among the tall reeds and whispered about the routes they would take. They had no idea of the ponds and marshes and streams which lay in their way, and the villages and guard stations through which they would have to pass. In the black sky not a single star lay visible. Each one had brought a shirt torch,[1] but in the enveloping darkness they seemed to see eyes glaring at them, and they knew that the slightest light shown by them would call for a bullet from the enemy. And if the enemy knew that they

---

[1] A small, short torch that can be tucked inside one's shirt.

were passing along the river, the lives of all those who followed them on the bamboo rafts would be endangered.

After a while they decided not to take the road over the hills, but to follow the path which lay along the edge of the river. The flood water had receded° during the past few days, and now the path was dry. Besides, there was always the chance that they would come across a sampan° or canoe left somewhere along the bank.

The small path wound through bushy reeds. The earth was muddy and slippery underfoot, and there was a strange smell, a smell which grew inexplicably° stronger as they went forward.

"Mind your steps! There's probably another body some-where around. Don't fall over it."

"I forgot to feel the pockets of the fellow under the raft. Probably he was one of our comrades."

"Who else could it be?"

"Now I remember. The message of number seventy-four was stitched into the back of his trousers, the message of thirteen was hidden in a cigarette, and. . . ."

"Rubbish! Don't talk. We are still under close watch. Look out, because we don't want to have two more corpses in the place."

Lu-Yi was embarrassed by the strange smell, and thought the corpse could hardly be more than five yards away from them. He held his torch in his hand, and made as though he was going to flick on the light but the boy prevented him. They pricked up their ears and listened intently. They heard the approaching splash of rhythmic oars. They were about five feet away from the river, but thick bushes of reeds screened them from sight. They were both aware of the critical situation they were in, for it was evident that the approaching boat was patrolling the river to prevent the guerrillas from using it as a means of communication. If the patrol boat had reached the bend in the river and discovered the raft and their footprints, they would be followed immediately, and God knows what would happen then. Fortunately, they were already on land. . . .

At that moment, frightened by the steps of the two

wanderers or by the splashing of the oars in the river, a waterfowl rose, flapped its wings, and flew up into the dark sky. And then, after describing aimless and purposeless evolutions,° it darted towards the opposite bank of the river. They heard whispers among the oarsmen; probably they had already suspected the presence of strangers among the reeds. But the boat, instead of pursuing them, followed in the direction of the waterfowl, and they heard the leisurely pad of oars as the boat went towards the other bank.

The two wanderers lay on the bank with their pistols pointed in the direction of the boat. They were calm and determined, but when they heard the boat moving into the distance, they held out their hands silently at the same moment and clasped one another's hands with excitement and relief. Then they went on.

They could still smell the corpse, which was evidently lying somewhere to their left, away from the path. Suddenly Lu-Yi felt a hand snatching at his sleeve.

"Devil take you! What do you want?" he groaned.

"I think it is comrade seventy-four. Let me go and feel his body. A minute, or half a minute. . . ."

Without waiting for an answer from the older man, who was clearly displeased by the suggestion, the boy bent down and ran swiftly towards the place in the bushes where the heavy fetid° smell came from. He was back half a minute later.

"It's him all right," the boy said. "And it smells like him. He was a daring and dauntless fellow when alive, and now, even in corruption, his smell is terrific."

"What have you got?"

"A handful of maggots."°

"Are you sure it is him?"

"Yes, I tore off his collar. The papers are there. I knew it right away."

"Nice fellows—both of you!"

They strode along the path in silence. They were soon out of the bushes, but new dangers seemed to be lying in wait for them. Soon they came to a hillside, where the path diverged,° one road leading down towards the ford, and the other winding strangely among the battlemented rocks. A few lights were shining above the ford: evidently the place was well guarded. They gazed into one another's faces and neither could decide which pass was more dangerous or easier to get through.

Each minute gained gave them more hope, but they had no time to lose. They knew that the path to the ford was more familiar to them, and, if necessary, they could wade or swim across the river. They made a dash for the river. The boy saw that a fire was going out, and was probably unattended, but the older man held him back.

"Don't go near the fire, boy!"

"Don't worry. The fire must have been left behind by the patrols who boarded the boat. Probably they left it intentionally, to make us think they were there."

Once more the boy won the older man's consent. Crawling on all fours, they made their way towards the dying embers. They passed the fire unharmed, and found themselves before a long smooth road which wound along the edge of the hills and the river. They were light-hearted now, and all the danger forgotten, until some minutes later the boy thought he heard the clop-clop of a horse's hooves along the road. Lu-Yi listened. He, too, heard the sound and imagined that the enemy was approaching, followed perhaps by a wolfhound trained to smell out strangers at night. They decided to hide in the woods which bordered the hill, and blindly they crawled among the shadows of rocks and trees. Later, they heard the sound of hoof-beats along the road at the place where they had been, and they even imagined they could see the sparks from under the horse's feet and the white, thick vapour coming from the horse's mouth, and the sleek shadow of its back.

On his way down the slope, Lu-Yi twisted his ankle, but he knew that he would have to go as fast as possible if they were to avoid the guard station.

The sound of cocks crowing was wafted down the river. They decided, then, to bury their automatics among the reeds and swim downstream. If they could once pass the pontoon bridge, they would find themselves in safe territory less than a quarter of a mile away. But Lu-Yi knew that with his twisted ankle, it would be impossible for him to swim. They could go over the hills, but the tracks there were unknown to them, and hardly visible even in broad daylight. Moreover, beyond the hills lay precipitous° slopes looking down over a ravine, and it would be easy for the enemy patrols to pick them out.

Knowing that the position was hopeless, Lu-Yi broke out into angry remonstrances.°

"Boy, it's a trick played by devils. I know I am going to die here, and become a mess of worms. Next time you pass this way, better feel my collar as well. I can't walk. My right leg hurts abominably,° and I am sure I can't swim. You go downstream, and I'll go to the hills—and give me your pistol."

"No, if you are hurt, I'll go with you. We'll go up the hill and die together if we have to."

"Why should we die together, my dear little devil?" Lu-Yi answered, in a tone of annoyance. "Give me your pistol, and make your own way downstream."

The boy was silent. The older man repeated his command.

"I'll do as you say," the boy answered at last in a low voice. He unslung his belt, and all the time he was wondering how anyone could climb up hills and down valleys with only one good leg. He hesitated before handing the pistol over. They had gone on many dangerous errands together, and they had worked well together, and now Lu-Yi had to take the most dangerous road of all. He hardly dared to leave his companion. Lu-Yi saw this, and tried to console him.

"Boy, don't worry about me. With two pistols I shall kill many before I am killed. I prefer climbing to swimming, and in any case your journey will be hard. There may be barbed wire rising from the bottom of the river near the pontoon bridge. You may have to climb over the bridge— that's dangerous. I think I shall find my way easily enough over the hill, and when I find you I shall give you your pistol back. We'll meet again, my dear little devil."

Both knew that he was lying. Hardly had Lu-Yi finished speaking when he stepped forward and helped the boy untie his pistol belt and the bandolier° of bullets which fell down from his shoulders. Then he patted the boy on the arm and asked him to jump into the water before he himself went uphill. The kindly dogmatism° of the older man, the deep friendship which existed between them, and the strict discipline which existed among the guerrilla troops, all these exhorted the boy to slide down the embankment and into the water without another word.

The stream murmured quietly and coldly, and the boy threw himself in the water, imitating the cry of a wildfowl to show that he was already on his way, and meanwhile the older man, as a sign of final greeting, threw a pebble which landed a little way from the boy's foot. Thus, for the last time, they bade each other farewell and went on their ways.

The boy exerted all the strength of his young limbs, and cautiously moved downstream. He saw fires burning at each end of the pontoon bridge, and each fire cast a dazzling shadow on the water. The bridge was formed of a number of sampans and fishing boats fastened together with iron thews;° there was a sentry at each end, and there were also three or four soldiers patrolling the bridge. With his face showing only a little above water, the boy attempted to surrender to the force of the water, hoping to slide under the bridge without making the slightest sound. Suddenly he heard a whistling sound from the hilltop, and a moment later there was the sound of shooting. He knew then that the whereabouts of his friend had been discovered, but what puzzled him was that there was no answering fire from his friend. The bridge was only two yards away from him, shining in the light of the flares. He dived swiftly. There were no obstacles rising from the bottom of the river. Three yards past the bridge he came to the surface, and at that very moment he heard the automatic pistol shooting seven times in rapid succession. Soon afterwards he heard four successive pistol shots, and for the moment there were no more sounds.

Later he heard three rifle shots, then there was silence,

followed by a solitary pistol shot. Immediately afterwards he heard a shrill scream from someone on the bridge. A torchlight swept over the bridge, and all around. Once more the boy dived, and when he came to the surface again all was silent in the boundless darkness except for the interminable° murmur of the water beneath his body. The black night air permeating° all the space overhead seemed to press down on the river and penetrate through his skin and into his veins. He knew that the safety zone lay less than a quarter of a mile away.

He saw a camp fire blazing through the darkness, and the recognition of the friendly light and the illusory warmth which came from the fire gave him new strength.

"Password!"

"Nine . . . ty, with both feet wrapped in cloth."

"Why only one? Where's your companion?"

"Ask the ghost of your ancestor."

"Is he lost then?"

There was no reply. Only a splashing sound was heard when the boy climbed up the river bank.

Do especially Questions 48, 51, 78, 82, 83, and 84. Consult the Short Story Model on page 156.

SHEN T'SUNG-WEN   1902-

Shen T'Sung-Wen is a very modern Chinese author. His education consisted of a military, rather than the conventional academic background. A prolific novelist and critic, Shen T'Sung-Wen edited *Ta-Kung pao* literary supplement. Perhaps the best known work among his some sixty novels, volumes of stories, and other works is *The Chinese Earth*. Since the People's Republic was set up in China in 1949, however, little has been heard from established writers like Shen T'Sung-Wen.

A Weary Hour

THOMAS MANN Translated by H. T. Lowe-Porter

He got up from the table, his little, fragile writing-desk; got
up as though desperate, and with hanging head crossed the
room to the tall, thin, pillar-like stove in the opposite
corner. He put his hands to it; but the hour was long past
midnight and the tiles were nearly stone cold. Not getting
even this little comfort that he sought, he leaned his back
against them and, coughing, drew together the folds of his
dressing-gown, between which a draggled lace shirt-frill
stuck out; he snuffed hard through his nostrils to get a little
air, for as usual he had a cold.

It was a particular, a sinister cold, which scarcely ever
quite disappeared. It inflamed his eyelids and made the
flanges of his nose all raw; in his head and limbs it lay like
a heavy, sombre intoxication. Or was this cursed confinement to his room, to which the doctor had weeks ago condemned him, to blame for all his languor and flabbiness?
God knew if it was the right thing—perhaps so, on account
of his chronic catarrh° and the spasms in his chest and belly.
And for weeks on end now, yes, weeks, bad weather had
reigned in Jena—hateful, horrible weather, which he felt
in every nerve of his body—cold, wild, gloomy. The
December wind roared in the stove-pipe with a desolate
god-forsaken sound—he might have been wandering on a
heath,° by night and storm, his soul full of unappeasable°
grief. Yet this close confinement—that was not good either;
not good for thought, nor for the rhythm of the blood, where
thought was engendered.°

The six-sided room was bare and colourless and devoid
of cheer: a whitewashed ceiling wreathed in tobacco
smoke, walls covered with trellis-patterned paper and hung
with silhouettes in oval frames, half a dozen slender-
legged pieces of furniture; the whole lighted by two
candles burning at the head of the manuscript on the

writing-table. Red curtains draped the upper part of the window-frames; mere festooned wisps of cotton they were, but red, a warm, sonorous red, and he loved them and would not have parted from them; they gave a little air of ease and charm to the bald unlovely poverty of his surroundings. He stood by the stove and blinked repeatedly, straining his eyes across at the work from which he had just fled: that load, that weight, that gnawing conscience, that sea which to drink up, that frightful task which to perform, was all his pride and all his misery, at once his heaven and his hell. It dragged, it stuck, it would not budge — and now again ... ! It must be the weather; or his catarrh, or his fatigue. Or was it the work? Was the thing itself an unfortunate conception, doomed from its beginning to despair?

He had risen in order to put a little space between him and his task, for physical distance would often result in improved perspective, a wider view of his material and a better chance of conspectus.° Yes, the mere feeling of relief on turning away from the battlefield had been known to work like an inspiration. And a more innocent one than that purveyed by alcohol or strong, black coffee.

The little cup stood on the side-table. Perhaps it would help him out of the impasse? No, no, not again! Not the doctor only, but somebody else too, a more important somebody, had cautioned him against that sort of thing — another person, who lived over in Weimar and for whom he felt a love which was a mixture of hostility and yearning. That was a wise man. He knew how to live and create; did not abuse himself; was full of self-regard.

Quiet reigned in the house. There was only the wind, driving down the Schlossgasse and dashing the rain in gusts against the panes. They were all asleep — the landlord and his family, Lotte and the children. And here he stood by the cold stove, awake, alone, tormented; blinking across at the work in which his morbid self-dissatisfaction would not let him believe.

His neck rose long and white out of his stock° and his knock-kneed legs showed between the skirts of his dressing-gown. The red hair was smoothed back from a thin, high

forehead; it retreated in bays° from his veined white
temples and hung down in thin locks over the ears. His
nose was aquiline, with an abrupt whitish tip; above it the
well-marked line of the brows almost met. They were
darker than his hair and gave the deep-set, inflamed eyes
a tragic, staring look. He could not breathe through his
nose; so he opened his thin lips and made the freckled,
sickly cheeks look even more sunken thereby.

No, it was a failure, it was all hopelessly wrong. The
army ought to have been brought in! The army was the root
of the whole thing. But it was impossible to present it
before the eyes of the audience—and was art powerful
enough thus to enforce the imagination? Besides, his hero
was no hero; he was contemptible, he was frigid. The
situation was wrong, the language was wrong; it was a dry
pedestrian lecture, good for a history class, but as drama
absolutely hopeless!

Very good, then, it was over. A defeat. A failure. Bank-
ruptcy. He would write to Körner, the good Körner, who
believed in him, who clung with childlike faith to his
genius. He would scoff, scold, beseech—this friend of
his; would remind him of the *Carlos*, which likewise had
issued out of doubts and pains and rewritings and after all
the anguish turned out to be something really fine, a
genuine masterpiece. But times were changed. Then he
had been a man still capable of taking a strong, confident
grip on a thing and giving it triumphant shape. Doubts and
struggles? Yes. And ill he had been, perhaps more ill
than now; a fugitive, oppressed and hungry, at odds with
the world; humanly speaking, a beggar. But young, still
young! Each time, however low he had sunk, his resilient
spirit had leaped up anew; upon the hour of affliction had
followed the feeling of triumphant self-confidence. That
came no more, or hardly ever, now. There might be one
night of glowing exaltation—when the fires of his genius
lighted up an impassioned vision of all that he might do
if only they burned on; but it had always to be paid for
with a week of enervation° and gloom. Faith in the future,
his guiding star in times of stress, was dead. Here was the

despairing truth: the years of need and nothingness, which
he had thought of as the painful testing-time, turned out
to have been the rich and fruitful ones; and now that a
little happiness had fallen to his lot, now that he had
ceased to be an intellectual freebooter and occupied a
position of civic dignity, with office and honours, wife and
children—now he was exhausted, worn out. To give up,
to own himself beaten—that was all there was left to do.
He groaned; he pressed his hands to his eyes and dashed
up and down the room like one possessed. What he had
just thought was so frightful that he could not stand still
on the spot where he had thought it. He sat down on a
chair by the further wall and stared gloomily at the floor,
his clasped hands hanging down between his knees.

His conscience . . . how loudly his conscience cried out!
He had sinned, sinned against himself all these years,
against the delicate instrument that was his body. Those
youthful excesses, the nights without sleep, the days spent
in close, smoke-laden air, straining his mind and heedless
of his body; the narcotics with which he had spurred himself on—all that was now taking its revenge.

And if it did—then he would defy the gods, who decreed
the guilt and then imposed the penalties. He had lived as
he had to live, he had not had time to be wise, not time to
be careful. Here in this place in his chest, when he breathed,
coughed, yawned, always in the same spot came this pain,
this piercing, stabbing, diabolical little warning; it never
left him, since that time in Erfurt five years ago when he
had catarrhal fever and inflammation of the lungs. What
was it warning him of? Ah, he knew only too well what it
meant—no matter how the doctor chose to put him off. He
had no time to be wise and spare himself, no time to save
his strength by submission to moral laws. What he wanted
to do he must do soon, do quickly, do today.

And the moral laws? . . . Why was it that precisely sin,
surrender to the harmful and the consuming, actually
seemed to him more moral than any amount of wisdom and
frigid self-discipline? Not that constituted morality: not
the contemptible knack of keeping a good conscience—

rather the struggle and compulsion, the passion and pain.

Pain ... how his breast swelled at the word! He drew himself up and folded his arms; his gaze, beneath the close-set auburn brows, was kindled by the nobility of his suffering. No man was utterly wretched so long as he could still speak of his misery in high-sounding and noble words. One thing only was indispensable; the courage to call his life by large and fine names. Not to ascribe his sufferings to bad air and constipation; to be well enough to cherish emotions, to scorn and ignore the material. Just on this one point to be naïve,° though in all else sophisticated. To believe, to have strength to believe, in suffering. . . . But he *did* believe in it; so profoundly, so ardently, that nothing which came to pass with suffering could seem to him either useless or evil. His glance sought the manuscript, and his arms tightened across his chest. Talent itself—was that not suffering? And if the manuscript over there, his unhappy effort, made him suffer, was not that quite as it should be—a good sign, so to speak? His talents had never been of the copious, ebullient° sort; were they to become so he would feel mistrustful. That only happened with beginners and bunglers, with the ignorant and easily satisfied, whose life was not shaped and disciplined by the possession of a gift. For a gift, my friends down there in the audience, a gift is not anything simple, not anything to play with; it is not mere ability. At bottom it is a compulsion; a critical knowledge of the ideal, a permanent dissatisfaction, which rises only through suffering to the height of its powers. And it is to the greatest, the most unsatisfied, that their gift is the sharpest scourge. Not to complain, not to boast; to think modestly, patiently of one's pain; and if not a day in the week, not even an hour, be free from it—what then? To make light and little of it all, of suffering and achievement alike—that was what made a man great.

He stood up, pulled out his snuff-box and sniffed eagerly, then suddenly clasped his hands behind his back and strode so briskly through the room that the flames of the candles flickered in the draught. Greatness, distinction,

world conquest and an imperishable name! To be happy
and unknown, what was that by comparison? To be known
—known and loved by all the world—ah, they might call
that egotism,° those who knew naught of the urge, naught
of the sweetness of this dream! Everything out of the
ordinary is egotistic, in proportion to its suffering. "Speak
for yourselves," it says, "ye without mission on this earth,
ye whose life is so much easier than mine!" And Ambition
says: "Shall my sufferings be vain? No, they must make
me great!"

The nostrils of his great nose dilated, his gaze darted
fiercely about the room. His right hand was thrust hard and
far into the opening of his dressing-gown, his left arm hung
down, the fist clenched. A fugitive red played in the gaunt
cheeks—a glow thrown up from the fire of his artistic
egoism: that passion for his own ego, which burnt un-
quenchable in his being's depths. Well he knew it, the
secret intoxication of this love! Sometimes he needed
only to contemplate his own hand, to be filled with the
liveliest tenderness towards himself, in whose service he
was bent on spending all the talent, all the art that he
owned. And he was right so to do, there was nothing base
about it. For deeper still than his egoism lay the knowledge that he was freely consuming and sacrificing himself
in the service of a high ideal, not as a virtue, of course, but
rather out of sheer necessity. And this was his ambition:
that no one should be greater than he who had not also
suffered more for the sake of the high ideal. No one. He
stood still, his hand over his eyes, his body turned aside in
a posture of shrinking and avoidance. For already the
inevitable thought had stabbed him: the thought of that
other man, that radiant being, so sense-endowed, so
divinely unconscious, that man over there in Weimar,
whom he loved and hated. And once more, as always, in
deep disquiet, in feverish haste, there began working
within him the inevitable sequence of his thoughts: he
must assert and define his own nature, his own art, against
that other's. Was that other greater? Wherein, then, and
why? If he won, would he have sweated blood to do so?

If he lost, would his downfall be a tragic sight? He was no hero, no; a god, perhaps. But it was easier to be a god than a hero. Yes, things were easier for him. He was wise, he was deft, he knew how to distinguish between knowing and creating; perhaps that was why he was so blithe and care-free, such an effortless and gushing spring! But if creation was divine, knowledge was heroic, and he who created in knowledge was hero as well as god.

The will to face difficulties. . . . Did anyone realize what discipline and self-control it cost him to shape a sentence or follow out a hard train of thought? For after all he was ignorant, undisciplined, a slow, dreamy enthusiast. One of Caesar's letters was harder to write than the most effective scene — and was it not almost for that very reason higher? From the first rhythmical urge of the inward creative force towards matter, towards the material, towards casting in shape and form — from that to the thought, the image, the word, the line — what a struggle, what a Gethsemane! Everything that he wrote was a marvel of yearning after form, shape, line, body; of yearning after the sunlit world of that other man who had only to open his godlike lips and straightway call the bright unshadowed things he saw by name!

And yet — and despite that other man. Where was there an artist, a poet, like himself? Who like him created out of nothing, out of his own breast? A poem was born as music in his soul, as pure, primitive essence, long before it put on a garment of metaphor from the visible world. History, philosophy, passion were no more than pretexts and vehicles for something which had little to do with them, but was at home in orphic° depths. Words and con-ceptions were keys upon which his art played and made vibrate the hidden strings. No one realized. The good souls praised him, indeed, for the power of feeling with which he struck one note or another. And his favourite note, his final emotional appeal, the great bell upon which he sounded his summons to the highest feasts of the soul — many there were who responded to its sound. Freedom! But in all their exaltation, certainly he meant by the word both more and less than they did. Freedom — what was it? A self-respecting middle-class attitude towards thrones and princes? Surely not that. When one thinks of all that the spirit of man has dared to put into the word! Freedom from what? After all, from what? Perhaps, indeed, even from happiness, from human happiness, that silken bond, that tender, sacred tie....

From happiness. His lips quivered. It was as though his glance turned inward upon himself; slowly his face sank into his hands.... He stood by the bed in the next room, where the flowered curtains hung in motionless folds across the window, and the lamp shed a bluish light. He bent over the sweet head on the pillow ... a ringlet of dark hair lay across her cheek, that had the paleness of pearl; the childlike lips were open in slumber. "My wife! Beloved, didst thou yield to my yearning and come to me to be my joy? And that thou art.... Lie still and sleep; nay, lift not those sweet shadowy lashes and gaze up at me, as sometimes with thy great, dark, questioning, searching eyes. I love thee so! By God I swear it. It is only that sometimes I am tired out, struggling at my self-imposed task, and my feelings will not respond. And I must not be too utterly thine, never utterly happy in thee, for the sake of my mission."

He kissed her, drew away from her pleasant, slumbrous warmth, looked about him, turned back to the outer room. The clock struck; it warned him that the night was already far spent; but likewise it seemed to be mildly marking the end of a weary hour. He drew a deep breath, his lips closed firmly; he went back and took up his pen. No, he must not brood,° he was too far down for that. He must not descend into chaos;° or at least he must not stop there. Rather out of chaos, which is fullness, he must draw up to the light whatever he found there fit and ripe for form. No brooding! Work! Define, eliminate, fashion, complete!

And complete it he did, that effort of a labouring hour. He brought it to an end, perhaps not to a good end, but in any case to an end. And being once finished, lo, it was also good. And from his soul, from music and idea, new works

struggled upward to birth and, taking shape, gave out light
and sound, ringing and shimmering, and giving hint of
their infinite origin — as in a shell we hear the sighing of the
sea whence it came.

---

*Do especially Questions 45, 50, 75, 89, 91, and 105. Consult
the Short Story Model on page 156.*

THOMAS MANN   *1875-1955*

Regarded by many critics as one of the outstanding novelists
of the twentieth century, Thomas Mann was educated in a military school, with a view to becoming a merchant. After his father's
death he worked as a fire insurance clerk in Munich, but quickly
tired of business life and began auditing courses at the University
of Munich. Soon he moved to Rome where he wrote his first
novel, *Buddenbrooks,* which helped bring him fame and in 1929
the Nobel prize for literature. In 1938 the German novelist fled
to the United States where he became an American citizen. But
after the Second World War ended, he returned to the culture of
the Old World, and died in Switzerland in 1955. Mann's short
story "A Weary Hour," an attempt to show the struggle of an
author as he endeavors to create, will challenge even the most
mature reader. In the central figure we recognize a strong resemblance to Mann himself who said: "I myself am completely
taken aback; for I have never yet set forth a book without being
convinced that it was unreadable."

The Train from Rhodesia

NADINE GORDIMER

The train came out of the red horizon and bore down toward
them over the single straight track.

The stationmaster came out of his little brick station with
its pointed chalet° roof, feeling the creases in his serge
uniform in his legs as well. A stir of preparedness rippled

through the squatting native vendors waiting in the dust; the face of a carved wooden animal, eternally surprised, stuck out of a sack. The stationmaster's barefoot children wandered over. From the gray mud huts with the untidy heads that stood within a decorated mud wall, chickens, and dogs with their skin stretched like parchment over their bones, followed the piccanins[1] down to the track. The flushed and perspiring west cast a reflection, faint, without heat, upon the station, upon the tin shed marked "Goods," upon the walled kraal,[2] upon the gray tin house of the stationmaster and upon the sand, that lapped all around, from sky to sky, cast little rhythmical cups of shadow, so that the sand became the sea, and closed over the children's black feet softly and without imprint.

The stationmaster's wife sat behind the mesh of her verandah. Above her head the hunk of a sheep's carcass moved slightly, dangling in a current of air.

They waited.

The train called out, along the sky; but there was no answer; and the cry hung on: I'm coming . . . I'm coming . . .

The engine flared out now, big, whisking a dwindling body behind it; the track flared out to let it in.

Creaking, jerking, jostling, gasping, the train filled the station.

Here, let me see that one — the young woman curved her body further out of the corridor window. Missus? smiled the old boy, looking at the creatures he held in his hand. From a piece of string on his gray finger hung a tiny woven basket; he lifted it, questioning. No, no, she urged, leaning down toward him, across the height of the train, toward the man in the piece of old rug; that one, that one, her hand commanded. It was a lion, carved out of soft dry wood that looked like spongecake; heraldic, black and white, with impressionistic° detail burnt in. The old man held it up to her still smiling, not from the heart, but at the

[1] Small children.
[2] A small native village.

customer. Between its Vandyke teeth, in the mouth opened in an endless roar too terrible to be heard, it had a black tongue. Look, said the young husband, if you don't mind! And round the neck of the thing, a piece of fur (rat? rabbit? meerkat?); a real mane, majestic, telling you somehow that the artist had delight in the lion.

All up and down the length of the train in the dust the artists sprang, walking bent, like performing animals, the better to exhibit the fantasy held toward the faces on the train. Buck, startled and stiff, staring with round black and white eyes. More lions, standing erect, grappling with strange, thin, elongated warriors who clutched spears and showed no fear in their slits of eyes. How much, they asked from the train, how much?

Give me penny, said the little ones with nothing to sell. The dogs went and sat, quite still, under the dining car, where the train breathed out the smell of meat cooking with onion.

A man passed beneath the arch of reaching arms meeting gray-black and white in the exchange of money for the staring wooden eyes, the stiff wooden legs sticking up in the air; went along under the voices and the bargaining, interrogating the wheels. Past the dogs; glancing up at the dining car where he could stare at the faces, behind glass, drinking beer, two by two, on either side of a uniform railway vase with its pale dead flower. Right to the end, to the guard's van, where the stationmaster's children had just collected their mother's two loaves of bread; to the engine itself, where the stationmaster and the driver stood talking against the steaming complaint of the resting beast.

The man called out to them, something loud and joking. They turned to laugh, in a twirl of steam. The two children careered° over the sand, clutching the bread, and burst through the iron gate and up the path through the garden in which nothing grew.

Passengers drew themselves in at the corridor windows and turned into compartments to fetch money, to call someone to look. Those sitting inside looked up: suddenly

different, caged faces, boxed in, cut off, after the contact
of outside. There was an orange a piccanin would like...
What about that chocolate? It wasn't very nice...

A young girl had collected a handful of the hard kind,
that no one liked, out of the chocolate box, and was throwing
them to the dogs, over at the dining car. But the hens
darted in, and swallowed the chocolates, incredibly quick
and accurate, before they had even dropped in the dust, and
the dogs, a little bewildered, looked up with their brown
eyes, not expecting anything.

— No, leave it, said the girl, don't take it...

Too expensive, too much, she shook her head and raised
her voice to the old boy, giving up the lion. He held it up
where she had handed it to him. No, she said, shaking her
head. Three-and-six? insisted her husband, loudly. Yes
baas! laughed the boy. *Three-and-six?* — the young man was
incredulous. Oh leave it — she said. The young man
stopped. Don't you want it? he said, keeping his face
closed to the boy. No, never mind, she said, leave it. The
old native kept his head on one side, looking at them sideways, holding the lion. Three-and-six, he murmured, as
old people repeat things to themselves.

The young woman drew her head in. She went into the
coupé and sat down. Out of the window, on the other side,
there was nothing; sand and bush; a thorn tree. Back
through the open doorway, past the figure of her husband
in the corridor, there was the station, the voices, wooden
animals waving, running feet. Her eye followed the funny
little valance° of scrolled wood that outlined the chalet roof
of the station; she thought of the lion and smiled. That bit
of fur round the neck. But the wooden buck, the hippos, the
elephants, the baskets that already bulked out of their
brown paper under the seat and on the luggage rack! How
will they look at home? Where will you put them? What
will they mean away from the places you found them?
Away from the unreality of the last few weeks? The man
outside. But he is not part of the unreality; he is for good
now. Odd...somewhere there was an idea that he, that
living with him, was part of the holiday, the strange places.

Outside, a bell rang. The stationer was leaning against the end of the train, green flag rolled in readiness. A few men who had got down to stretch their legs sprang on to the train, clinging to the observation platforms, or perhaps merely standing on the iron step, holding the rail; but on the train, safe from the one dusty platform, the one tin house, the empty sand.

There was a grunt. The train jerked. Through the glass the beer drinkers looked out, as if they could not see beyond it. Behind the fly-screen, the stationmaster's wife sat facing back at them beneath the darkening hunk of meat.

There was a shout. The flag drooped out. Joints not yet coördinated, the segmented body of the train heaved and bumped back against itself. It began to move; slowly the scrolled chalet moved past it, the yells of the natives, running alongside, jetted up into the air, fell back at different levels. Staring wooden faces waved drunkenly, there, then gone, questioning for the last time at the windows. Here, one-and-six baas! – As one automatically opens a hand to catch a thrown ball, a man fumbled wildly down his pocket, brought up the shilling° and sixpence and threw them out; the old native, gasping, his skinny toes splaying the sand, flung the lion.

The piccanins were waving, the dogs stood, tails uncertain, watching the train go: past the mud huts, where a woman turned to look, up from the smoke of the fire, her hand pausing on her hip.

The stationmaster went slowly in under the chalet.

The old native stood, breath blowing out the skin between his ribs, feet tense, balanced in the sand, smiling and shaking his head. In his opened palm, held in the attitude of receiving, was the retrieved shilling and sixpence.

The blind end of the train was being pulled helplessly out of the station.

The young man swung in from the corridor, breathless. He was shaking his head with laughter and triumph. Here! he said. And waggled the lion at her. One-and-six!

What? she said.

He laughed. I was arguing with him for fun, bargaining—
when the train had pulled out already, he came tearing
after.... One-and-six Baas! So there's your lion.

She was holding it away from her, the head with the open
jaws, the pointed teeth, the black tongue, the wonderful
ruff of fur facing her. She was looking at it with an expression of not seeing, of seeing something different. Her face
was drawn up, wryly, like the face of a discomforted child.
Her mouth lifted nervously at the corner. Very slowly,
cautious, she lifted her finger and touched the mane, where
it was joined to the wood.

But how could you, she said. He was shocked by the
dismay of her face.

Good Lord, he said, what's the matter?

If you wanted the thing, she said, her voice rising and
breaking with the shrill impotence° of anger, why didn't
you buy it in the first place? If you wanted it, why didn't
you pay for it? Why didn't you take it decently, when he
offered it? Why did you have to wait for him to run after
the train with it, and give him one-and-six? One-and-six!

She was pushing it at him, trying to force him to take it.
He stood astonished, his hands hanging at his sides.

But you wanted it! You liked it so much?

—It's a beautiful piece of work, she said fiercely, as if to
protect it from him.

You liked it so much! You said yourself it was too expensive—

Oh *you*—she said, hopeless and furious. *You*... She
threw the lion on to the seat.

He stood looking at her.

She sat down again in the corner and, her face slumped
in her hand, stared out of the window. Everything was
turning round inside her. One-and-six. One-and-six. One-
and-six for the wood and the carving and the sinews of the
legs and the switch of the tail. The mouth open like that
and the teeth. The black tongue, rolling, like a wave. The
mane round the neck. To give one-and-six for that. The

heat of shame mounted through her legs and body and sounded in her ears like the sound of sand pouring. Pouring, pouring. She sat there, sick. A weariness, a tastelessness, the discovery of a void made her hands slacken their grip, atrophy[3] emptily, as if the hour was not worth their grasp. She was feeling like this again. She had thought it was something to do with singleness, with being alone and belonging too much to oneself.

She sat there not wanting to move or speak, or to look at anything, even; so that the mood should be associated with nothing, no object, word, or sight that might recur and so recall the feeling again. . . Smuts blew in grittily, settled on her hands. Her back remained at exactly the same angle, turned against the young man sitting with his hands drooping between his sprawled legs, and the lion, fallen on its side in the corner.

The train had cast the station like a skin. It called out to the sky, I'm coming, I'm coming; and again, there was no answer.

[3]Waste away from disuse.

Do especially Questions 11, 15, 44, 57, 75, 76, 107, 109, and 149. Consult the Short Story Model on page 156.

NADINE GORDIMER 1923-

One of the most promising young writers of this era is Nadine Gordimer. While her productivity is somewhat limited, a review of her short story collection, *The Soft Voice of the Serpent* (1952), reveals a series of selections both meticulous and subtle in their development. Miss Gordimer began writing fiction in her childhood years, and, by her mid-teens, she was publishing stories in several magazines in her native city, Johannesburg. She attended the University of Witwatersrand, located in that city, in which she continues to reside.

Miss Gordimer's writing centers around local scenes of South Africa, both city tales based on Johannesburg and those set in the brush country and mining towns of the outer regions. In both she is able to maintain a fine balance between careful, accurate description of the area under scrutiny, and keen insight into the nature of the individuals with whom she populates her works. Most of these character images come in the form of compound sketches, found in her several stories, although she has written one successful novel, *The Lying Days* (1953). Still a relatively young woman, she remains a writer from whom much may well be heard.

PROBLEM QUESTIONS

1. Why is the woman in Nadine Gordimer's story so angry about the purchase of the wooden lion? What do we learn about her through her anger?

2. Was the rat-trap maker in the Lagerlöf story truly the captain in question? If not, why did he sign his name as he did?

3. What accounts for the changes in attitude of the narrator and his daughter toward the fruit peddler in "The Cabuliwallah"?

4. What problem suggested in the Galsworthy story is closely related to that of our modern, automated age?

5. What is the fat traveler in "War" saying about the difference between youth and age? Why does he break down into uncontrollable sobbing at the end of the story?

6. In "The Apple Tree" why did the father become so greatly excited about his tree? What changed his feelings toward it?

7. What may the Italian writer Alvaro be saying about the value of "precious" things in "The Ruby"? Of what different values was the ruby in the story?

8. Describe the nature of the relationship between the two men in "Under Cover of Darkness." Why does Lu-Yi frequently call the boy a "little devil"? What do you think the boy's feelings are at the very end of the story?

9. What does Thomas Mann have to say about man's inhumanity to man, and his inhumanity to himself in "A Weary Hour"? Relate these issues to the main character and find specific examples of both.

10. Most of the characters in the stories of this unit show the impact upon them of an experience of another person. In "The Sculptor's Funeral" what effect does the experience of meeting his friend's family and townspeople have upon young Steavens?

How does Big Liam in "The Quiet Man" draw out the best qualities in Shawn Kelvin? What influence does the fruit peddler in "The Cabuliwallah" have upon both Mini and her father?

11. Which of the writers in this unit have attempted to analyze a character under the stress of an intense emotion? Compare the theme and structure of two stories in which the author presents such a psychological study.

12. What characteristics do you see in the stories of this unit that identify them as twentieth-century stories rather than of the nineteenth century?

Preface to the Dictionary of Questions

The "Dictionary of Questions for Understanding Literature" is an organized set of the important questions that can be asked about any work of literature. It will serve throughout the four years of high school as the basic source for the questions that teachers and students will be asking about the literature they read. In view of this long-continued reference to the "Dictionary," it seems reasonable to suppose that you will develop the habit of asking yourself these important questions when you come to read independently of teachers and textbooks.

The *organization* of the questions in the "Dictionary" is simple. You move from your first general impression of a work to classification and a tentative statement of the theme; you then analyze the literary techniques used to express and develop this theme; you conclude with a final evaluation of the work in the light of the earlier steps in the process.

The *purpose* of the "Dictionary of Questions" is simply to teach habits of critical reading. It is devised to help you form those habits which will serve you in whatever reading you will have to do. Such habits will enable you to read more intelligently and critically anything from the daily newspaper or reports of a business meeting to the latest significant novel or play. They will help you formulate and express what would otherwise be vague feelings of satisfaction with a significant novel or general feelings of disappointment with a silly movie. In short, the purpose of the "Dictionary of Questions" is to accustom you to ask yourself the important questions you must answer if you are to evaluate properly whatever you read.

The following comments about each of the seven steps will give a quick overall view of the "Dictionary."

The *First View* elicits your first and perhaps superficial reaction after reading the work. In this View you try to familiarize yourself with the piece and begin to express your thoughts on it. The *Second View* asks you to classify the work among the various types of literature, a necessary step before any further analysis can take place. In the *Third View* you are asked a few general questions which will help you to state, at least in rough preliminary form, the theme of the work.

The *Fourth View* contains a series of questions which help you determine the overall structure of the work and the function each of its major divisions has in developing the theme. The *Fifth View*, which contains more than half of the questions in the "Dictionary," seeks a more detailed analysis of such points as style, imagery, figures of speech, characterization and plotting, and so forth. You will find in this View large blocks of questions relating specifically to lyric poetry, fiction, the drama, the film, television productions, and so forth.

The *Sixth View* contains questions about areas outside the work—history and biography, for example—which will help you to understand the work further and relate it to the culture that produced its author.

The *Seventh View*, the last one, offers questions for a final evaluation of the work in terms of comparison with other works and according to your own philosophy of life.

It would be an impossibly large task if all questions were to be asked of each work. There is a core of questions which will apply to any work of literature; but many questions are clearly labeled as applying only to one or other of the literary genres. Therefore, many of the 157 questions are eliminated early, when you decide (in the Second View) that the work belongs under one literary type rather than another.

The following consideration also reduces the number of questions that can be asked about any particular piece. Let us suppose that the work to be analyzed is a rather abstract essay. In that case you would skip over the questions relating to imagery and figures of speech, and concentrate more

SUMMARY OUTLINE

on those questions which analyze the thought processes
and evaluate the moral and intellectual issues. On the other
hand, if the poem is a simple lyric, the opposite will be
true. There may be very little moral or philosophical
content to the poem, whereas the imagery and figures will
be the all-important carriers of the author's emotion. Sum-
marily, not all 157 questions *can* be asked of every literary
work.

SUMMARY OUTLINE OF THE
DICTIONARY OF QUESTIONS

1. FIRST VIEW: **What is my first impression of the work as a
   total unit?** (Ques. 1)

2. SECOND VIEW: **Under which literary type would I classify
   the work from a first reading?** (Ques. 2-10)

3. THIRD VIEW: **What is my tentative expression of the *theme*
   of the work at this point?** (Ques. 11-20)

4. FOURTH VIEW: **How in general is the theme developed by
   the main parts of the work?** (Ques. 21-42)

5. FIFTH VIEW: **How in particular do the theme and its develop-
   ment give meaning to every part of the work?** (Ques. 43-132)
   A. *In all works* — **by feeling and thought, style, figures of
      speech and symbols?** (Ques. 44-61)
   B. *In poetry* — **by imagery, meter, rhyme?** (Ques. 62-72)
   C. *In narratives* — **by setting, plot, character?** (Ques. 73-117)
   D. *In drama* — **by dialogue, gesture, dramatic conventions?**
      (Ques. 118-127)
   E. *In movies and television plays* — **by pageantry, camera,
      editing?** (Ques. 128-132)

6. SIXTH VIEW: **How is the theme further clarified by knowledge of elements outside the work itself, such as the author's
   life and times?** (Ques. 133-146)

7. SEVENTH VIEW: **What is my final evaluation of the work?
   How does the work clarify, support, or contradict my own
   concept of what the "Good Life" is?** (Ques. 147-157)

Dictionary of Questions for Understanding Literature

BY VERNON RULAND

FIRST VIEW

I. **What is my first impression of the work as a total unit?** I must try first to understand rather than to judge, to read the work with an open mind, to approach the author on his own terms no matter how much he might seem at first to differ with me.

SECOND VIEW

II. **Under which type in the following scheme would I classify the work from a first reading? Why?** I must remember, of course, that many works defy simple classification, even after much study. Placing a label on a work is not an end in itself, but merely a temporary decision about the direction my later questions for understanding will have to follow.

   A. *An important preliminary:* **Does the work stand before me in its original state?** Although the editor's introduction will often answer this question, I must realize my distance from the original work in all my later analysis of this work. An author's vapid style might be merely the translator's; his apparent brevity might be the result of an editor's condensation.

   1. **Is the work before me in its original language, or is it a translation or "modernization" of the original? If a translation, is it an adequate one?**

   2. **Is my copy a "revised student edition" or an adaptation from which passages have been omitted? Is it an abridgement, a "Digest"?**

   3. **Is this work a chapter or excerpt from a complete work?**

   4. **Is this work meant primarily to be read, or to be heard as a poem read aloud and interpreted, or to be heard and seen as a drama in a stage performance?** Perhaps the work was written for an open Elizabethan stage, and loses much of its effect on our contemporary stage.

   5. **Is the present edition of the work accurate and trustworthy? What influence do its format, print, and illustrations exert on my analysis of the original work?**

1

2

3

4

5

6

7

8

B. Is the *complete* work before me *nonimaginative* (nonfiction prose) or *imaginative* (prose fiction or poetry)? In *nonimaginative works (nonfiction)* the author records and reports as scientist, scholar, historian, biographer: he develops already existing material and aims for factual accuracy in his work. In *imaginative works (prose fiction or poetry)* the author creates a world of his own; he forms his experience into an artistic whole that is more properly called a work of literature than is the nonfictional work.

C. **Under what more specific heading is the work best classified?**

TYPES OF LITERATURE

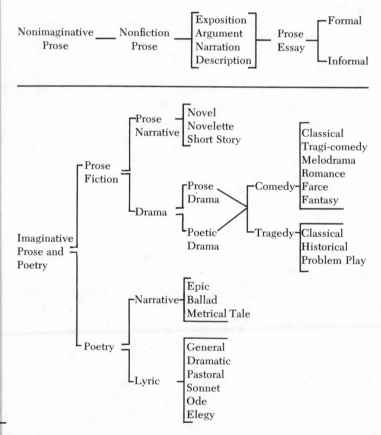

THIRD VIEW

III. **What is the theme of the work?** The theme of any work, best stated in a declarative sentence, is the essential meaning of the subject matter; it is the author's judgment about or attitude towards his subject matter. Any expression of a theme is correct that can justify itself from evidence in the work. Trying to state the theme of a work is *not* an effort to extract a moral or lesson from the work, nor should my statement be so final that it cannot be modified or enriched by further understanding.

With the work already classified in my Second View, the following chart determines my choice of questions for the Third, Fourth, and Fifth Views. Answers to all questions are no stronger than the evidence quoted from the work to support them.

Type of Literature	*3rd View*	*4th View*	*5th View*
I. Nonimaginative Prose (or Nonfiction Prose)	Questions		
A. Exposition	12-14	22-31	44-61
B. Argument	12-14	22-31	44-61
C. Narration	15-20	22-31, 35-42	44-61, (73-117)
D. Description	12-14	22-31, 32-34	44-61
II. Imaginative Prose & Poetry			
A. Prose Fiction	15-20	35-42	44-61
1. Prose Narrative	15-20	35-42	73-117
2. Drama	15-20	35-42	44-61, 73-117, 118-127
3. (Movie & Television Drama)	15-20	35-42	44-61, 73-117, 118-127, 128-132
B. Poetry	15-20	35-42	44-61, 62-72, 73-117, 118-127
1. Narrative Poetry	15-20	(32-34) 35-42	44-61, 62-72, 73-117
2. Lyric Poetry	12-14	32-34	44-61, 62-72

11

A. *Questions for a Nonnarrative Work (12-14)*

1. What in the subject matter causes the author to feel as he does—entranced, aloof, etc.? Or

2. Why is the subject matter important to the author? What does it mean to him? Or

3. What new insight into man and his world does the work seem most concerned about?

B. *Questions for a Narrative Work (15-20)*

1. What does the author want me to generalize about the central character(s)?

   a. First, who is the central character?

   b. Next, what of major importance happened to him? (State the importance of the event in a declarative sentence with the central character(s) as subject.)

   c. Finally, is it probable that the author wants me to extend my preceding statement to "all men"; or to "every man in such a situation"?

2. Or what important change or revelation occurred in the central character(s)?

3. Or what new or significant vision of the world did I grasp through the eyes of the central character(s)?

FOURTH VIEW

IV. How in general does the theme give order to the whole work?

A. *Questions for All Nonimaginative Prose (22-31)*

1. If the work is book-length, how does the theme of each chapter develop the theme of the whole book?

   a. What is the theme of the whole book? What chapter best expresses it?

   b. What is the theme of each chapter?

2. If the work is a reasonably short essay, how is its theme developed?

   a. What is the topic paragraph?

   b. What overall pattern or method best explains how the remaining paragraphs develop the topic paragraph? E.g., enumeration, cause and effect, comparison and contrast, circumstances, examples, repetition, etc.

   c. How does each paragraph fit into this unified scheme?

12

13

14

15

16

17

18

19

20

21

22

23

24

25

26

27

28

    d. What method of *coherence* best explains the connection between successive paragraphs in this essay?

    e. By what method(s) of *emphasis* does the essay give importance to the topic paragraph?

  3. In the development of any given paragraph, how does the author achieve unity, coherence, emphasis, variety? How effective is the topic sentence?

B. *Questions for Descriptive Prose and Lyric Poetry (32-34)*

  1. What in the work is the dominant physical *viewpoint* and the mental *viewpoint* (the author's attitude towards what he describes—sympathetic, ironic, casual, hostile, etc.)?

  2. Record any noticeable shift from one physical or mental viewpoint to another, from one sense-appeal to another, from one emotional state to another. How do the theme and its method of development explain these changes?

  3. If the work is a poem, do differing emotional states succeed one another and mark the poem into divisions? Does the poet use stanza divisions to mark changes in feelings and viewpoints, or does the theme develop independently of such divisions?

C. *Questions for All Narratives (35-42)*

  1. What events or historical incidents are handled in each chapter of the book, or each scene and act of the drama?

  2. If the work is biography, what important facts and judgments about the subject's life fall into the following time-divisions: (a) his cultural and family background, (b) his youth, (c) his education, (d) his maturity, (e) his decline, (f) his death, (g) a general analysis of his personality, (h) his achievements, and his effect on his own and later generations?

  3. If the work is history, what important data belongs to one or more of the following convenient divisions?

    a. Year-by-year, or century-by-century, or term-by-term of kingship or presidency or in terms of some characteristic hero of the period?

    b. The data pertinent to the history of one nation, then another?

    c. Subject-by-subject—the data of religious importance, then political, cultural, economic, etc.?

29

30

31

32

33

34

35

36

37

38

39

40

4. If the work is prose fiction or narrative poetry, can I divide the material to indicate the growth and release of tension according to the following graph?

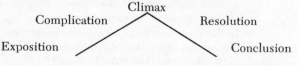

5. Similarly, if the work is tragedy — drama or nondrama — can I construct a graph giving the exposition, rising action, climax, falling action, and catastrophe? What are the various inciting forces to account for the hero's rising action, the tragic forces accounting for the hero's falling action, the turning point in the climax, etc.?

FIFTH VIEW
V. How in particular do the theme and its development give meaning to every part of the work?

   A. *Questions for Understanding All Works (44-61)*
     1. What feeling and thought does the work evoke?
       a. What emotions dominate the work — as signified in my expression of the theme? What emotions stand out in each division of the work — stanza or paragraph, for example — and how do they harmonize with the dominant feeling of the entire work?
       b. Are such emotions as strong as the subject matter and theme warrant, or are they excessive or deficient?
       c. Does the theme in any way so contradict my basic beliefs and convictions about man and the world, and man's place in the world, that I am hindered partially or entirely from sharing the feelings of the work? Or does it strengthen my beliefs and increase my sympathy for the work?
     2. How does the author's general style contribute to the development of the theme?
       a. What does the style tell me about the author's personality, and about the social caste, age group, and mentality of his audience?
       b. Are there qualities in the style that appear to be an aid or liability in developing the theme? Why?
       c. Is the style on a consistent level throughout the work, or does it shift to a higher or lower level of expression?
       d. Is the diction clear, simple, fresh, intense, subtle, purposeful; or labored, self-conscious, hackneyed, etc.?

e. In expository and argumentative literature, is the logic lucid, mature? Does the author appeal to intellect and feelings both, or strictly to the intellect? Does he indulge in "loaded language" and in the other common fallacies of false argument?

3. Why does the author prefer the denotations and connotations of one word rather than those of another in developing his theme?

a. What does the dictionary record as the exact logical definition, the pronunciation, syllabification, and etymology of the word?

b. Assuming that the author chooses each word intelligently, preferring it to various synonyms, how does the meaning of any particular word affect a given context?

4. How does the author's use of figurative language and symbols affect the development of the theme?

a. *Figures of speech* — What is their contribution to the theme?

(1) Do I recognize the following figures of speech?

(a) *Simile* — expressed comparison with "like" or "as" — "They went by like a jet."

(b) *Metaphor* — implied comparison — "a snowball development" or "He has a thin jackal face."

(c) *Personification* — giving human qualities to the nonhuman — "Death dropped in for a visit."

(d) *Synecdoche* — part designates whole, whole a part — "All hands on deck!" *Metonymy* — word designates an associated relation — "I read Blake."

(e) *Irony* — intended meaning is opposite of literal word-meaning — "I just love to lose a fight!"

(f) *Hyperbole* — exaggeration for effect — "a night of pure hell."

(g) *Litotes* — understatement for effect — "I finished the delicate little snack of five hamburgers."

(h) *Paradox* — an apparent contradiction which is true upon examination — "We must die in order to live."

(i) *Apostrophe* — words spoken in direct address to some abstract quality or nonexistent person — "Sing, Heavenly Muse! that on the secret top of Oreb ..."

60

(2) **Once identified, is each particular figure of speech fresh and effective? If a literal prose statement were substituted in this passage for the figure, what values would be added or lost?**

b. *Symbols* — (A *symbol* is a word, person, action, or object which takes on a meaning in the work far beyond its ordinary meaning; allegory, fable, parable, and symbol are all extended metaphors.) **What is their contribution to the theme? Is there any central symbol or metaphor that gives organic unity and life to the work?**

61

B. *Questions for Understanding Poetry (62-72)*

1. Any short passage of a poem demands careful study of word denotations and connotations, figures of speech, symbols; turning complex grammatical constructions into normal word order; explaining difficult allusions. Once these preliminaries are finished, the most important questions remain: **Why did the author use this word or image or technique rather than another? What is the relationship between this brief passage analyzed on one hand—and on the other, the theme and the dominant feeling of the entire poem?**

62

2. **How does the imagery of the poem contribute to the shaping of the theme? Does the imagery unify the poem or merely enrich it as an ornament?**

a. **How varied and sharp is the appeal to each of the five senses?**

b. **What are the areas of experience that provide the sources for the metaphors, similes, and allusions in the poem?**

3. **How does the metrical pattern of the poem help shape the meaning of a particular passage or the total meaning of the poem?**

a. **How closely can I describe the general metrical pattern?** The four common *poetic feet* are:

Iambic (∪/)—"With whát | Ĭ móst | enjóy | con- | tén- | tĕd leást."

Trochaic (/∪)—"Laḱe aňd | rí-věr | bŕeak ă- | sún-děr."

Dactylic (/∪∪)—"Whére iš mў | lovelў oňe | whére iš mў | lovelĭeš̌t"?

Anapestic (∪∪/)—"Aňd thĕ míght | of thĕ Gén- | tĭle, un-smóte | bў thĕ sẃord."

67

A verse of one foot is monometer, two is dimeter, three is trimeter, four is tetrameter, five is pentameter, six is hexameter, seven is heptameter, eight is octameter.

b. The important question is: How do the tensions and pace of the metrical techniques in this poem contribute to its theme and effect? Would the effect be enhanced or weakened if I were to alter these techniques?

4. How do rhyme and other audial techniques contribute to the effect of a particular passage or the entire poem?

a. What is the rhyme scheme of the poem?

b. Is the rhyme scheme conventional to the stanza the poet has chosen? If no rhyme is used, are other audial effects used purposively? E.g.,

Alliteration—repetition of initial consonants—"brainy but bashful."

Assonance—similar vowel sound in two or more syllables (rhyme is exact in consonant—"wake-take"; assonance is approximate—"wake-fate").

Onomatopoeia—sound of words suggests their meaning—"sizzle" or "screech."

Refrain—a phrase or sentence of one or more lines repeated at intervals in a poem, often at the end of a stanza. See Jonson's "Hymn to Cynthia" in which the closing line of each stanza is "Goddess excellently bright."

c. Are rhyme, meter, imagery, and other techniques used with balanced regularity and variety?

C. Questions for Understanding All Narratives (73-117)

1. If the work is prose fiction or narrative poetry, what is the proportion of dialogue to description and comment? Is the plot cluttered by excessive descriptive detail? Does the story tell itself, or does the author himself intrude to editorialize or moralize?

2. In a brief paragraph, give a summary of the plot. What incidents are essential to the theme, which merely contributory?

3. Is the work primarily one of incident and surprise, character problems, or mood and local color; or are plot, character, and setting of equal importance?

4. How is the setting integrated with the theme?

a. What are the details of setting?

(1) The historical period, season, time of day?

(2) The nation, city, or section of the nation?

68

69

70

71

72

73

74

75

76

77

78

79

(3) The social class and occupation of the characters?

(4) The mood or atmosphere — tense, gloomy, care-free, etc.?

b. Are these details clearly presented? What is the contribution of the opening sentence to the setting? The closing sentence of the work?

c. What incidents in the story could have happened only in this particular setting; what could have happened at any time or place?

d. If the narrative begins in the middle of events, how does the author provide the reader with sufficient knowledge about characters' past lives and other incidents in order to follow the present story?

e. Are later plot changes in time and locality essential to the development of character and plot?

f. Does the environment described in the setting bring such social, economic, political, religious pressures to bear on the lives of the characters that these elements become essential to the shaping of the theme?

5. How is the plot integrated with the theme?

a. If the story has a single plot, are any episodes introduced that seem inessential — or even irrelevant — to the theme, characterization, or thread of the story?

b. What conflicts constitute the main action of the story? One emotion or state of mind against another, or one man against another, or man against his physical environment and society — or a combination of these conflicts? How are these conflicts resolved in the work? If unresolved, does some incident in the plot prevent a solution within the work, or does the author apparently want me to leave his work with a problem I must solve for myself?

c. What is the *climax* of the plot, and what bearing does it have on the theme of the work? Does the story end with the climax? If not, would the ending be more effective if the climax came earlier than it does?

d. If there is a *denouement* following the climax, does it attempt to squeeze an obtrusive moral from the story, or does it answer important questions raised in the work, summarize, hint at future events in the characters' lives?

e. *Foreshadowing and suspense*—What is their function in the work?   **92**

   (1) How and with what success does the author employ dramatic foreshadowing and suspense to grip the reader and urge him on to future movements in the story? Does he use *dramatic irony*?   **93**

   (2) If the work has a surprise ending, is the surprise essential to the theme of the story?   **94**

f. Is the plot convincing and plausible? If the work constructs a fantastic world of romance, does it sustain that world throughout the work? If the work strives for realism, on the contrary, is it marred by coincidences improbable in real life?   **95**

g. Are there significant contrasts in the work—between incidents in the plot (winning the first, losing the second game)? **Between characters** (the vindictive old woman and the congenial doctor)? **Between moods** (carnival gaiety followed by the terror of murder)? **Do these contrasts contribute comic relief, irony, symbolism, or surprise to the total effect of the work?**   **96**

h. How does the passage of time function in the plot?   **97**

   (1) Approximately what portion of the story is devoted to exposition, to the complication, to the climax, to the denouement?   **98**

   (2) Does the pace of the story entice the interest of the reader, but still allow sufficient time for plausible character growth and progress of events?   **99**

   (3) Does the plot progress chronologically, or are there skips ahead in time which are later filled in by "flashback" techniques?   **100**

6. How are the characters integrated with the theme?   **101**

a. Who is the central character in the work? How does the theme evolve out of this character in action? Is the work mainly the story of the central character's development or deterioration?   **102**

b. What are the dominant traits of the central character?   **103**

   (1) What is significant about his physical appearance, clothes, social status, personal habits?   **104**

   (2) What are the characteristics of his thoughts, speech, and actions?   **105**

(3) What is the relation between the character's judgment of himself and the judgment of him by others?

(4) What is the character's philosophy of life – his convictions and beliefs about man, the world, and human destiny? Does the author seem favorably inclined, critical, or noncommittal towards this philosophy?

(5) Do all these character traits harmonize into one plausible personality?

c. Who are the important subordinate characters? What are their chief traits? Are they distinct personalities, or are they mere surface types?

d. If the work is comedy, what is the exaggerated trait in the character of the hero or other characters which causes the complications of plot or provokes comic satire? If the work is tragedy, what personality trait is the "tragic flaw" from which the catastrophe emerges?

e. Is there real character change during the course of the work, or gradual self-realization and revelation of hitherto unknown qualities of character?

7. From what point of view is the story told?

a. Is the narrator the first or third person?

b. If first person, is the narrator an observer only or a participant in the action? If third person narrator, is the author omniscient – inspecting the most hidden motives of his characters, trying to keep his own personality out of the story – or does he tell the story only from inside the mind of one character?

c. Does the author maintain one consistent point of view throughout the story, or does he change it during the narrative – and, if so, does he do it plausibly?

d. What advantages and disadvantages result from the point of view chosen in this particular work?

8. Is it possible throughout the work to sympathize with the feelings of the central character(s) and the character through whose viewpoint the story is filtered? What in the work accounts for the ease or difficulty of my identification with the central character or others?

D. *Questions for Understanding Drama (118-132)*

1. What is the total effect of the play as a combined venture by author, director, actors, and stage technicians?

a. How closely does the stage performance achieve the ideals of the author's original script? | **119**

b. How effectively do author and director employ scenery, props, costumes, lighting, make-up, stage-groupings of characters, exits and entrances, etc.? | **120**

c. What are the names of the actors and the director? Are the actors well-cast — in physical appearance, voice, intelligent interpretation? Do they interact well as a unit? | **121**

2. How does the work *as a drama* develop its theme in setting, plot, and character? | **122**

a. How does the author respect the limitations and exploit the advantages of stage, television, radio, etc., in comparison with the novel or short-story form into which he might have chosen to cast his subject matter? | **123**

b. To what extent are the divisions (into scene and act) or lack of divisions in the play necessitated by the medium in which the author is creating? | **124**

c. How effectively do dialogue and gesture accomplish what the novelist more readily achieves by simple narrative and comment — viz., reveal internal states of mind, emphasize character differences, speed the pace and sustain the interest of the play? | **125**

3. How successfully does the author exploit the various dramatic stage-conventions to accomplish his theme and effects? E.g., asides and soliloquies, confidants, raisonneur, prologue and epilogue, Greek chorus, etc.? | **126**

4. If *poetic drama*, are the lines good poetry and good drama both? Do they become at times too reflective and complex to communicate themselves to an audience that is normally alert and experienced in appreciation of poetic drama? | **127**

E. *Questions for Understanding Movies and Television Plays (128-132)*

1. Is the film merely a photographed play that might just as well have been performed in a theater, or does the camera create a work with unique artistic value in itself? | **128**

2. Give examples of successful camera techniques — particular close-up studies of a face, fade-outs, etc. What is the effect of each technique on character portrayal, pace, setting, mood? | **129**

3. Does the pageantry of the setting have a value in itself, apart from plot and character? | **130**

131

132

4. Has the film been successfully edited to achieve continuity, pace, variety?
5. What contribution to the total effect of the work is made by the sound-track, color, the wide screen, or other techniques? Is the background music of good independent artistic value, or is it mere sound effects — muted violins for love scenes and kettle drums for suspense?

SIXTH VIEW

133

VI. How does my knowledge of elements outside the work contribute to further understanding of the work itself? Study beyond the limits of the work itself can suggest areas of scrutiny in the work I might otherwise have overlooked.

134

A. How do the author's notebooks, correspondence, and other comments on his own work shed light on his theme and other elements of the present work? Does this evidence limit, extend, or merely confirm my present conclusions?

135

B. What light do critical and biographical studies of the author shed on the meaning of the work?

136

1. Do these studies show me how the present work fits chronologically into the output of the author's entire career? Do his other works shed further understanding on this work, and this work shed further understanding on the others?

137

2. How does the present work agree with or contradict the author's philosophy of life — both as revealed in the general themes of his works, and as recorded in other documents?

138

3. Do the author's earlier editions or later revisions of the present work give insight into the meaning of the work?

139

4. How does a knowledge of the sources and analogues of the work contribute to a further understanding?

140

a. Are there people and experiences in the author's own life which bear close resemblance to — or have directly inspired — people and situations in the work?

141

b. Is the present work an adaptation of another's work, or has the author used his sources creatively?

142

5. How do the individual critic's reactions and interpretations of the work add to my understanding of the work?

143

C. How do other bodies of knowledge help me to understand the work?

1. How does the knowledge of the history of literature and the other arts contribute to my understanding of the work?   **144**

2. How does a knowledge of history and other sciences contribute to interpreting the work? Was the theme of the work—and the issues treated—something timely when the work first appeared? Are these issues vital today?   **145**

3. How does my understanding of the present work, on the other hand, contribute to an understanding of the politics, sociology, religion, etc., of the period? How does it contribute to further understanding of life in general? Does the author force me to reëvaluate institutions (marriage, the home, civil law, etc.) and philosophies that I respect? That is, are my ideals reaffirmed or are they attacked and ridiculed?   **146**

SEVENTH VIEW

VII. What is my final evaluation of the work? How does the work clarify, support, or contradict my own concept of what the "Good Life" is? I have a mental picture, vague or definite, of what would be for me an ideal life. In determining how this work of literature affects my idea of this life, I must first consider what kind of person I am, what kind of person I should like to be, what kinds of lives I admire, what ideas I respect. I am then concerned about whether the work helps me to understand my own personality, the character of others, or the nature of the world. I must consider whether the work disturbs me because it presents values and sympathies different from my own, whether it awakens in me a yearning for a different kind of life, or whether or not it makes me content with my present way of life.   **147**

A. How does a final reading of the work (considering it as a total unit after all of the analytical study has been completed) compare with my first unanalyzed impressions in the First View?   **148**

B. Is the development of the theme handled so intelligently that the work helps me to understand aspects of life previously confusing and inexplicable to me? Or, on the other hand, do the theme and important elements in the work represent, in my judgment, such an immature, distorted philosophy of life that I feel the work to be *artistically* inferior? When I compare the author's theme or view of a certain aspect of life with my own view, do I conclude that his notions are not only different from mine but also so extremely distorted that he has therefore produced a work of literature which is an artistic failure?   **149**

C. **How does the theme as it is developed in the work agree with my moral principles?** The following questions pertain chiefly to mature reading-experiences in later life, reading material beyond the scope of the present text-books.

1. Am I judging the work solely on its own merits, unswayed by the author's known principles and conduct in his private life?

2. Characters in many realistic works use vulgar, obscene, blasphemous language. Is such language used with artistic purpose for realistic characterization? May it perhaps incite the normal reader to sensual thoughts or immoral behavior?

3. Are the scenes that describe immorality handled with restraint and artistic distance, and are they a true insight into the nature of immorality?

4. Is the immorality portrayed in the work presented as *some* type of human evil, or is it presented as the result of social pressures, or as a result of a personality flaw? Does the author recognize immorality as such, even if his characters do not? Moreover, in his work does he punish characters for their immoral behavior — if not, should he have done so? Is the immorality presented as evil only in a certain sense of the word? Is the main conflict in the work between actual moral good and evil, or between what is merely good and bad, pleasant and unpleasant, or socially or politically acceptable and unacceptable, etc.?

5. Does the work present a set of values so advanced or objectionable that it is to be recommended to mature readers only, or perhaps with a caution to others? Are the scenes or passages to which I object necessary to the artistic integrity of the work, or would the work be seriously mutilated by the omission of such passages?

6. How does my personal evaluation of the work compare with the judgment of other, more experienced, critics? In general, are my usual moral evaluations of literature more liberal or conservative — more tolerant or more severe — than their evaluation? In what ways might their conception of the normal reader's problems be more accurate than mine? In what ways less accurate?

D. **How does the present work, as I understand it, compare with other works I have read?** What difference, if any, is there between the rank I finally assign the work among my favorites, and the objective rank I have assigned it among the world's great pieces of literature?

Index